BONHOEFFER FOR A NEW DAY

Bonhoeffer for a New Day

Theology in a Time of Transition

Papers Presented at the
Seventh International Bonhoeffer Congress
Cape Town, 1996

edited by

John W. de Gruchy

WILLIAM B. EERDMANS PUBLISHING COMPANY
GRAND RAPIDS, MICHIGAN / CAMBRIDGE, U.K.

© 1997 Wm. B. Eerdmans Publishing Co.

255 Jefferson Ave. S.E., Grand Rapids, Michigan 49503 /

P.O. Box 163, Cambridge CB3 9PU U.K.

Printed in the United States of America

02 01 00 99 98 97   7 6 5 4 3 2 1

Library of Congress Cataloging-in-Publication Data

International Bonhoeffer Conference (7th : 1996 : Cape Town, South Africa)
Bonhoeffer for a new day : theology in a time of transition : papers
presented at the seventh International Bonhoeffer Congress,
Cape Town, 1996 / edited by John W. de Gruchy.
p.   cm.
Includes bibliographical references.
ISBN 0-8028-4284-4 (paper : alk. paper)
1. Bonhoeffer, Dietrich, 1906-1945 — Congresses.
I. De Gruchy, John W.   II. Title.
BX4827.B57I58   1997
230'.044'092 — dc21   97-8918
CIP

Contents

v

CONTENTS

Contents

"Are We Still of Any Use?"

JOHN W. DE GRUCHY

Dietrich Bonhoeffer's soul-searching question, "Are we still of any use?" provided the theme for the Seventh International Bonhoeffer Congress held in Cape Town, South Africa, in January, 1996. Those of us who gathered for that historic event considered the question in a variety of ways, not all of them in the mind of Bonhoeffer when he first penned the words. This volume of essays from that Congress is, in many respects, an attempt to answer the question from various perspectives and contexts with specific reference to Bonhoeffer's own legacy.

There can be no doubt that Bonhoeffer's legacy of life and thought has had a major impact on Christianity and the ecumenical church since his martyrdom fifty years ago. But can it be said that he is still of significance for us today as we stand on the brink of a new millennium in a rapidly changing world? Bonhoeffer certainly anticipated that the world he knew would change in fundamental ways. Yet even he could not have foreseen the extent of those changes, and the crises and challenges which would accompany them. In all honesty, then, is an interest in Bonhoeffer today anything more than nostalgic loyalty to a remarkable person? Can it be that he still has something to say to us today in our many different historical contexts, often far removed from his time and place? The more than two hundred participants from six continents at the Cape Town Congress, whether long-standing devotees or not, had little doubt that this was the case. But what did Bonhoeffer himself have

1

in mind when he asked the question of himself and his compatriots in the German resistance?

The question comes at the end of his evocative essay, "After Ten Years," which was a Christmas gift to his brother-in-law Hans von Dohnanyi and his close friends Hans Oster and Eberhard Bethge in 1942. In it Bonhoeffer reflected on what he and his companions in the resistance had learned during that past tumultuous decade. The cause for which they had fought was clearly right and just, but the means which they were sometimes forced to adopt was often morally ambiguous. Of necessity, responsible action had meant the sacrifice of any claim to ethical righteousness. Consider the passage:

> We have been silent witness of evil deeds; we have been drenched by many storms; we have learnt the arts of equivocation and pretense; experience has made us suspicious of others and kept us from being truthful and open; intolerable conflicts have worn us down and even made us cynical. Are we still of any use?[1]

The conspirators had, to quote Martin Luther, "sinned boldly." Their hands were sullied. They were now exhausted by a process which went against everything for which they had previously stood. Was it possible, then, that they could still be of any use in the reconstruction of Germany and Europe once the present nightmare had ended?

Bonhoeffer's question is one which many people, both Christians and others, who have been engaged in the struggle for political liberation, know only too well. Many tactics employed in the anti-apartheid struggle in South Africa were morally ambiguous even though the liberation movement managed so well to maintain the moral high ground. But armed struggle and resistance, whether above or below ground, invariably led to actions which were ethically problematic. Indeed, sometimes the struggle led to actions which were not condoned by the liberation movement itself. These have now become the subject of investigation by the Commission on Truth and Reconciliation set up by the post-apartheid government to deal with the gross violation of human rights during the years of apartheid on all sides. "Are we still of any use?" is a question which faces us as a new generation arises, less tainted by the

---

1. Dietrich Bonhoeffer, "After Ten Years," *Letters and Papers from Prison* (London: SCM, 1971), 16.

past and full of new energy and vision to shape the future. Should we, many of us compromised by past events, now stand aside and let others take on the task of building a new nation?

Bonhoeffer might well have asked the question of the church in Germany, indeed, of the Confessing Church. Would that church which, in many ways, so courageously opposed Hitler and yet which failed to show solidarity with the victims of Nazism still have a role to play in the future? Bonhoeffer also pondered the future of Christianity in the western world as a whole. Had not its time run out? If there was to be renewal, might it not come from beyond Christendom, from India and the peace testimony of Gandhi? In many ways this has happened as the center of gravity for a vibrant and expansive Christianity has shifted from Europe and the west to Latin America and Africa since the end of Bonhoeffer's era. Yet those of us who were involved in the church struggle in South Africa, and who know something of the vitality of Christianity in our context, are also aware and ashamed of the legacy of Christianity's connivance with colonialism and apartheid and patriarchy. Is it possible that the church in South Africa can overcome that tainted past and truly make a contribution to the shaping of the new South Africa?

Given the many different historical and ecclesial situations represented at the Congress in Cape Town, it would have been surprising if all those in attendance had considered or answered the question of Bonhoeffer's continuing relevance in the same way. Indeed, right at the outset, in the opening service at St. George's Cathedral, Dr. Beyers Naudé, doyen of church leaders in the struggle against apartheid, reminded us that Bonhoeffer himself would have had serious problems with the question as posed by us. The question he would have us ask does not concern his own significance, but the significance of Jesus Christ. The basic question with which he addresses us remains the one which he asked himself, his students, and his readers time and again: "Who is Jesus Christ, for us, today?" Only as Bonhoeffer helps us to answer that question does he remain of any use for the task of Christian witness and doing theology today. Which is not, by any means, to deny the many-sided character of Bonhoeffer's legacy.

International Bonhoeffer Congresses are, so the faithful maintain, rather special events. In many respects they reflect the polyphonic character of Bonhoeffer's life, interests, and thought. Invariably they include times of worship and celebration as well as cultural and political events.

Moreover, the first six Congresses were attended by various members of the family, notably Eberhard and Renate Bethge, as well as some of Bonhoeffer's students from Berlin and Finkenwalde. Maria von Wedemeyer, his fiancée, was present at the second Congress held in Geneva in 1976. All of this gave those Congresses a sense of continuity with Bonhoeffer, and made them occasions of profound enrichment. Cape Town proved to be the exception in this regard. Eberhard Bethge, in his eighty-fifth year, and his wife Renate, Dietrich's niece, were unable to make the long journey from Germany to South Africa. But Cape Town, so we were told by many overseas participants, was a remarkable Congress nonetheless. Participants had an opportunity to visit Robben Island and the prison cell in which President Nelson Mandela spent nineteen years of his long imprisonment. They visited black townships, worshipped in St. George's Cathedral (center of so much resistance and protest in the past), listened to African music, and shared an evening banquet with Archbishop Desmond Tutu and Dr. Beyers Naudé.

Bonhoeffer Congresses are all this. But they are also opportunities for theological discussion and debate at a high level. Cape Town was no exception in this regard. The programme included six plenary sessions, the first five of which were devoted to major themes in Bonhoeffer's legacy. The speakers invited (Peter Selby, Konrad Raiser, Chung Hyun Kyung, Jean Bethke Elsthain, and Barney Pityana) did not claim to be Bonhoeffer specialists. They were invited to speak on major themes in Bonhoeffer's legacy because the organizers of the Congress believed, rightly so it proved, that they would best help us focus on the relevance of Bonhoeffer for today from their own very distinct perspectives. All of these plenary papers have been included in this volume, though not in the order in which they were given. Indeed, we have placed Chung Hyun Kung's letter to Bonhoeffer at the beginning because she, perhaps more than anyone, raised the question of Bonhoeffer's significance for us today most sharply. Although Eberhard Bethge was unable to present his presidential lecture at the Congress, we are delighted that he has made it available for publication.

There were also thirty seminar papers. These ranged from highly specialized presentations to more popular expositions, and much in between. Our selection of essays for this volume was determined not only by the quality of the papers but also by their appropriateness in dealing with the theme under the categories which form the three parts of the volume. Those seminar papers not included have been listed in an

4

appendix and, along with the papers of previous Congresses, are located in the Bonhoeffer archives housed in the library of Union Theological Seminary in New York.

The organizers of the Congress were asked by the International Bonhoeffer Society to ensure that participants would be exposed to the theology which had emerged in the course of the struggle against apartheid. This was attempted at two plenary sessions. The first took place on Robben Island when several leading South African theologians (Charles Villa-Vicencio, Denise Ackermann, Molefe Tsele, Frank Chikane, and Buti Tlhagale) reflected on the different theologies and assessed their ongoing significance. Then, on the final morning, a plenary session was devoted more specifically to Bonhoeffer's contribution to theology and witness in South Africa. A panel, reflecting on the week that had passed, considered whether or not Bonhoeffer was still of any use for us in South Africa at this time of nation-building and reconstruction. It is always difficult to recapture what is said on such occasions since much of the comment is extempore. But we have included, as a conclusion to the volume, Russel Botman's compilation of the presentations which took place at the final plenary session. This indicates that the discussion about Bonhoeffer and his contemporary significance, and the attempt by the Congress to answer his question, remains open-ended, at least in South Africa.

The Congress would not have been possible without the support and encouragement of many friends, colleagues, and donors. Included among them are Bill and Sam Eerdmans of Wm. B. Eerdmans Publishing Company, who not only attended the Congress and helped fund the banquet, but who also warmly agreed to publish this volume. What remains is to say a special word of thanks to those who have helped prepare the manuscript for publication, notably Steve Martin, Elsie Steel, and Gillian Walters.

John W. de Gruchy
Editor and Congress Convenor
Cape Town,
Easter 1996

CHRISTIANITY
IN A WORLD COME OF AGE

Dear Dietrich Bonhoeffer

CHUNG HYUN KYUNG

11 January 1996
Cape Town
South Africa

Dear Dietrich Bonhoeffer,

How are you? I hope you are well wherever you are. Let me introduce myself first to you for our communication. My name is Chung Hyun Kyung. I come from Seoul, Korea. I am an Asian eco-feminist postmodern liberation theologian who teaches at Ewha Women's University, the largest women's university in the world. I have 20,000 women students studying with me.

Well, you may be puzzled by such a grandiose introduction. I am sure you never heard of such a creature as me in your own time. I am living in a different time from yours. In my time, for theologians to "name" themselves in their social location as honestly as possible is the first step in any dialogue. In my theological community, people do not accept any universal assumptions anymore. No poker face dialogue is allowed. You have to show all your cards at the dialogue table before you begin communication.

Since I would like to dialogue with you, I have to let you know more about myself. I am a product of the Korean Christian Student movement. The experiences and questions arising from that movement led me to pursue theological studies. Since then, my love for the people's movement has continued through my participation in the feminist and ecological movements, as well as the citizens' movement for grassroots democracy.

I have studied widely in many different theologies: traditional Euro-American male theology, Latin American Liberation theology, feminist, womanist, Minjung theology, Black theology, Asian theology, eco-theology, and theology of life.

Then, at the "no-exit" dead end of my political intellectual search, I became a student of Zen meditation practice, Taoist "Ki" mind-body practice, and goddess-dance practice. Now I receive most of my outrageous theological imagination from my artist friends: dancers, painters, actors, poets, playwrights, filmmakers. I also get much inspiration from artistic and cultural critiques. From them I am reminded what a Native American elder prophesied a long time ago: "Eventually genuine beauty will save us all."

I am therefore a theologian who wants to integrate the pathos of the people's movement, serious theoretical analysis of the intellectual community, the spiritual opening of meditation, and the breakthrough imagination of the arts in our time.

This has been quite a long introduction. Now I will tell you how I got to know you as a person and a theologian.

My first encounter with you was through the Korean Student Christian movement. You were the major theological mentor of our movement, not because we understood the details and nuances of your theology but because we were inspired by your life story: a young pastor who fought for justice and (out of his faith in Jesus Christ and love of people) participated in the project to assassinate Hitler, and was then caught, imprisoned and executed by the principalities and powers of the world.

We understood you immediately when we read about "costly discipleship" because we also had to pay a heavy price for our participation in the student movement. Many of us were tortured, imprisoned, and killed. We knew it could cost our lives to speak for justice and democracy. Many burned themselves to death as martyrs. We also understood your well-known phrase "without God, before God, with God" because we knew there was no magic problem-solver God up there who would protect us from military torture. We found the face of God in the faces of the most oppressed as we worked with them and built communities based on right relationships.

From your influence came a blooming of political theology, the theology of secularization, and Minjung theology — and most of all the blooming of a resistance movement among socially conscious Christians.

However, people started to lose interest in the middle of the seventies because your theological orientation could not help anymore. We found your theology too embedded in traditional western doctrines of Christ and your ethics did not offer us much imagination for concrete political actions, processes, and ideologies. At that point many young people turned to Latin American liberation theologians, learning from their Marxist social analysis.

So we forgot you for a long time. Only at the end of the eighties and in the early nineties, when young pastors in the Minjung Church and the Minjung movement tried to find the meaning of Christian identity in the midst of the rapid secularization of Korean religious culture, did we begin to talk about you again. This is the short history of how Korean young people and theologians have received you in general in our context.

Now I will tell you more personal stories of my encounter with you. Frankly I remembered you again because organizers of the Bonhoeffer Conference asked me to give a plenary speech on "Costly Discipleship" at their Seventh Congress. I accepted the invitation not because I had any vested interest in your theology but because of my deep interest in South Africa, its people, its legacy of struggle, and its fate as a nation. (Please don't take this personally.)

Since I had to give this speech, I began to search for your books on my bookshelves. They looked like antique books. They were full of dust and the papers had become yellow since I had not touched them for the last fifteen years. In the beginning, your books did not awaken much interest in my spirit. Your theological language and expressions are so very European male and orthodox in my eyes. After I finished my Ph.D. I stopped reading dead white European men's theologies and memoirs since there are so many interesting theologies to read from the explosion of the people's movement and of new theological imaginations.

So in order to awaken some interest within me about you, I made an investment. I bought an expensive, hard-covered picture book on your life from the Union Theological Seminary bookstore a year ago as a Christmas gift to myself. (It was more than 40 dollars!)

I wanted to know who you are as a person. As a feminist I firmly believe that "personal is political." From that book I discovered that you came from a very rich family, almost aristocratic. Your father was a well-known physician. You had nine brothers and sisters. You grew up in a happy family in a protective environment. Then I found that you were born in February 1906 and executed in April 1945. You were 39 years old when you were killed. I am 39 years old. This makes me feel much closer to you. Then I went through my east and west astrological chart. According to the eastern chart you were born in the boundary of the year of the horse and the year of the snake. I understood why you emphasized action so much like a galloping horse and made contemplative statements such as "without God, before God, with God" like a wise snake. According to the western chart you are Aquarius — Ah! *that's* why you were a musician who played the piano well. You had a free spirit compared to Karl Barth's, and that's why you were so unpredictable: you were a pacifist . . . but then suddenly you joined the group of people who attempted to assassinate Hitler.

Not only that, I discovered you were born fifty years earlier than me. And fifty years have passed since you died.

Since I am Asian, I believe that nothing that happened to you was an accident. There was some meaning in it. I started to like this interesting connection between you and me.

Then your book came alive to me. I also searched out several Bonhoeffer scholars in Korea and interviewed them to discover your legacy in their theology.

Finally I had to decide on the format of our dialogue. I made a decision that it should be a Shamanic journey of making a connection with you.

Why?

Because, according to my Korean tradition, you are a man of very bad Karma. Every person has pity on you.

In our tradition, it would be understood that a person like you did something gravely wrong in your previous life. Otherwise you would not have been killed like that. You had all the components of bad Karma such as:

1. dying an unnatural death such as in an accident;
2. dying young;
3. dying in some alien place outside of your home without any family near.

We believe that the spirit of a person like you cannot rest because of what happened to you but wanders the universe with much *Han* (what we call spirit). We listen to the agony of such beings and bless them to release their Han and enter eternal peace.

I wanted to talk to you and connect with you. Of course, I worried about comments from some of my colleagues:

"Oh what is she doing. I don't have any idea what she is doing."

"She is not academic enough."

"There is no substance in her talk."

"Where is the meat in her theology?"

(Sorry. I am a vegetarian. I do not require any meat.)

For those who doubt my method of presenting theological reflection, I will recommend a best-selling book called *Living Ideas of Dead Economists*. It was written by a Harvard professor. He evoked dead economists like Karl Marx, Adam Smith, and John Maynard Keynes in order to discuss with them today's economic problems. People do academic work very differently nowadays.

OK, now I have finished my groundwork for dialoguing with you, Mr. Bonhoeffer. Let us begin our dialogue.

First, I will let you know how I critically evaluate and appropriate your work for my theology.

Then you have to tell me what you think of my reflection on your work. How will you talk to me? I don't know. Maybe through the audience here. I truly hope that some members of this audience can become a medium of your speech — like Whoopie Goldberg in the movie "Ghost."

Let us begin . . .

When I flew from Kuala Lampur to Cape Town via Johannesburg, my eyes opened wide because most of the passengers were white. After all, I was traveling to South Africa where black people make up eighty percent of the population. All the pilots were white. All the flight attendants were Asian. All the cleaners were black. When I arrived in Cape Town a very friendly white man waited for me to take me to the conference center. When I registered at the hotel, the receptionists were handsome white men and women. Then I came to the Bonhoeffer Conference and eighty percent of the participants were white.

Then I walked around the harbor. Almost ninety percent of pedestrians and shopkeepers were white. The city was visibly a white city. I felt like I was in some European capital.

When I came back, I discovered that the people who served the tea for our conference were black women. When I went to the restaurant all the waiters were white. I felt like I had walked into the segregated South of the U.S. in the fifties.

Something became clear to me. Maybe black South Africans are not very much interested in Bonhoeffer's theology. He must be important mainly to white theologians and pastors. Or was the registration fee too high?

My one-day exposure to South Africa made me think seriously about the social location of theology and theologies. Why am I speaking here? Are these people my main theological audience?

What's the point of my talking here?

Well, the point seems to be that I have to expose the "politics of difference" in theology so that we understand where we are together in this much-divided world, and I need to forge connections among us in order to make this world more life-affirming.

You see, Mr. Bonhoeffer, I raise these kinds of questions in my theological work. Since I have been asked to talk at this Conference specifically on the theme of the "Costly Grace of Discipleship" from a women's perspective, under the big theme of "Are We Still of Any Use?" I will evaluate some of your major theological concerns from an Asian eco-feminist postmodern women's perspective.

First, I understand that your core message of costly discipleship is summarized by your words, "Men for others." Jesus was the example *par excellence* for your words. You urged members of the German church to wake up from the cheap grace of misinterpreted Lutheran theology — the theology of justification by faith alone. These people were doing nothing, just waiting for God's grace. You urged them to become agents of change, Christians who took responsibility for their sinful complicity in the unjust world. You especially emphasized the need for maturity on the part of adult Christians who could solve the problems of their own life.

For you, following Jesus meant emptying your self and caring especially for the most oppressed of your time. When I think about the emphasis on autonomous man after the European enlightenment and reflect on the last five thousand years of patriarchy, a man who became a "man for others," lowering himself to relieve the suffering of others, seems very heroic, messianic and holy.

Therefore, I appreciate your confession of the core of costly dis-

14

cipleship — that is, being a man for others. Especially a man like you: white European, upper-class, elite man.

Now let's take the time-machine to our time.

Let's think about "*Women* for others."

How does it sound? Does it sound spiritual? Ethical? Holy? Does it sound heroic? Messianic? Beautiful?

"Women for others" doesn't give me any new theological imperative or inspiration. Why? Because that is what we women have been for the last five thousand years of patriarchal history. Remember our mothers', grandmothers', and great-grandmothers' lives? They sacrificed their life for others: their husbands, their children, their communities.

Let's add some adjectives to this term "Women for others."

Think about "*Asian* women for others."

What image comes up in your head. The images that come up in my head are Korean comfort women under Japanese militarism; Vietnamese, Filipino, and Thai prostitutes; migrant women workers from the Philippines, Sri Lanka, and Bangladesh who are maids in First World countries; Asian picture brides in the catalogues widely circulated in Europe, North America, and Australia.

Then let's change the adjective again.

"*Black* women for others."

What images come up in your head?

I remember black slave women who were forced to give birth and then to put their babies up for sale. Black women cleaners, maids, and nannies who work for others.

This is what contemporary feminist theologians are asking about, Mr. Bonhoeffer!

It seems that your phrase "Men for others" needs to be analyzed in this light in order to make the meaning of your words come alive. Why do you think African Americans shout with their soul, "I discovered God within me and I loved her fiercely."

For some of us who were colonized in our body, mind, and spirit by the oppressive forces of sexism, racism, classism, and cultural imperialism, it seems we have to unlearn "Women for others" for a while and relearn "Women for herself first, then for others and for her community by choice."

Mr. Bonhoeffer, I also have a problem with this concept, "others."

In our time, many feminists recognize that "the other" ideology is the core of patriarchy. Men with power defined all who were different from them as "others" in order to control and dominate them: less powerful men, women, children, and even the natural world. Simone de Beauvoir talked about this extensively in her book *The Second Sex.*

Edward Said talks in a similar way about "Orientalism" — the mythical representation of the east by the west, whereby eastern people are defined as "irrational," "emotional," "feminine," and "erratic" in contrast to those from the west who are defined as "rational," "orderly," "masculine," and "autonomous."

In my few years of immersion in Asian spirituality in my own land from the Buddhist, Taoist, and Hindu traditions, I have learned that "the Other" is a conceptual flaw. There is no "other." I am you, and you are me. There is no separation; separation is an illusion. Everything is interconnected in the web of life: atoms, mountains, amoebas, trees, men, women, God. Therefore, there are no men for others. We are all life-energy striving to be born into fullness.

Second, your understanding of Jesus Christ and the meaning of his suffering seems the center of your theology. It almost seems circular. Jesus means costly grace. Costly grace means his dying on the cross. Dying on the cross is the consequence of following Jesus. Following Jesus means costly discipleship. Costly discipleship means martyrdom.

It worked for you. I can see it in your life under Hitler's domination and in the Holocaust situation where following Jesus meant suffering and martyrdom.

From the beginning of the Christian church, martyrdom has been praised as virtuous Christian action. Therefore most Christians suffer from the guilt of not suffering enough and from a messianic complex. We are often asked in our churches, "Can you die for Jesus as Jesus died for us?"

And let's face it, the ideology of suffering has been used in the Christian church and in Christian culture to domesticate people with lesser power. It has been used as the weapon of domination to make people obey and suffer rather than resist. This ideology of suffering is used in Korea to invigorate male heroism.

For example, when Korean women theologians challenged Korean male Minjung theologians for not including the writing of any women theologians in the book *Minjung Theology,* some of them said:

First, we can't find any good, intellectually equipped women theologians;

Second, when women paid the same price of discipleship as men, such as being tortured and imprisoned, we will include you.

Of course, the women were furious. We shouted, "When you went to prison, we took care of your children, your old parents, and family. We worked to bring food for our family."

And we women also know how brave women can be through the labor movement and the Chipko movement. Women are the last ones to give up because they do not have much to lose compared to men.

What we women want is not to glorify the suffering death of a messiah. What we want is to abolish all kinds of capital punishment, whether the electric chair, the gallows, the guillotine, or the cross. We ask not what we can die for, because our children's lives are dependent on us. We ask rather what we can live for?

Asian American feminist theologian Rita Nakashima Brock boldly said Jesus' suffering death did not save anybody. Through his vision for life, for the kingdom of God (we say now kin-dom of God!) and the erotic power of his life in community, we empower one another for our salvation.

When Asian women, scholars, and theologians got together for an EATWOT christological meeting, we found consensus about what made Jesus the Christ. We confessed that Jesus' vision and his uncompromising "no"' to injustice in the world gave life to "the kin-dom of God." Unlike you, Dietrich Bonhoeffer, we found the centrality of Jesus in our life to be a major stumbling block in working with friends and comrades from other religions (which constitute more than 97 percent of Asia's population). We carry the burden of the christological doctrine of Jesus, the only Savior. When you live in Asia, you know that's not true.

What I most like about your theological imagination is your "without God, before God, and with God." Your words come alive more than ever in this time of so-called postmodernity. We cannot find a wholesome, orderly, powerful god anymore. It seems as if the whole world is worshipping in the sanctuary of a global free market in a religion of savage capitalism. Its ultimate god is Mammon. We keep asking where the good God is who once gave us so much security. When our god loses its definite character our enemy loses its definite character too.

I envy your clarity in defining Hitler as the enemy you had to defeat. You said, "When mad, Hitler drove a car with innocent people in it. This mad driver has to be stopped. Conducting funerals for these people as the pastor is not enough." Yes, in your time the enemy was clear.

But how about our time?

In our time we do not have a Hitler character. Our enemies are often so beautiful, attractive, even sexy. They dominate us with the power of seduction, allure, and attraction rather than military force. When I look at today's situation of globalization, CNNization and marketization, I can see that the driver is mad. But the passengers and the person who tried to save them are also slightly mad. We all are to some degree insider-outsiders in this madness of globalization. We are victims and we are also complacent. And we also resist.

"Victim," "Complicit one," and "Resister" are embedded in all of us to some degree.

Therefore, in our time we cannot find any heroic solution because nobody's hands are clean. Of course there are differences between more dirty hands and less dirty hands. Our solution seems more tedious. It seems as if we have had to make an ant and spider strategy rather than a more heroic lion and tiger strategy.

We make holes in this humungous free market system by developing a grassroots democracy economy. We have also to make connections like spiders with the enemy's fax machines — electronic freedom fighters!

We cannot see reality through the eyes of modernity — divide, analyze, objectify, observe. Rather we have to make many connections, emphasize *with*, and participate passionately.

In my time I want to change your words as follows:

"Without Life, before Life, with Life."

What is at stake in our time is Life itself. The solution is to find the way to invigorate Life in our midst.

So, in conclusion, I go back to your question: "Are we still of any use?"

Maybe we Christians will be of some use, but only if we deconstruct our Christendom, Christian superiority, Christian cultural imperialism, and christocentric mentalities.

Yes. We will be of some use if only we retain memories of the Jesus movement and incarnate God within us as Jesus did for his God, and complete the ever-changing body of God in our midst. We should

18

not just follow Jesus but become a new Christ, a new Christ in our communities of resistance, hope, and celebration.

What will be the name of theology coming out of this experience? Life theology? Inter-living theology?

Dietrich Bonhoeffer. What's your response to my non-stop talking? "Shut up and meditate more?" I am waiting for your response.

Yours in Christ,
Chung Hyun Kyung

Who Is Jesus Christ, for Us, Today?

PETER SELBY

These words are written in winter for delivery in summer. Would that all contrasts were as easy to handle as seasonal ones. For it is also true that these are words written in Durham for delivery in Cape Town. Can words produced in Britain, where the shape of transformation is as hard to define as the need of it is palpable, resonate in the new South Africa, where transformation is the obvious and accepted agenda? Curiously, the title and subtitle of this Congress seemed to me to reflect those contrasts and that difficulty: "Are We Still of Any Use?" feels like a wintry question for a British audience; *Bonhoeffer for a New Day* more like the manifesto for a South African summer.

Such an opening is not intended to convey the impression of self-pity, let alone of the illusion that the pains of South Africa are now all in the past, emptied in the delight of a new and democratic society. Nonetheless, I think I may not be the only person here with a sense of being a visitor from an old world to a new one. With that goes the sense that this is something of a dream, and certainly an experience for which "privilege" is a rather bland and inadequate term. Nonetheless, the contrasts of feeling and agenda have to be faced, and in a sense are the

---

The argument presented in this essay is developed more fully by the author in his book *Grace and Mortgage* (London: Darton, Longman and Todd, 1997).

context for my handling of the root christological question, "Who is Christ, for us, today?" For that question, which we all know so well, puts before us two different kinds of agenda.

A Twofold Agenda

In the first place, this christological question asks about the continued vitality, truth, and relevance of the Christian tradition. Indeed, in its original context in Bonhoeffer's letter of 30 April 1944, the question of the identity of Christ is presented as equivalent to the question of the essence of Christian faith. In those familiar words, he says:

> What is bothering me incessantly is the question what Christianity really is, or indeed who Christ really is, for us, today. The time when people could be told everything by means of words, whether theological or pious, is over, and so is the time of inwardness and conscience — and that means the time of religion in general.[1]

Such is the struggle of a theologian confronted with modernity: What does this inheritance mean in the nonreligious world we now inhabit? Paradoxically, it is of course a question most people would regard as "religious"; you would not ask it if you were not yourself steeped in, and deeply preoccupied with, Christianity itself and its possibilities for today. Indeed, it is precisely the situation of today that appears to vindicate Bonhoeffer's early perception, one in which he appears very much to speak with a Barthian voice, that there is a profound contrast between the revelation and the community of which Christ is the agent, on the one hand, and the realm of religion and religious community, on the other. As he wrote in *Sanctorum Communio:*

> This was not a new religion seeking adherents, which is a picture drawn by a later time. But God established the reality of the church, of humanity pardoned in Jesus Christ. Not religion, but revelation, not a religious community, but the church: that is what the reality of Jesus Christ means.[2]

1. *Letters and Papers from Prison* (London: SCM, 1971), 279.
2. *Sanctorum Communio: A Dogmatic Inquiry into the Sociology of the Church* (London: Collins, 1963), 111f.

Yet this form of the christological question, the apologetic agenda, contrasts strongly with another one which is equally christological but is presented, it would seem, in quite a different tone of voice. This second agenda brings with it a different kind of passion, that of obedience and discipleship. Here is that agenda as it was expressed in one of Bonhoeffer's very earliest public utterances, his statement to the congregation in Barcelona. Here are words of an assistant pastor merely twenty-two years of age. This person is not wondering whether in this time Christ might have relevance, only how that relevance can be expressed and responded to. This is not the Christ whose relevance to today's world is in any doubt; all that is in doubt is whether we shall make an adequate response:

> Whether in our time Christ can still occupy a place where we make decisions on the deepest matters known to us, over our own life and over the life of our people, that is the question we will consider today. Whether the Spirit of Christ has anything final, definitive, and decisive to say to us, that is what we want to speak about. We all know that Christ has, in effect, been eliminated from our lives. Of course we build him a temple, but we live in our own houses. Christ has become a matter of the church, or rather of the churchiness of a group, not a matter of life. Religion plays for the psyche of the nineteenth and twentieth centuries the role of the so-called Sunday room into which one gladly withdraws for a couple of hours but only to get back to one's work immediately afterwards. However, one thing is clear: we understand Christ only if we commit ourselves to him in a stark "Either-Or." He did not go to the cross to ornament and embellish our life. If we wish to have him, then he demands the right to say something decisive about our entire life.[3]

Here is a form of the christological agenda which resonates much more immediately with the needs of those faced with structures of oppression requiring resistance. The "decisions about our lives and the lives of our people" are surely decisions about justice and truth in our relations with one another, about our participation in the ordering of our society and about our responsibility within the teeming variety of

---

3. "Jesus Christ and the Essence of Christianity" (Address of December 11th, 1928), in G. B. Kelly and F. B. Nelson, eds., *A Testament to Freedom* (San Francisco: HarperCollins, 1990), 53.

the living and material world. Here is a voice that echoes in the experience of the churches of the poor and their theologians of liberation who have followed on in the history of resistance since Bonhoeffer. This is not the perplexity of a post-Christian, post-Enlightenment, European Christianity, but a summons for the hour of radical discipleship.

The contrast of these two agendas, old world perplexity and new world resistance, is perceived clearly in the way in which John de Gruchy explains the nature of Bonhoeffer's relevance for South Africa in the days of its struggle:

> We have not referred at all in this essay to Bonhoeffer's thinking in prison about Christianity in a "world come of age." The reason for this is that his earlier writings appear to be more relevant to our present situation. Moreover, there is a sense in which the Enlightenment as an historical event has passed us by at the southern tip of Africa, and therefore we are still a religious rather than a secular society.[4]

So the question with which his essay ends, "Who is Jesus Christ, for you in South Africa, today?"[5] surely has quite a different feel there from what it conveys when asked by Bonhoeffer in general terms in his April 1944 letter. It certainly sounds very different from the way in which I heard it, along with many of my contemporaries, when Dietrich Bonhoeffer first entered my consciousness.

For my knowledge of Bonhoeffer belongs to the period which de Gruchy designates that of the "creative misuse of Bonhoeffer."[6] That is to say, I am conscious of belonging to the generation of those whose introduction to Bonhoeffer came through the flurry of debate occasioned by John Robinson's *Honest to God*. It was by this means, as a student in 1963, that I found myself grasping hold of the notions of "a world come of age" and "religionless Christianity" with enthusiasm. I had in those days little time for what I thought was the very conservative overreaction of the practitioners of theology, a subject I had not then studied. Not only did the New Testament scholar Dr. George Caird declare in an Ascension Day sermon that St. Luke had pulled Dr. Robinson's leg and it had come off in

---

4. "Bonhoeffer in South Africa," an exploratory essay, in Eberhard Bethge, *Bonhoeffer: Exile and Martyr* (London: Collins, 1975), 41.

5. *Ibid.*, 42.

6. John de Gruchy, ed., *Dietrich Bonhoeffer, Witness to Jesus Christ* (London: Collins, 1988), 36.

his hand; but a few months later this douche of cold water threatened, as I saw it, permanently to wash away my excitement:

> There is an immense amount of material in the Fathers, both western and eastern, which, taken along with the insights of the great mystical writers and masters of the spiritual life, should remind us first very sharply and then very profitably of the scandalous poverty of much modern "theism." The true extent of the scandal is peculiarly well shown by the fact that not only does the theism against which [Bishop John Robinson] protests seem to very many people to be recognisably the theism of the Christian Church (and the only possible theism — hence the need for atheism) but he seems to be trapped in this belief himself.[7]

Those words were written by David Jenkins, whom I then supposed to be some kind of a reactionary, such was the heat generated in that debate which seems so long ago![8] Part of the reason the debate seems so distant in the current British situation is the sense of religious optimism which pervaded much of what liberal theologians were saying at that time. We now know the truth of Michael Ramsey's comment to the Conference of Modern Churchmen only four years after *Honest to God,* when he drew attention to a secularism far more radical than the liberal theological tradition was disposed to take into account. That conference was entitled, significantly for our purposes, *Christ for Us Today.* Ramsey pointed out how profound was the skepticism which the secularism of that period was bringing to such an agenda. In his opening sermon he said:

> It is not only how we understand the story of Jesus in relation to God and man, and how we find Jesus to be meaningful. Rather are men and women asking how man is meaningful at all, and whether the idea of meaningfulness has any validity in the world in which we live.[9]

7. David Jenkins, "Concerning Theism," in John A. T. Robinson and David L. Edwards, eds., *The Honest to God Debate* (London: SCM Press, 1963).

8. Jenkins was not of course primarily referring to the Bonhoeffer component in Robinson's theology but rather to the extensive use of Tillich's categories "ground of being" and "ultimate reality."

9. A. M. Ramsey, "Sermon to the Modern Churchmen's Conference, 24 July 1967," in *Christ for Us Today: Papers from the Fiftieth Annual Conference of Modern Churchmen,* Somerville College, Oxford, 24-28 July, 1967 (London: SCM Press, 1968), 12.

Nearly thirty years later we know how hardened many of our societies are to such questions, let alone to the answers which Christianity has offered to them. We have also seen the flourishing of fundamentalisms, Christian and otherwise, which suggest that for many the proper response of religion to modernity is strident confrontation. All of this implies a need to transcend the kind of reading of Bonhoeffer which characterized the way many of us came to know him.

If our religious situation is different from that of 1943 (or 1963), the politics with which many of us are confronted has altered too. Writing this paper, as I have said, in Britain for delivery in South Africa raises this question sharply. In common with many of you, I have come to this Congress in large measure to discover how the Bonhoeffer who has been read as the resistance hero, the anti-racist martyr, will be read in this society. For in common with many of South Africa's well-wishers we pray, with some fear and trembling based on our own experience, that the victories which have been so painfully achieved against an ideology of racial domination will not be snatched from its grasp with the aid of the sophisticated tools of modern capitalism. In his account of *Christianity and Democracy,* John de Gruchy occasioned for me a shiver of recognition when he wrote about the ambiguous relationship between democracy and the free market ideology.

> Neo-conservatives such as Friedrich von Hayek and Milton Friedman, and other proponents of the new world order such as Francis Fukuyama are adamant in their insistence on a market free from any kind of social control. For this reason, many advocates of the free market, such as Hayek, resist the checks and balances of democracy, even while using the freedoms it offers to achieve their own goals.[10]

It is not hard to read such an account as a description of what has happened in Britain in the last decade and a half.

More to the point, his words reminded me of a meeting I attended at a hotel in downtown Bulawayo where a large gathering of business people — almost all white — was addressed by a spokesperson of a large South African corporation. His message was simple and clear: "You people have done good business here; we need a settlement with the

---

10. John W. de Gruchy, *Christianity and Democracy* (Cambridge: Cambridge University Press, 1995), 25f.

ANC and we'll have good business too, and yours will be even better." My rejoicing at the power of economic pressure to change racist policies was, to say the least, tarnished somewhat by the equal foreboding at the capacity of those with economic power to exploit the possibilities — and avoid incurring the costs — of almost any political change.

We see, therefore, two somewhat different readings of Bonhoeffer, the prophet of humanity come of age, and the martyr of the resistance to racist tyranny, both in some measure vulnerable to the pressure of this new day. Like any prominent person whose life and thought are used to suit the various purposes of subsequent generations, Bonhoeffer is likely to survive these more or less "creative misuses" and be read again; but for us the question presses hard: *Are we* (as his present-day readers) *still any use?*

The famous form of the christological question as it was posed in the April 1944 letter and which was given to me as the title of this session offers its own particular way of addressing the crucial matter of our continuing usefulness. It offers three words, "who?" "us," and "today," to pose thereby three profound challenges to our continuing usefulness, the challenges of identity, solidarity and discernment; it is to these three challenges that I shall attend in the next three sections.

"Who?" — The Challenge of Identity

The question, Who? runs like a thread through the whole history of Bonhoeffer's christological thinking. So in his reconstructed Christology lectures he begins his "positive Christology" with the statement: "The question may not run, 'How is it possible to conceive of the Incarnate?' but 'Who is he?'"[11] Similarly, later on in considering the humiliation and exaltation of Christ, he says, "The question is no longer, '*How* can God be humiliated man?' but rather '*Who* is the humiliated God-man?'"[12]

In coming to this point, he has followed the lines he had sketched out for himself early in the lectures:

The question "Who" is the question of transcendence. The question "How?" is the question of immanence. Because the one who is ques-

11. Dietrich Bonhoeffer, *Christology* (London: Collins, 1966), 106.
12. *Ibid.,* 111.

tioned here is the Son, the immanent question cannot grasp him. Not, "How are you possible?" — that is the godless question, the serpent's question — but "Who are you?" The question "Who?" expresses the strangeness and otherness of the encounter and at the same time reveals itself as the question of the very existence of the enquirer himself.[13]

He highlights the significance of this point in his reference to what a factory worker might mean in asking about Jesus. Is Jesus (he would want to know) the one in solidarity with the worker in his opposition to the oppressions of capitalism, or is he the one so commonly represented by the church as settled into bourgeois society?[14] Bonhoeffer also presents the issue of identity through the person of Dostoyevsky's *Idiot*:

The idiot does not keep himself apart, but clumsily causes offence everywhere. He has nothing to do with the great ones, but with the children. He is mocked, and he is loved. He is the fool and he is the wise man. He endures all and he forgives all. He is revolutionary, yet he conforms. He does not want to — but he draws attention to himself simply by being there. Who are you? Idiot or Christ?[15]

We must note that the question of identity is mutual; those who examine the identity of Christ will find their own identity questioned. Thus the encounters we see in the Gospels go to the heart of the question of identity. Jesus' audience asks of him, "Who is this?" only to find themselves facing basic questions about who *they* are; the answer to "Are you the Christ?" is inevitably, "Are you first of all a rich person, or a landowner, or a fisherman? Or are you first of all a human being?"

Such are bound to be the issues faced if we ask, Are we still of any use? We are drawn away from questioning about how the God-man, the first claim on our life and loyalty, is possible, and toward the issue of *who?* The discipleship of prayer and action cuts through the doctrinal quest for how a Christ might be possible to the requirement of discerning *who* this is — Christ or idiot? And having discerned, to face the question, Who are *you?*

13. *Ibid.*, 30f.
14. *Ibid.*, 35.
15. *Ibid.*, 36.

The question asked in prison is not different from this: In a world that is *mündig,* who is Jesus Christ? Is he among those who still acknowledge their need of religion, or is he to be found among those who manifest their *mündigkeit,* living *etsi deus non daretur,* as God requires, before God without God. Such persons are not particularly the puzzled religious questioners of Britain in the 1960s; they are just as much the workers he mentions in his Christology lectures, not least those who do not even think the question worth bothering with at all. For the question of identity, ours and Christ's, arises with special force in a world where *religious* identity and identifiability can no longer be assumed. Who are you, Christ? Fanatic? Moralist? Market leader? Refugee? Bankrupt? And the response is the question put to us, Who are we?

"Today" — The Challenge of Discernment

Bonhoeffer's christological question appears in the context of a statement about our historical situation. The Christ whom he seeks is a Christ for *today,* and we can easily read this as meaning that time has some absolute quality, that it exists independently of our values and purposes, and supremely that it exists independently of Christ. A world where the accuracy of a watch with a quartz movement is within the grasp of most people in prosperous societies is a world where we can easily suppose that the more accurately we know it the more constructively we shall use it.

Yet we also know that the speed with which time passes varies: Christmas seems ages away to our children waiting to unwrap their presents and all but imminent for parents who have yet to buy them. We know that the couple of minutes it takes the dentist to drill a cavity seems much longer, as does the ten minutes we are kept waiting for an appointment on which a great deal hangs for us. We are aware that whether my lecture seems to last a long or a short time depends on many factors other than how many actual minutes it consumes, and that when we are in severe pain just a few minutes can seem an eternity.

Our consciousness has also been greatly affected by an entirely different set of time scales, those of the cosmic history of the universe and of humankind. Alongside our obsession with accuracy to the last second is the knowledge we now have of a massive pre-history that dwarfs our civilization with its sheer expanse and has to be measured in spans of years that defeat our imagination. Alongside that is the sense of a darker future millions of years hence when the universe is destined to run down and time itself will cease. What has all that to say about our concern to know exactly which second in which minute it is so that we can be sure to fill it?

So time has no absolute status: it measures out our lives not primarily in days and months and years but in what we can do with our days, the past we can remember or would rather forget, and the future we can dread, or plan. And whether or not we are religious enough to know that "the times and seasons are in the Father's hand," we certainly know they are not in ours. Everyone involved in business knows that the least predictable economic reality is timing, and that even if you could be reasonably sure there would be a recovery some day, there are no easy ways to get the timing right, and right means not the right second and minute but the right time in relation to the launching of a new product or the calling of the next election. How or when the teenager who is glad to be thought a year or two older than she is turns into an adult who likes to feel and look young will vary from person to person, but it comes to us all, does it not? Yet even that is determined by aspects of culture that vary greatly from society to society and time to time, and our feelings about ourselves are greatly affected by whether we are surrounded by a cult of youth or of age.

We also need to remind ourselves that as well as a culture there is also a *politics* of time. In the absence of constructive and properly rewarded work time hangs heavy upon people; ways to fill it are hard to find and mostly cost money; and the days to the next welfare cheque can seem to last forever. We know as a matter of experience that who keeps whom waiting, who has time *in* his or her hands, and who is supposed to have time *on* his or her hands are very good indications of where the power lies in a situation. We know that some people get thanked for "giving up their valuable time," the clear implication being that other people's time is not valuable. We also know very well that such value is not merely an intrinsic or psychological value: "time is money," we say, knowing that some people's time is better paid than others. We also say that time varies in its quality, and accuse ourselves of not giving our nearest and dearest what we very accurately call "quality time."

It is crucial, in efforts to produce change as well as in the natural grain of life, the rhythm of days and seasons, to work with the grain of social movements in order to manipulate the levers of history. Ideas have times when their hour comes; there are historic movements, not always open to us to know or to direct, which determine whether an idea or a program will simply be confined to the dustbin of wasted human endeavor or will be decisive for the future course of events. The revolutionary developments in Eastern and Central Europe and the recent politics of my own country and of this one are obvious examples of the coming to fruition of ideas that had been around for a long time but whose hour came and was grasped — for better and for worse. In that sense, it is important to say that even ideas whose hour has not come, so far as one can tell, lie there in the store of memory able to be summoned into usefulness when some particular, usually unpredictable, conjunction of events gives them a relevance and a dynamic which really bring about change. The cry, "How long, O Lord?" is very often the cry of those who are out of time, whose ideas and convictions seem both obviously just and true and evidently destined to be ignored until some unknown future time.

The claim to know what today is, its cultural shape and character, is ultimately a claim to prescribe the framework into which Christ must be fitted. The claim is inevitably patrician: the today that is being referred to is the today of those in power today, the shapers of the culture of today. Theirs will not be the descriptions of the today of the dispossessed, of those who spend today in terror of their lives or in such pain that they cannot wait for it to end. Such is the fate of all todays: to turn out in the end to be the today of those who shape today. This was even true of quite recent attempts to describe the biblical shape of time and to assert that it is the pattern of timekeeping for the world. So in his classic *Christ and Time,* Oscar Cullmann writes:

> Our system of reckoning time does not number the years in a continuous forward-moving series that begins at a fixed initial point. That method is followed, for example, in the Jewish calendar, which thinks it possible to fix the date of the creation of the world and simply numbers forward from that point. Our system, however, does not proceed from an initial point, but from a centre; it takes as the midpoint an event which is open to historical investigation and can be chronologically fixed, if not with complete accuracy, at least within a space of a few years. That event is the birth of Jesus Christ of Nazareth.

30

Thence proceed in opposite directions two enumerations, one forward, the other backward: "after Christ," "before Christ."[16]

Such sentiments we read with embarrassment. They describe a world of Christendom and of massive insensitivity to the desire of Jews and others to have their time, their "today," taken with full seriousness. Such words read as the assertion of the preeminence of the Christian "today," and claim the calendar for an eternal and exalted Christ. Yet Bonhoeffer's perception of the humiliated God-man is of one whose "today" is found not with those who control the calendar, not even those who control the calendar allegedly in his name, but with those whose urgencies are treated as of no account.

Such was the today into which Bonhoeffer felt compelled to immerse himself in his famous commendation of life lived fully with God in the world, words which sum up the position he had expounded in his *Ethics*:

> [I]t is only by living completely in this world that one learns to have faith. One must completely abandon any attempt to make something of oneself, whether it be a saint, or a converted sinner, or a churchman.... By this-worldliness I mean living unreservedly in life's duties, problems, successes and failures, experiences and perplexities. In so doing we throw ourselves completely into the arms of God, taking seriously not our own sufferings, but those of God in the world — watching with Christ in Gethsemane.[17]

Thus the "today" of Bonhoeffer's question can be read in liberal or radical mode: it may be the today of those who are sure of their own today and ask how Christ may fit into it, or it may be that "today" is "today" as Christ the "humiliated God-man" sees it and asks us to see it. On the one hand we may see today from the perspective of an old world perplexed as to whether Christ can be understood today, or we may seek to see it from the viewpoint of those whose today is that of the humiliated one whose perspective on today is of no account. Among

---

16. O. Cullmann, *Christ and Time* (1946; revised English edition, London: SCM Press, 1962), 17.

17. From the letter of 21 July 1944, quoted in Haddon Willmer, "Bonhoeffer's Sanctity as a Problem for Bonhoeffer Studies," in *Celebrating Critical Awareness: Bonhoeffer and Bradford 60 Years On* (n.p.: International Bonhoeffer Society, 1993).

those we must, of course, include generations yet unborn, those who have no voice in decisions about how our world is to be used and abused in the service of those who rule, and shape, our "today."

"Us" — The Challenge of Solidarity

The preacher's text, Romans 8:31, "If God is for us, who is against us?" could have led in a number of directions at an ordination; but this preacher, Bishop Simon Phipps, chose to present the Christian life, and Christian priesthood, as having above all to do with the meaning of "us."[18] He began with an account of an event portrayed on television: an aircraft had crashed into the sea, though remaining watertight. When one of the crew offered to leave through a hatch and attempt to surface with a transmitter, a passenger who was an experienced diver offered to go with him. His wife remonstrated with him, but he responded, "It's for the good of all of us?" That prompted the very human reply, "Us? Who's 'us'? *We're* us. This is just a bunch of strangers."

"Who's 'us'?" is neither an elegant nor even a grammatical question. I distinguish it from the other question, "Who are we?" for that question asks for characterization, for a statement of identity such as we considered earlier. As such it can be a very profound question; but it is not the one with which we are concerned here. For the question of "us" is the issue of the boundaries of our solidarity, the territory beyond which all we see is "just a bunch of strangers."

I do not have to elaborate here on the relevance of Bonhoeffer's life and thought to the issue of "Who's 'us'?" or of the implications and inspiration derived in the resistance to racist ideologies from his stand in relation to the Jews. Propelled as he was into many of the positions which he took by an ideology of race which proved singularly attractive to the majority of his Christian fellow-citizens, he has been an obvious person to call in aid for those seeking in the name of Christ to confront such ideologies in the intervening decades. John de Gruchy has both led and chronicled the relationship of a theological dialogue with Bonhoeffer and the political resistance to apartheid in South

18. Simon Phipps, unpublished ordination sermon, June 1990. I am grateful to Bishop Phipps both for a very significant address, and for refreshing my memory with his notes.

Africa,[19] and, quite apart from the analogy with Nazism, we know the extent to which Bonhoeffer himself was moved by the situation of Black Americans during his time in New York.[20] In the context of the nationalisms of our time, writers such as Keith Clements have resorted to him in the search for a true patriotism.[21]

The refusal of Christ to accommodate to any self-chosen "us," and his demand that the identity of "us" should be the one that appears in the light of Christ, remains a pressing issue. Naturally it is not usually a matter of controversy among believers that in theory human rights should be accorded to all citizens irrespective of ethnic origin. That level of understanding may carry weight within the life of the nation-state. But its inadequacy becomes evident when we consider the increasing number of people who are driven from their homelands by the pressures of war and oppression and are left to beg for rights of abode and sustenance at the hand of other nations who retain their right to determine who "us" is. In a European context there is no sign of fundamental questioning of the right of human communities to decide the boundaries of their solidarity and the identity of their "us."

It is not hard to recognize the politics of the current determination in my country to "tighten up" on immigration procedures under the guise of barring the door to "bogus asylum seekers." The weasel words whereby the object of such proposals is to "safeguard community relations" cannot conceal the fact that when legislation is introduced that assumes that asylum seekers are likely to be liars a statement is also being made about all the recent arrivals in European countries to the effect that they were probably liars too. To give as one of the answers to Bonhoeffer's question that Jesus Christ for us today is a *refugee* is not after all to say anything that is not clearly rooted in the Gospel of Matthew. Any political judgment about the power of the nation state to administer its borders must at some point come face to face with the claim of Christ to a decisive voice in the matter of deciding who "us" is.

19. See, e.g., John W. de Gruchy, *Bonhoeffer and South Africa: Theology in Dialogue* (Grand Rapids: Eerdmans, 1984).

20. See Eberhard Bethge, *Dietrich Bonhoeffer: A Biography* (London: Collins, 1970), 109ff.

21. See Keith Clements, *A Patriotism for Today: Love of Country in Dialogue with Dietrich Bonhoeffer* (London: Collins, 1986).

Yet in seeking to honor Bonhoeffer's legacy we cannot only take up the points where there are obvious parallels between the issues we face and the racism he found necessary to resist. It is precisely the areas of our current political situation which he does *not* appear to address which we may need to take up. In a world in which nationalisms and ethnic division continue to be occasions of hatred and bloodshed, it may seem almost bizarre to suggest that there are other ways in which the issue of boundaries to our solidarity — the question "Who's 'us'?" — is arising which are more sinister and hold yet more menace for the future of humankind.

I take you back to the meeting in a Bulawayo hotel to which I referred earlier. The message of that meeting and a host of other pieces of evidence make it clear to us that the ideology of racism *can* be opposed by the instruments of the marketplace (though in noticing that we must never forget the role of those who put their lives on the line in a far more direct way than those who only abstained from eating South African oranges). In the end it was surely clear that the prosperity even of those who were enjoying it would not be able to continue unless apartheid were dismantled.

Yet I believe there is a profoundly sinister aspect to that development. We were all assured that the trends in the world economy were all ultimately beneficial, provided unnecessary and old-fashioned restrictions could be removed. The world was moving, we were told, in the direction of a free market, of low taxation, of the exportability of capital and know-how. Was this a world in which the challenge of "Who's 'us'?" would finally have been answered? Or is it not rather a world in which the power to decide who "us" is has been handed over to those who have the capacity to succeed in the market, and ultimately to control it?

It is here, surely, that we come up against Bonhoeffer's fundamental stance in his approach to the question who Jesus Christ is for us today. In his critique of Bultmann in the letter of 5 May 1944, he calls Bultmann's approach "still a liberal one (i.e. abridging the gospel)" in contrast to his own, which is "trying to think theologically."[22] That is, the question of who Jesus Christ is for us today cannot be interpreted so as to mean that we know who "us" is and the question therefore is how Jesus Christ is somehow to be accommodated to that "us." Rather, in the language of the Barcelona address, if Jesus Christ is to have something decisive to say about

22. *LPP*, 285.

the deepest decisions we have to take concerning us and our people, he has to be able to be decisive precisely about who the "us" is.

In contrast to what "thinking theologically" must mean, the attraction of the market is that it appears to offer a method for deciding who "us" is apart from Christ. It is a response not to the question of who "us" is, but to its own quite different question, what is the best method for deciding who is of "us" and who is not (that is to say principally, who shall inherit the riches of the earth and who shall not)? Do we not have here precisely what Bonhoeffer means by the "godless question, the question of the serpent," which supplants the "transcendent" question who Christ is for us with the "immanent" question of how, the question by which Christ cannot ever be grasped. We are reminded here surely very directly of the lawyer's question, "Who is my neighbor?" (by which he meant, of course, Who am I free to regard as *not* my neighbor?), to which the only possible response was a story that raised an entirely different question.

If the question, Who is Jesus Christ, for us, today? is to be addressed, therefore, it has to be on the basis that Jesus Christ is not the one who accommodates himself to prior decisions, reached predominantly through the instrument of the market, about who "us" is, but on the basis that only in and through him is the decision about the boundaries of our solidarity to be made. When we know him we know who "us" is, and without submitting our decisions about who "us" is to him we shall not know who he is.

In this connection I think it most important that we address the context which Bonhoeffer was considering in raising the question who Jesus Christ was for us today. His concern is with Christ and the world come of age. This *mündigkeit* he explicates in terms of the end of the religious *a priori*, of humanity's accountability for itself, and of the end of the "alibi" of God. He sees that as a historical development, and a benign one. In its English translation, "come of age," it is not surprising that *mündigkeit* should be seen as the result of a progressive human self-emancipation, a process as irrevocable as the growing up of an individual person is.

Yet the metaphor of *mündigkeit* makes a more profound point. Its reference is to the point where someone is a legally responsible person, able to speak for herself and enter into obligations on her own account. In most cases, of course, that point is arrived at through the passing of years, when a person reaches the age of majority and is not any longer regarded as, to use the Latin metaphor, *in-fant*, unable to speak. But there are categories of people besides the young who are denied the right to speak for themselves: the imprisoned, those certified as insane, not to mention the whole list of *Unmenschen*, non-persons who have been the creation of the Third Reich — and not just the Third Reich.

Once we remove the connotations of inevitability and irrevocability from our perception of the human situation in the modern era, the language of a world "come of age" can hold out, in a contemporary reading and appropriation of the legacy of Dietrich Bonhoeffer, a vision that is both realistic and challenging. We shall not be naïvely blind to the possibility that people, societies, and communities will be put back "under guardianship" willingly or unwillingly, deprived of autonomy and the right to act responsibly, *entmündigt*, put under administration, reduced to the level where their own decisions count for nothing. Thus understood, the high cost and the tremendous fragility of the declaration that the world is *mündig geworden* come very quickly and clearly before our eyes, as does the great difficulty which human beings have in bearing that reality.

In particular, the claim of the market to be a symbol of human freedom and responsibility comes under the judgment of all those who are restricted and bound, *entmündigt* by its operation: What else can we say about the nations of the two-thirds world and the structural adjustment programs forced upon them? How else can we regard the whole communities within the world's more prosperous societies for whom the market is neither the symbol of nor the key to their freedom, but the means by which they are reduced, as all debtors in history have been reduced, to incapacity and ultimately to effective slavery. Most serious of all is the fact that since what happens to them appears to come about through the operation of the "free market," there is added to the injury of their overwhelming poverty the insult of the conviction that they are to blame.

If we are to be of any use, then, we shall need to engage with the market. We shall need to assert, for our time, the unique right of Christ to the definition of "us," and that means refusing that right to institutions in society, however useful they may seem to be for certain purposes, to provide that definition. Just because the market seems to have been a useful instrument for ending the power of a racist state, we need to see how it too has the capacity to offer itself as an idol, as an alternative Christ, asserting its own claim and creating its own "us" and its own "bunch of strangers." Thus the question, Who is Christ for us today? turns out to have more to do with his claim upon our obedience than with our perplexity about his relevance to us.

Christ and the New Day

I have endeavored in constructing this paper to relate various kinds of evidence as I perceive them. There is the world as I see it, in my own country. There is the world of this society as I read about it and see it portrayed. There is what I know of the context and content of Bonhoeffer's writing.

But there is also the evidence of an inner tension, heightened enormously for me in the process of putting these words down for this occasion. On the one hand I am the product of a liberal theological culture as a result of which I first heard the question, Who is Jesus Christ, for us, today? The perplexity which that gave me about how Christ might be understood and related to my world of today remains, and the climate in which the question has to be faced is, if anything, more hostile than when I first heard it.

At the same time, I hear Bonhoeffer himself, whom I have gotten to know more closely since I first heard that question express my perplexity, speak with a different voice. It is a voice which seems to me to be the authentic bearer of the Christian vocation to discipleship, and a witness to a Christ who (as the title Christ implies) continues to make the decisive claim expressed in the Barcelona address. He continues to make it, furthermore, not with the power of the market leader or the force of state coercion, but as the humiliated God-man.

As such, he is uniquely able to tell us about our "today," for he has dined with those who have had no part in shaping the culture out of which we voice our perplexity. As such he can ask us about the boundaries of our "us" because he has lived and died outside them. As such he is able to turn our question to him, "Who are you, for us, today?" into his question, "Who are you?"

The day is indeed new, and not just for this society. The new day brings new perplexities in the form of issues about democracy, about the economy, about the vision of humanity which informs our common life. Among those who face the new day will be those who, like some of us gathered at this Congress, have questions and perplexity about the identity of Christianity, and indeed of Christ himself, in our time. In Dietrich Bonhoeffer we have someone who was both close enough to his own culture to feel its perplexity in the face of its coming of age, and yet sure enough of the claim of Christ among the excluded of his time to be a disciple. Sometimes tensions paralyze us and, in particular, cause us not to see the possibilities of a new day. Sometimes, however, we need the determination to hear two voices clearly, the voice of the culture that has given us our questions and the voice of those who have no part in that culture. That, I am suggesting, is probably the only way we shall still be of any use.

The Nonreligious Scientist and the Confessing Theologian: The Influence of Karl-Friedrich Bonhoeffer on His Younger Brother Dietrich[1]

EBERHARD BETHGE

The fiftieth anniversary of Dietrich Bonhoeffer's murder on April 9, 1945, evoked a broad and intense interest in him from the *Washington Post* to the *New Zürich*, from Rome to Trient, from Coventry to Adelaide, from Flossenbürg to Berlin. His whole person came up for discussion: the pastor and the pacifist, the prophet and the pietist, the conspirator and the patriot.

In an impressive memorial address on April 9, Jürgen Schmude, a former Minister of Justice and now Präses of the Synod of the *Evangelische Kirche* (EKD), reminded us that there has still not been any official rejection of those judges of the Third Reich who had blood on their hands. Nor any rejection of their judgments. The same is true of the present Lower House of the German Federal Parliament *(Bundestag)*. There are, at the same time, groups in Germany today who plead for such a declaration. Of course, this can hardly be the concern of those who were associated with the condemned. No declaration will bring them to life again, and those murderous judges are either as old as the hills or dead. The honor of the members of

---

1. The original German title of this lecture given in the State Library in Berlin on 19 July 1995 was "Spannung zwischen Dogmatik und Ethik in der Widerstandszeit: Die Beziehung zwischen Karl Friedrich Bonhoeffer, dem a-religiösen Psysiko-Chemiker und seinem Bruder Dietrich, dem Theologen." It has been translated and edited by Robert Steiner and the editor.

the resistance, moreover, does not need such a vindication. For Germany, however, such a declaration is important since the decision of Flossenbürg is still regarded as legitimate. We are much more concerned, then, with handing on the memory of their martyrdom to a new generation. There are encouraging developments in this regard today amongst theologians, church leaders and historians, journalists and the media, as was evident at the last *Kirchentag*.[2]

All of this has demonstrated that Bonhoeffer's writings, and especially his letters from Tegel *(Letters and Papers from Prison)*, have lost nothing of their freshness and fascination. On the contrary! Critics have wrongly assumed that Bonhoeffer's analysis of a "nonreligious world come of age," which was discussed so widely in the 1960s, has been disproved, and that we can therefore disregard Bonhoeffer. Such a step would deprive us of a unique theologian of this century.

The letters which Bonhoeffer smuggled out of his Tegel cell in 1944 include meditations on how and why his belonging to Jesus of Nazareth was the source of his ethics of conspiracy. The meditation in the letter of April 30 that year begins with the fundamental question: "Who is Jesus Christ, for us, today?"[3] The emphasis lies on "for us, today." But who is the "us"? Generally speaking, the heirs of the Enlightenment. But, in a more specific and concrete sense, his own family, his parents and siblings who were irreversibly involved in the resistance.

Bonhoeffer's fundamental question received a very simple answer: Jesus Christ is "the person for others."[4] This interpretation of his "credo in Christo," formulated in that situation — "I believe in Christ as the person for others"[5] and therefore also in his "body," the church as the community of human beings for others — was the foundation of his participation in the resistance. It provided the basis for the ethics of conspiracy and its implementation. If this is the case, then the reverse is equally obvious, namely that an apparently correct dogma which refrains from such an ethic of political resistance on behalf of others is mere verbalism and the degradation of theology. With Bonhoeffer we too are

2. An annual congress held by the EKD in Germany since the end of the Second World War, which is attended by thousands of laypeople and pastors.

3. *LPP,* 279.

4. *Ibid.,* 381.

5. Today we may prefer to say "with others" in order to express the reciprocal rather than the patriarchal character of our relationship with Jesus Christ.

searching for a Christology which can support such an ethic, an ethic which he discovered in Christ as the person for, or with, others. It is no coincidence, then, that Bonhoeffer makes his remarks about the relationship between dogmatics and ethics — in a much more profound way than can be discussed here — to a theological friend.[6]

The Tension between Dogmatics and Ethics

The tension between dogmatics and ethics illustrates precisely the relationship between the oldest and the youngest brother within the larger circle of Bonhoeffer siblings: Karl-Friedrich, the renowned physical chemist, born in January 13, 1899 (died in 1957), and Dietrich, the pastor and theologian, born in February 4, 1906. The latter had chosen the church and theology as his vocation, though by no means with the enthusiastic support of the family. Yet this did not affect the good relationships which always existed within the family. Indeed, especially during the Nazi period, an interest in one another together with a natural, unrestricted sharing of advice prevailed.[7]

There was considerable correspondence between Karl-Friedrich and Dietrich, since the former lived quite far away (Frankfurt, Leipzig, and the U.S.A.). Of special interest are the regular birthday letters which Dietrich sent to his brother and which have been scattered in the various Bonhoeffer volumes. Now they can be read together in the new edition of *Widerstand und Ergebung.*[8] On reading these birthday letters, one realizes how the younger brother tried to give an account of his profession to his older brother. One also recognizes the momentary character of Dietrich's theological reflections and the decisions he made during the church struggle.

It was very significant for Dietrich that a member of a family so

---

6. Eberhard Bethge is referring here, of course, to himself, to whom the prison letters which dealt with these issues were addressed [editor].

7. Some years ago, Renate Bethge (née Schleicher), Bonhoeffer's niece, pointed out the importance of this relationship between Dietrich's theology and his family connection. "Bonhoeffer's family and her importance for his theology," in *Beiträgen zum Widerstand 1933-1945,* 2nd ed. (Gedekstätte Deutsche Widerstand, 1995), 30.

8. *Widerstand und Ergebung,* ed. Eberhard Bethge, Renate Bethge, Christian Gremmels, and Jürgen Henkys, *DBW,* vol. 8 (Munich: Chr. Kaiser Verlag). This is the German title of *Letters and Papers from Prison.*

deeply rooted in the humanism of the Enlightenment, an agnostic natural scientist, should act in so ethically correct a manner under the circumstances prevailing under Nazism. (Karl-Friedrich offered protection and shelter to Jewish colleagues in his institute right up to 1945.) Equally important was the fact that his own Confessing Church, despite its partial resistance and achievements, was struck with a fatal and continuing blindness regarding the persecution of the Jews. Of course, Dietrich himself, in criticizing the later synods of the Confessing Church and in taking part in the conspiracy, did not have the support of the Councils of Brethren *(Bruderräten)*. The resistance clearly meant not just refusal to bring into line but the elimination of the regime. So it was exceedingly difficult to live with the tension between dogmatics and ethics. But it is exactly this experience that stands behind the theological reflections in his *Letters and Papers from Prison*. And, in this regard, the steady presence of his family, and especially his brother Karl-Friedrich, was probably more motivating and important than that of many theological colleagues like Emil Brunner, Friedrich Gogarten, and even Karl Barth.

The Renowned Scientist

Who was Karl-Friedrich Bonhoeffer? As a theologian I lack the competence to show that he was one of the great, internationally acknowledged physical chemists of this century. But what of the opinion of others? His mother maintained that "if Karl-Friedrich had not been the first of my children, the rest wouldn't have come out right." Others have reminded us that he refused to sign a declaration of loyalty and obedience toward Hitler, something he could afford because of his international reputation. Karl-Friedrich had established this reputation with his work on two modifications of the hydrogen molecule whereby he was able to obtain pure para-hydrogen out of the natural mixture of ortho- and para-hydrogen for the first time. He stopped his work as a specialist in "heavy water" when the importance of this material for the construction of the nuclear bomb became known. At the beginning of the war he transferred his interest to electrochemistry. He received invitations to the most important professorates of physics in Germany: in 1930 to Frankfurt and in 1934 to Leipzig. There he was engaged with the passivity of metals and the kinetics of electrode processes, before moving on to the investigation of periodic chemical reactions as models of life processes.

After the war, in 1947, Karl-Friedrich returned to his scientific roots, first to the University of Berlin, where he also took over the managment of the Kaiser Wilhelm-Institute of Dahlem, then to the Max Planck-Institute. Finally he built the new Max Planck-Institute for biophysical chemistry in Göttingen that is now named after him. His managment of this institute led to a new flourishing of work in this field and to the enhancement of his own international reputation, helped by the fact that he was also regarded as a person of political integrity. In 1955 the Bunsen Society awarded him a medal in recognition of his work, and at his death in 1957 the Max Planck-Society spoke of him as a great scholar and a man of character. W. Jaenicke commented: "His scientific achievements made him well-known — but while there are quite a few excellent scientists, characters like him are too few."[9] Jaenicke, who belonged, until 1943, to those "half-Aryans" who had been successfully protected, added: "The same love of his country with which Karl-Friedrich Bonhoeffer went into the field as a volunteer in 1917 made him wish the defeat of Germany in the second World War."

Indicative of his personality was Karl-Friedrich's relationship with Fritz Haber, an important scientist and colleague who emigrated to Switzerland in 1933 and died there the following year. On hearing of Haber's death, he wrote a letter of condolence to the children:

Dear Mr. Haber, dear Ms. Haber,

I have just learned from the newspaper of the death of your respected father. I am so dismayed by it that I can hardly find words. [I am so sorry] that he had to die at this moment. Everything good and beautiful which I owe to him comes back to me, and I cannot suppress the feeling of bitterness at our powerlessness to support him in these last difficult years. I shall always remember his wisdom and goodness, and as long as I live I shall do everything in my power to nurture and keep his memory alive in our field. I am grateful to the fate which for many years brought me close to such an extraordinary man as your father, and I hope that I will have an opportunity to express publicly how much Germany owes to him and also what I feel for him. Since I do not know where his grave

9. *Physikalische Blätter* 13 (1957): 369f.

is, I intend to have a wreath laid at the Haber-Linde as a sign of my gratitude.

With deep sympathy, always your Karl-Friedrich Bonhoeffer

Karl-Friedrich helped organize a memorial event for Fritz Haber with the Kaiser Wilhelm-Society in Berlin in 1935, and even wrote a speech for it. This led to fierce conflicts between the Society and the Nazi Ministry of Education and Culture. The result was that while Karl-Friedrich courageously gave the memorial address at an unofficial funeral ceremony in Dahlem, he was not allowed to do so at the official ceremony even though he had prepared the speech. In fact, he stood at the door of the overcrowded hall when his speech was read by Otto Hahn.

One can imagine how Dietrich both loved and feared this older brother — heir of the Enlightenment and its scientific achievements, and critic of the encrusted and insulated theism of the church and its servants. Dietrich always let Karl-Friedrich know that he understood his critical reservations and, yes, even approved them from the time that theological blindness led to the justification of the Aryan Clause in 1933, with all its fatal consequences. Dietrich was well aware that he could not involve either his father or his siblings in the life of the church, and he never tried. But he was glad when his family began expressing interest in the start of the Confessing Church. He certainly did not regard their increasing attendance at Martin Niemöller's church in Dahlem as simply motivated by political considerations. But he was also well aware that the members of his family circle would not accept tutelage any longer on vital ecclesiastical and theological questions — particularly when the majority of theologians had morally denied their credo in failing to protect persecuted Jews.

Examining the Correspondence

The American Letter

Before we look at the various birthday letters of Dietrich to Karl-Friedrich I would like to refer to a passage in a letter from the beginning of 1931. Both brothers stayed in the United States in 1930/31. In his letter, Dietrich writes about racism in America, but he does not mention the antisemitism in Germany. He was fascinated by his experiences amongst African Americans in Harlem and Washington. Indeed, he wrote: "I spent more time with them than on anything else" during the year at Union Theological Seminary. Karl-Friedrich, for his part, had just turned down an invitation to Harvard University. His reason was that he could not imagine living with his children in the racist context of the United States. He clearly did not think at that time that anything comparable could take place in Germany. Dietrich then focused on his brother's philosophical interests, informing him about the reading which formed part of his study program. This included mainly the writings of William James, the American pragmatist who regarded religion as valid only to the extent of its ethical usefulness. Dietrich wrote: "I have come to know American philosophy fairly thoroughly, and in doing so I have often thought of you, Karl-Friedrich." Nonetheless, the gap between this utilitarian philosophy and his own theology, so influenced by Karl Barth, was obvious: "Even though I do not believe in it all much more than previously, I have learned a great deal from it. James is especially interesting to read."[10] Dietrich never forgot empiricism's modern way of thinking and, through his oldest brother, it remained an ongoing challenge. Eventually, in Tegel prison in 1944, he finally had to come to terms with it. This is one of the reasons the prison letters are so interesting even today. Indeed, we must read those fifty pages of theology in *Letters and Papers from Prison* with much more awareness of the unseen presence of Karl-Friedrich, the scientist and ethical example as well as the representative of the empiricism of William James.[11]

The First Letter from London (1934)

The next extant letter was sent from London to Frankfurt in January 1934. Now everything had changed. Disappointed by his church's mild reaction toward the Nazification of its synods, its main committees and

10. *Barcelona, Berlin, Amerika,* ed. Reinhart Staats and Hans Christoph von Hase, *DBW,* vol. 10 (Gütersloh: Chr. Kaiser/Gütersloher Verlag, 1991), 250.
11. See Ralf K. Wüstenberg, *Glauben als Leben. Dietrich Bonhoeffer und die nichtreligiöse Interpretation biblischer Begriffe* (Frankfurt/M.: Peter Lang, 1996).

also its theological faculties, Dietrich started his pastorate in London among the German-speaking community. By this time both brothers were busy trying to help Jewish emigrants. In this birthday letter Dietrich wrote:

> Being in England is actually a disadvantage. One is too close not to want to participate, and too far away in order to really be actively involved. This has bothered me a lot during the past weeks. I have recently read of Barth's dismissal in the *Times* (13.1.34). I still cannot believe it. But if it is correct, I might have to return so that at least someone still says those things at the universities.[12]

Dietrich continued:

> Somehow I experience this stay in England more as an intermezzo, though I enjoy the work very much with its very limited scale. I only thought that the next step would bring me at last to India and to the east.[13] It seems to be much closer from here. And since I am daily more strongly convinced that Christianity will come to an end in the west — at least in its present form and interpretation — I would like very much to go to the east a second time, before I return to Germany. Besides my pastoral work, I also have had talks and discussed plans with English church leaders, as well as with some very interesting politicians.[14] Furthermore I have had an immense number of visits from Germans, mostly Jews, who know me from somewhere and ask me for something. . . . Otherwise, Hildebrandt is with me . . . moreover a student from Berlin. In that way I don't become lonely. The numerous phone calls from here to Berlin and from Berlin to here also prevents that.[15]

12. See Karl Barth's tract *Theologische Existenz heute* (Munich: Chr. Kaiser Verlag, 1933).

13. He attempted to go to India in 1928/29 from Barcelona and again in 1931 from New York.

14. Lord Lothian, later ambassador in Washington, who asked Bonhoeffer through Bell for an analysis of the Church Struggle for *The Round Table*. See Eberhard Bethge, *Dietrich Bonhoeffer*, 290.

15. *London 1933-1935*, ed. Hans Goedeking, Martin Heimbucher, and Hans-Walter Schleicher, *DBW*, vol. 13 (Gütersloh: Chr. Kaiser/Gütersloher Verlag, 1994), 75.

The Second Letter from London (1935)

The most interesting of the birthday letters was sent a year later from London, but this time to Leipzig. By now the German Church struggle had taken a decisive turn under strong constraints. The Confessing Church took two steps which had serious consequences. First, in the Barmen Declaration at the end of May 1934, the Barmen confessors declared that the official church was guilty of heresy if it continued to mix the message of the gospel with teutonic racism and the *Führer* ideology. Then, at the synod of Dahlem in October 1934, the Confessing Church called for obedience to the emergency organizations of the Confessing Synods and the Councils of Brethren instead of the "heretics." This meant that they had to accept a position of illegality, something for which they had not previously been prepared, and which was especially difficult for younger pastors who had not yet been placed in congregations. It also required an unusual degree of commitment to confession and sacrifice on the part of congregations in supporting the emergency church authorities, expressed in the signing of red or green cards. This commitment played a special role in the extended Bonhoeffer family. Some of the women (Paula and Susanne) signed the "red card" in Dahlem. For other members such a confessional and doctrinal commitment remained problematic. To what degree could identification be expected at this point?

In order to understand this birthday letter it is important to recall that shortly before it was sent a family meeting occurred at the parents' house on Wangenheim Street. Both Dietrich and Karl-Friedrich were present, the elder brother being at that time in the midst of the heated dispute about the memorial lecture for Fritz Haber. It is against this background that Dietrich wrote the letter of January 14, 1935:

> . . . In recent years we have seen frightfully little of each other. So I especially appreciated those days recently. It may be that in some things I seem to you somewhat fanatical and crazy. Sometimes I am somewhat afraid of that myself. But I know that if I were more reasonable, the next day I would have to hang up my whole theology to be honest. When I started with theology, I imagined something different, perhaps more an academic affair. Now something quite different has come of it all. But I believe I finally know that, at least for once, I am on the right track — for the first time in my life. And that

47

often makes me very happy. I am just often afraid that out of fear of other people's opinions I won't keep moving, but will get stuck. I think I know that I will only achieve inner clarity and genuine integrity if I really begin to take the Sermon on the Mount seriously. This is the only source of strength which could finally explode all the magic and ghosts until only a few burned-out remains are all that is left of the fireworks. The restoration of the church will surely come from a kind of new monasticism, which has in common with the old kind only the uncompromising nature of life according to the Sermon on the Mount, following Christ. I think that it is about time to gather the people for this. . . .

Apologetically, he continued:

Please excuse these rather personal comments, they happen to flow from my pen as I thought about our being together recently. And, anyway, we are interested in each other in this way, too. I still just can't imagine that you really think all these thoughts are completely crazy. There just are some things which are worth standing up for without compromise. And I think, peace and social justice, or actually Christ, is such a thing. . . . By chance I recently came across the fairy tale of the Emperor's New Clothes — it really fits these times. All we are missing is the child at the end. We really should perform it sometime. I hope I will hear from you again soon. In any case, my birthday is coming soon. . . .

The "rather personal comments" for which Dietrich thinks he needs to apologize are unusual. But there are exciting hints about fresh developments in his thinking and acting. Indeed, this is the time when he was drafting the first notes and outline for *The Cost of Discipleship*, a work which the later Rhenish Präses Beckmann referred to as the most important theological book of this century, and the most profound interpretation of the Barmen Declaration. That was the time when, in Germany, the Reformation doctrine of *sola gratia* had been so mockingly used to permit racist theories to penetrate the church's teaching and practice, yes, even the church's order. One could no longer counter with mere words. Renewal and a transformed lifestyle were necessary. The book being planned would not have a traditional theological title such as, for example, "Sanctification" or "Doctrine of Justification" or "Faith and Works" but one which referred to the gift of relationships established between God and the person, between the person and God, and between one person and another; hence Bonhoeffer's choice: *Nachfolge,* in English, discipleship or "following Christ."

Binding Ethics and Dogmatics Together

I return to the letter that predated Dietrich's visit to Berlin. The conversations on that occasion would not have revolved only around the escalation of Nazi policies — 1935 was the year of the Nuremberg Laws — and probably not just around the memorial event for Fritz Haber; they would also have touched on those problems that arose for some of the family out of their new association with the language of the Barmen Declaration. These included their relationship to the theology of the Confessing Church which resulted from signing the green card.

A few months later, in a letter to his brother-in-law Rüdiger Schleicher, a liberal jurist from Swabia, Bonhoeffer shows an awareness of these difficulties which originated in the neo-orthodoxy in the Confessing Church.[16] He explains in detail, and in a remarkably personal way, his own attitude toward "Holy Scripture" and the "Word of God." He concludes: "Whether we have the right to speak in the way I have to you, will only be shown through being put to the test. And I think that we still have to prove that."[17]

The most exciting aspect of the letter to Karl-Friedrich of 1935 is how Dietrich passionately binds ethics and dogmatics together in one single sentence: "Peace and social justice . . . or, actually, Christ." He almost forces these together. These three basic elements are inseparable, just as he and Karl-Friedrich were bonded together. If the basic insight of his dissertation *Sanctorum Communio* (1927), "Christ existing as the congregation," does not have anything to do with peace and justice, then this very Christ is already denied. So it is that the prison theology begins with the question "Who is Jesus Christ, for us, today?" as expressed in the letter of April 30, 1944. This "us, today" refers, on the one hand, to his scientist brother, the liberal jurist and brother-in-law, and all those in Dietrich's environment for whom they stood and, on the other hand,

16. April 1936, *GS,* vol. 3, ed. Eberhard Bethge (Munich: Chr. Kaiser Verlag, 1966), 26ff.
17. *Ibid.,* 31.

the theologian of *The Cost of Discipleship*, who is now entangled in the conspiracy. In a single sentence Dietrich forces together his beloved, agnostic, but ethically exemplary brother Karl-Friedrich and his own faith and spirituality in the process of reformulation. Therefore, already in this letter of 1935, the ground out of which the prison theology would later grow was being prepared.

The Letter from Finkenwalde (1937)

While this last letter of 1935 from London dealt with difficulties in the circle of siblings because of the new ideas and changes in lifestyle of their youngest brother, the next letter resolutely protests against the attempts of the family to divert him from pursuing the path of illegality. It is not a birthday letter and originates from November 1937, a time in which Dietrich found himself in a very dangerous situation in his engagement in the church struggle. In 1935, when he began to build Finkenwalde, he was involved in an illegitimate act of disobedience toward the heretical Reichsbishop and his administration. But now it was an act of disobedience toward the state, its ministerial decrees, and police prohibitions.

Finkenwalde had been running for two and a half years, the lectures on *Nachfolge* had been given, and a disciplined "monastic" life had been lived. Since the autumn of 1935 the "House of Brethren" had been in operation to ensure the continuity of the spiritual life of the ordinands, who changed every half year. Then in September 1937 the seminary was closed down by the police, following decrees issued by Himmler and Kerrl.

Dietrich and I were convinced that the work of training of the Confessing Church would have to be continued under all circumstances and for two months in Berlin we looked for a new way of doing this under disguise. We finally found a way in the so-called "collective pastorates" *(Sammelvikariate)* in the backmost part of Pomerania. Two brave church superintendents (in Schlawe: Eduard Block; in Köslin: Friedrich Onnasch) received candidates as assistant pastors in their church districts, which could still be regarded as legal, and gathered them during the week in their parsonages for the training which we gave. This worked until March 1940 when the Gestapo arrived at Sigurdshof and closed the seminary for the last time after we had left for the holidays.

At Christmas 1937 the list of Protestant clergy arrested by the Gestapo reached new lengths.

Karl-Friedrich was worried about the health of his mother at this time. This was not least because the family of his sister Sabine, Dietrich's twin, who was married to a so-called non-Aryan, Gerhard Leibholz, became increasingly threatened by Nazi legislation, and emigration became more and more necessary. Therefore Karl-Friedrich asked if Dietrich really wanted to begin the seminary again under the obviously worsened circumstances. Dietrich responded:

Dear Karl-Friedrich,

Many thanks for your letter. I am always sorry whenever Mama gets so upset and pulls others into it, too. But there really isn't any reason for it at all. We really mustn't get upset any more at the possibility that Himmler's decree might mean for me what it has already meant for hundreds of others. We cannot continue to struggle for the church's cause without making sacrifices. All of you who went to war sacrificed a great deal more. Why shouldn't we do it for the church, too? And why does everybody try to stop us? Of course, no one is keen to go to prison. But if it comes, then it will be — I hope, at least — a joy, because the cause is worth it. We will start again the beginning of next week. How are the little one and Grete? Did you receive the little book?

Greetings to all of you, your Dietrich.[18]

The "little book" to which Bonhoeffer refers was, of course, *The Cost of Discipleship*, which appeared at Christmas 1937.

The Final Four Fragments

Four further short letters from Dietrich to Karl-Friedrich reflect the stations along the path he had now begun to travel. Karl-Friedrich, who was teaching physical chemistry in Leipzig, was frequently in Berlin at his parents' home and was thus well informed about Dietrich's steps and decisions. A belated birthday letter of January 1939, from the collective

18. *GS*, vol. 2, ed. Eberhard Bethge (Munich: Chr. Kaiser Verlag, 1959), 295.

pastorate in Gross-Schlönwitz in the Schlawe district of Pomerania, written at a time of great danger for the illegal ministerial candidates, reads:

> . . . I wish you and the others a good New Year, and in any case no more disturbance than last year. The reason I did not write in time was that there is a lot going on here again right now. Partially it has been really depressing in recent weeks to have to see how many [pastors] use all sorts of pretexts and reasons to get peace and security at all cost. In such times, which come every now and then, there is always a lot to do with visits, lectures, etc. I am sure that for the church everything depends on whether we can stand fast, even at great sacrifice. The greatest sacrifices are small compared to what we would lose by conceding anything. I really would not know what today would be worth investing everything for, if not for this. It certainly does not matter, how many remain, but that there are some who still stand fast. Of course, some things are more difficult for those who are married, but sometimes I think that much easier, too. I very often admire the courage of pastor's wives who are prepared to accept any consequences rather than advise their husbands to give in. Parish members are also often much clearer and more determined than their pastors. Very important decisions will be made here during these days. — I am well. I would like to visit Sabine in March, if it is still possible. . . .

Already, then, Bonhoeffer announces an intended visit to the Leibholz family, the family of his twin sister Sabine, who meanwhile had emigrated to England. During that trip he wanted to seek the advice of his friend, George Bell, the great ecumenical leader and bishop of Chichester, to find out what possibilities there might be for him to find a meaningful existence outside of Nazi Germany. These considerations eventually led to Bonhoeffer's journey to New York in the summer of 1939, a time when Karl-Friedrich himself also lectured in the United States, as had been the case eight years before.

A postcard which Dietrich wrote to his brother in the United States was sent after Dietrich's own painful decision to return to Germany. He discussed the problems of returning home, returning to his students, and returning to his family. Members of the family were already in the conspiracy and its new mode of resistance, namely participating in covert preparations for a *coup d'état*. No risky public words from the pulpit were permitted. The card from New York to Karl-Friedrich on June 26, 1939, reads:

... Things here are as follows: I have turned down the offers made to me here, for many reasons. So I am now completely in control of my time. I can stay or return as I want. Under normal circumstances, I would have participated in the Summer School here, which lasts until August and for which I was expected. But I find the political news from Europe so appalling that I am seriously considering returning earlier. I don't want to be over here in case war should begin, but back to Germany. I have thought that over during these weeks, especially since I now do not have any specific work to do here. So I am thinking that perhaps I will travel together with you on the eighth as far as England from where I could get home much more easily. . . .

The next surviving lines are written by Dietrich in January 1940 after having returned to Germany and resumed his teaching in the illegal seminary of the Confessing Church. The card was sent from the frozen forests south of Schlawe. He tells his brother about reading a book which relates to his physicist brother's profession and world of thought. The sentences from this short greeting from Sigurdshof of January 15, 1940, read:

... By the way, I must tell you that I am currently reading the book *Science Breaks Monopolies* with real enthusiasm like reading a novel. If only we had been told such things in school or somewhere later! For me it is practically changing my world view; at least it is making a great impression on me and giving me much joy. . . .

Dietrich was fascinated by Zischka's *Science Breaks Monopolies,* a book encouraged by the Nazis because it praised German independent scientific achievements. Dietrich was not disturbed by that in his desire to gain information about advancements in the field of natural science. Unfortunately, we do not know if and how Karl-Friedrich responded to these sentiments of his youngest brother, who was always hungry for knowledge. But we remember how later on in his Tegel prison cell (through the slowly increasing opportunities of reading material from the prison library) Dietrich tried to continue to educate himself in this direction by reading C. F. von Weizsäcker's *On the World-View of Physics* in May 1944.

At that time in prison, Dietrich was not permitted to send letters through the censor to anyone — and therefore also not to his brother Karl-Friedrich — except to his parents and his fiancée. Smuggling letters to the family, as he often did to me on army service from November 1943 onward, would have been too dangerous because of the possible censorship of the family's mail. But in one of those smuggled letters he wrote: "I am now reading with greatest interest Weizsäcker's book and hope to learn a great deal from it for my own work."[19] He went on to say: "how wrong it is to use God as a stop-gap for the incompleteness of our knowledge. . . . We are to find God in what we know, not in what we don't know. . . . That is true for the relationship between God and scientific knowledge."[20] Is it not now quite obvious how significant was the influence of Karl-Friedrich in motivating Bonhoeffer's prison theology?

The last surviving birthday greeting from Dietrich is his relatively punctual card of January 17, 1941, sent while he was on one of his conspiratorial trips in Bavaria. He was en route to the Benedictine monastery in Metten whose abbot, Hofmeister, like Dietrich, had a military deferment to serve in the military intelligence *(Abwehr)*. The greeting, posted from Landshut, reads:

Dear Karl-Friedrich!

Many greetings for your birthday, slightly late, and many good wishes for you all in the New Year. At the moment I am travelling to the Benedictine monastery in Metten, where I will have a lot to discuss in the matter which now concerns me. Next week I expect to travel to Switzerland for several weeks. After that I will come back to Berlin briefly. All good wishes to you all!

Your Dietrich.

Here Bonhoeffer gives notice of the first of his three trips to Switzerland on behalf of the conspiracy, made possible by the military intelligence, which were to enable him to establish contacts with England. But what excited him most, and what he looked forward to most eagerly, was his meeting with Karl Barth and Willem Visser 't Hooft in Geneva and Basel. And Barth, in turn, was interested not only in Bonhoeffer's new attempt to write a book of ethics, but also to hear at first hand about the resistance in Germany.

19. *LPP,* 308.
20. *Ibid.,* 311.

These, then, are the surviving letters from Dietrich to Karl-Friedrich. But the contacts and the vivid and intensive interest in one another did not end with the correspondence. With the closing down of the seminary in Pomerania in 1940, the center of personal decisions for Dietrich was transferred back to his parents' home in Berlin. Karl-Friedrich also traveled now more often from Leipzig to Berlin, since he worked as a consultant for Osram and always stopped at the Marienburger Allee. In other words, he knew quite well about Dietrich's increasing involvement and planning in the military intelligence in Tirpitzufer and his activities in the underground cell of Colonel Hans Oster and Hans von Dohnanyi.

When Karl-Friedrich struggled back again for the first time from Leipzig to Berlin in June 1945 after the family catastrophe, he wrote to his children. This letter forms the epilogue which has concluded *Letters and Papers from Prison* since the 1970 edition. In it he indicates that he knew that Dietrich had been sent from Regensburg at Flossenbürg, but he still did not know about the murder. The epilogue concludes with the anxious question: "Why isn't he here yet?"[21]

Theological Reflections in Prison

Theology is absent from Karl-Friedrich's letters to Dietrich in Tegel prison. But Dietrich is intensively occupied with his new project, outlining and drafting sketches of his proposed book on Christianity in a world come of age. Smuggled out of prison, Bonhoeffer's letters reflecting this new theological interest reached me on the Italian front in the summer of 1944. But much of the motivation for these theological reflections came from Karl-Friedrich's reservations concerning Christian dogmatics and his ethical convictions and actions. They became creatively fruitful in Dietrich's mind.

In those terrible days after the failed assassination of Hitler on the 20th of July and the darkening of every horizon for the conspirators, their families, and friends, Dietrich was surprisingly free and sovereign with his topic. On October 8, when he was transferred to a cell in Prinz-Albrecht Street, he took the work which he had already begun, and once there he worked on the theme again and again. A genuine

21. *Ibid.*, 410.

theology was now required to provide a dogmatic foundation for the dangerous ethics of the conspiracy, namely an answer to the basic question: "Who is Jesus Christ, for us, today?" This much Dietrich felt he owed his family and friends. So, in the midst of the heaviest air-raids in the Prinz-Abrecht Street cell, and aware that the *coup d'état* had failed, he developed many pages of new thoughts on Christian faith "for us today." This continued until his death. Huppenkothen, the Gestapo captain responsible for Bonhoeffer and Dohnanyi, burned Bonhoeffer's posthumous work on April 9, 1945, in Flossenbürg. Thus Bonhoeffer left us only fragmentary and preliminary meditations which invite us to continue thinking with, against, and for him.

In a time of change from a theocentric to a scientifically shaped, indeed, materialistically oriented world, together with accompanying forms of misanthropy, Dietrich Bonhoeffer became a theologian of the conspiracy, conditioned somewhat by the pervasive presence of his scientist brother. After fifty years his concern has not yet been finally dealt with; in fact, it is probably only at its beginning. It continues to make an impact, and its topicality even seems to be increasing. During a series of lectures by American and German teachers at the Humboldt-University in Berlin on February 2, 1995, Helmut Reihlen,[22] professor and engineer, and presently the president of the Berlin-Brandenburg Synod, spoke of Bonhoeffer as the one who helped him as an adult to speak both as an engineer and a member of the church at the same time, and with the same self-confidence. He continued:

> It was his readiness to engage in the world in the way it is . . . that he did not allow his personality to be split up . . . scientists, engineers observe nature, recognize its laws . . . and make its powers serve one's own purpose. And many scientists . . . became homeless in our church. . . . So it was a liberation when Bonhoeffer, after having read Carl-Friedrich von Weizsäcker's *On the World-View of Physics,* out of his prison cell rejected "the use of God as a stop-gap for the incompleteness of our knowledge."

22. Reihlen was the recipient of the Union Theological Seminary medal for his work in establishing the Dietrich Bonhoeffer Chair at the Seminary in 1994.

Religionless Christianity: Dietrich Bonhoeffer's Tegel Theology

RALF K. WÜSTENBERG

In May 1944 Dietrich Bonhoeffer wrote to his friend Eberhard Bethge from Tegel prison: "I am thinking about how we can reinterpret in a 'worldly' sense — in the sense of the Old Testament and of John 1:14 — the concepts of repentance, faith, justification, rebirth, and sanctification. I shall be writing to you about it again."[1] In subsequent correspondence the two friends discussed those concepts which would subsequently become so well known to us: the conviction that a *religionless time* had arrived, and that the *world had come of age* since it began to exist without God as a *stop-gap* for the incompleteness of our knowledge.

In introducing these terms, Bonhoeffer wanted to provide a hermeneutic whereby Christ would become Lord of the world again. This form of interpretation, which implies that religion is no longer a condition of justification, was designated both a *worldly* and a *nonreligious* interpretation. By this, however, Bonhoeffer, did not mean a metaphysical form of interpretation, but rather the reinterpretation of *biblical concepts*. So what, then, does it mean to interpret biblical concepts in a nonreligious way? Has the world really become religionless at this historical epoch? What does Bonhoeffer mean by the term *religion* when he writes about a nonreligious form of interpretation?

A large number of publications have dealt with these questions,

---

1. *LPP*, 287.

often misunderstanding what Bonhoeffer actually meant. For talking about a religionless time, some interpreters like Harvey Cox have called him an "atheist," others a "secularist" (A. Loen).[2] Bernd Jaspert and John Macquarrie believed that Bonhoeffer himself had a "religious nature,"[3] while for William Hamilton and others, Bonhoeffer was the "father of the God-is-dead theology."[4] Such interpretations clearly reflect the religious or the secular perspectives of the interpreters rather than the assumptions of Bonhoeffer himself. He was, in fact, made a participant in the debate about secularism.

Many of the misinterpretations of Bonhoeffer in the 1960s owed to the failure to take into account how profoundly his theology was informed by his Christology. As Thomas Torrance stated:

> . . . the tragedy of the situation is that . . . instead of really listening to Bonhoeffer many . . . have come to use Bonhoeffer for their own ends, as a means of objectifying their own image of themselves. . . . In this way Bonhoeffer's thought has been severely twisted and misunderstanding of him has become rife, especially when certain catch-phrases like "religionless Christianity" and "worldly holiness" are worked up into systems of thought so sharply opposed to Bonhoeffer's basic Christian theology, not least his Christology.[5]

Ignoring the christological center in Bonhoeffer's theology inevitably means misconstruing him altogether. The same rule applies to the nonreligious interpretation of biblical concepts. Gerhard Ebeling was ultimately right to presume that the nonreligious interpretation meant for Bonhoeffer a christological interpretation.[6] This basic insight has often been quoted in the publications of the last four decades, but it has not been put in concrete form. If to interpret nonreligiously at the same

2. A. E. Loen, *Säkularisation. Von der wahren Voraussetzung und angeblichen Gottlosigkeit der Wissenschaft* (Munich, 1965), 205ff.

3. B. Jaspert, *Frömmigkeit und Kirchengeschichte* (Erzabteil St. Ottilien, 1986), 76f.; John Macquarrie, *God and Secularity* (London: SCM, 1968), 72ff.

4. William Hamilton, "A Secular Theology for a World Come of Age," *Theology Today* 18 (1962): 440; cf. J. A. T. Robinson, *Honest to God* (London: SCM, 1963).

5. Thomas F. Torrance, "Cheap and Costly Grace," *God and Rationality* (Oxford: Oxford University Press, 1971), 56-85, 74.

6. Gerhard Ebeling, "Die 'Nicht-religiöse Interpretation biblischer Begriffe,'" *Zeitschrift für Theologie und Kirche* 52 (1955): 296-360; quotation from Eberhard Bethge, ed., *Die Mündige Welt*, vol. 2 (Munich: Chr. Kaiser Verlag, 1956), 12-73, 20f.

time means to interpret christologically, what does this form of interpretation imply in a more concrete way?

In what follows I shall focus on the content and the meaning of religionless Christianity. As a first step I will concentrate on Bonhoeffer's own writings to determine what these sources say about "religion."

Bonhoeffer's View of Religion

If we take into account all of Bonhoeffer's statements, we can see three quite distinct views of religion. Firstly, there is the *positive* view, which appears in his early writings and owes to the influence of liberal theology. As a student,[7] Bonhoeffer adopted a positive understanding of both religion and culture from his teachers, notably Adolf von Harnack and Reinhold Seeberg. However, from 1925 Bonhoeffer came under the influence of Karl Barth. Discovering dialectical theology meant changing his opinion of religion as well. So, secondly, there is Bonhoeffer's *critical* view of religion, which appears for instance in his doctoral dissertation *Sanctorum Communio.* The year of its publication, 1927, marks the change from a positive to a more critical view of religion. But Bonhoeffer went further. From his critique of religion he, thirdly, developed his *nonreligious* interpretation. Assuming that the time of religion was finished, he proclaimed a religionless Christianity. Bonhoeffer did more than criticize religion in a *theological* way; he supposed that the time of religion had run its *historical* course. So he proposed a Christian faith that is not "anti-" but "a"-religious.[8]

In his writings, then, Bonhoeffer speaks about "religion" in three different ways — positively, negatively, and historically — as a phenomenon that has run its course. Statements reflecting these three different ways of perceiving religion appear unsystematically and at times even side by side. For instance, as late as 1944, in his letters from prison,

---

7. See Bonhoeffer's essays "Luthers Stimmungen gegenüber seinem Werk in seinen letzten Lebensjahren. Nach seinem Briefwechsel von 1540-1546," in *Jugend und Studium 1918-1927*, ed. Hans Pfeifer, Clifford Green, and Carl Jürgen Kaltenborn, *DBW*, vol. 9 (Munich: Chr. Kaiser Verlag, 1986), 271-305, 300; also: "Referat über historische und pneumatische Schriftauslegung," *ibid.*, 305-23, 321.

8. R. Bernhardt, *Der Absolutheitsanspruch des Christentums. Von der Aufklärung bis zur pluralistischen Religionsauffassung,* 2nd ed. (Gütersloh, 1993), 68.

Bonhoeffer still speaks of Christianity as "true religion," though he has obviously been under the influence of Barth's critique of religion since at least 1927. Bonhoeffer, as we have said, does not reflect on religion systematically but neither does he ever attempt to establish a theory of religion. For Bonhoeffer, religion was never a problem *of* or *within* theology; he wanted to speak of God without religion — in "nonreligious terms," as he put it.

Bonhoeffer used the word "religion" in such a way that its content cannot be clearly determined. To put it dogmatically, the meaning of religion in Bonhoeffer's writings is not "univocal." In fact it seems that Bonhoeffer had no interest in describing the meaning of religion; he used the term only in a formal way. In a lecture he gave in 1931 he explicitly said that the time for theology to use a *concept* of religion was over ("keinen allgemeinen *Begriff* von Religion (kann es) mehr geben").[9]

In not integrating religion into a theological system he distinguished himself both from the dialectical theology of Karl Barth and from the recent theology of Wolfhart Pannenberg.[10] For both these theologians, though in different ways, humanity is understood religiously. Bonhoeffer, however, wanted to grasp what it meant to be human not *with* but *without* religion. According to him religion was going to disappear from theological language. Where, then, in a dogmatic system, he asked, can "religion" find a place? "What is the place of worship and prayer in a religionless situation?"[11] If in a religionless situation religious practices like worship and prayer have lost their meaning, how can that vacuum be filled? Bonhoeffer answers such questions with reference to the "discipline of the secret" or *disciplina arcana*.[12] He believed that the rediscovery of this ancient discipline would help to save such religious praxis from profanation. Religious practices such as worship and prayer, he argued, should not be given up but should be engaged in terms of the *disciplina arcana*.

9. "Die Systematische Theologie des 20. Jahrhunderts," *Vorlesung aus dem Wintersemester 1931/32*, ed. Eberhard Bethge, *GS*, vol. 5 (Munich: Chr. Kaiser Verlag, 1972), 181-227, 219.

10. See Wolfhart Pannenberg, *Systematische Theologie* (Göttingen: Vandenhoeck & Ruprecht, 1988), vol. 1, 133ff.

11. *LPP*, 281.

12. *Disciplina arcana*, normally translated as "secret discipline" in the English versions of Bonhoeffer's writings, has been more accurately translated as "discipline of the secret" in the *DBWE* [editor].

At the same time, worship and prayer in "secret" ought always to be followed by responsible action in the world. If the discipline of the secret was one side of the dialectic,[13] the other was Bonhoeffer's nonreligious interpretation of Christianity. He proposed, thus, a dynamic dialectic of dogmatics and ethics, of indicative and imperative, of faith and deed. You cannot, he argued, have one without the other. Likewise you cannot agree with religionless Christianity and not accept prayer and worship on which the Christian indicative is based. The discipline of the secret is to religionlessness — in the language of the prison letters — as prayer is to righteous action;[14] or, in the words of the *Ethics,* as "the last things" are to "the things before the last."[15] The two sides must be brought together in the Christian life.

In a first step on the way to explaining what religionless Christianity really means, I have drawn attention to Bonhoeffer's own statements on religion, concluding that he neither defines religion systematically nor develops a theory of religion. This means two things for our understanding of religionlessness. Firstly, it means that we cannot deduce its meaning merely from Bonhoeffer's view of religion, simply because for him a *Religionsbegriff* does not exist. Secondly, it means that we have to go a step behind the sources and ask where the critique of religion and the proposal about religionless Christianity come from. What was Bonhoeffer reading when he developed his thoughts on the "nonreligious interpretation of biblical terms"?

The Origin of "Nonreligious" Interpretation

The young Bonhoeffer's critique of religion must be interpreted against the background of dialectical theology. His reading of Barth started with *Das Wort Gottes und die Theologie,* in which Barth declares in an essay from 1920: "Jesus has nothing in common with religion" ("Jesus hat mit Religion einfach nichts zu tun").[16] In the second edition of Barth's *Letter to the Romans* (1922), faith and religion were set in opposition to each other,

---

13. Andreas Pangritz, "Aspekte der 'Arkandisziplin' bei Dietrich Bonhoeffer," *Theologische Literaturzeitung* 119 (1994): 755-68, 765.

14. *LPP,* 300.

15. *Ethics* (New York: Macmillan, 1971), 120ff.

16. Karl Barth, *Das Wort Gottes und die Theologie* (Munich, 1924), 94.

since the "Word of God" meant the judgment of all religious efforts made by human beings. The "freedom of God" stood in opposition to "human religion,"[17] making sin obvious.[18] "Religion" was for Barth the opposite of grace.[19]

In essays that Bonhoeffer wrote as a student for his seminars in 1925/26 there are a number of references to Barth's *Römerbrief,* particularly with regard to this distinction between grace and religion. In *Sanctorum Communio* (1927), his doctoral dissertation written under the supervision of Reinhold Seeberg, the influence of both Barth and liberal theologians such as Albrecht Ritschl is evident.[20] Dialectical and liberal theology coexisted. But with *Act and Being* (1929) things have begun to change. I shall demonstrate this with reference to the term "religious *a priori.*"

As Bonhoeffer understood it, Reinhold Seeberg took a Kantian approach to theology in arguing that "God is the supramundane reality transcending consciousness, the Lord and creator." How, then, can man understand God? This is the point where Seeberg's use of Ernst Troeltsch's notion of a "religious *a priori*" came into play: "Man," according to Seeberg, "is charged with the capacity for becoming directly conscious of pure mind. . . ." The religious *a priori* was said to be fundamentally open to the divine will. There is a mould in human beings wherein the divine content of revelation may be poured. In other words, revelation must become religion; that is its nature. Revelation is religion. But this view represents a movement from pure transcendentalism (Kant) to idealism.[21]

Kant had sought to show that human understanding is limited to the phenomena of sensory experience. Transcendent objects, such as God, freedom, and immortality, lie beyond human modes of perception and so are unknowable. Bonhoeffer detects a lack of logic in Seeberg's Kantian approach in introducing Troeltsch's idea of a religious *a priori.* This, Bonhoeffer argues, is idealist thought according to which God

---

17. Karl Barth, *Der Römerbrief,* 13th ed. (Zurich, 1984), Beleg 236.
18. *Ibid.,* 228.
19. *Ibid.,* 212.
20. See *Sanctorum Communio,* ed. Joachim von Soosten, *DBW,* vol. 1, 97, and Albrecht Ritschl, *Rechtfertigung und Versöhnung* 3 (Bonn, 1888), 508: "Jede gemeinsame Religion ist gestiftet."
21. *Act and Being* (New York: Harper & Row, 1961), 45f.

could be understood by human beings on the basis of their religious *a priori* rather than through God's revelation in Jesus Christ. The distance between God and human beings was bridged, therefore, by the religious *a priori*. But for Bonhoeffer the deep gulf between God and human beings can only be overcome through God's self-revelation. This, of course, is not Bonhoeffer's insight alone but reflects the influence of Barth's "Word of God" theology in its opposition to liberal theology.

For Barth, God as he is in himself *(an sich)* cannot be recognized except through self-disclosure. The gap between God and humanity can only be overcome by God. Where Hegel mixes revelation with religion and Seeberg uses the human term "religious *a priori*," Barth focuses solely on God's revelation in his Word, Jesus Christ. By 1929, when Bonhoeffer wrote *Act and Being*, he had become fully initiated into the dialectical theological movement. He was influenced not only by Barth's *Römerbrief* but also by many of his other writings, such as *Unterricht in der christlichen Religion* (1924) and *Christliche Dogmatik im Entwurf* (1927). Like Barth,[22] Bonhoeffer argued that religion is, in the first place, a problem of modern times, that is to say, the *Religionsbegriff* had a beginning and must have an end at some stage of history. The word "religion" was introduced by the English Deists. What the Reformation called "faith" began to take on a different meaning from the seventeenth century onward when the word "religion" came into being. In fact, the term "religion" came to replace "faith." This change found its clearest expression in nineteenth-century liberal theology. Theology became anthropology, as Barth observed in his lecture on Feuerbach.[23]

It is evident, then, that every critical statement on religion that can be found in Bonhoeffer's writings is based upon Barth's theology. The critique that Bonhoeffer learned from Barth is the critique of the Word of God on religion, the antagonism between religion and grace. But what is the origin of Bonhoeffer's thoughts on religionlessness?

It would seem that this question must be answered in the light of the philosophy which Bonhoeffer adopted.[24] Through Barth and his

---

22. See Prolegomena, "Unterricht in der christlichen Religion," in Karl Barth, *Gesamtausgabe* 17/2 (Zurich: Theologischer Verlag, 1985), 224.

23. Karl Barth, *Protestant Theology in the Nineteenth Century* (London: SCM, 1972), 534-40.

24. See Ralf K. Wüstenberg, "Bonhoeffer on Theology and Philosophy," *ANVIL* 12/1:45-56.

dialectic theology, Bonhoeffer discovered the importance of Kantian terminology and philosophy for theological statements, particularly with respect to revelation. Then in New York in the early 1930s he became familiar with a different philosophical strain. At Union Theological Seminary he discovered the philosophy of William James, labelled "pragmatism." In a review of James's *Varieties of Religious Experience*, Bonhoeffer commented:

> It is not true to say that the religious individual does not care as much about the reality as about the efficiency of God. The reality of God is, of course, for most religious people not a philosophical question but a basic conviction. 2. Concerning the term "subconsciousness" we must ask: if subconciousness is to be satisfactory for the religious experience of the outside, then it must be considered really outside of the individual person. But if it is not really outside then the religious experience of the outside is an illusion. . . . So it seems to me not possible to find a mediating term between religion and science.[25]

In this comment Bonhoeffer makes an obvious effort to include James within the framework of the philosophy with which he is accustomed. But it does not seem to work. Particularly in his second comment concerning the term "subconsciousness," Bonhoeffer misses the transcendental aspect, that which is "really outside," as he puts it. Subconsciousness and the "really outside" do not go together and cannot be linked within a philosophical framework. The link for Bonhoeffer is God — really outside — which leads him back to both Kantian philosophy and Barthian theology.

On the other hand, Bonhoeffer found something fascinating in James's pragmatic philosophy. It was certainly not merely James's view of religion — which, as in liberal theology, was still a positive one — but the way that James put religion and life together. James's argument is the following: if religion is true, it has meaning in life, but if it has no meaning in life, then it is false. This pragmatic argument is important for Bonhoeffer in terms of the value that James attributed to life, and more generally of the earthboundness of pragmatism as a philosophy of life.

In trying to answer more precisely *what* Bonhoeffer's observation

25. "Concerning the Christian Idea of God," *GS,* vol. 3, 100-109, 109.

of a time of no religion is based on and *where* the roots of religionless Christianity are, I would argue, in summary, that there were three philosophers of importance to Bonhoeffer's philosophical theology, namely Kant, James, and then Wilhelm Dilthey. Discovering pragmatism as a life-philosophy in 1930 meant, for Bonhoeffer, the opening of theology toward a new philosophical strain which found its conclusion in Wilhelm Dilthey's historicism. Bonhoeffer adopted this in 1944, and Dilthey strongly influenced his view of religion and life in his prison theology.

German Bonhoeffer researchers in the early 1970s were of the view that, besides Kant, Dilthey, with his *historicism,* had a great impact on his arguments about a world that has come of age since the Renaissance and Reformation. Dilthey could be regarded as a second Kant, for he developed a critique of historical reason in accordance with Kant's critique of pure reason. Unlike Kant, however, Dilthey explained human autonomy *historically.* According to Dilthey's *historicism,* humans began thinking autonomously from the time of the Renaissance and the Reformation. Since then they no longer used God as a stop-gap, but began to use autonomous reason to explain politics (Niccolo Machiavelli), law (Hugo Grotius), natural sciences (Galileo Galilei), and other subjects.

Bonhoeffer read Dilthey during his imprisonment, and as Ernst Feil and Christian Gremmels have discovered, he adopted Dilthey's argument.[26] He began to articulate theological problems such as the criticism of religion within a historical framework. He stopped setting revelation over against religion (as Barth had done) but felt more fundamentally that the *time of religion* was over.

> The time when people could be told everything by means of words, whether theological or pious, is over, and so is the time of inwardness and conscience — and that means the time of religion in general.[27]

In particular the historical passages in Bonhoeffer's letters from June and July 1944 indicate the extent to which he made use of Dilthey's historical

---

26. See Ernst Feil, *The Theology of Dietrich Bonhoeffer* (Philadelphia: Fortress Press, 1985).

27. *LPP,* 279; Ernst Feil has shown that the term "inwardness," like "metaphysics," has been taken directly from Wilhelm Dilthey by Bonhoeffer; see E. Feil, "Der Einfluß Wilhelm Diltheys auf Dietrich Bonhoeffers *Widerstand und Ergebung,*" *Evangelische Theologie* 29 (1969): 662-74.

thinking and terminology. One of the most famous reflections on autonomy and history can be found in the letter of 8 June 1944:

> I'll try to define my position from the historical angle. The movement
> that began about the thirteenth century . . . towards the autonomy of
> man (in which I should include the discovery of the laws by which
> the world lives and deals with itself in science, social and political
> matters, art, ethics, and religion) has in our time reached an undoubted
> completion. Man has learnt to deal with himself in all questions of
> importance without recourse to the "working hypothesis" called
> "God." In questions of science, art, and ethics this has become an
> understood thing at which one now hardly dares to tilt. But for the
> last hundred years or so it has become increasingly true of religious
> questions; it is becoming evident that everything gets along without
> "God" — and, in fact, just as well as before. As in the scientific field,
> so in human affairs generally, "God" is being pushed more and more
> out of life, losing more and more ground. . . . The question is: Christ
> and the world that has come of age.[28]

German researchers discovered that Bonhoeffer's critical use of the
terms "metaphysics" and "inwardness" came from Dilthey's volume *Weltanschauung und Analyse des Menschen seit Renaissance und Reformation*. Yet,
it is interesting to note that, in addition to the two terms mentioned, the
word "religionless" is also used by Dilthey explicitly, namely in his
Einleitung in die Geisteswissenschaften. Bonhoeffer had known of this book
from at least 1931, for he quoted it in a lecture which he gave at Berlin
University at that time. In the Dilthey text, however, "religionlessness"
has a meaning different from that which Bonhoeffer gave it.

Dilthey thought that a historical understanding of a "religionless
time" was not possible, since humanity is always religious. For Dilthey,
the positive understanding of religion and culture, as introduced to
German Protestantism by Schleiermacher, was still valid. Bonhoeffer
makes use of Dilthey in a critical way. He takes up the term "religionlessness" formally and fills it with new content, namely with the
criticism of religion. Adopting Dilthey's historical argument, that in
modern times, that is, in the *Neuzeit*, human beings have come of age,
he combines it with a critique of religion. If the world came of age,

28. *LPP*, 325f., 327.

religion would lose its meaning—a time of "a religionlessness" would begin, in which Jesus could become "Lord of the world" anew.

Concluding this second section, we are now able to say *where* the "nonreligious interpretation of biblical concepts" comes from *historically*. On the one hand, the nonreligious interpretation is determined by the theology of Karl Barth, especially as far as the criticism of religion is concerned. On the other hand, the nonreligious interpretation is based upon the philosophy of Wilhelm Dilthey, particularly in terms of the *historicism* which is made manifest in Bonhoeffer's prison theology by concepts like worldliness, inwardness, or metaphysics. With the concept "religionlessness," Bonhoeffer brings together Barth and Dilthey. In presuming that the "nonreligious" interpretation comes from Barth *and* Dilthey, its origin is explained *historically*. The question then is: What does religionlessness mean *dogmatically?* What does it mean to speak of God in nonreligious terminology?

"Religionless" Christianity

Bonhoeffer learned to criticize religion in the light of faith on the basis of the antagonism between religion and grace. Yet in Tegel prison things changed. Writing to his friend Bethge, he remarked: "The 'religious act' is always something partial; 'faith' . . . is involving the whole of one's life." Bonhoeffer thus understood faith as an act of life. He continued: "Jesus calls men, not to a new religion, but to life."[29] The antagonism between religion and grace had now become an antagonism between religion and "life." Faith was interpreted in the light of "life"; the concept of faith had become a concept of life. How does Bonhoeffer come to this position?

In Tegel, Bonhoeffer is concerned with a this-worldly form of faith in daily life. Thus he reminds us: "I believe that we ought so to love and trust God in our *lives*, and in all the good things that he sends us."[30] The quest for the "Good" brings us back to Bonhoeffer's *Ethics*. At the end of 1943, Bonhoeffer expressed the opinion that his only remaining task would be to finish writing his *Ethics*. But then he changed his mind and began to read Dilthey. The preparation for studying Dilthey came

29. *Ibid.*, 362.
30. *Ibid.*, 168.

through his reading of José Ortega y Gasset, the Spanish pupil of Dilthey. Under the influence of the literature that he requested for his prison cell in Tegel, Bonhoeffer began to ask new questions concerning the church and theology in the twentieth century. "What is bothering me . . . is the question what Christianity really is, or indeed who Christ really is, for us, today."[31] The quest for Jesus Christ links the prison theology with the *Ethics* manuscripts, for Christology is essential to both.

In his *Ethics*, for example, Bonhoeffer insisted that "Jesus is not *a* man. He is *the* .man"[32] ("Jesus ist nicht *ein* Mensch, sondern *der* Mensch"). In a letter from prison, he takes up this sentence, which was from the section "Ethics as formation," and uses it critically in relation to "religion": "To be a Christian does not mean to be religious in a particular way . . . , but to be a man, not *a* . . . man, but *the* man that Christ creates in us."[33] In contrast with what he did in the passage from his *Ethics*, Bonhoeffer here combines a christological statement with a critique of religion. As far as his view of worldliness and autonomy is concerned, Bonhoeffer moves further in his letters from prison. Whereas in a manuscript from the *Ethics* the world, which is in the process of "coming of age," is regarded negatively in terms of "nihilism," in the prison letters Bonhoeffer reflects positively on the autonomy of the world, humanity, and life. What caused his view of autonomy to change?

In the autumn of 1943, Bonhoeffer requested a number of essays by Ortega y Gasset to be brought to his prison cell. Dilthey's basic insight, namely that *history* tells us what humanity is ("was der Mensch ist, sagt ihm seine Geschichte"),[34] Bonhoeffer learned from Ortega y Gasset's essay "Geschichte als System," which was published in 1941. This prepared the way for the Dilthey studies that Bonhoeffer undertook in the spring and summer of 1944. Bonhoeffer now began to read Dilthey in the light of the "philosophy of life" and, in a letter on 21 May 1944, he spoke about the value of "a multi-dimensional and polyphonous" life.[35]

Studying Dilthey's volume *Weltanschauung und Analyse des Menschen seit Renaissance und Reformation*, Bonhoeffer reflected on the historical

---

31. *Ibid.*, 279.
32. *Ethics*, 72. See *Ethik*, ed. Ilse Tödt, Heinz Eduard Tödt, Ernst Feil, and Clifford Green, *DBW*, vol. 6, 71.
33. *LPP*, 361.
34. See Wilhelm Dilthey, *GS*, vol. 8, 224.
35. *LPP*, 311.

development that led humanity to an autonomous understanding of the world in modern times. Dilthey observed the striving of humanity after autonomy in a variety of subjects. In doing so he always put the emphasis on the *actual life* of people in their period. With concepts such as *Lebensgefühl, Lebensführung, Lebenshaltung,* or *Lebensstimmung,* Dilthey unfolds his *Lebensphilosophie*[36] or philosophy of life. Petrarch, for instance, was to Dilthey the most original of the philosophers of life because he was prepared to give up all scholastic spider's webs for a moment of full living (". . . alle scholastischen Spinnewebe für einen Moment vollen Lebens hinzugeben bereit war").[37] Opposite to the concept of life was metaphysics. This insight Dilthey demonstrated again and again in many examples from history throughout *Weltanschauung und Analyse.* His critique of metaphysics was determined by his philosophy, namely that there is no theoretical knowledge beyond life. To have knowledge of humanity means to have knowledge of human life depicted in history. Knowledge, life, and history are thus closely linked in Dilthey's philosophy. Bonhoeffer, in fact, not only adopted Dilthey's historicism but also his view of life.

In his letter of 8 June 1944, Bonhoeffer described the striving of humanity for autonomy in the fields of morality and law. His dependency upon Dilthey can also be shown here. "In ethics," he wrote, "it appears in Montaigne and Bodin with their substitution of rules of life for the commandments."[38] Bonhoeffer observed that Dilthey's historical understanding was based upon his understanding of life, which for Dilthey was not that a general meaning of morality and ethics became autonomous but that rules of life were no longer bound to the commandments.

There is no passage in the letters from prison in which Bonhoeffer speaks of autonomy in a general way. On the contrary, following Dilthey, he always had the autonomy of humanity or of life in mind. What was true for ethics also applied to law. Dilthey showed that the concepts of law as developed by Hugo de Groot are concepts of life. These concepts are meaningful irrespective of whether or not God exists and, therefore, cannot lose their meaning, even if there is no God. Quoting Dilthey, Bonhoeffer observes, "we cannot be honest unless we recognize that we

---

36. See Wilhelm Dilthey, *Weltanschauung und Analyse des Menschen seit Renaissance und Reformation* (*GS,* vol. 2), 17, 18, 20, 43, 50.

37. *Ibid.,* 20.

38. *LPP,* 359.

have to live in the world *etsi deus non daretur*."[39] Referring to Dilthey again, he writes on 21 July 1944 that "it is only by living completely in this world that one learns to have faith."[40] And here we observe again that Bonhoeffer is not reflecting on a mere understanding of this-worldliness, qualifying the historicism with the concept of life; Bonhoeffer is concerned with *living* in this world.

The concept of life is, however, determined by a christological framework. Bonhoeffer does not mean "the shallow and banal this-worldliness of the enlightened, the busy, the comfortable, or the lascivious, but the profound this-worldliness, characterized by discipline and the constant knowledge of death and resurrection."[41] Thus by interpreting the concept of life christologically, Bonhoeffer distinguishes his view from the philosophy of life. In terms of a philosophical understanding, life is ambiguous; in the light of revelation life is definite through Jesus Christ. Bonhoeffer thus takes up the concept of life from Dilthey and gives it a theological meaning. Life thereby takes on a different meaning; it stops being merely joy and fun. Life means participation in the sufferings of God in the world. Bonhoeffer reminds us that the Christian shares "in God's sufferings through" his life.[42] If the Christian lacks suffering, the Bible calls for repentance. If participation in Jesus' being for others is absent, the Christian lacks integrity. Thus the biblical concept of repentance, nonreligiously interpreted, means nothing but "ultimate honesty" — "ultimate" because it could only apply through faith.[43] Bonhoeffer understood by faith that "the whole of the earthly *life* is claimed for God."[44] Interpreting in a nonreligious way means interpreting Christianity not through religion but in terms of *life*. From the concept of faith defined as participation in the being of Jesus, Bonhoeffer deduces the concept of life as being there for others. Life is ontologically linked with Christology through faith.

So, in conclusion, we have to put Gerhard Ebeling's argument, which we mentioned at the beginning of this essay, in concrete form: to interpret nonreligiously implies a christological form of interpretation

---

39. *Ibid.,* 360.
40. *Ibid.,* 369.
41. *Ibid.*
42. *Ibid.,* 370.
43. *Ibid.,* 360.
44. *Ibid.,* 374.

which is made concrete by taking into account the decisive concept of life. "Nonreligious" interpretation means a form of interpretation by which modern *life* that has come of age in the modern era and Christian *faith* are brought together in a new relation. In his "Outline for a Book" Bonhoeffer describes the task of the church today in words that are easy to follow: the church "must tell men of every calling what it means to *live* in Christ, to exist for others."[45]

45. *Ibid.*, 383.

The Wound of History:
Reading Bonhoeffer after Christendom

BARRY HARVEY

Near the end of the section in his *Ethics* entitled "Ethics as Formation," Dietrich Bonhoeffer refers several times to a wound inflicted
among the nations of the western world. This wound, inflicted when
these nations defected from the one who, as the form of our true humanity "was ready to take form in us and to lead us to our own true form,"
manifests itself in violence, avarice, and injustice. According to Bonhoeffer, the cicatrization of this wound, though not the removal and
forgiveness of the guilt that is the result of "the defection from Christ,"
will only take place through the justification and renewal of the west, a
process that will unfold indirectly, through the faith of the church in its
submission to, and participation in, the form of Christ.[1]

Signs of this wound are all too apparent wherever one goes in
our rapidly shrinking global village. Those who live in what remains
of the so-called western world habitually find themselves, as political
scientist Ronald Beiner observes, "barbarized by an empty public culture, intimidated by colossal bureaucracies, numbed into passivity by
the absence of opportunities for meaningful deliberation, inflated by
absurd habits of consumption, deflated by the Leviathans that surround
us, and stripped of dignity by a way of living that far exceeds a human

1. *Ethics*, 110-19.

scale."[2] In places such as South Africa, the social, political, and cultural circumstances are in some ways quite distinctive, but the overall patterns that determine the course of everyday life are not all that different from those in North America and Europe. While the shackles of apartheid have finally been removed, the terrible human toll exacted by that regime continues to be staggering. Racial, ethnic, and economic divisions continue to rend the human fabric of the country.

With his image of a wound, an opening in the body that threatens its life and drains its vitality, Bonhoeffer points the church in the right direction as it struggles to come to terms with a world come of age, and especially with its conception of history. The pioneers of the modern age sought to create an opening between the finite world and the infinite, that is, to depict history as an enclosed, self-contained space that contains and defines all finite entities and events in isolation from all considerations of the infinite. In contrast, classical thought had always "understood finite limitation in terms of its relationship to the infinite. Our knowledge of the infinite was considered to be imperfect, but, by the same token, our knowledge of the finite to be limited also. Yet, at the same time, a metaphysics, or a representation of the permanent circumstances of the relation of finite to infinite, was still considered possible."[3]

While this opening is not solely an innovation of modernity (according to Augustine, its origins may be traced in the pagan practices of the earthly city back to Babylon),[4] it takes on a new and malevolent quality with the world's coming of age. Once finitude was severed from the realm of the "sacred," modern thought could effectively lay sole claim to an exhaustive, once-for-all representation of the essential properties of this "secular realm." The ultimate aim of this project was to transform history into a sphere of operations that is subject to a calculus of power relationships. Whatever occupies the position of the "subject" within this space (a proprietor, an enterprise, a city, a scientific institution, an army), says Michel de Certeau, "assumes a place that can be circumscribed as proper . . . and thus serve as the basis for generating relations with an exterior distinct from it (competitors, adversaries,

2. Ronald Beiner, *What's the Matter with Liberalism?* (Berkeley: University of California Press, 1992), 34.

3. John Milbank, *Theology and Social Theory: Beyond Secular Reason* (Cambridge, MA: Basil Blackwell, 1990), 280.

4. St. Augustine, *City of God* 16.4.

'clientèles,' 'targets,' or 'objects' of research). Political, economic, and scientific rationality has been constructed on this strategic model."[5]

There is, however, a second and very different sense suggested by this image. Due to the potential confusion between a subjective and an objective reading of the English preposition "of," the wound of history can also refer to the participation of the church, as Bonhoeffer puts it, "in the being of Jesus."[6] In this respect the mission of the church, in whom "Jesus realizes his form in the midst of the world,"[7] is the interruption of the modern opening of history. This interruption occurs as the infinite divine love made flesh (and so made to suffer) is sacramentally manifested in, with, and under in the community of Christ. As this community shares in the messianic suffering of God, confronting the strength of the modern world with the weakness of the cross, it embodies an alternative configuration of time and space that creates yet another opening, this one within the domain of what a world come of age calls history, which now bears the wound. But as Scripture indicates, this wound is for the healing of the nations (cf. Isaiah 53:5; Revelation 22:2).

The Eclipse of the Penultimate in the Fiction of History

We begin our inquiry into the nature of this wound in the *Ethics*, where Bonhoeffer takes up the question of the last things, the things before the last, and the relationship that binds them together. He characterizes the ultimate or last word in good Lutheran fashion: "The origin and essence of all Christian life are comprised in the one process or event which the Reformation called justification of the sinner by grace alone. The nature of the Christian life is disclosed not by what humankind is in itself but by what it is in this event. The whole length and breadth of human life is here compressed into a single instant, a single point." In this event, and as a consequence of this process, human beings are free for God and their brothers and sisters. We become aware that there is a God who loves us, that our brothers and sisters are standing at our sides, whom

---

5. Michel de Certeau, *The Practice of Everyday Life*, trans. Steven Rendall (Berkeley: University of California Press, 1984), xix.

6. *LPP*, 381.

7. *Ethics*, 111.

God loves as God loves us, and that we have a future with the triune God, together with the church.[8]

Bonhoeffer is careful to point out that the ultimate does not exist by itself, hermetically sealed in a sterile environment to protect it from contamination, as it were. It stands rather in a distinctive and generative relationship with the things before the last, the penultimate. To be sure, these things before the last, which Bonhoeffer identifies as "being human *(Menschsein)* and being good," possess no separate, autonomous existence: "There is . . . no penultimate in itself, as though a thing could justify itself in itself as being a thing before the last thing; a thing becomes penultimate only through the ultimate, that is to say, at the moment when it has already lost its own validity." But it is equally the case in the economy of God's Word that the penultimate of necessity precedes the ultimate, and so "the relationship is such that being human precedes justification, and that from the standpoint of the ultimate it is necessary that it should precede it." Indeed, Bonhoeffer goes so far as to say that for the sake of the ultimate the penultimate must be preserved: "Any arbitrary destruction of the penultimate will do serious injury to the ultimate."[9]

From Bonhoeffer's standpoint, then, the idea of history is intelligible only within the paradigmatic framework established by the relationship between ultimate and penultimate. A world come of age, however, does not recognize this conception of history or the penultimate as such, for the things before the last have that status solely as a consequence of the last things to which they are related. According to Robert Jenson, the project of the Enlightenment was in large part to deny this connection. To be sure, the architects of modernity assumed

> that the world "out there" is such that stories can be told that are true *to it.* And modernity supposed that the reason narratives can be true to the world is that the world somehow "has" its own true story antecedent to, and enabling of, the stories we tell about ourselves. . . . Put it this way: the way in which the modern West has talked about human life supposes that an omniscient historian could write a *universal* history, and that this is so because the universe with inclusion of our lives is in fact a story written by a sort of omnipotent novelist.[10]

8. *Ibid.,* 120.
9. *Ibid.,* 133-34.
10. Robert Jenson, "How the World Lost Its Story," *First Things* 36 (October 1993): 21.

Modernity sought to sustain this realist faith in a narratable world, though, while at the same time withdrawing allegiance "from the God who was that faith's object." Jenson contends that there is no mystery about the source of this secularized faith in a narratable world in Jewish and Christian practice, according to which the universe is in actuality a story written by a sort of omnipotent novelist, namely, God. But if there is little doubt as to the source of this faith in a narratable world, neither is there much mystery about how that faith has been lost in a growing pathos that currently haunts modernity, since it was essentially "defined by the attempt to live in a universal story without a universal story-teller."[11]

In place of the practical ligatures that in the Jewish and Christian traditions bind together ultimate and penultimate in a generative relationship, the inventors of modern society imagined, and then set out to construct, a carefully circumscribed space that contains and defines all finite entities and events. They supposed that it was possible to provide a more or less complete inventory of the categories that constitute the essential properties of this space *etsi deus non daretur,* even if there were no God. This realm of the finite, to which the name history is appended, is analogous to the space which takes form within a scientific laboratory, in that both strive for more precise control and prediction of all that is contained within their technical apparatuses. A world come of age dogmatically posits this opening as a given in all matters dealing with being human and being good.

Immanuel Kant gave definitive theoretical expression to this conception of history. Kant was convinced, and also convinced generations to come, that it was possible to identify precisely the limits of human knowledge, to list once and for all the *a priori* categories, both conceptual and intuitive, which define the essential properties of both the natural and social worlds. This rounding off of finitude also meant that these categories could not be speculatively extended to obtain a knowledge of the transcendent in itself, supposedly heralding the end of the age of metaphysics as such. Access to the infinite was still available, but now only through the direct presence of freedom in the apperceived self, thus rendering the ultimate a sublime reality that is, as Bonhoeffer observes, "relegated to a realm beyond the world of experience."[12] In other words, Kant claimed

11. Jenson, "How the World Lost Its Story," 21.
12. *LPP,* 341.

76

that it was possible to represent totally the bounds of finitude in the finite subject, while at the same time protecting the so-called "human sphere," though only at the margins of life, where our capacity to manipulate, control, and predict physical phenomena gives out.

As many have noted, an ongoing engagement with the modern philosophical tradition of transcendental subjectivity definitively shapes the intellectual contours of Bonhoeffer's theology, and in particular his understanding of human identity and sociality.[13] However, as Bonhoeffer indicates in his "Outline for a Book," the philosophic explication of the self as a self-positing, world-constituting subject develops in concert with the construction of the technical organization that sets a world come of age apart from every other culture. In this tantalizing passage he locates this coming of age within the effort to safeguard life against "accidents" and "blows of fate." The aim is to make human life independent of the menace of nature, which had formerly been dealt with through "spiritual" means, but in the modern era it has been "conquered . . . by technical organization of all kinds." Our immediate environment is therefore no longer nature, but organization. "But with this protection from nature's menace," he warns, "there arises a new one — through organization itself." Sadly, we no longer possess the spiritual force to cope with this peculiarly modern menace. The question that plagues us, then, is: "What protects us against the menace of organization? Humanity is again thrown back on itself. It has managed to deal with everything, only not with itself. It can insure against everything, only not against humanity."[14]

It was this dramatic interplay between technical organization and philosophic speculations that keyed the development of the modern idea of the self as transcendental subject. In other words, this idea of the self as an autonomous subject is the lead (though somewhat shadowy) character in an ongoing work of fiction entitled *History* by its authors. This story is set within the technical configurations of the factory, office, school, shopping center, and the other institutions that uniquely characterize a world come of age. To call this story a work of fiction is not to say that history is imaginary, existing "only in the head," as it were. The principal difference between the genres of history and fiction is that

13. See, for example, Charles Marsh, *Reclaiming Dietrich Bonhoeffer: The Promise of His Theology* (New York: Oxford University Press, 1994).
14. *LPP,* 380.

the latter is governed by the trope of irony, whereas we are serious about the former. To be human, in other words, is necessarily to indwell (and tacitly contribute as co-author to) one or another fiction, which then scripts our self-identity in relation to the many roles each of us plays in everyday life. The story that is the peculiarly modern tale is serious fiction indeed — deadly serious.[15]

The Colonization of History

Anthony Giddens's sociological analysis of modernity as a risk culture helps to identify the main plot of the modern fiction. Giddens does not mean to suggest that social life is intrinsically more dangerous than it was in the past. For most people in the developed areas of the world this is not obviously the case, fears about the dangers of modern urban life (often exacerbated by sensational reports in the media) notwithstanding. His point is rather that in contrast to other forms of life, the centrality of the concepts of risk and risk calculation to the way that both lay actors and technical specialists reflexively organize the social world pushes to the periphery of life traditional notions of providence, fortune, destiny, and fate, ideas for which spiritual means are solely appropriate.[16]

The modern fiction thus seeks to strip basic human trust of all "religious" connotations, to insure that the daily activities, habits, and allegiances that give shape and direction to our lives are no longer formed in and around the practices and institutions of church, mosque, synagogue, or temple. Once this is accomplished, trust may be reinvested in the knowledge environments that form a technical cocoon to guard the self in its dealings with everyday reality. This cocoon "brackets out" potential occurrences which, were the individual seriously to contemplate them, would produce a paralysis of the will, or feelings of "engulfment." Giddens rightly concludes that the exchange of the concept of risk for that of fate or providence, signified by the reorientation of basic trust, "represents an alteration in the perception of determination and

---

15. See Milbank, *Theology and Social Theory,* 91, 185, 265.

16. Giddens, *Modernity and Self-Identity* (Stanford: Stanford University Press, 1991), 3. Giddens notes that the terms "risk" and "chance" first appear in English only in the seventeenth century: *The Consequences of Modernity* (Stanford: Stanford University Press, 1990), 30, 34.

contingency, such that human moral imperatives, natural causes, and chance reign in place of religious cosmologies."[17]

According to Giddens, this radical shift in how modern society deals with questions of determinacy and contingency is rooted in two characteristics that distinguish its fictional rendering of the human agent from all competing narratives: the particular ways that its social systems bind time and space, and the peculiar role that reflexivity plays (both institutionally and individually) in the creation of knowledge environments. With respect to the former, Giddens describes in some detail how, within the technical setting of modernity, "time and space are organised so as to connect presence and absence." Essential to this dramatic project is the triumph over time, which has been achieved through the creation of "empty" time. In contrast to pre-modern societies, in which time was organically interrelated with place (usually in ways that were imprecise and variable), the invention of the mechanical clock and its rapid diffusion to most members of the population made possible the separation of time from place, enabling the former to be quantified into uniform (and therefore empty) units. The uniform measurement of time in turn authorized uniformity in the social organization of time, exemplified in the worldwide standardization of calendars.[18] The concerted efforts to master time extend to the periodization of history (modern, pre-modern, etc.), so that the past and future may be properly managed. The modern regime thus seeks to isolate past events and future prospects from the social contexts formed within particular locations and narratives, and to assimilate them into a goalless, unitary present.

Coordination across time forms the basis of another facet of the the technical organization of modernity — the creation and control of abstract space. As with time, space and place largely coincide in pre-modern societies, such that "the spatial dimensions of social life are, for most of the population, and in most respects, dominated by "'presence' — by localised activities."[19] By means of techniques that allow (1) the representation of space without reference to a a particular place, and (2) the possibility of substituting between different spatial units, modern institutions foster social relationships between "absent others,"

17. *Modernity and Self-Identity*, 3, 109-11; *The Consequences of Modernity*, 30, 34.
18. *Ibid.*, 14, 16-18.
19. These activities are misread if they are viewed solely as anticipations of modern forms of social interaction and economic exchange.

divorced from face-to-face interaction. Once emptied of the content dictated by the traditions and institutions of specific locales, time and space can not only be quantified, but also endlessly recombined in forms that allow "precise time-space 'zoning' of social life" by selected technical mechanisms.[20]

The social mechanisms of time-space distantiation help to constitute the strategic break between the self-positing, world-constituting subject and its "environment," making possible a mastery of places through sight, or as de Certeau puts it, "a *panoptic practice* proceeding from a place whence the eye can transform foreign forces into objects that can be observed and measured, and thus control and "include' them within its scope of vision. To be able to see (far into the distance) is also to be able to predict, to run ahead of time by reading a space."[21] Giddens refers to this process as the *colonization of the future.* A territory in time, as it were, is carved out to be colonized. Severed from its contextual connections with particular locales, "the future is continually drawn into the present by means of the reflexive organisation of knowledge environments," where it "becomes a new terrain — a territory of counterfactual possibility. Once thus established, that terrain lends itself to colonial invasion through counterfactual thought and risk calculation."[22]

The dismembering of traditional societies is achieved through the disembedding of social systems, that is, the "lifting out" of social relations from the particularities of contexts of presence (where they are subject to the constraints of local practices and institutions), and restructuring them across indefinite spans of time-space, where other, less apparent but more pervasive ligatures govern their sense and significance. As a result, particular locales increasingly become *phantasmagoric,* "thoroughly penetrated by and shaped in terms of social influences quite distant from them. What structures the locale is not simply that which is present on the scene; the "'visible form' of the locale conceals the distantiated relations which determine its nature."[23]

According to Giddens, two types of disembedding mechanisms are involved in the development of modern social institutions. The first he names symbolic tokens, which are "media of interchange which can be

20. Giddens, *Consequences of Modernity,* 14-19.
21. de Certeau, *Practice of Everyday Life,* 36.
22. Giddens, *Modernity and Self-Identity,* 3, 111.
23. Giddens, *Consequences of Modernity,* 18f., 21.

'passed around' without regard to the specific characteristics of individuals or groups that handle them at any particular juncture." Money is perhaps the principal symbolic token of modernity. According to Giddens, money is not, as some have argued, a medium of circulation that flows in time, but a means of bracketing time and space so as to lift transactions out of particular milieux of exchange where they are subject to local (and therefore "unreasonable") limitations. In other words, "money is a means of time-space distantiation." This omnipresent token of a world come of age couples instantaneity and deferral, presence and absence.[24]

The other disembedding mechanism of modernity takes form in the proliferation of expert systems, that is, networks of technical or professional expertise that continuously organize large areas of the material and social environments in which we live today. Like symbolic tokens, expert systems remove social relations from the immediacies of context, furthering the separation of time and space so characteristic of a world come of age. Most of us know little or nothing about the codes and techniques of knowledge used by architects, engineers, economists, etc., and yet every day in countless ways we place our faith in what they do. Simply by riding in a car, buying a house, or consulting a book on parenting, we not only involve ourselves in a series of such systems, we seemingly have no choice but to place our trust in them.[25] The demise of traditional goods and virtues that occurs as these "experts" assume control over virtually every aspect our lives, and the faith we habitually place in their technical expertise, lead to an abdication of the need on the part of the rest of us to make substantive moral judgments. The triumph of these expert systems in the modern regime may be seen in the ways the idioms of therapeutic and managerial expertise increasingly colonize the realms of politics, education, religion, and law enforcement.

The pervasiveness and centrality of expert systems lead us to the second characteristic of modernity: the pivotal role assigned to radical reflexivity. To be sure, says Giddens, all human beings have, as a matter

---

24. *Ibid.,* 22, 24. Another symbolic operation of time-space distantiation with an immediate connection to the theology of Bonhoeffer is the concept of religion. This term serves to separate the diverse practices and convictions of the various historical traditions from the communities that bear them, and transform them into symbolic conventions that bear universal significance at the level of the abstract individual and at the level of the social organism.

25. *Ibid.,* 27-28.

of routine, "kept in touch" with the grounds of what they do as an integral element of doing it. At work in the modern world, however, is a radically different conception of reason from that which prevailed prior to the Enlightenment. One no longer defines reflexivity substantially in terms of our relationship to the living and creating God (as Bonhoeffer does, for example) but procedurally, in terms of the standards by which we construct technical environments that protect us from the menaces of nature. Reflexivity thus takes on a radically different character with the reconfiguration of finitude around the instrumental axes of distinct knowledge domains. Indeed, says Giddens, modernity is constituted in and through the reflexive organization of knowledge environments. The practice of radical reflexivity, introduced into the very basis of system reproduction "such that thought and action are constantly refracted back upon one another,"[26] combines with various disembedding mechanisms to prise social relations away from the particularities of local contexts of presence and restructure them across indefinite spans of time-space. Radical reflexivity, "the regularised use of knowledge about circumstances of social life as a constitutive element in organisation and transformation,'[27] ushers a world come of age across a distinctive threshold where, as Michel Foucault puts it, "the formation of knowledge and the increase of power regularly reinforce one another in a circular process."[28]

Radical reflexivity is not limited to the level of institutions, for, as Giddens points out, "In the settings of . . . 'high' or 'late' modernity — our present-day world — the self, like the broader institutional contexts in which it exists, has to be reflexively made." The reflexive project of the self, which Kant assumed emanated spontaneously from the convergence of reason and freedom within the transcendental subject, is actually located "in the context of multiple choice as filtered through abstract systems." Due to the "openness" (that is, the disembedding) of social life today, lifestyle choice is increasingly important, and not merely for affluent groups or classes: "Reflexively organised life-planning, which normally presumes consideration of risks as filtered through contact with expert knowledge, becomes a central feature of the structuring of self-identity."[29]

26. *Ibid.,* 36-39.
27. Giddens, *Modernity and Self-Identity,* 20.
28. Foucault, *Discipline and Punish,* 224.
29. Giddens, *Modernity and Self-Identity,* 5.

In short, people have little choice but to choose who and what we will be. The paradox is thoroughgoing: as traditional ways of life lose their hold and daily life is reconstituted in terms of the technical interplay of the local and the global, individuals are increasingly required to negotiate lifestyle choices among a diversity of options. But this pluralism of lifestyles is strictly confined to the private level, for the ultimate good is predetermined by the modern state and its commercial republic, which collaborate to impose and enforce a particular set of goods: the role of the market as sole manager of the heterogeneity of interests, the superlative value of scientific progress, the sovereignty of choice itself.[30]

The scripting of self-identity as a reflexively organized endeavor and the universalization of lifestyle planning have not resulted in the general increase of freedom and human flourishing that was anticipated. Instead, our increasing dependence on expert systems, and in particular the triumph of managerial and therapeutic systems, coupled with modernity's unswerving (and for that reason most uncritical) faith in technique, has actually had the opposite effect. We seem to be caught "in a web of powers that is one of our own making yet not under our control."[31] As the so-called helping professions have increasingly taken over our lives, we no longer trust our own tradition-formed intuitions about happiness, fulfillment, and child-rearing.[32] Along with the collapse of local standards and the erosion of political ties beyond the expediencies of voluntary associations and lifestyle enclaves, the goal of autonomy has led to a form of life that fits perfectly into the instrumental, bureacratic world over against which it supposedly stands.

History and the Poetizing Memory of Jesus

The other reading of the phrase "the wound of history" is found in Bonhoeffer's description of the God "who wins power and space in the world by his weakness." This opening, unlike the dismembering of time

30. *Ibid.*, 1, 5; William T. Cavanaugh, "A Fire Strong Enough to Consume the House: The Wars of Religion and the Rise of the State," *Modern Theology* 11 (October 1995): 409.

31. Stanley Hauerwas, *Against the Nations: War and Survival in a Liberal Society* (San Francisco: Harper & Row, 1985), 169.

32. Charles Taylor, *Sources of the Self: the Making of Modern Identity* (Cambridge, MA: Harvard University Press, 1989), 508.

and place that occurs at the hands of a world come of age, irrupts within the penultimate as humans are "caught up into the messianic suffering of God in Jesus Christ." Put somewhat differently, this other space takes form in the body politic of the Christian community, where the word of the incarnate, crucified, and risen Christ "confronts us in its entirety in the message of the justification of the sinner by grace alone. Christian life means being human through the efficacy of the incarnation; it means being sentenced and pardoned through the efficacy of the cross; and it means living a new life through the efficacy of the resurrection."[33]

The opening that the ultimate secures through its encounter with the penultimate inhabits a very different "fiction," and thus posits a very different conception of history, than that presupposed by a risk culture. The roots of this alternative understanding are very ancient. Indeed, as Martin Buber suggests in his fascinating discussion of Gideon's legendary refusal of hereditary kingship in deference to the divine rule (Judges 8:22), it is the story of Israel that originally invents the idea of history as such. The beginning and end of that story, and of that people, says Buber, is the kingship of God. Gideon thus declares that neither he nor his sons, but only YHWH, would rule over Israel. According to Buber, the theocratic motif in this story does not refer, as some have suggested, to the institutionalized rule of consecrated elites, nor is it merely an "ideal" or regulative concept. It is rather what Buber calls a poetizing memory, that is, a disposition to know and to will that is "of a religious and political kind in one." This memory educated Israel to "know history as the dialectic of an asking divinity and an answer-refusing, but nevertheless an answer-attempting humanity, the dialogue whose demand is an *eschaton*." This divine-human interchange, moreover, is not embodied at the sublime boundaries of life, "but in the midst of the whirl of political actualities."[34]

To be sure, says Buber, Gideon's declaration represents an original form of this poetizing insight that is naive and non-reflecting, but nonetheless basic to the increasingly complex developments that constitute the biblical story. Those who first represented the case for divine rulership against the resistance and defiance of "history" encountered in the

33. *LPP*, 361; cf. *Ethics*, 132-33.
34. Martin Buber, *The Kingship of God*, 3rd ed. (New York: Harper & Row, 1967), 58, 63-65, 139.

whirl of political actualities the first tremors of eschatology.[35] These tremors recur with increasing intensity throughout the story, beginning with the conflict between the advocates of monarchical institutions and the proponents of God's kingship, and continuing through the crisis of the Exile, the practices and institutions of diasporic Judaism, the probing inquiries of Ecclesiastes and Job, the extension and radicalization of the prophetic oracles of judgment and redemption by the apocalyptic writers, and then, according to the New Testament, reaching its denouement in the incarnation, crucifixion, and resurrection of Jesus. But the basic contours and eschatological tendencies of Israel's poetizing memory detailing the confrontation of the penultimate by the ultimate are never rejected in Scripture in favor of another depiction of history.

For Bonhoeffer, the power and space that God secures in the penultimate through the messianic sufferings of Jesus display the historical form of this divine-human interrogatory, most definitively in the response of faith to "the message of the justification of the sinner by grace alone." This message is not, however, a distillation of abstract theological formulas, which by themselves are but "a partial extension of the world." Bonhoeffer instead focuses on a series of encounters between Jesus and those he calls and heals: the call of the twelve to discipleship, table fellowship with tax collectors and harlots, the conversion of Zacchaeus, the healing of the sick, the centurion of Capernaum, the rich young ruler.[36] Through such encounters, says Rowan Williams, "people are concretely drawn into a share in the vulnerability of God, into a new kind of life and a new identity. They do not receive an additional item called faith; their ordinary existence is not reorganized, found wanting in specific respects and supplemented: it is transfigured as a whole."[37]

This message of justification, embodied in the poetizing memory, or more specifically, the poetizing *re-membering* of Jesus, is extended in, with, and under the life of the church (the *other* body of Jesus) by the power of the Spirit in a strategically dis-membered world. Through the eucharistic polity and piety of the church, the message of the justification of the sinner

35. *Ibid.,* 63-65, 139.
36. *LPP,* 341f., 361f., 381.
37. Rowan Williams, "Postmodern Theology and the Judgment of the World," in *Postmodern Theology,* ed. Frederic B. Burnham (San Francisco: Harper & Row, 1989), 108.

by grace alone continues to confront the penultimate with a word of judgment and of redemption. This word does not pertain to some esoteric realm which is merely, in Bonhoeffer's words, "the religious rounding-off of a profane conception of the universe,"[38] but addresses the concerns and celebrations, the actions and passions, that characterize everyday life in all its particularity and contingency. Mundane existence is not merely surveyed, categorized, inventoried, and supplemented as needed by religious discourse; it is rather transfigured as a whole.

The transfiguration of our existence means, first, that in the poetizing memory of Jesus the penultimate encounters the first human being. That is to say, the humanity that enters into reality through the incarnation is not, as Bonhoeffer so rightly puts it, "the corroboration of the established world and of the human character as it is." Such conceptions lead directly to the compromise solution to the problem of the relation of the penultimate with the ultimate in Christian life, which Bonhoeffer regards as "an eternal justification for things as they are . . . the metaphysical purification from the accusation which weighs upon everything that is."[39] The incarnation is therefore not the affirmation of God's approval of the human as defined by the penultimate, but God's breaking through such definitions to establish "a new and formative definition of the human."[40]

Embodied in this new and formative definition of the human is, as Bonhoeffer puts it, "a twofold condemnation of humankind, the absolute condemnation of sin and the relative condemnation of the established human orders." This "death sentence upon the world"[41] does not refer to a word of condemnation from God, but rather, as Williams observes, is executed via the dramatic event of Jesus' interaction with people. Such interactions give "the persons involved definitions, roles to adopt, points on which to stand and speak. They are invited to 'create' themselves in finding a place within this drama — an improvisation in the theater workshop, but one that purports to be about a comprehensive truth affecting one's identity and future."[42]

---

38. *Ethics,* 189.

39. *Ibid.,* 127-31.

40. Stanley Hauerwas, "Jesus: The Story of the Kingdom," in *A Community of Character: Toward a Constructive Christian Social Ethic* (Notre Dame, IN: University of Notre Dame Press, 1981), 48-49.

41. *Ethics,* 131-32.

42. Williams, "Postmodern Theology and the Judgment of the World," 96-97.

The poetizing memory of Jesus is not, however, only a death sentence executed upon the world, for in the incarnation we also learn of God's love for creation. According to Bonhoeffer, the incarnation "means that we have the right and the obligation to be human beings before God."[43] Jesus was thus, in Herbert McCabe's words, "the first member of the human race in whom humanity came to fulfilment, the first human being for whom to live was simply to love — for this is what human beings are for." The rest of humanity fears being fully and completely human, because it demands that we abandon ourselves to others, that we be at their disposal, that we receive ourselves at the hands of others, that we find our true flourishing in the contingent (and therefore utterly unpredictable) relations of love. It demands, in other words, that we refuse the divine summons to regard the entirety of our lives, not as given but as gift.[44]

We refuse the summons, and recoil in fear and trembling, because we prefer the safety and predictability of the person that each of us has become, the familiarity of what each of us has made of herself or himself, within the framework of the penultimate. We do not love, and so fail to live a fully human life. Jesus, in contrast, "was the first human being who had no fear of love at all; the first to have no fear of being human." He had no fear of being human "because he saw his humanity simply as gift from him whom he called 'the Father'. . . . His whole being and death was a response in love and obedience to the gift of being human, an act of gratitude and appreciation of the gift of being human."[45] To be human — something that is not a given, but which only takes form in the midst of the penultimate through participation in God's messianic suffering — is therefore to love.

"What you give someone when you give them love," says McCabe, "is the gift of yourself. And what does that mean? What it means is that you give them space. You give them a place where they can be themselves. To give someone love is to give her herself, to give him himself, to let him be. . . . Love is the space in which to expand, and it is always a gift. In this sense we receive ourselves at the hands of others. Of course this is true in innumerable ways — we have to be born of others, for a

---

43. *Ethics,* 131.

44. Herbert McCabe, O.P., *God Matters* (London: Geoffrey Chapman, 1987), 94-95.

45. *Ibid.,* 95.

start—but our growth, our personal development, also takes place only in the space that others provide by their love."[46] To love, in other words, is to respond *in* love and obedience to the gift of being human by giving a place where those whom you love "can be themselves."

Put another way, to love is repeat differently, and thus to repeat exactly, the drama enacted by the poetizing memory of Jesus. The relations of charity, understood as participation in the being of Jesus — that is, in the re-membering of Jesus by the Spirit in the church — do not leave either party unaffected, for both find their place within the transfigurative story of God. The poetizing memory of Jesus within the body politic of Christ is therefore a form of *mimesis,* a nonidentical repetition which is both faithful to what is repeated *and* poetic, that is, which allows this memory to go on and on.

The reciprocating patterns of the divine love made flesh do not emerge out of nothing, but are the result of the practices of local Christian communities. These practices foster a common life in response to the same vicissitudes of earthly life and from the same range of finite goods as faced by penultimate communities, but to distinct ends, since each operates according to "a different faith, a different hope, a different love."[47] The Christian life thus flows from, and subsists in, the improvisations of charitable relations "via the construction of a common space of intersecting and overlapping practices."[48] These relations of charity "particularize the universality of Jesus Christ in a community of differences . . . as the provisional representative of all humanity before God and neighbor."[49] Hence not only do we love because God first loved us (1 John 4:19), but we also *are* because God loves: *Deus amat, ergo sumus.* To be sure, we may resist the giftedness of our very being. Indeed, according to Buber, such resistance helps to drive history toward its eschaton. What creatures cannot do, however, is refuse this gift altogether.

---

46. *Ibid.,* 108.

47. St. Augustine, *City of God* 17.54.

48. John Milbank, "The End of Dialogue," in *Christian Uniqueness Reconsidered: The Myth of a Pluralistic Theology of Religions* (Maryknoll, NY: Orbis Books, 1990), 187-88. Bonhoeffer's appeals to the arcane discipline of the early church, as well as the practices recounted in *Life Together,* provide crucial guidance for discerning this divine improvisation, through which Christ takes form in, with, and under his ecclesial body.

49. James J. Buckley, "A Field of Living Fire: Karl Barth on the Spirit and the Church," *Modern Theology* 10 (January 1994): 91.

In contrast, the principal trait "given" to everyday human existence by Descartes's *cogito, ergo sum* consists in its self-isolation, which is the result of a decision that, as Bonhoeffer states in *Act and Being,* "is . . . constantly in process of being taken, because it has already been taken."[50] The peculiar give-and-take of this decision is the product of the performative interplay that takes place within modern institutions to shape the sinews of both corporate and individual life. The habits and relations fostered by these institutions deny to self-positing subjects a distinctive *place* or *persona* in the divine-human drama where they can be themselves, that is, where they receive themselves as gifts that are in turn to be given to others. Instead, the modern subject, trapped with the Machiavellian void, is forced either to sacrifice itself or colonize the other. Tragically, when either self or other is defined in this manner, the humanity of its counterpart is also obliterated.

Gift Relations in the Body of Christ

We also encounter in the isolation of self and other another vestige of the modern fiction — the distinction that is regularly drawn in our society between legal contract and gift.[51] In contrast to the operations of the symbolic tokens that make the antagonisms of the contract the principal means of social interchange, a gift is formally defined as unilateral (that is, untainted by the expectation of return), noncompulsory (and therefore characterized by a complete absence of constraint upon the spontaneity of the giver), and completely indifferent as regards content (since, according to Kant, purity of will is all that really matters in any moral act, and so we are constantly admonished that "it is not the gift but the thought that counts"). The justification of the sinner by grace, as the gift of God which demands nothing of you except "that you accept the fact that you are accepted,"[52] is frequently cited as the paradigmatic instance of this unilaterial and formalist definition of gift.

What is crucial to take note of in this rigid distinction between

---

50. *AB,* 166.

51. In the section that follows I am deeply indebted to what John Milbank lays out in his essay, "Can a Gift Be Given?" *Modern Theology* 11 (January 1995): 119-61.

52. Paul Tillich, *Systematic Theology* (Chicago: The University of Chicago Press, 1957), vol. 2, 177-79.

contract and gift is the way that it relegates gift (and therefore grace) to the boundaries of life, where it exists outside the normal media of interchange — that is, the symbolic tokens of liberal capitalism. Indeed, the idea of gift may best be described in the modern fiction as a symbolic token, for the gulf fixed between private and public spheres, the inner or personal and the social, the sacred and the secular, is enshrined in the distinction between gift and contract. And from a theological perspective, this symbol misleadingly isolates agapeic love from the question of the giver's own well-being, from the desire to be with the recipient of one's love, and from all considerations of justice or power.[53]

In contrast, social relationships in pre-modern cultures (that is to say, in communities where these relations have not been severed from the particularities of contexts of presence, but remain subject to the constraints of local practices and institutions) are best characterized by the idea of gift-exchange.[54] Gift relations (including the divine gift that is creation) differ from the purely economic interchanges that characterize the symbolic tokens of modernity in several ways. First, gift relations normally involve balanced yet nonidentical reciprocation that binds both giver and recipient in a social relation which can best be described as organic (i.e., a body politic). Second, the suitability of a gift's content — whether or not it is a "good" gift — is contextually determined. A third trait concerns the inalienability of the giver from the gift, while at the same time its quality as a gift preserves the otherness of the giver. Finally, a resituating of the self takes place in gift relations through the address of others, embodying "a recognition of ineradicable connection with others and a desire for its furtherance."[55] Social contexts characterized by the giving and receiving of gifts are therefore not free of assumptions of moral obligation and debt, a point that Bonhoeffer tacitly recognizes when he notes that a consequence of the divine gift of love made flesh is that we have "the obligation to be human beings before God."

What does all this mean theologically for the church in a "post-Christian" era? The end of the so-called Christian age, as John H. S. Kent states, means that the church has reached

53. Milbank, "Can a Gift Be Given?" 132.
54. See, e.g., Marcel Mauss, *The Gift* (London: Routledge, 1990), 5, 36, 72-73; and Bronislaw Malinowski, *Argonauts of the Western Pacific* (New York: E. P. Dutton, 1961), 167ff.
55. Milbank, "Can a Gift Be Given?" 132.

the end of a line of growth, an end which neither Marxism nor Christianity can prevent, not even when they combine in "liberation theology," which would like to see itself as legitimizing an ecclesiastical take-over of a post-revolutionary situation, but which may be more correctly interpreted as a theology of nostalgia — the characteristic theology of the twentieth century — a harking back to the style of the *ancien régime,* however paradoxical this may sound, to a society in which the churches regarded themselves as the spiritual form of a material community.[56]

One not only hears in these words echoes of Bonhoeffer's critique of liberal theology's anxious efforts to reserve some space for God, but also a concise summary of what the "age of Christianity" was all about. Whenever Christians identify the mission of church with that of the modern nation-state, and thus accede to the role of spiritual form for this community, we effectively efface our identity as the body politic of Christ. If this happens, it will deprive the people of the gift relations that only the church is in a position to give, forcing them to rely exclusively on the institutional mechanisms and symbolic tokens of modernity, as every nation in our global village does, in its attempt to fashion a unity among disparate peoples. To the degree that this attempt dominates the mission of the churches in South Africa, for example, the legacy of apartheid will be replaced, not by a democratically inspired sister- and brotherhood, but by further fragmentation, self-isolation and disparity that are the offspring of the modern fiction of history. Steadfast love and faithfulness will remain estranged; righteousness and peace will not embrace (cf. Psalm 85:10).

Within the body of Christ, questions of identity and interaction should neither be confused nor separated. Only a community that knows it is a diasporic people, "held together in Jesus Christ alone, having become one because they remember *him* [and thus *re-member* him] in the distant lands,"[57] can heed the word of God spoken by Jeremiah to the exiles in Babylon to "seek the welfare of the city where I have sent you into exile, and pray to the LORD on its behalf, for in its welfare you will find your welfare" (Jeremiah 29:7). Only a church that refuses to be typed

56. John H. S. Kent, *The End of the Line? The Development of Christian Theology over the Last Two Centuries* (Philadelphia: Fortress Press, 1982), viii.

57. Dietrich Bonhoeffer, *Life Together* and *Prayerbook of the Bible,* ed. Geffrey B. Kelly, *DBWE,* vol. 5 (Minneapolis: Fortress Press, 1996), 28.

as the spiritual form of a material community, thus taking seriously its biblical designation as a member of a commonwealth whose mission is to be "a light to the nations" (Isaiah 49:6), is able to foster transcendent patterns of charity "in the middle of the village"[58] that allow the rulers and authorities of this age to see what is the plan of the mystery for creation hidden for ages in God (Ephesians 3:9-10; Philippians 3:20). Only the city whose pentecostal citizenship relativizes without annihilating "the ties of common history, of blood, of class, and of language"[59] can be the sacrament of union with God and of unity among humankind.[60] Only a people that mimetically embodies the divine love made flesh within the sinews of penultimate existence understands that reconciliation is empty without justice, and justice is directionless apart from reconciliation.[61] Only a body politic that is formed by the sharing of bread at the eucharist, so that it extends the boundaries of solidarity that normally are restricted to the family to include the widow, the orphan, the alien, and the poor, is capable of signifying the presence of a history in which differences — such as differences of color — are related harmoniously through the receiving and giving of gifts, rather than antagonistically, via the disembedding mechanisms of modernity.

Finally, the messianic suffering of God reintroduces the tragic nature of existence to all who once sought refuge from this reality in the knowledge cocoons of modernity. A world come of age, its lofty aspirations notwithstanding, has not changed the fact that we "have made a world in which there is no way to be human that does not involve suffering."[62] Bonhoeffer understands this all too well, which is why he places at the beginning of *Life Together* a quote from Luther that states, in part, "To rule is to be in the midst of your enemies. And whoever will not suffer this does not want to be part of the rule of Christ."[63] Of course, it is the wound of Jesus' crucifixion, which, as Bonhoeffer says,

58. *LPP,* 282.

59. Bonhoeffer, "The Church and the People of the World," in *A Testament to Freedom: The Essential Writings of Dietrich Bonhoeffer,* ed. Geffrey B. Kelly and F. Burton Nelson (San Francisco: HarperCollins, 1990), 240.

60. Austin Flannery, O.P., ed., *Vatican Council II: The Conciliar and Post Conciliar Documents,* new rev. ed. (Northport, NY: Costello Publishing Company, 1992), 68-69.

61. Paul Lehmann, "Metaphorical Reciprocity between Theology and Law," *The Journal of Law and Religion* 3 (1985): 189.

62. McCabe, *God Matters,* 93.

63. *LT,* 27.

"contains within itself the rejection of the whole human race without exception," that dramatically specifies both the tragic nature of life within the penultimate, and the direction of the divine judgment upon it. And yet, because "the crucifixion of Jesus does not simply mean the annihilation of the created world,"[64] the tragic nature of our engagement with the penultimate does not mean that it is unworthy of our time or labor. It simply places it in proper context, that is, in relation to the ultimate. We dare not be mistaken about this aspect of the wound of history, for as Bonhoeffer reminds us, "When Christ calls a person, he bids that one to come and die."[65]

---

64. *Ethics,* 132.

65. Dietrich Bonhoeffer, *The Cost of Discipleship* (New York: Macmillan Publishing Company, 1960), 99.

"Waiting for the Word": The Churches' Embarrassment in Speaking about God

FRITS DE LANGE

It's an unconscious waiting for the word of deliverance,
though the time is probably not yet ripe for it to be heard.
But the time will come. . . .[1]

This paper offers a reconstruction of Dietrich Bonhoeffer's conception of "God-talk," using as a basis the letter he wrote from prison in May 1944, on the occasion of the baptism of his godchild. Bonhoeffer's "Thoughts on the Day of Baptism of Dietrich Wilhelm Rüdiger Bethge"[2] still represent a fascinating text. In these few condensed pages Bonhoeffer, with an almost prophetic perspicacity, shows himself to be aware of the churches' continuing embarrassment in speaking about God.

We know that there are cultural reasons for that awkwardness: religious skepticism and relativism seem to affect not only (post)modern culture in general, but also the churches' preaching. Another, and perhaps even more disquieting fact we have to acknowledge is the persistent inability of the churches to stand by the Word they proclaim. How can the church deal honestly with its past without obscuring the liberating presence of God? Talking freely about God seems to be more and more

1. Letter dated 25 March 1944. *LPP*, 240.
2. *Ibid.*, 294-300.

94

problematic in our days. The Reformed confession that "the Proclamation of God's Word *is* God's Word" *(Praedicatio verbi divini est verbum divinum, Confessio Helvetica)* seems to be a presumptuous overstatement. Maybe negative theology offers a more viable solution for Christian churches today. Is not all we can say about God that we can say nothing about him?

We focus on the "Thoughts on the Day of Baptism," assuming this text to be crucial in Bonhoeffer's theological evolution. As a persistent — although critical — ally of Karl Barth's dialectical Word of God theology, Bonhoeffer had developed his own version of a theology which creates room for a speaking God. Accordingly, the Baptism Letter refers to the liberating power that lies in the Word of God. But at the same time, Bonhoeffer observes in this text the actual impasse in the church's speaking of God's Word.

In his critical analysis of the reasons for that impotence, there is another side of Bonhoeffer that comes to the fore. Here we meet a modern, secularized theologian who sharply diagnoses the failure of Christianity before a changed world. For that reason, the Baptism Letter represents a crucial moment in the testing of Bonhoeffer's theological theory of the Word. It may be regarded as a point of transition in his theological biography.

The letter was conceived after more than one year of captivity in Tegel. It originates from the period in which Bonhoeffer pressed his friend Eberhard Bethge progressively with his new theological insights on a "world come of age" and a "nonreligious interpretation of biblical concepts." "What is bothering me incessantly is the question what Christianity really is, or indeed who Christ really is, for us, today," he writes as a running start to those theological explorations, in the famous letter bearing the date 30 April 1944.[3] Bonhoeffer must have composed his Baptism Letter in the following days. It was sent out of prison as a substitute for the sermon and the sacrament, which he was not able to render to his new-born nephew because of his captivity. The preaching of God's Word in a nonreligious world: it is this combination of Reformation orthodoxy on the one hand and cultural sensibility on the other that make this letter from prison still an intriguing and inspiring document.

3. *Ibid.*, 279.

The Performative Power of the Word of God

The Baptism Letter opens with the observation that in western civilization radical changes are transpiring which will imply the definite end of bourgeois culture. When the child that receives baptism today is grown up, Bonhoeffer states, bourgeois life will be "a vanished world." An era is closing. Although Bonhoeffer considers himself a product of this era, he does not want to look back in a nostalgic way; on the contrary, he directs his view hopefully to the future. He is convinced that the substance within the fading cultural patterns, which has proved to be reliable in the past, will also survive the new age. "The old spirit, after a time of misunderstanding and weakness, withdrawal and recovery, preservation and rehabilitation, will produce new forms." This assurance enables Bonhoeffer to meet the future with tranquillity. "So there is no need to hurry; *we have to be able to wait*," he writes.[4] "The old spirit will create itself new forms," but when that will happen, and how, and in which shape these forms will finally manifest themselves we do not yet know. We shall have to wait for it confidently. This last statement is important as regards the vision of the future of Christian faith which Bonhoeffer developed in prison.

Bonhoeffer continues his letter with a set of theological observations which can be read in obvious correlation to his cultural analysis. According to Bonhoeffer, bourgeois culture and Christianity are, in a certain sense, sharing an analogous destiny. We read about an era that comes to an end and about the dawning of a new one, not only for culture in general but also with regard to Christian faith. Bonhoeffer talks about "earlier words," bound to "lose their force." At the same time he expresses his expectation of "a new language," "liberating and redeeming."

Before I comment on this fragment more extensively, I want to quote it at length:

> Today you will be baptised a Christian. All those great ancient words of the Christian proclamation will be spoken over you, and the command of Jesus Christ to baptize will be carried out on you, without your knowing anything about it. But we are once again being driven right back to the beginnings of our understanding. Reconciliation and redemption, regeneration and the Holy Spirit, love of our enemies,

4. *Ibid.*, 295. Author's emphasis.

cross and resurrection, life in Christ and Christian discipleship — all these things are so difficult and so remote that we can hardly venture any more to speak of them. In the traditional words and acts we suspect that there may be something quite new and revolutionary, though we cannot as yet grasp or express it. This is our own fault.

Bonhoeffer then goes on to speak about the radical renewal of Christian thought, speech, and action which he envisaged:

Our church, which has been fighting in these years only for its self-preservation, as though that were an end in itself, is incapable of taking the word of reconciliation and redemption to mankind and the world. Our earlier words are therefore bound to lose their force and cease, and our being Christians today will be limited to two things: prayer and righteous action among men. All Christian thinking, speaking, and organizing must be born anew out of the melting-pot, and any attempt to help the church prematurely to a new expansion of its organization will merely delay its conversion and purification. It is not for us to prophesy the day (though that day will come) when man will once more be called so to utter the word of God that the world will be changed and renewed by it. It will be a new language, perhaps quite non-religious, but liberating and redeeming — as was Jesus' language; it will shock people and yet overcome them by its power; it will be the language of a new righteousness and truth, proclaiming God's peace with men and the coming of his kingdom. "They shall fear and tremble because of all the good and all the prosperity I provide for it" (Jeremiah 33:9). Till then the Christian cause will be a silent and hidden affair, but there will be those who pray and do right and wait for God's own time. May you be one of them, and may it be said of you one day, "The path of the righteous is like the light of dawn, which shines brighter and brighter till full day" (Proverbs 4:18).[5]

Attentive reading shows that Bonhoeffer does not plead for a theological break with Christian tradition. On the contrary, according to him our earlier words still possess a revolutionary potential. Bonhoeffer seems to assign to traditional faith a meaning surplus rather than a lack of meaning. God does not keep silence; Bonhoeffer's confidence in the God who wants to express his Word through the mouth of people seems

5. *Ibid.*, 299-300.

unbroken. The day will come that it will be spoken again, shocking, liberating, and redeeming. Language almost explodes when Bonhoeffer expresses the revolutionary power of the Word of God.

Adopting a helpful distinction familiar in modern language theory, one can say that in Bonhoeffer's view biblical God-talk uses a *performative* language.[6] Genuine speaking of God creates and transforms the human situation in a liberating way. Bonhoeffer does not reproach current God-talk for having a lack of descriptive adequacy, as if the traditional words of Christian faith have lost their referential meaning. His first intention is to point to the transforming effect of God-talk, be it religious or eventually even nonreligious, not to its semantic content.

From which source does this redemptive new language Bonhoeffer hopes for originate? The Baptism Letter is quite plain about that: the new language owes its performative force to Christ himself. "It will be liberating and redeeming — as was Jesus' language," Bonhoeffer states. Hearing Jesus' gospel is a shocking event that transforms one's entire being because it represents a confrontation with the Lord himself and his coming kingdom.

"It Is Our Own Fault"

The question arises as to why in Bonhoeffer's days the church had become incapable of speaking the liberating Word of God. What is the reason for this inability? Why was Jesus' language — and that of the apostles' — once capable of enacting redemption, whereas ours is not? Again, Bonhoeffer is very clear about the reason. He states tersely: "That is our own fault." The church's proclamation of the gospel misses the *exousia* which the language of Jesus once possessed. Why is this? Once more, not because of its

---

6. A *constative* speech act refers to an existing state of affairs. It describes the reality of what is the case. On the other hand, a *performative* speech act creates reality that did not exist before. Opening or closing a meeting, baptizing a child (or an ocean steamer), judging a criminal or a student, are common examples. Promising represents a significant performative activity. It creates a relationship of mutual expectations and obligations which did not exist before the promise was pronounced. It is "a performance of an act *in* saying something" (J. L. Austin, *How to Do Things with Words,* 2nd ed. (Oxford: Oxford University Press, 1975), 99-100; cf. J. R. Searle, *Speech Acts: An Essay in the Philosophy of Language* (Cambridge: Cambridge University Press, 1969), 22ff.

referential lack of clarity or ambiguity, but because of the Word's proclaimer; the Word of God is powerless, not because it lacks its object (the absence of God), but rather because those who proclaim the Word no longer support its original authority with their total existence.

In this context linguistic theory provides us with some useful analytical tools. When we say that our God-talk lacks *meaning,* we are pointing to its *semantic* aspect. In his diagnosis Bonhoeffer contends, however, that the real origin of this factually experienced weakness is not to be looked for in semantics, but rather in the *pragmatic dimension;* its source lies in the defective link between the speaker and the word spoken, not in the relation between the word and God's reality it tries to depict. That we cannot grasp any more the meaning of words such as reconciliation and redemption, cross and resurrection is merely symptomatic for a disease that has its roots elsewhere: in the incredibility of the church which proclaims them. "It is our own fault."

Modern philosophy of language stresses the social imbeddedness of language and the relevance of the pragmatic context for linguistic communication. According to Wittgenstein, culture incorporates a variety of language games which are located in shared social practices and a variety of forms of life. Language (also religious language) appears to be structured and regulated by the conventions and institutions in which people live. That means — we are still employing the linguistic idiom here — that the performance of a speech-act can only be successful if certain conditions concerning this pragmatic context have been met. A pragmatic setting in general consists of three elements, dependent on the scope one has in view: (1) the speaking person, as well as the person addressed (personal level); (2) the institutional framework in which the communication occurs (institutional level); and (3) its broader historical and cultural setting (situational level).

Going back to our text, we read how Bonhoeffer blames his church for "fighting in these years only for its self-preservation, as though it were an end in itself." Precisely there he situates the reason for its kerygmatic impotence. "Our earlier words are *therefore* bound to lose their force and cease," he concludes.[7] We shall see below that Bonhoeffer's grievance against his church concerns the three aspects of the pragmatic context, by which the liberating proclamation of God's Word should be supported.

---

7. Author's emphasis.

In stressing Bonhoeffer's accent on the pragmatic, rather than on the semantic, reasons for the churches' embarrassment in speaking about God, I want to make room for the thesis that Bonhoeffer, even in his last letters from prison, retains his belief in the power of God's Word. In doing so, he confirms until the end his allegiance to the theological concept of the Word of God, as developed by Barth. Bonhoeffer adopted this position in the midst of the twenties, and apparently never abandoned it afterward. It should be added, however, that already in his first writings he accentuated, more strongly than Barth ever did, the intrinsic relation between the Word of God and the configuration *(Gestalt)* of the church. "Effective preaching only is possible in the sanctorum communio," we read in his dissertation of 1927. "The community creates the Word, as the Word creates the community into community."[8] This indissoluble tie between church and Word is confirmed and retained throughout Bonhoeffer's entire theological biography, including the letters and papers from prison. But at that time, Bonhoeffer was forced to recognize that not only the German church in general, but also his Confessing Church, had failed. There seemed to be no subject left any more to speak the Word of God.

Bonhoeffer is thus confronted with an aporetical situation: he stresses human incompetence in speaking rightly about God, but simultaneously he does not want to detach himself from his theological heritage, the Barthian Word of God theology, firmly rooted in the dogmatic and homiletic tradition of the Reformation. For him, at this very moment, the only way one could still speak authentically about God was through silence, a kind of linguistic moratorium until further notice. Speaking about God becomes synonymous with waiting on God, until the day when God might be revealed in human language again.

Apparently Bonhoeffer solved his theological dilemma, not by easing its pressure, but, on the contrary, by incorporating the aporetic situation with which he was confronted in the core of his theology: the *aporia* (to speak about God, knowing that one must do so inadequately) is not conquered dialectically nor seen as an avoidable consequence of certain wrong theological premises, but lies at the heart of theology itself in the age to come. It follows that Bonhoeffer challenges the aporetic situation above all in a practical way, not by constructing another theory;

8. *Sanctorum Communio. Eine dogmatische Untersuchung zur Soziologie der Kirche* (1927), ed. Joachim von Soosten, *DBW*, vol. 1 (Munich: Chr. Kaiser, 1986), 159.

according to him a different-based *praxis pietatis* ("pray and do right") is needed in the first place.

Before elaborating this thesis in greater detail, we might note that the Bonhoeffer interpretation here presented assumes, firstly, a relative continuity in his theological development; secondly, it distances itself somewhat from the attempt — particularly popular among representatives of the so-called theology of secularization — to consider Bonhoeffer above all things as a model for linguistic innovation in theology. In my opinion, his project of a nonreligious interpretation of biblical concepts has never been worked out sufficiently to satisfy that claim.

Deus Dixit: Karl Barth's "a priori"

The theological presupposition which lies at the foundation of Bonhoeffer's defense of the performativity of the Word of God was borrowed from Karl Barth. One can summarize it in two words: *Deus dixit*. The phrase implies that God takes the initiative in revelation (in another metaphor: "speaks"), and that God does so decisively in Jesus Christ, the unique *Logos Theou*, Word of God. This means that theological speaking about God should be preceded by the act of listening to God's own Word. Before we talk about God, God talks to us. All our theological speaking is speaking in hindsight; our words about God will only be trustworthy when they find their source in God's own self-revealing Word. It follows that the genuine subject of our theological knowledge is not the theologian, but God.

How strongly Barth really did influence Bonhoeffer is still a matter of discussion.[9] It is a fact, however, that this influence was decisive and radical in any case. Since 1925, when Bonhoeffer the student read Barth's *Das Wort Gottes und die Theologie*, his thinking was deeply affected by the critical reorientation Barth introduced in theology. In a seminar paper from 1925 Bonhoeffer affirmed without reservation Barth's epistemological ground decision: "The equal can only be known by equal, God by God." How is human speaking about God then still possible? Bonhoeffer's solution is Barth's: "The object of

---

9. Cf. Charles Marsh: *Reclaiming Dietrich Bonhoeffer: The Promise of his Theology* (Oxford: Oxford University Press, 1994), 7-33.

knowledge creates organs in the subject for knowing in the act of knowledge itself."[10]

Some years later, Bonhoeffer gives, as a teacher at the Berlin University, an extensive explication of the turn *(Wende)* Barth accomplished in theology. His lectures on the "History of Systematic Theology in the Twentieth Century" (1931-1933) show how deeply and personally Bonhoeffer was affected by this subject. It was Barth's intention, Bonhoeffer states, to create room again in theology for God's free and sovereign acting:

> Only where God speaks himself, we know something about him. No retrospectively postulated concept of revelation makes him speak. Only from the self enacting revelation we know God as the origin, which can not be founded elsewhere and founds everything. . . . The Word of God is pre-eminently *petitio principii. Deus dixit* — assuming that is the beginning of all real theological thinking. . . . The only object of theology is the *Logos Theou,* the self grounding acting of God. Behind this origin we cannot go back any more.[11]

Here Bonhoeffer follows Barth completely. But in his emphatic christological concentration he lays his own accents. God's self-revelation occurs in the person of Christ, namely in an intelligible way. This word, Christ, is really God's self-disclosure in total freedom, yet at the same time wrapped up in the cloak of history, humanity. Indeed, "God is totally different *(ganz anderes)* than humanity. But when God speaks, God does so in a hidden way, that is to say in a human way."[12]

In this christological intensification, Bonhoeffer's criticism of Barth, already expressed in his dissertation and especially in his *Act and Being* (1931), resounds. There, Bonhoeffer criticizes Barth's epistemology as actualistic and individualistic. According to Bonhoeffer, the *locus* for the knowledge of God is not the faith of the individual believer, but the

---

10. "Referat über historische und pneumatische Schriftauslegung" (1925), *DBW,* vol. 9, 305-24, 312.

11. "Die Geschichte der systematische Theologie des 20. Jahrhunderts" (1931/32), in Dietrich Bonhoeffer, *Ökumene, Universität, Pfarramt 1931-1932,* ed. E. Amelung and C. Strohm, *DBW,* vol. 11(Gütersloh: Chr. Kaiser/ Gütersloher Verlag, 1994,), 140-213, 199.

12. *Ibid.*

community of the church. God has *given* the Word, he stresses in *Act and Being*. God's sovereignty does not imply a withdrawal, but rather a self-binding in free will to people. "God is not free from humankind; He is free *for* it. Christ is the Word of the freedom of God."[13] In the proclaimed Christ, he is "tangible." He is "to be had" in the church. The church, Bonhoeffer had already claimed in *Sanctorum Communio*, coining a Hegelian formula, is "Christ existing as community." By means of this Christology-based ecclesiology Bonhoeffer accentuates the continuity of revelation, against Barth's actualism. In the church as the Body of Christ the revelation is more or less "possessed."[14]

We see that already in his earlier theology Bonhoeffer links the presence of God indissolubly to the concrete existence *(Gestalt)* of the church. The free and sovereign God acts through the creative and transforming word spoken in and by a community of people. We observe that the same concept still determines the Baptism Letter, though it is stretched there to its ultimate limits.

Throughout his theological writings, Bonhoeffer ascribes to the Word of God a strong performative force. Though decisively spoken in Christ, Bonhoeffer states in his lectures on *Creation and Fall*, its transforming power originates, in fact, in God's act of creation. "And God spoke: 'let there be light'" (Genesis 1:3). "In the beginning was the Word . . . and all things were created by the Word" (John 1:1-3). Biblically speaking, the original Word of God is a *dabar*, a deed-word *(Tatwort)*. It creates what it says. Our human words, however, have lost that force; they have become symbols, signs, ideas, or meanings; they are used to refer to reality but they do not create it.[15]

So it becomes impossible for us to be the intermediary of God's Word to this world any more. Human sin must be held responsible for that loss of power of speech. "The fallen creation is not the creation of the first, creating word any more."[16] Christ, however, represents the renewed Word, which God wants to address to humankind, in the midst

---

13. Dietrich Bonhoeffer, *Akt und Sein: Transzendentalphilosophie und Ontologie in der systematischen Theologie* (1931), ed. H.-R. Reuter, *DBW*, vol. 2 (Munich: Chr. Kaiser, 1988), 85.

14. *Ibid.*, 109.

15. Dietrich Bonhoeffer, *Schöpfung und Fall* (1933), ed. M. Rüter and I. Tödt, *DBW*, vol. 3 (Munich: Chr. Kaiser, 1989), 38-40. Cf. 39, note 7, referring to Ps. 33:9: "Das Wort selbst ist die Tat."

16. Dietrich Bonhoeffer, *Christologie* (1933), *GS*, vol. 3, 166-242, 188.

of its silent world. "The Logos is a powerful Creator's word."[17] The *Logos Theou* is not an idea but a person; he represents the forgiving and commanding appeal *(Ansprache)* of God to humankind.

In his lectures on *Christology* (1933), Bonhoeffer retains the link between Christology and ecclesiology, pointed out earlier, by stating that this new Word of God, Christ, is spoken to us by means of the concrete forms of the living church, differentiated as: firstly, the proclamation of the gospel, in interpreting the Scriptures that give witness of Christ; secondly, the sacraments; and thirdly, the congregation itself as a social community. In this variety of forms, the church represents the given Word of God. The church is *Christus praesens*.

Briefly summarizing the Word theology Bonhoeffer develops in his early years, one can say that according to him the one Word of God takes four different forms. First of all, it is the creating and sustaining Word of God as spoken in the beginning. Then, this Word is spoken again in the incarnate Logos, Christ, and subsequently in the Scriptures bearing witness to him. Finally — and here we see Bonhoeffer, contra Barth, putting a deliberate accent on ecclesiology [18] — the church in its proclamation of the gospel and its social configuration, through which the first three forms of the Word of God are actualized in the present situation. In the Word preached in the church, God himself brings us anew in contact with our origins, transforming and recreating our sinful existence. In his Finkenwalde lectures on homiletics Bonhoeffer declares preaching to be "the happening truth. It creates itself its own form of existence."[19] The church embodies that form of existence. With Luther, Bonhoeffer considers the Word of the church (perhaps we can also say now: the Word *as* church) to be a *verbum efficax;* a creative Word of God which has regained its original force.

---

17. *Ibid.,* 193.

18. Cf. Barth's theory of "the Word of God in its threefold form," in Karl Barth, *Kirchliche Dogmatik,* vol. 1/1 (Zurich: Zollikon: 1932), par. 4.

19. "Finkenwalder Homiletik" (1935-1939), ed. Eberhard Bethge, *GS,* vol. 4 (Munich: Chr. Kaiser, 1975), 237-89, 252.

"The Church Was Silent When She Should Have Cried Out"

A theology which identifies the Word of God with Christ and subsequently considers the church to be its form of existence, ties the performative force of God's Word indissolubly to the pragmatic context of the ecclesiastical community. The tension between the presumed meaning surplus of God's Word and the simultaneous confirmation of the lack of effectiveness of human God-talk can increase to such an extent that the theological concept that virtually identifies them is bound to break down. This is precisely what seems to happen in Bonhoeffer's theology from prison, especially in his Baptism Letter. We have already distinguished within a pragmatic situation a personal, an institutional, and a historical-cultural level. In his letters from prison we observe how Bonhoeffer underscores the shortcomings of the church on all these three levels. Some illustrations may be helpful.

On the personal level, a Christian believer should stand for the trustworthiness and the life-transforming power of the Word of God. In his "Outline for a Book," however, written in Tegel, Bonhoeffer observes the common confessing believer, rather, to be characterized by "standing up for the church's cause, but little personal faith in Christ."[20] For Bonhoeffer, faith is not a matter of being intellectually convinced of certain propositions concerning divine reality. According to him, the question "What do we really believe?" needs to be intensified: "I mean, believe in such a way that we stake our lives on it."[21] Christian faith demands total commitment. "To live in the light of the resurrection — that is what Easter means," Bonhoeffer writes to Bethge on the occasion of Easter 1944. "If a few people really believed that and acted on it in their daily lives, a great deal would be changed." What he observes, instead, is a great *perturbatio animorum* among people. They do not actually know what they really live by. And already anticipating his Baptism Letter he states: "It's an unconscious waiting for the word of deliverance, though the time is probably not yet ripe for it to be heard. But the time will come. . . ."[22]

The church lives out of the story of Jesus, the man for others. In his "Outline for a Book," however, Bonhoeffer observes: "Jesus is disap-

---

20. *LPP*, 381.
21. *Ibid.* ("Outline for a Book"), 382.
22. *Ibid.*, 240-241 (Letter from 25 March 1944).

pearing from sight. . . . The decisive factor: the church on the defensive. No taking risks for others."[23] Here we meet the second element in the pragmatic context of the church, the institutional framework. Words have to be personally trustworthy, but they must also be sustained and legitimated by social conventions and practices. When the word of deliverance spoken in the pulpit is not supported by a corresponding social structure that liberates people accordingly, it will be spoken in vain. Yet in this regard Bonhoeffer is obviously disappointed in his own Confessing Church.

The Confessing Church showed courage in its fight for room within the totalitarian State, fortifying its own position vis-à-vis the pressures of Nazism. But it failed in its lack of political resistance for the sake of others, namely the Jews. From April 1933 — when the so-called "Aryan-paragraph," which prevented the Jews from holding public office, was introduced — and throughout the church struggle Bonhoeffer himself spoke up for the Jews, as did some other individual members. "Open your mouth for the speechless" (Proverbs 31:8) was the text Bonhoeffer frequently quoted.[24] The Confessing Church as a whole, however, did not step into the breach for the Jews — even to defend Jewish Protestant pastors. The demonic process that started with the Jews' loss of civil rights and ended up with their deportation and annihilation, was not stopped nor even frustrated by the church. The total silence of the church after the synagogues burned on Crystal Night (10 November 1938) represented a sad low point in this regard.

In a Confession of Guilt, written in 1940, Bonhoeffer laments of the church: "She was silent when she should have cried out because the blood of the innocent was crying out to heaven. She has failed to speak the right word in the right way and at the right time."[25] The church still kept preaching, praying, and singing under the Nazi dictatorship. But Bonhoeffer coined an aphorism in these years. "Only he who shouts for the Jews, is allowed to sing Gregorian."[26]

23. *Ibid.* ("Outline for a Book"), 381.

24. Cf. Eberhard Bethge, *Dietrich Bonhoeffer. Eine Biographie* (Munich: Chr. Kaiser, 1967), 323, 474, 559, 596, 603. Cf. also *GS,* ed. E. Bethge (Munich: Chr. Kaiser, 1958ff.), vol. 1, 42; vol. 2, 144, 415; vol. 3, 323-324; Dietrich Bonhoeffer, *Nachfolge,* ed. M. Kuske and I. Tödt, *DBW,* vol. 4 (Munich: Chr. Kaiser, 1989), 253.

25. *Ethics,* 113. Compare as a striking contrast Bonhoeffer's discussion of "silence before the Word," *Life Together, DBWE,* vol. 5, 65ff.

26. Bethge, *Dietrich Bonhoeffer,* 506.

Not only faithful personal commitment or institutional trustworthiness, but also attentiveness to the historic and cultural situation — the third, more general level of the pragmatic context — is needed in order to speak powerfully about God. Speakers and hearers must want to participate within each other's cultural horizon in order to communicate successfully. That means that they have to acknowledge each other as persons, as "the people they are now." Otherwise their conversation deteriorates into a dialogue of the deaf. Those who proclaim the gospel must submit to these conditions. Inasmuch as the message is *addressed*, one must know to whom it is directed. According to Bonhoeffer, this condition of cultural sensibility was not met by his church. "People as they are now simply cannot be religious any more," Bonhoeffer notes in his famous letter of 30 April 1944.[27] It is the first of a sequence of letters in which he explores the contours of the modern world disclosed behind the horizon of the war, a world whose "coming of age" has significant consequences for theology.[28]

Bonhoeffer foresees a religionless world in which the common words of the church will have become pointless. "The time when people could be told everything by means of words, whether theological or pious, is over, and so is the time of inwardness and conscience — and that means the time of religion in general."[29] The theological explorations Bonhoeffer undertakes in the following months are just as challenging as they are indefinite. His ambitious program for a religionless interpretation of biblical concepts unfortunately remains unfinished and fragmentary. His intention, however, is clear. The Word of God cannot be heard in a language which is not understood and spoken by ordinary people. God-talk has to be popular, in both senses of the word.

Already in *Sanctorum Communio* Bonhoeffer had criticized the German Lutheran church for being a bourgeois and elitist institution.[30] In prison he radicalizes this criticism. When the masses use a more direct language of body and images instead of intellectual vocabulary, why not speak their tongue and use their semiotics? God's presence is not made known by God by means of the terminology of upper-class intellectuals only.

27 Author's emphasis.
28. *LPP*, 279.
29. *Ibid.*
30. *Sanctorum Communio, DBW*, vol. 1, 299ff.

Yet Bonhoeffer's cultural diagnosis in his letters from prison manages only to point out a direction. The concepts "coming of age," "religious," and "religionless" — however challenging they might be — are perhaps too ambiguous in view of the complicated cultural scene of postwar western culture. Postmodernism seems to give room again to religion, although in rather untraditional and hidden forms.

Whatever one might think of Bonhoeffer's sketch of modern culture, however, his thinking led him to adopt positions diametrically opposed to those taken by his church. In his "Outline for a Book" he examines the church's shortcomings in cryptic style:

> The Protestant church: Pietism as a last attempt to maintain evangelical Christianity as a religion; Lutheran orthodoxy, the attempt to rescue the church as an institution for salvation; the Confessing Church: the theology of revelation; a *dos moi pou stoi* over against the world. . . . Sociologically: no effect on the masses — interest confined to the upper and lower middle class. A heavy incubus of difficult traditional ideas.[31]

The church is obviously missing what Bonhoeffer himself considers to be a necessary condition for any competent speech about God: a contextual cultural hermeneutic.

A New Language?

What does this mean for Christian preaching? It seems clear that the liberating "new language" Bonhoeffer envisions in his Baptism Letter implies more than alternative theological semantics. The apparent lack of forceful impact of the gospel is basically — though perhaps not exclusively — located in the pragmatic setting of its proclamation. The story told by the church will only be experienced as credible if the church itself and its members turn out to be standing by their cause. Hermeneutics and ethics in Bonhoeffer, though they cannot be easily identified, are indissolubly intertwined.

Does not Bonhoeffer in his high-tensioned ecclesiology expect too much of the church? Perhaps he does. In order to prevent any more

---

31. *LPP*, 381.

frustrations and disappointments he might have adopted another ecclesiology and reconsidered his concept of church. Why not stress more expressively the fact that the church is a *corpus permixtum* of saints and sinners? Why not discuss ecclesiology in the more flexible language of pneumatology instead of invoking the very demanding concept of *Christus praesens?* The relationship between Christ and the believer would then be freed from that risky and overly-demanding identification. Bonhoeffer chooses, however, to maintain rather than to change his ecclesiology; but he does so by radicalizing his original view on God-talk. His clear insight into the weakness of the church's speech about God leads him in prison not to a less demanding ecclesiology, but rather to a renewed evaluation and re-estimation of the language of silence. In this, Bonhoeffer remains within the central presupposition of Word theology, as adopted by him in 1925: God's self is revealed concretely in human language, God's Word is to be spoken by human beings.

Does the fact that human language has actually eluded its performative force mean that God is condemned to stay speechless forever? No. Bonhoeffer's theology is far too Christ-centered to permit such an idea. Christ is the Logos of God and remains so. A God who kept silence from now on would be like a God undoing the incarnation.

Bonhoeffer thus consciously construes an aporetic tension between the actual impoverishment of the church's God-talk and his ongoing belief in the abundance of God's creative power. His prevailing *Christus praesens* ecclesiology keeps him from searching for an easy solution. On the contrary, it leads him to a strong emphasis on the act of silent waiting as the outstanding Christian attitude. "Until God's Word is spoken as a new language," the Baptism Letter concludes, "the Christian cause will be a silent and hidden affair, but there will be those who pray and do right and wait for God's own time."[32]

In this emphasis on keeping silent Bonhoeffer draws on insights which he developed much earlier. For Bonhoeffer, keeping silence is not the expression of some accidental embarrassment, but rather the appropriate Christian attitude vis-à-vis the living God. Indeed, human silence is the dialectial counterpart of God's speaking, not the mere consequence of taciturnity. In the opening of his lecture on *Christology*, which takes up the concept of Christ as Logos, he exhorts his hearers:

32. *Ibid.,* 300.

> Be silent, it is the Absolute! (Kierkegaard). . . . The silence of the church is silence before the Word. . . . Speaking about Christ means being silent, being silent about Christ means speaking. The appropriate speaking of the church that originates in an appropriate silence is proclamation of Christ.[33]

Similarly, in *Life Together* (1938), the fruit of the spiritual experiment in Finkenwalde, we find penetrating insights regarding the theological role of silence:

> . . . silence means nothing other than waiting for God's Word and coming from God's Word with a blessing. . . . The silence of the Christian is listening silence, humble stillness that may be broken at any time for the sake of humility. It is silence in conjunction with the Word.[34]

For Bonhoeffer, being silent before God is an equivalent of persistent and attentive listening. This vigilant way of being silent in the absence of the speaking God he once called "qualified."[35]

We can observe this same "qualified" sense of the concept of silence returning in the Baptism Letter, although this time no longer as a spiritual exercise of the individual believer (as in Finkenwalde) but as the strategy of the church as a whole. Bonhoeffer's plea, elsewhere in his letters from prison, for a renewed introduction of the *disciplina arcani,* the "discipline of the secret" of the church in its first centuries, has to be situated in this context as well.[36]

The Christian disposition Bonhoeffer supports represents a paradoxical combination of passivity (waiting for God) and activity (praying and doing good). It means a stretching out of one's whole existence toward God and neighbor; here, mysticism and ethics intertwine.[37] "God" appears to be no more — if God ever was — available. His transforming presence can no longer be invoked on call. The only way we can meet God is by embracing unconditionally the world God created,

33. *Christologie, GS,* vol. 3, 167.

34. *Life Together, DBWE,* vol. 5, 85.

35. Dietrich Bonhoeffer, "Zur theologische Begründung der Weltbundarbeit" (1932), *DBW,* vol. 11, 327-44, 330, 334.

36. *LPP,* 281, 286, 300.

37. Cf. Simone Weil, *Waiting on God* (1942; English translation, London: Routledge, 1951).

and taking part in its ongoing struggle for justice and peace. This stance represents at the same time an act of faith and repentance. The act of "praying and doing good" expresses the total submission to and approval of this religious dispossession. Under these conditions there is only one way left to be religious; it is in recognizing that one can be no longer religious in the traditional sense of that word. According to Bonhoeffer, the only good Christian is a "worldly" Christian, who takes, without reservation, her or his responsibilities in building up a just and humane society.

This high-tensioned theology from prison cannot be explained without resort to paradoxes. Certainly Bonhoeffer could have avoided them, by leaving his embarrassments aside and constructing a far more "easy" theology — a theology in which the absence of God does not represent the reverse side of God's powerful presence, but simply God's eternal essence. A theology in which the only thing one can tell about God is that there is nothing to tell. A theology in which the church constitutes at most a religious association and not the body of Christ, the Logos of God in this world.

Yet Bonhoeffer sticks to his basic intuitions until the end. Is this because of an intractable German temperament? I rather think it was because he had learned from Luther that good Christian theology is *theologia crucis.* A theology which remains *logos* about God, but is born out of despair *(Anfechtung)* about God's hiddenness. In this theology, God's strength is revealed in the midst of human weakness.

God and World: The Possibility of the New[1]

JAMES R. COCHRANE

A t the end of his life, in his *Letters and Papers from Prison,* Dietrich Bonhoeffer opened up a range of new options for Christianity in a postmodern, post-metaphysical era. He was unable to explore them very far, of course, and his theological impulses are open to a wide range of interpretations. It is his impulse toward a worldly, nonreligious interpretation of Christianity upon which this paper builds. However, my goal is not to find a new, nonreligious language for Christian faith, but to go behind the issue of languages and mythologies to the metaphysical foundations of modern Christianity in order to suggest that God-language, as it arises in the context of a local base community, drives us toward a destabilization of that very language for the sake not of God, but of human beings.

Reference to the God-language of a South African local base community will serve the heuristic purpose of raising the necessary questions. The "answer" will be to suggest, first, that there is no answer; second, that this answer drives us toward a recovery of a contemporary meaning for the apophatic tradition in theology; and third, that this links our knowledge (whether of God or not) to the ontological status of possibility

---

1. The ontological arguments presented in the latter two thirds of this essay have appeared in different form in James R. Cochrane, *Belief on the Boundaries: Dogma, Domination and the Recovery of Incipient Theologies.* Forthcoming.

in the actualities of the world which we more or less take for granted. One might say that the end result points toward an ontological eschatology, perhaps in ways that might have met some of Bonhoeffer's searching questions toward the end of his life.

Characteristically, Bonhoeffer's questions about God arise from "concreteness," from taking responsibility in the midst of actuality rather than from the point of view of abstract principle. Anticipating an insight that would in our time become a major paradigm in theology, Bonhoeffer also recognized the importance of seeing reality from the point of view of the marginalized, and taking our point of departure epistemologically there. This is a key element in my own reflections which, though developed here at a second-order level of theory, have been deeply shaped by the local base community to which I have referred. It is worth quoting Bonhoeffer on this point:

> There remains an experience of incomparable value. We have for once learnt to see the great events of world history from below, from the perspective of the outcast, the suspects, the maltreated, the powerless, the oppressed, the reviled — in short, from the perspective of those who suffer. . . . We have to learn that personal suffering is a more effective key, a more rewarding principle for exploring the world in thought and action than personal good fortune.[2]

We know that his thoughts about "religionless Christianity" are developed in prison in his encounter with people who face suffering, and people who extract suffering from others. Bonhoeffer clearly envisages suffering as a key to the structure of life and not simply as an experience of personal pain. He later criticizes any emphasis on "spiritual suffering," particularly that which the church sometimes likes to claim as the cost of proclaiming the gospel. Even his own imprisonment for something he felt he had to do as a Christian does not qualify: "No, suffering must be something quite different, and have a quite different dimension, from what I've so far experienced."[3]

The important point is the question of our primary interlocutor in our understanding of reality, and our related theological constructions. Feminist theologians, Black theologians, and others who in fact suffer in

2. *LPP*, 17.
3. *Ibid.*, 232.

the ontological sense that Bonhoeffer seems to point toward, are clearly uncomfortable with the metaphor of suffering to define the appropriate perspective, partly because so often Christianity has used the notion of "suffering for the gospel" as part of the discourse of domination, and partly because it is a negative term defining a condition rather than a positive term defining the goal of emancipation. It is important to keep in mind, therefore, that the question of one's primary interlocutor, of a defining perspective, is at stake here, rather than the ethos of suffering itself. Still, as Paul Ricoeur reminds us in *Oneself as Another,* the human being as "acting and suffering" is the key to ethics.[4]

In all of this the name of God becomes questionable, and the Israelite refusal to name God moves gradually to center stage: "(this) makes me think, and I can understand it better as I go on."[5] In a subsequent letter, Bonhoeffer goes further, claiming in typical dialectical fashion that one can only utter the name of Jesus Christ "when one knows the unutterability of the name of God."[6] But this theological statement is immediately connected to a statement about the world, for what it means now to utter the name of Jesus Christ is to "love life and the earth so much" that only then does it make any sense to speak of resurrection and a new world.

Here the apophatic strand is directly tied to worldliness.[7] In this lies a paradigm upon which much of the rest of this paper will touch, namely, that our language of God must first and foremost be language about worldly reality because — and this is the critical point — we cannot speak God's name. This forces us away from religiosity, where God's name is our shield from reality, our way of avoiding God's absence which calls us to responsibility. It forces us into responsibility, into naming things as they are, and thus, for the sake of God, into concrete thought and action.

This kind of dialectic, clearly shaped by the early Barth, among others, is familiar to students of Bonhoeffer. It plays itself out further around the notion of God in a religionless Christianity too. Bonhoeffer

---

4. Paul Ricoeur, *Oneself as Another* (Chicago: University of Chicago Press, 1992).

5. *LPP,* 135.

6. *Ibid.,* 157.

7. In this respect, a conventional picture of the apophatic tradition, the *via negativa* in theology, changes, with a strong link to historical, activist engagement.

therefore questions what it means to speak of God today "without religion, i.e. without the temporally conditioned presuppositions of metaphysics, inwardness, and so on."[8] In this context, God cannot be spoken of only beyond the boundaries of human knowledge, but must somehow be located at the center of our knowing. But because we cannot speak the name of God, this knowing is simultaneously a radical unknowing. God must be spoken of "not at the boundaries where human powers give out, but in the middle of the village," or "in what we know, not in what we don't know."[9]

Now the boundaries he mentions here, in keeping with previous arguments, are those which confront us at our weaknesses, our points of ignorance, guilt, and sin. Yet Bonhoeffer has spoken of other boundaries, too, which he obviously does not mean here: the unknowingness and ambiguity of all God-language, the suffering of the marginalized, the victim, and so on. It is these latter boundaries that are of interest to me. What I want to ask about is what, in a later discussion criticizing Barth's "positivist doctrine of revelation,"[10] Bonhoeffer calls the "discipline of the secret" which "must be restored whereby the *mysteries* of the Christian faith are protected against profanation." At the same time, Barth's critique of religion, so easily forgotten by the Confessing Church, stands. There can be no retreat into "conservative restoration," nor can religion be made "a precondition of faith."[11]

In South Africa the temptation to retreat from the lessons learned in resistance to apartheid is no less great than the temptation for the German church in Bonhoeffer's time. Whereas there was an internationally recognized willingness to take risks, at least by enough Christians in enough places, during the struggle against apartheid, it is common knowledge today that the powerful ecumenical dynamics which supported these risks and gave them substance are disappearing with alarming rapidity, while an all too frequent notion that the churches may now "go back to being church" indicates a strange forgetfulness of the ecclesial implications of the struggle against apartheid. We may well be

---

8. *LPP*, 280-82.

9. *Ibid.*, 311. The apparent contradiction is readily resolved if we recognize that what Bonhoeffer is pushing for is a realization of the sacred in the profane, rather than in some separate metaphysical or linguistic sphere of reality.

10. *LPP*, 286.

11. *Ibid.*, 328f.

moving back to a time when, to use Bonhoeffer's analysis of his situation, there is a "heavy incubus of difficult traditional ideas" gaining prominence in the church, and the "decisive factor" is a "church on the defensive. No taking risks for others."[12]

What might it mean to speak of God — taking concrete contexts seriously without losing that which transcends these contexts (without which we would be stuck with "what is" and unable to imagine "what is not")? Put in different terms, how might we understand the incarnation of God in concrete actuality without ignoring the importance of new possibilities not yet actualized which drive us toward a completion or fulfillment of reality? And without depending on the metaphysics which Kant sabotaged some time ago, or on the nominalism which marks the materialist reduction of the world in our time (whether from a conservative or a radical theory of human being)?

In asking these questions, I am already expressing an interest somewhat different from, though not unrelated to, the industrialized world's concern about the question of God. I am writing from the South African context. These questions are cast in the terms of my experience in this context, particularly within the paradigm of "contextual" theology as it has been shaped here (for me) by a long-standing encounter with black theologians, an involvement in what has come to be known as "Kairos theology," and a long-standing destabilization of all orthodoxies from the side of feminist theologians. Here, however, I depend upon work done in relation to the "incipient theologies" of a local base community in Natal.[13]

The community is a typical *favella* or peri-urban informal shack settlement. Poverty is predominant, and the history of the community has been described as besieged, fractured, and contested.[14] During the 1980s and early '90s, the community was under siege from the apartheid state and its proxies, facing an external "enemy." At the same time, various property relations, ranging from absentee landlords to subtenants, and varying economic opportunities, produced tensions and

---

12. *Ibid.,* 381.

13. See *Belief on the Boundaries.* "Incipient" suggests that theology in this case is "beginning to appear," but remains to be completed by a conscious and critical link to the wider church (synchronically) and to the tradition of the church (diachronically).

14. Martin Mandew, *Power and Empowerment: Religious Imagination and the Life of a Local Base Ecclesial Community* (Ph.D. dissertation, University of Natal, 1993).

conflicting interests which fractured the community internally. In addition, political contestation between the bantustan-based Inkatha movement and groups linked either with the United Democratic Front or the African National Congress bedeviled relations. In this context, where unemployment is also high and infrastructure largely absent, the local base community engaged in weekly Bible studies over several years, trying to understand and cope with immediate reality through this discursive activity.

In respect to our topic here, though, more important is the role of "contrast experiences"[15] through which subjugated knowledge and ontological absences in the dominant discourses and related practices — that which has been concealed — are revealed. Contradiction and paradox become clues to the nature of reality, and only through them can adequate strategies evolve to reconstruct the new out of possibilities in the present. In theology, I believe this drives us toward recognizing and working with the foundational *aporiai* of the tradition, which are also the *aporiai* of reality seen from within the history of this tradition. It is this clue that I now wish to follow in speaking of God.

The contradictions and paradoxes which confront the local base community, like the *aporiai* of theology, are perplexities which we seek to systematize into a single view but which continually force us to open up that view again in the gap that remains. As suggested earlier, the most fundamental *aporia* lies in our speech about God, which, when probed more deeply, leaves us silent about God. It is essentially parabolic language, speech, or writing which points to a reality which cannot be apprehended directly. As T. S. Eliot says in his *Four Quartets*, "every phrase and sentence that is right . . . is an end and a beginning, Every poem an epitaph."

To think of theology in this way is to participate in the contemporary philosophical suspicion of any correspondence theory of truth, a suspicion based in an analysis of the irresolvable ambiguity of language and language-like activity. It is to suggest that reality — our understanding of reality — is based not on some discernible essence, but on constructions of our mind. More, these mental constructions are not the isolated acts of an islanded subjectivity, but the result of a prior insertion into a world of discourse which "members" us in a community of dis-

15. Per Frostin, *Liberation Theology in Tanzania and South Africa: A First World Interpretation* (Lund: Lund University Press, 1988).

course.[16] Of course, these constructions have to conform to a number of tests by which we eliminate ignorance and madness.[17] Even then, however, what we are left with is not reality itself, but a picture of reality. We may be able to map the picture with greater or lesser accuracy, and this is not unimportant. But, as Jonathan Smith puts it, "the dictum of Alfred Korzybski is inescapable: 'Map is not territory' — but maps are all we possess."[18]

To think of the theological task in terms of silence and parabolic language is to be part of a long history, albeit one somewhat forgotten among the positive theologies of modernity. This is the history of apophatic theology, in which the absence of God, the shadows of our language about God, the vacant places in our understanding of God are incorporated into our sense of God. Radical unknowing challenges all claims to know. Revelation is found to conceal as much of reality as is disclosed, and that recognition itself becomes part of the disclosure. Theology itself is destabilized for the sake of theology.

We may locate some of the implications of this position quite directly in the plurality of theological discourses which arises in the confrontation of contexts, an encounter with the Other across the boundaries of what is known and remembered, a meeting which characterizes and challenges particularist perspectives. In South Africa after apartheid, the challenge may be stated thus: How are we to theologize without relinquishing what we have learned (for to do so would be to disrespect history, which would be to dishonor those whose sacrifices in the past enable important possibilities in the present). Here I attempt to reflect on three ontological paradoxes, or *aporiai,* which open up new possibilities for imagining the theological task in a "post-apartheid" era. These are the oppositions between space and time, between body and spirit, and between truth revealed and truth concealed.

16. Theologies which privatize religious truth I would characterize as reductionist and untenable, at least as theology, that is, as forms of reflection on faith.

17. Following Habermas we may say that these tests may be understood generally as tests of truth (propositional assertions which can be tested), of truthfulness (the comprehensibility, well-formedness, and rule-correctness of normative rightness), and of sincerity (expressive authenticity). Jürgen Habermas, *Reason and the Rationalization of Society: The Theory of Communicative Action,* vol. 1 (Boston: Beacon, 1984).

18. Jonathan Z. Smith, *Map Is not Territory* (Chicago: University of Chicago Press, 1993), 309.

The first opposition helps us to answer the question: Has the liberation paradigm in theology become obsolete? The second opposition poses the problem of the Cartesian split between mind-body, God-world, internal-external, personal-social which has so bedeviled our theological work in South Africa and so limited our capacity to account for reality as one. The third opposition undermines all attempts either to close down communication between ourselves and the Other on the grounds that we have the truth, or to impose upon the Other our understanding of reality in the name of truth. This last opposition poses the question of apophatic theology in its most acute form, namely: Can we live out of faith without requiring that we possess it for our own? If we can, then our encounter with the Other in the meeting of contexts may be fruitful in reshaping the theological task, and that is what I will argue.

Freedom in Space and Time

What interests us here is the nature of resistance and control, the forms of power expressed in relation to the battle over space and time.[19] Freedom in space — the paradigmatic core of liberation theories of the last decades — may not be the same as freedom in time, the latter a theme more likely to be found in mystics than in systematic analysts. The former paradigm has tended to be skeptical, if not downright contemptuous, of the latter, with the result that both ontological and epistemological mistakes are made in assessing the importance of spirit, of personhood, and of myth.

A useful and important study of this problem within the framework of the notion of *kairos* is that of Robin Petersen.[20] I would like to draw upon this study to make certain points about the link between space and time as it affects "contexts of translation." The particular kind of translation of concern to Petersen is that between the context of liberation

---

19. See Jean and John Comaroff, *Of Revelation and Revolution: Christianity, Colonialism and Consciousness in South Africa* (Chicago: University of Chicago Press, 1991); James Scott, *Domination and the Arts of Resistance: Hidden Transcripts* (New Haven, CT: Yale University Press, 1990).

20. Robin Petersen, *Time, Resistance and Reconstruction: Rethinking Kairos Theology in South Africa* (Ph.D. dissertation, University of Chicago, 1995).

theologies and the context of popular indigenous "churches of the Spirit" or African Initiated churches (particularly of the Pentecostal or Zionist type).

Petersen shows that *kairos* and *chronos* are not as distinct as is often assumed by theologians adopting Paul Tillich's influential use of the term. *Kairos* is not simply a time of crisis, nor is it linked only to prophetic discernment and ethical action. Petersen wants to recover a different, more nuanced understanding of *kairos* without setting aside the important lessons drawn from a politically committed Kairos theology. This opens up room for reconceptualizing the link between freedom as the conquest or reconquest of space (land, jobs, housing, governing institutions — the realm of the physical and the material), and freedom as the unshackling of time (ritual, liturgy, celebration, creative imagination — the realm of the spiritual and the ideal). Petersen's central concern is to find an understanding of resistance which is capable of taking into account both intentional, conscious emancipatory action and unintentional, semiconscious ritual; or, in another formulation of the problem, to find a unity between prophetic and mystical theology.

Liberation theologies, which Petersen subsumes under the category "prophetic," typify this problem in an overdetermination of the *ethical* imperative of liberation, leaving the *cultural* terrain inadequately theorized. Yet on the cultural terrain the struggles of everyday life are often expressed in forms of creativity which "speak to human social and spiritual needs; practices that make the inhuman human, that heal the diseased body, that exorcise the demonic possession of the principalities and powers of apartheid capitalism, that create new people from the discarded of society."[21]

Drawing on an argument that *kairos* in Greek thought is connected to *metis* (cunning intelligence), one may say that *kairos* includes a way of knowing which combines "flair, wisdom, forethought, subtlety of mind, deception, resourcefulness, vigilance, opportunism, various skills, and experience acquired over the years." *Kairos* is then the terrain of time within which a struggle of resistance may also be carried out.[22]

In order to arrive at the resolution of the relation between time understood mystically and time understood prophetically, Petersen endeavors to show that religious practices such as those characteristic of

21. *Ibid.*, 41.
22. *Ibid.*, 46.

AICs are internally coherent with the religiously motivated praxis so important to liberation theologies. He does this by turning to the work of Moishe Postone in his neo-Marxist reconstruction of time as a sphere of domination under the conditions of modern capitalism. Postone, arguing that our modern understanding of time is a construction not found in pre-capitalist societies, posits two forms of this modern construction: abstract time and historical time.[23] These two forms of time are opposed to time as "concrete," that is, time tied to concrete events and cycles (concrete time could be linear or cyclical — this is not the key distinction) in which one may speak of good or bad time, profane or sacred time.

Abstract time is tied to the social necessity of measuring and quantifying value in production. Handled as a commodity under the conditions of exchange characterized by a market economy (whether this is a state-controlled market or not), abstract time becomes hegemonic, that is, it becomes an unseen, totalizing form in which power is organized and taken for granted. The clock, a mechanical device which counts out time into discrete, controllable entities, is the symbol of commodified time, and a form of control. Historical time, understood as a directional dynamic, also functions under modern economic conditions as controlling in what Postone refers to as the "treadmill" of modern life which presses more and more into any unit of time, so that an experience of an hour a century ago has been radically intensified.

What makes this distinction interesting for our purposes is that forms of domination, following the theory of hegemony and consciousness posed by the Comaroffs, must be accompanied by forms of resistance. The dispersal of power across the continuum of hegemony and ideology is always in flux, as is the related dispersal of consciousness and its representations. This flux is the stuff of contestation, sometimes overtly political, sometimes indirectly cultural. As the Comaroffs insist, resistance must therefore be understood as more than a self-conscious activity against a consciously grasped form of domination. Resistance arises not only in attempts to conquer space by establishing a place of freedom. It also arises in the sphere of time as the repossession of concrete time against abstract time and against the alienated form of historical time characteristic of capitalism. This is what Petersen calls *kairotic* time:

23. *Ibid.*, 205ff.

. . . it takes the form of resistant time; resistant in the sense that it inserts a discourse which contests, subverts, undermines and challenges the totalization of time. This resistance is, however, also regenerative, for it points beyond the time of resistance to the time of liberation, when time will no longer dominate but be subordinated to the human good.[24]

Petersen thus points to what he calls "resistance in two keys," the former being in the familiar field of ethical activity and the struggle for a place, the latter breaking open a reduced, limited reading of resistance to incorporate religious experiences which are not ethically motivated. Construing the latter as *kairotic,* and not just the former, situates the two forms "on a continuum, rather than seeing them as mutually excluding the other."[25]

Abstract time is thereby subordinated to sacred time, to ritual time, and an attempt is made to bring it back under human control. For example, Petersen links the AIC stress on religious healing practices to resistance understood as the contestation of the body as a commodity (in labor and in nonholistic medicine). The remystification of reality in ritual cannot then be understood merely as a return to superstition, an incapacity to enter into modernity, but as a contestation with the terms of modernity itself.

Finally, a link is made between a prophetic use of *kairos* and resistance to time as the closure of history. Against the closure of history in systems of control which deemphasize subjugated memories and naturalize commodified forms of time, *kairotic* time "inserts a discourse of Messianic time, of eschatological time, which resists this closure."[26] Here we are back with the prophetic stream of thought in theology. Here too we encounter freedom in space articulated as freedom in time.

The tension between the two dimensions, however, is not collapsed. And in the gap between them, the boundaries between prophetic theology and mystical theology may be both recognized and mutually related. This forces us, too, to recognize that "theology is first and foremost a living out of, a listening to, and an adjudicating of *aporiai* in the human

24. *Ibid.,* 223.
25. *Ibid.,* 224.
26. *Ibid.,* 224.

odyssey of faith."[27] A contextual theology which works with this gap offers the hope of translation between two paradigmatic contexts in the service of a richer conception of life and thus of that redemption which offers life more abundantly.

Theology's Split Personality

Space-time is not the only *aporia* fundamental to the world of theological discourse. Another is the link between body and spirit, a link severed by Montanism and the gnostic forms of Christianity which so challenged the early Church and led it to formulate its claims in terms of a unity of body and spirit. The split has also become characteristic of our modern world under the influence of Cartesian dualisms, primarily that between subject and object, but also that between the personal and the social, between the internal and the external, and — in theology — between God and the world. These splits are also the source of several problems in South African contextual theologies. Most of these problems may be traced to a particular epistemology determined by an emphasis on the second term in these polarities, and a typical inability by "political" or "contextual" theologies to account adequately for the first term.

The Cartesian epistemology is now under attack in many quarters. It is not necessary to summarize its weaknesses or the arguments now ranged against it in the name of postmodernism, postcolonialism, or any similar position. But one approach to the problem which seems to offer a point of attack is that of McGaughey. He challenges the epistemology undergirding modernism while simultaneously opening up space for the more fluid, ambiguous understanding of truth demanded by a contextualized theology.

Clearly, a traditional interpretation of Plato which treats universals as rationally established absolutes will not offer us much help. But this interpretation of Plato is no longer uncontested. One source of such contestation becomes the basis of the argument that follows on the unity of body and spirit. I take for granted a contemporary acceptance of the importance of body, of material reality, in contextual theologies. This is clearly evident in their emphasis on the physical, economic, and political

27. Douglas R. McGaughey, *Strangers and Pilgrims: On the Role of Aporiai in Theology* (forthcoming), 96.

realities of unfreedom. What has proven more intractable for contextual theologies is an inability to incorporate an adequate vision of spirit. It is to this task that I turn.

McGaughey's argument essentially attacks materialist epistemologies and the resultant "mathematization of reality." Primary reality is here seen as quantifiable, measurable, observable, predictable, manipulable; rationality is understood as causal, calculation.[28] The paradigmatic shift came with the rediscovery in Europe of the Aristotelian corpus. Modern thinking since Descartes has been dominated by Aristotelian nominalism, argues McGaughey. Epistemologically, this is most simply stated as the requirement that there be "evidence" for the truth. This evidence must be located somewhere, that is, it must be accessible in a particular place. "Place" is material, actual. Nominalism therefore requires that our nonmaterial experience be discounted as evidence.

Because nominalism thus denies that our names for things are anything more than pointers to reality which lies outside the naming process (our consciousness, mind, *nous*), truth must be constituted through a verification, or falsification, of that to which our names point — an external reality. There must be a correspondence between what is thought and what is externally "sense-able" (that is, externally determinable). If one cannot show an externally sense-able correspondent to experiencing and what is thought, then the experiencing or thought are assumed to be false.

Theology makes this move too. Truth, for modern theologies, generally means verification, either in the text of Scripture (a tangible object), in the dogmatic tradition (likewise a discernible object), in appropriate behavior (the observable results of faith, a strong theme in both pietism and liberal theology), or in the positing of another realm of reality which reaches to us "from beyond" (thus even a concept of revelation which depends upon some other metaphysical "place" as the source of experience seeks a truth that can be verified in its effects on us). Ironically, despite all attempts to define theology as a spiritual discipline, its modern forms thus partake of a materialist epistemology. That which goes on in the consciousness, in mind, in *nous* — that which is spirit — is nonobservable, nonsensible, nontangible, nonverifiable. It cannot therefore offer proof of anything, at least within this paradigm.

28. *Ibid.*, 196ff., 443ff.

As should be clear, the division between what is "internal" (consciousness, mind, *nous,* experiencing) and what is "external" (accessible to the senses or objectively available) parallels the fatal divisions between the seen and the unseen, body and mind, eternal realm and worldly realm, the divine and the human. These divisions are alien to Africa. The same epistemological fault is responsible, McGaughey argues, for the clash between science and theology on the one hand, and the apparent harmonization of the two along the lines that they deal with different spheres of truth on the other. Either way, a dividing line is drawn between the two, analogous to the divide between internal and external reality.

All of these approaches to truth which I have characterized as dependent upon the epistemological foundations of nominalism find their reference in actualities: texts, observable behavior or action, language, the deposit of history, and the like — all object-like manifestations of the "real." But McGaughey argues with some force that the "real" includes not just actualities; it also includes possibilities. In order to understand this, McGaughey suggests a recovery of the notion of truth found in Plato's simile of the line in *The Republic* used to distinguish between mind and body, spirit and world, ideas and material. The first term in each of these pairs refers to what is above the line, the second term to what is below. Spirit, now, is equivalent to consciousness, mind, or *nous.* But *nous* or spirit is not simply ideation or reflection. Rather, it is that which serves the first principle of the whole — the Good — in grasping and illuminating reality itself. *Nous* is neither restricted to ideas nor reducible to calculating or contemplative reason, neither self-contained mind nor abstract reason separated from a world of engagement. It incorporates imagination, understanding, and reflection, but is not reducible to them.

Spirituality must therefore also be defined in this relation. But spirituality is not, as many interpreters of Plato hold, separate from body, world, or materiality, nor is it superior in any formal or ontological sense. It is, first, different, because it is consciousness appropriating reality (indirectly). Second, it is also the basis of the possibility of any experience, because without consciousness we would have no experience, no ordering of the sense phenomena of the material world (they would overwhelm us). But it can never be separated from experience — from body and world — without being destroyed in the process. A free-floating consciousness is quite literally inconceivable.

McGaughey's analysis produces the following insights, each of which I will subsequently employ in defining Christian God-language.

1. Reality consists in the whole of the line, that is, consciousness (or spirit, mind, *nous*) above the line, and the sensible world (materiality) below the line. The truth of reality is reached only in grasping the material and the spiritual simultaneously. Reality is a *Gestalt* of mind and body, spirit and world.

2. Spirit *(nous)*, that which produces universals and paradigms, pertains to possibilities ("what is not") in the world, and as such opens up actualities ("what is"), enabling us to transcend them. However, spirit does not engender transcendence from world or body, society or person (above, outside), but transcendence within world or body, society, or person. Spirituality is thus central to human being and becoming, an elevation of what is into that which is not yet; the motor of what is new and the source of human being (beyond our participation in nature as particular kinds of animals).

3. World or body, as actuality, constrains us. It is an equally inescapable part of reality (the insight of pragmatism). This is why an idealist epistemology or ideology fails to grasp the material conditions of human being.

4. Neither consciousness nor knowledge of the world provides guarantees of truth, for both are filled with ambiguity and unknowability. Consciousness operates with ultimately indefinable universals (an insight first stated by Socrates), whereas knowledge of the world is inescapably framed within limited interpretive paradigms.

5. The universals with which consciousness operates are not metaphysically universal, that is, ontologically guaranteed absolutes. Rather, they remain "hypotheses" (Plato). Thus all appeals to universals have the character of tentative approximations, still and always to be confirmed.

6. Nevertheless, universals do not float in the air unattached to any historical experience. First, the meaning of an idea/universal is not grasped "without having grasped it as a possibility for understanding something particular."[29] Second, universals are deposited in human history in the form of language, which precedes us, and in

29. *Ibid.,* 463.

the form of traditions, which give us our identity. Because both language and tradition define the self in relation to others, universals are inherently social, the work of communicative action. Thus spirituality, in relation to *nous,* should never be taken to be merely private, individual, isolated from body and world.

Following these notions, we may now say that the loss of spirituality in modern times follows upon the Cartesian split of mind and body, spirit and world, and the triumph of an epistemology which values body and world. The corollary, of course, is that all that Plato would see as spiritual is regarded in the new epistemological framework as unreliable, as non-verifiable, as "mere emotion" or "illusory experience" incapable of guiding us to truth. The modern search for truth, then, must aim precisely at excluding, bracketing, or marginalizing as far as possible such "subjective" factors in order to arrive "objectively" at a truth which can be shown to correspond to an external occurrence or object.

What is forgotten here is that any investigation of material reality already depends upon a prior imaginative framework which is both limited and partial. Knowledge, whether material or spiritual, is irredeemably mediated. Drawing on Ricoeur, McGaughey defines this prior imaginative framework or paradigm as the "sedimented syntheses" of the past: "the labor of imagination is not born from nothing. It is bound in one way or another to the tradition's paradigms . . . deployed between the two poles of *servile application* (requiring a hermeneutics of suspicion) and *calculated deviation* (dependent upon a hermeneutics of restoration), passing through every degree of 'rule-governed deformation.'"[30]

The theological task I implicitly defend here may be described as a challenge to the "servile application" of the paradigms of the Christian tradition on the one hand, and a plea for a "calculated deviation" from those paradigms on the other. The challenge employs a hermeneutics of suspicion by analyzing factors of power and knowledge, relations of power, representation of the Other, and uncritical conversation in an engagement with particular contexts and the encounter between people from different contexts. It also employs a hermeneutics of reconstruction by locating the evidences of spirit in the midst of the world by which "what is" may be transcended in the anticipation and construction of "what is not" yet.

30. *Ibid.,* 450. Author's emphasis.

Spirit, understood thus, is emancipatory, and it is so in the world, embodied in persons among other persons. Moreover, it is emancipatory in two senses: in time as the imaginative grasp of possibility — an insight of mystical thought; and in space as the drive of emancipatory action — the insight of prophetic theology.

The Actual and the Possible

This leads to a proposal for understanding theological truth which binds possibility and actuality, a joining of the spiritual and the material. The "disclosure" *(aletheia)* of reality which ensues points to the nature of truth. McGaughey shows that truth as *aletheia* means to be noticed, "in the sense of arising out of that which eludes notice and is unnoticed."[31] Truth reveals what is concealed, but in doing so, new concealment's occur (other possibilities lurk there which have not been realized or which have been excluded). Here there is no marriage with a correspondence theory of truth in which what is revealed (what is actual) is taken to be a direct correlate of what is true, and what is concealed only the result of ignorance or error.

These thoughts can now be relayed to our understanding of Christian tradition. The first thing we may state is that tradition, the deposit of past commitments, is actual and, in this sense, material (fixed in texts, creeds, etc.). It constrains us to the heritage which defines us because it provides the language by which we may identify what it means to "put on the mind of Christ" (Paul, speaking precisely of *nous*). We are constituted by this heritage.

But if this is all, then it is a truncated reality, a dogmatic trap from which spirit strives to escape. This is tradition as "law." By the spirit, by "putting on the mind of Christ," by *nous,* we participate in the making of that tradition in the dialectic between what constitutes us and what we constitute. This is the epistemological foundation for a theology of unification between the actual and the possible. It requires that not all possibilities are congruent, and that the actualization of one possibility conceals or prevents the actualization of other available possibilities. This is why the tradition is not simply a harmonious record of the work of the spirit, but also the record of contestation for one possibility against others.

31. *Ibid.,* 464.

This is not a one-way street, however. The universals or paradigms of the received tradition remain as a deposit which particular persons, groups, or communities encounter and with which they must deal. Whatever possibilities may be actualized in the process of this encounter, other possibilities are prevented or concealed. The hermeneutic of restoration invoked by new possibilities does not leave behind the hermeneutic of suspicion which questions both what is actualized and what has been prevented or concealed.

The fourth point presses us to recognize that neither natural nor revealed knowledge gives us any guarantees. This paradox is inherent in the nature of our experiencing: we search for understanding, but we always encounter doubt or that which escapes our understanding, and not because of ignorance. The paradox lies in the fact that universals constitute the basis of our understanding: we inherit them in language which is "the great institution that . . . has preceded each and every one of us."[32] But simultaneously we constitute the universals out of the particulars of our experience.

Thus we cannot ultimately depend upon revealed or natural knowledge. As McGaughey notes, this forces us to live by faith. Reading the past, including Scripture, in which Christian tradition comes into being, we may then recognize that its truth lies in a profound record of the never-ending search of human beings for the wholeness which eludes them. The process is what counts. The content of that search — the words, sentences, ideas, and intentions deposited in the records of the tradition — provides us with no guarantees. It remains tentative, always pointing to our "profound unknowing," to a nonepistemic faith.[33] The route to certainty is blocked. Any attempt to smash down the walls which block us inevitably means that we smash other human beings or nature itself. This is the insight of faith, of non-knowing.

Moreover, the paradox of being constituted by the universals we inherit even as we constitute them out of the particulars of our experience has a further twofold implication for our understanding of Christian tradition, reinforcing what has already been said. First, at the point where we lay claim to being "Christian," we insert ourselves into the inherited language of the faith. As we learn more of this heritage, which we must to make any sense of the identity of being Christian (otherwise

32. Ricoeur, quoted in McGaughey, 462.
33. *Ibid.*, 459.

the claim is trivial), so we sink our roots into its universals. Second, we necessarily contribute to the establishment, confirmation, or alienation of these universals by constituting them in relation to our own particulars of experience. This process, of course, is the way in which the tradition got started and kept going in the first place. The dynamic of the development of tradition is its truth. Our participation in this dynamic is its requirement.

Another step may be added. If the Christian tradition is the linguistic (or language-like) deposit of the set of universals which define what it means to be Christian, then it must be recognized that these universals themselves are ultimately indefinable. They elude our grasp, and they do so systematically (that is, it is not a matter of ignorance but of the limit of our knowing). The implication is that no statements of this tradition which claim to "be the truth" may be taken as such in any final, certain, unambiguous manner. They guarantee nothing except our historical identity, which, if open to possibility or to new creation, cannot remain static. This, as I have already indicated, is a position indeed held within the Christian tradition for a long time, especially among the mystics whose theological paradigm is one of "search" or "quest" as opposed to "assertion" or "decree," but also in the implications of a fully grasped doctrine of the *sensus fidei.*

Revelation is thus not an event in the past, but an unfolding of the future in the present. Moreover, this unfolding is not anti-worldly but takes place within the real world — that is, within the constraints of actuality. Thus revelation simultaneously conceals the truth (other possibilities which might have been actualized but were not) even as it reveals it (the insertion of the new within the old, opening it up for further possibility). Theology, like the spirituality it accompanies, is thus an ongoing journey, a search for understanding, and not a repetition of the past, nor even simply a reinterpretation of the past. It takes the *creatio ex nihilo* quite literally as the bringing into existence (actualizing) of that which does not yet exist (possibility).

We move now to the fifth point, that universals are hypotheses about reality, or tentative approximations. If this is so, we may conclude that the Christian tradition, to the extent that we take it as our own, offers us one set of tentative approximations of reality, including our part in it. There are no grounds, in this case, for any fundamentalism, any hegemonic religious domination of others, any exclusive claims to truth. McGaughey's formulation of this point in relation to spirituality is precise and rich in implications: "The spiritual as well as the material dimensions of experience require us to speak of an odyssey of faith seeking understanding, because we do not have direct and immediate access to the material, and the spiritual, at the very least, is rooted in indefinables. But spirit is informed by a higher horizon of pragmatic faith."[34]

All such attempts are not only unworthy of the human spirit, particularly among those who claim that this spirit is made new in Christ and reaches out to all, but they are also inevitably damaging of the spirit and the humanity of others. This does not mean that a restless pluralism is best, and a noncommittal faith exemplary. It only means that we recognize our own limits, in spirit and in knowledge, taking on the humility which this requires as a systematic contribution to the world and to others of the love of which Jesus spoke and which the narratives of his life indicate he shared.

Revelation, in this view, must be brought into relation with concealment. What unmasks one aspect of reality (the point of conscientization or of social analysis in political/contextual theologies) must simultaneously be understood as hiding other aspects. Thus there is no path to truth as absolute, certain, or guaranteed, no clear and unambiguous grasp of the reality of the world. To quote McGaughey, "The truth of human experience is that it consists of a dynamic of the actual concealing the possible where the possible is constantly being projected by the human spirit into the future in acts of understanding."[35]

To conclude, if we understand the truth of tradition in terms of *aletheia* — the disclosure of that which eludes notice or is unnoticed — then it is possible to understand that translation across boundaries, between contexts of otherness, is not only interesting but vital for the truth Christians proclaim. What is unnoticed or eludes notice is key. It does not take much, in the paradigm of a contextualized theology which I have taken for granted in my reflections, to see that the most significant indicator of what eludes notice may be found in suffering, not as an abstract principle, but as embodied in the world among those who elude notice because they are not heard.

Truth as disclosure then has implications of a profound sort. It drives us to apprehend reality in its actuality (no cheap grace here!),

34. *Ibid.*, 473.
35. *Ibid.*, 38.

requiring a hermeneutic of suspicion. It calls us to imagine reality in its possibilities (no faint hope!), requiring a hermeneutic of reconstruction.

Drinking the Earthly Cup

The theological journey proposed by the juxtaposition of terms adopted in the above arguments, as I have tried to suggest in each case, is never certain. To paraphrase McGaughey once more, "the theologian is always and already in a groundless wagering in faith" rooted in paradox. Yet one's grasp of the paradoxical character of life may be less or more adequate, which is not unimportant: ". . . it is not as if one could choose not to wager. Faith has as much to do with our acting as it does with our understanding, and one cannot not act!"[36]

We do not undertake this journey without carrying a particular history. That history is both personal and communal, both local and general. It is also the stuff of identity inasmuch as we take into ourselves, either voluntarily or involuntarily, a tradition by which we name ourselves. If the theological task is our focus, then a religious tradition is what we remember and re-member. As we walk through the gate of the present into the future, we take this memory — embodied, reinterpreted — with us.

But as we pass through the gate, we enter again into an unknown territory. The maps we bring with us are our guide, but they remain provisional, even if they are all we have. They can and must be redrawn. In this sense theology itself cannot be anything else than situated in a context to be shaped by that context. It is part of the task of reconstruction. How we translate that task from one context to another is crucial. I have argued that it must be a tentative translation, a translation which recognizes boundaries but is capable of taking account of them. It is also a translation which works with the *aporiai* of theology as the epistemological basis of resistance to any totalizing form of discourse and any form of certainty in our religious discourse.

To conclude with Bonhoeffer, it seems right then to stress that the task of reconstructing God-talk as discussed above can never be separated from its basis in the concreteness of the world. Perhaps there are

36. *Ibid.*, 96.

no stronger words from Bonhoeffer in this respect than those which he
wrote to Eberhard Bethge from Tegel prison on 27 June 1944:

> The Christian, unlike the devotees of the redemption myths, has
> no last line of escape, but, like Christ himself ("My God, why hast
> thou forsaken me?"), he[she] must drink the earthly cup to the dregs,
> and only in his[her] doing so is the crucified and risen Lord with
> him[her], and he[she] crucified and risen with Christ.[37]

37. *LPP*, 337.

RESPONSIBLE FREEDOM

Ethics for the Renewal of Life: A Reconstruction of Its Concept

HANS PFEIFER

Despite the tremendous impact of Dietrich Bonhoeffer's life and theology, a great number of problems related to the reception of his work remain. These apply particularly to the *Ethics*. One reason for this is to be found in the unfinished character of these papers. But the difficulties have also to do with the very specific theological language[1] Bonhoeffer uses, and the new and unusual concept of the book. But precisely for these reasons, the *Ethics* presents a challenge which should not remain unanswered. I will therefore venture to offer a few theses on the question of how we can reach a better understanding of this legacy.

My conviction is that certain passages ought to be seen in the context which would have been given to them in the final book. Only in this way can their meaning be fully understood. It is not, of course, possible to reconstruct the book as it would have been had Bonhoeffer finished it. I have elected, rather, to deal with his ethical thought after 1940 and with its structure, which is significant for the understanding of the individual texts. I am quite aware that this is not the first attempt to

---

1. *Ethik*, ed. Ilse Tödt, Heinz Eduard Tödt, Ernst Feil, and Clifford Green, *DBW*, vol. 6 (Gütersloh: Chr. Kaiser/Gütersloher Verlag, 1992), 439. The English translations in this essay have been done by the author except where quoting from the English text.

do this, and I am indebted to many authors, of whom I mention only Eberhard Bethge. Many problems are involved which need careful examination. But when the question of "Bonhoeffer for a New Day" is raised, reflection on his most far-reaching ideas seems appropriate.

A Well-Constructed Unity

Edited in a very scholarly fashion, Bonhoeffer's *Ethics* has been presented anew in the series *Dietrich Bonhoeffer Werke*. The papers are now presented in a chronological order which has been established in a rather complicated way. But this new edition presents us with the question: To what extent are we able to draw conclusions on the concept and the structure of the planned book? Are we to see them as different approaches, maybe four in total, as Eberhard Bethge has proposed in his biography?[2] And are these to be dealt with alternatively? Does this mean taking the final attempt as the key to grasping Bonhoeffer's vision of a Christian ethics? Or are they chapters, which have to be put together as a whole, even if we cannot determine their final structure beyond any possible doubt? And what can we learn about the structure of the whole work from such an ordering?

The tentative assumption of the following investigation is that the material as a whole can be regarded as belonging to a well-constructed unity. We state this fully aware of the fact that we are far away from an agreement about the structure of Bonhoeffer's ethics even among those who consider the papers as different parts of a whole.[3] The question remains to be answered. I present a new concept of the structure, using at first Bonhoeffer's own sketches of the organization for the book.[4] These have to be brought into line with the papers Bonhoeffer actually wrote.

2. Eberhard Bethge, *Dietrich Bonhoeffer. Eine Biographie* (Munich: Chr Kaiser, 1967), 808-11. This assumption has now been dropped by Bethge, but it is maintained by others such as Robin Lovin and Larry Rasmussen, in *New Studies in Bonhoeffer's Ethics*, ed. William J. Peck (Lewiston/Queenston, Ontario: Edwin Mellen Press, 1987), 68 (Lovin) and 103 (Rasmussen). A different opinion is voiced by Clifford Green in the same volume, 3ff.

3. Cf. Green in *New Studies*, 58ff., and *DBW*, vol. 6, 455.

4. Particularly *Zettel*, no. 38 and 1. Cf. Dietrich Bonhoeffer, *Zettelnotizen für eine "Ethik,"* ed. Ilse von Tödt (Munich: Chr. Kaiser, 1993), 46. *Zettel* refers to Bonhoeffer's own notes and outlines.

They are basically identical with the proposed ordering given in the new edition in the *Dietrich Bonhoeffer Werke*.[5] When we compare Bonhoeffer's sketches of the order with the papers he actually wrote, we find that the concept has changed considerably during the process of writing. Some topics are not dealt with, others are not to be found in his early ordering, and still others have been placed differently from the original plan. This is particularly the case with regard to "Church and (the Formation of the) World."

But there is one further item to be taken into consideration. Every new chapter of the *Ethics* begins with a basic discussion of ethical matters, which gave rise to the notion that they might all be different approaches to the whole. Such chapters are "Christ, Reality and the Good," "Ethics as Formation," "The 'Ethical' and the 'Christian as Subject,'" "The Ultimate and the Penultimate," and "The Love of God and the Decay of the World." Indeed, we cannot avoid seeing three of these as laying out the twofold character of the foundation, and therefore locate them at the beginning of the whole work. Others, such as "The Ultimate and the Penultimate" and "The 'Ethical' and the 'Christian as Subject,'" open later parts of the book, because they are strongly connected with other papers. The basic nature of their discussions owes partly to the fact that every new part needs a new foundation, and partly to the development of Bonhoeffer's thinking during his writing.

Lastly, I will consider Bonhoeffer's theological thoughts in *Letters and Papers from Prison* — such as the topic of "religionlessness," his reading of Dilthey, and the "Outline for a Book," with its subject of a "Church for Others," and even his literary fragments of a drama and a novel. These are to be seen as representing a reconsideration of the *Ethics* and need to be taken into account particularly for the mainly unwritten last part of the book. This is obvious in the case of "What Does It Mean to Tell the Truth?"

The Interpretative Key

The main issue in understanding Bonhoeffer's *Ethics* lies in the interpretative key we choose. Some have suggested looking at the *Ethics* under certain general terms, such as "Peace Ethics" or "Ethics of Resistance."

5. *Ethik*, 455.

Others have called it "contextual ethics."[6] All of these suggestions find justification in Bonhoeffer's theology and in the texts, but none is sufficient in view of the whole work. They omit a clear hint, given in Bonhoeffer's first sketch of an order.[7] According to this, the opening passage was to be a very programmatic introduction "Ethics as Formation," containing an analysis of the general failure of all traditional ethical concepts and attitudes.[8] This would be followed by a passage, "Heritage and Decay," in which the author offers reasons as to why this is the case. These notes (*Zettel*, 38) make clear how much importance Bonhoeffer gave to this introductory paper when he was in an early stage of writing. No doubt it is significant that this passage reminds us of Spengler's famous book *Decay of the West*, written during the First World War, in which Spengler predicted the end of the West in the twentieth century. In this light, one can only do justice to Bonhoeffer's *Ethics* when one understands it as intended to be a totally new beginning. He starts with the conviction that Europe has entered into a complete crisis which affects all realms. This crisis has not been evoked by National Socialism but has found its final expression in it.

One should not be surprised by this, for the same view is found already in early ethical writings of Bonhoeffer, particularly those written for ecumenical youth conferences in 1931-32. They are characterized by a search for an entirely new concept of ethics. "Reality is the sacrament of Ethics," he wrote in 1932,[9] by which he made clear that he was in search of a whole new basis for ethics. Already then he was convinced of the end of traditional ethics. Following Karl Barth's theology, he could say that only in the Word of God, only in the preaching of God's concrete command, can human decision find a reliable orientation.[10] Already then he had rejected any given ethical concept. Neither Wilhelm Lütgert's "Ethic of Love"[11] nor Reinhold Niebuhr's ethical writings influenced him in the true sense of the word. I mention these two because Bon-

6. Rasmussen in *New Studies*.

7. *Zettelnotizen*, 46.

8. Cf. "After Ten Years," in Dietrich Bonhoeffer, *Widerstand und Ergebung* (Munich: Chr. Kaiser, 1977), 14ff. See *LPP*, 3ff.

9. *DBW*, vol. 11, 334.

10. Cf. his lecture on Christology: Dietrich Bonhoeffer, *GS*, vol. 3, 166ff., particularly 194.

11. Wilhelm Lütgert, *Ethik der Liebe*, Beiträg zur Förderung christlicher Theologie, series 2, vol. 39 (Gütersloh: Gütersloher Verlag, 1938).

hoeffer had studied with Niebuhr at Union Theological Seminary in 1930-31, and Wilhelm Lütgert was at that time the professor to whom Bonhoeffer was attached as assistant at the University of Berlin.

It is, however, worth mentioning that Bonhoeffer was greatly influenced by what we might call cultural critics like Kierkegaard, Spengler, Nietzsche, and Dostoyevsky. Even Karl Barth's book on Romans can be ranked in this category of writings.[12] Bonhoeffer had read the German philosopher Karl Jaspers's book *The Spiritual Situation of Our Time* immediately after it appeared in 1932, and he used it for his lecture on "The Concept of a Leader *(Führer)* and the Young Generation" in early 1933.[13] Jaspers's term "epoch-making consciousness" can well be applied to Bonhoeffer himself in the early 1930s. His studies had led him to see in the Enlightenment and in Idealism, which he understood as the continuation of the Enlightenment, the total emancipation of Europeans from a culture rooted in Christ. In Hegel's concept of the absolute consciousness he saw enlightened humanity come to a declared goal of boundless self-exaltation. And it was precisely here that Lütgert, who had written a critical history of Idealism, was important for Bonhoeffer.[14]

Therefore we would misrepresent the facts if we saw Bonhoeffer's writing on ethics in 1940 as merely provoked by the situation of resistance. Of course that situation cannot be ignored, particularly in the passages written late in 1941 and in 1942 which were influenced by Bonhoeffer's participation in the plot to overthrow Hitler's dictatorship. Some texts written in autumn 1942 were meant to be used after a successful disposal of the Nazis. But Nazi ideology and terror ranked only among the consequences of the crisis as he understood it. They were not its origin. One should not forget how little attention Bonhoeffer pays to Nazi values like the "Teutonic Master Race," the glorification of the fight for survival, or even the particular concept of absolute

12. Karl Barth, *Der Römerbrief,* 2nd ed. (Munich: Chr. Kaiser, 1922). Cf. Jan Roß, "Von einem, der auszog, das Scheitern zu lehren. Aus dem Schatten Nietzsches ins Licht der Ideengeschichte: Franz Overbeck, der Verfall des Christentums und der Anbruch der Gegenwart," *FAZ,* 13 December 1994, L13.

13. *GS,* vol. 2, 22ff. Cf. Karl Jaspers, *Die geistige Situation der Zeit* (Frankfurt, 1932), 48ff. and 92f.

14. Wilhelm Lütgert, "Die Religion des Deutschen Idealismus und ihr Ende," Beiträg zur Förderung christlicher Theologie, series 2, vol. 10. Cf. Ilse Tödt, *Dietrich Bonhoeffer's Hegel-Seminar 1933, Nach den Aufzeichnungen von Ferenc Lehel* (Munich: Chr. Kaiser, 1988).

authority. Bonhoeffer set out to write a new ethics for a new time. One is tempted to say "for the time of religionlessness," to use the famous phrase from the *Letters from Prison*. And in this lies the impact for us today, who are confronted with a universal breakdown of traditional culture and ethics.

The Foundations

If we take all this for granted for the moment, we can venture to consider the question of a general concept for Bonhoeffer's *Ethics*. What was the content of the foundations laid in the first part of this book? The texts present a very interesting twofold systematic approach. One is christological; the other involves a theology of history.[15] Research by the editors of the *Dietrich Bonhoeffer Werke* edition has made it clear that these two approaches are not to be seen as alternatives.[16] They are to be taken together. The passages written from the perspective of a theology of history, "Ethics as Formation," "Heritage and Decay," and "Guilt and Justification," were to be brought together with "Christ, Reality and the Good," "History and the Good," and "The Love of God and the Decay of the World." Bonhoeffer intended in this way to make clear that the crisis of the west is to be seen as a concrete expression of the fundamental crisis between God and humanity, which is the content of the theological concept of Fall. The fact of the Fall appears in all times, but always under very specific forms, and now in the garment of National Socialism. The relatively late passage, "The Love of God and the Decay of the World," appears to be where these two central concepts were to be brought together.

A similar structure can be found in Bonhoeffer's discussion of the "End of Religion." The denial of God is not peculiar to modern times. Human beings have always found ways to contradict God's authority, and at times they have used religion as a means to do so. In such an

---

15. Rasmussen also speaks of a twofold method, an ethics of the command of God and an ethics as formation, in *New Studies*, 111f. As we do, he sees Bonhoeffer's work as an attempt to bring these two together. However, we cannot follow Rasmussen in his distinction of an ethics of the command inspired by Barth (and not original) and another more originally "Bonhoefferian" ethics of formation. But of course Barth's influence on Bonhoeffer cannot be underestimated.

16. *Ethik*, 5.

instance it is better that religion come to an end. But one would be illusioned to think that with the demise of religion the sinful denial of God also comes to an end. The end of religion only serves to help us see more clearly. It can equally be said that the end of traditional ethics may serve to help us find a way to truly Christian ethics for this world, rooted concretely in reality and in the presence of God.[17]

What does all this mean for the reconstruction of Bonhoeffer's ethics? To begin with, Bonhoeffer did not deal with material questions. Even in "The Natural Life," where we find him especially taken up with concrete problems, this was not his primary concern.[18] Rather, his primary focus was on the renewal of the relationships in which the human being exists. The ethical subject (a phrase not altogether appropriate for Bonhoeffer's thinking) has to be brought into a new position, to become part of the new world revealed in Christ. Heinz Eduard Tödt has pointed out the principal character of the passage "Christ, Reality and the Good."[19] I am inclined to see two major highlights of the whole work in this section and in "History and the Good." First, the goal of history is seen in God's own self-revelation as the ultimate reality. And second, ethics deals with the question of how humans can become part of this new reality. All depends on recognizing the center of renewal in Christ — be it ethical thinking or acting. He alone is the source of all ethical understanding, of all acting, of all normative decisions, of all ethical values and aims.

Therefore, Bonhoeffer rejects any special social ethics, any ethics of motives or good will. Neither are we to distinguish between personal and objective ethics.[20] "What is necessary is to become part of the indivisible whole of God's reality" and "In Jesus Christ God's reality has became incarnate in the reality of the world."[21] Bonhoeffer turns back

17. Precisely the lack of such a twofold access to the principles of theology may have been the reason for Bonhoeffer's criticism of what he calls "Barth's revelational positivism." "Friß, Vogel, oder stirb" ("Take it or leave it") was not at all his own approach to these matters. Cf. *WE*, 306, 312. See *LPP*, 280, 286.

18. Here we differ somewhat from Rasmussen, in *New Studies*, 128.

19. *Ethik*, 435.

20. It is in this context that his rejection of Dilschneider's ethics is to be seen. Cf. *Konspiration und Haft, 1940-1945*, ed. Jørgen Glenthøj, Ulrich Kabitz, and Wolf Krötke, *DBW*, vol. 16, 1,11. The title of Dilschneider's book is: *Otto Dilschneider, Die evangelische Tat. Grundlagen und Grundzüge der evangelischen Ethik* (Gütersloh, 1940).

21. *Ethik*, 38f.

to his sharp criticism of a division of thinking into two spheres,[22] which we know already from his *Cost of Discipleship*.[23] Ethics has to do with God's accepting the whole world.

We can, however, see a development from Bonhoeffer's earlier writings. In the beginning of the 1930s he looked for an opportunity to preach God's will in unmistakable, concrete terms.[24] This line of ethical thinking was most convincingly demonstrated in his lecture at Fanø, where he called the churches of the world to come together in an ecumenical council and to make an unmistakable witness for the necessity of peace.[25] But now the experience of resistance and conspiracy had taught Bonhoeffer that, particularly in boundary situations, nothing can replace free, responsible action. Already in the *Cost of Discipleship*, the concrete preaching of God's will is replaced by a purely relational concept, relating the person directly to the person of Christ. "What is said about the meaning of discipleship? Follow me, run behind me! That is all. Follow him is something that has no content at all."[26] Now, in *Ethics*, the idea of relationship is deepened and broadened. In reality as a whole, reality transformed through Christ, lies the aim of ethical thinking and acting.

Reality is something more than an accumulation of pure facts.[27] Reality includes "The Good," as we shall see. But above, all human reality exists in relationships, to God and to the fellow human, as is minutely discussed in "The Structure of Responsible Life."[28] Relationship means stewardship; the human person is steward to fellow human beings and to God in carrying out discipleship. In relationship to fellow human beings, the responsible person seeks to grasp what is commanded. In Bonhoeffer's understanding the term "command" comes very near to what is meant by the will of God. Very seldom is his idea of command identical with one of the commandments. Answering the command is acting out one's responsibility in relationship to God and the other person. Again we see that ethics is basically without content. In "The 'Ethical' and the 'Christian as Subject'" this view is repeated: "An Ethics cannot be a dictionary for

22. *Ethik*, 41ff.
23. *Nachfolge, DBW*, vol. 4.
24. Cf. *DBW*, vol. 11, 331f., 345.
25. Dietrich Bonhoeffer, *London 1933-1935, DBW*, vol. 13, 30.
26. *Nachfolge*, 46.
27. Here Bonhoeffer comes near to the thinking of Nietzsche, whose rejection of "servile acceptance of facts" he affirms. *Ethik*, 221. Cf. note 16.
28. *Ethik*, 259.

guaranteed faultless moral action and the ethical thinker can't evaluate and judge competently every human action." Ethical thinkers direct attention to disturbances rather than to the normal situation. "By creating rooms they want to help us learn to live with each other."[29]

Construction

It is precisely the spheres in which responsible action is possible which provide the content of the second major part of Bonhoeffer's *Ethics*. He called it "construction" *(Aufbau)*. The transition from foundation to construction is carried out by the chapter "The Ultimate and the Penultimate." Here my own organization of the material differs from that of Clifford Green. "The Ultimate and the Penultimate" is not part of the foundation, but the beginning of the construction,[30] a fact which can be seen in a careful investigation of the two *Zettel*, 38 and 1. This, of course, has to be brought into line with the course of Bonhoeffer's thinking. The Ultimate is the content of the foundation. Now Bonhoeffer deals with the Penultimate, the Preparation of the Way. "Preparation for the Word is the concern of all that has been said about the Penultimate."[31]

In an exegesis of Isaiah 40, Bonhoeffer pursues the question of what is meant by this. Reality is not void, is not unstructured, is not merely a theoretical concept. It is concrete, relative, and limited. Reality has to be seen as the historical place where the person lives. Factual relevance and willingness to accept guilt are necessary. In the Penultimate, Bonhoeffer deals with some basic conditions for responsible action. He does this by reinterpreting the Lutheran doctrine of the Two Realms. We have already seen that the unity of the Christ-given reality is essential to his thinking. Therefore, he is no longer willing to accept the idea of two realms existing side by side. He substitutes a concept of two different but sequential stages of the same reality.[32]

---

29. *Ethik*, 372.

30. Cf. Clifford Green, "The Text of Bonhoeffer's Ethics," in *New Studies*, 30, 58ff.

31. *Ethik*, 153ff.

32. Cf. Dietz Lange, *Ethik in Evangelischer Perspektive* (Göttingen, 1992), 56-61; Hartmut Rosenau, "Dietrich Bonhoeffers Mandatenlehre. Grundmodell einer erdverbundenen Ethik," *Deutsches Pfarrerblatt* 9 (1995): 446f.

This reinterpretation of an old doctrine is one of the most interesting results of Bonhoeffer's new thinking about ethics. It is not, however, without anticipation in his earlier writings. When Bonhoeffer rejected the Lutheran doctrine of Orders of Creation *(Schöpfungsordnungen)* and asked for its replacement by a concept of Orders of Maintenance *(Erhaltungsordnungen)*,[33] the eschatological concept of reality was already present. But now the Penultimate makes room for a reevaluation of historical and natural facts as part of Christian ethical decision. Ultimate and Penultimate are not differing realms but different stages of the same reality. The Ultimate is reality in its Christ-given renewal out of sin and decay; the Penultimate sets the stage for ethical decision and action in the concrete situation.[34]

Intrinsically connected with and written immediately after the passage on the "Ultimate and the Penultimate" is a discourse on "The Natural Life." Penultimate conditions are dealt with from an individual perspective.[35] In dealing with the question of the "Natural," Bonhoeffer found much insight in Catholic ethical writings. In the monastery of Ettal, where he stayed during this time, he engaged in discussions with Catholic theologians and was able to draw on some aspects of Catholic moral theology. But equally important, this was the period in which the Nazis began the annihilation of mentally-ill persons, a practice which they called "euthanasia." Nazi terror was also in sight when Bonhoeffer dealt with the question of freedom and the death penalty.[36]

But again he looks at this question much more basically.[37] The right to life is an essential part of the Penultimate. Ethics cannot begin

33. *DBW*, vol. 11, 339-42. Cf. *Ethik*, 171.

34. A new emphasis on the divine act of forgiveness that is the goal and terminus of all history. Characteristically Bonhoeffer invokes this eschatological concept, "not to deprive human choices of their importance, but precisely to give them their proper value in themselves" (Lovin, in *New Studies*, 94).

35. Cf. *Zettelnotizen*, 47, under the heading "Der neue Mensch" (the New Person).

36. The question of war is not really discussed. This may be partly due to the fact that this was especially problematic for Bonhoeffer given his general objection to war, but also because this question was considered from a perspective quite different from that of his close friends. Cf. the sermon of mourning for Hans-Friedrich von Kleist-Retzow, 3.8.41, *Konspiration und Haft 1940-1945*, ed. Jørgen Glenthøj, Ulrich Kabitz, and Wolf Krötke, *DBW*, vol. 16, iii, 6; also Bell's diary, *DBW*, vol. 16, i, 169, 313 in the manuscript.

37. Cf. William J. Peck, "The Euthanasia Text-Segment," in *New Studies*, 141ff.

with concrete questions of command or abstract theories of the ethical person. Ethics has to deal with what enables humans to take responsibility. Freedom of decision must be possible: a slave cannot act freely; therefore he cannot act responsibly. Equally important is the protection of life itself. Human rights are an essential basis for ethical freedom. "The rights of natural life are the reflection of God's glory as creator in the midst of a fallen world."[38] Thus life becomes one of the most essential values in a Penultimate world. And even though Bonhoeffer had some reservations about the concept of "human rights,"[39] it is here that the contemporary insight concerning the significance of human rights[40] finds one of its roots. And it is a sign of Bonhoeffer's understanding of the necessary social conditions for human freedom that he had planned the passage on "Natural Life" to be followed up by one on the "Right of Mental and Spiritual Life" and wanted also to deal with the necessity of education for a truly human life.[41]

Clifford Green has suggested, with good reason, that the passage on "History and the Good" belongs here, in the context of the Penultimate.[42] History is part of the Penultimate. The Penultimate includes the historical condition of human beings. And inasmuch as life itself is necessary for ethics, the historically given "Good" has its relevance. In this context, Bonhoeffer notes (somewhat surprisingly) an experience which has great importance. In times of terror, when all rights are suppressed, existing values become homeless and look for shelter within the church.[43] Protection of life and the consideration of traditional values are presuppositions for the human person waiting for God's coming. Bonhoeffer was sharply critical of the common Protestant defamation of "The Good."[44] But, strictly speaking, neither "The

---

38. *Ethik,* 174.

39. *Ethik,* 105 and 108.

40. Cf. e.g., Heinz Eduard Tödt and Wolfgang Huber, *Perspektiven einer menschlichen Welt* (Munich, 1988); also *Ethik,* 438.

41. *Ethik,* 216. Cf. *Zettel,* 1, where the catchword "Education" is found. *Zettelnotizen,* 45. And compare Karl Jaspers, *Die geistige Situation der Zeit,* 92. Jaspers gives expression to his doubts that uneducated masses are able to act in a truly democratic way.

42. Green, in *New Studies,* 58f.

43. *Ethik,* 343f.

44. Cf. *Ethik,* 301: "the Good — in its bourgeois sense — was given away to laughter."

Good" nor "Natural Life" was central to Bonhoeffer's view of the aims or values of ethical action.

In a later passage he definitively rejected "The Good" as an ethical aim.[45] In the context we are dealing with at the moment, we should consider "The Good" as being rather than as command. Here Bonhoeffer shows the influence of late Thomistic ethics, where "The Good" is seen as part of being itself.[46] This concept fits quite well into his idea of an ethics corresponding to reality. Bonhoeffer pursued this idea of the significance of life and the good even in the time of imprisonment, when he read Dilthey again.[47] But for the continuation of his work on the Penultimate another insight was essential. The historical situation and its demand for ethical action cannot be dealt with on an individual level alone. There needs to be a reflection on another concept: the mandates.

The Mandates

The historical, penultimate form of reality contains not only individual presuppositions but also collective ones. Instead of speaking about "orders," as he still did in his paper "State and Church"[48] written in 1941, he chose the term "Mandates" for the *Ethics*. The reason for this may have been the same as mentioned before. The term "Order," particularly in the German theological tradition, suggests quasi-ontological and therefore fixed structures, independent of any actual development and inappropriate for obedience to any direct divine command. Like the command itself, the mandates find their justification only in the directly and actually received Word of God. But they are necessary beside the direct command to avoid the atomization of reality. Rasmussen calls them "the media of conformation,"[49] by which he means that ethical response is not exempt from a consideration of the status of the individual. This view is underlined in the introductory chapter "The

45. *Ethik*, 301: "Christian ethics recognizes even in the possibility of knowing about good and evil the falling away from the origin." Cf. *Schöpfung und Fall, DBW*, vol. 3.

46. Cf. Lovin, in *New Studies*, 70f.

47. See Ralf Wüstenberg, "Dietrich Bonhoeffer on Theology and Philosophy," *ANVIL* 12/1 (1995).

48. *DBW*, vol. 6, 2, no. 10.

49. In *New Studies*, 118.

'Ethical' and the 'Christian as Subject,'" written early in 1943. The individual is not always and everywhere called to make ethical decisions. This would itself contradict the limited and relational character of the Penultimate. The individual is located in concrete realms, such as family, church, labor and the state. The mandates structure reality.

Originally, it seems, Bonhoeffer planned to speak about "institutions" when dealing with the mandates. But he refrains from doing so, partly because the concept of the Penultimate has liberated him from the old doctrine of State and Church, and partly because the institutions are no less corrupted by the Fall than the individual. More importantly, the mandates are themselves historically shaped and open to change — they are changeable forms in Spengler's and Goethe's sense.[50] And so Bonhoeffer can say, "The word of God revealed in Jesus Christ is delivered to us in the church, in the family, in labour and in the authority of the state."[51]

The renewal of the collective structures of reality can come only from above, directly through God's Word. There is a tendency to move from above to below in ethics;[52] Bonhoeffer here demonstrates a certain affinity with the perspective of conservative circles in the resistance movement. He shared his generation's disappointment in democratic forms of government — after all, the masses had voted Hitler into power. At least for some time he seems to have favored the reintroduction of monarchy.[53] His concept of politics was shaped by the idea that it is necessary to find room for responsible decision-making between the ruling powers and the masses. Gerhard Ritter's understanding of the demonic character of power and Jaspers's analysis of mass society are clearly in the background of his thinking.[54] But we must remember that at this time the conspiracy against Hitler was also strongly on his mind. Conspiracy demands secrecy and cannot be legitimized by public vote. What is more significant is that Bonhoeffer follows Barth in seeing revelation as God's word coming from above. He did not want to make a distinction between privileged and nonprivileged ethical persons, and

50. Oswald Spengler, *Untergang des Abendlands*, vol. 1, Introduction.

51. *Ethik*, 383.

52. *Ethik*, 376.

53. Cf. Bell's diary, *DBW*, vol. 16, 1, 169; in the manuscript 313.

54. Gerhard Ritter, *Machtstaat und Utopie, vom Streit um die Dämonie der Macht seit Macchiavelli und Morus* (Munich, 1940); Jaspers, *Die Geistige Situation der Zeit*. Cf. *Ethik*, 238f.

God-given authority is not limited to monarchy alone. Thus the concrete character of the political mandate is subject to historical changes like all the others. There is no permanently given order for it.

The mandates are related to institutions, particularly to the state and the church. Bonhoeffer only expressed what this meant for the mandate of the church. But everything necessary to understand what he would have thought about the state can be found in "State and Church." There he wrote that the state is legitimized by Christ; its very goal is Christ. This fact is independent of the question of how the state originated, whether democratically or in an authoritarian way: it is the function of the state to serve Christ's reign. It is also independent of the question of whether the state knows about this or not or whether its functionaries are Christians or not: even an anti-Christian state can be a state in the true sense. It serves Christ as long as it cares for the protection of life on earth. "As the historical entanglements in the guilt of the past are great and can't be overlooked in all governmental decisions, the judgement on the legitimacy of any single decision usually cannot be carried out. Here it is necessary to take the risk of responsibility."[55]

But if the legitimacy of action is clearly left aside, then the mandate of the state is given into the hand of individual persons or groups which fight for the righteous fulfillment of the state's task. Here is where the mandate of the church calls it to intervene. The church's calling is the proclamation of the gospel and the concrete preaching of God's command. The church does this by preaching Christ as Lord and Savior of the world. The church is not itself called to reign but to serve. And as such it needs the protection of the state. Neither the division of church and state nor an established relationship is to be favored. The judgment rests exclusively on the question of how Christ's reign is best carried out.

Looking back on the concept of the mandates, it can clearly be seen that Bonhoeffer remains strictly committed to his fundamental concept of one reality, rooted in God's incarnation in the world. Even his rather problematic passages on the function and authority of the state have to be seen in this light. Under no circumstance would Bonhoeffer have exempted any of the aforementioned mandates from this essential presupposition. Thus he remains faithful to his insistence on the oneness of reality in the Penultimate as well as in the Ultimate. The section of the *Ethics* which deals with given structures for ethical responsibility now

55. *Ibid.*, 365.

150

seems to be complete. The content of ethical teaching, however, remains undisclosed.

"The Law"

Though they are unfinished, it is possible to provide a rather complete picture of the first two major sections of Bonhoeffer's *Ethics*. This is not the case for what is to follow. From this point on, in what we shall hypothetically call part three, reconstruction is even more hypothetical. The editors of the *Dietrich Bonhoeffer Werke* edition indicate that Bonhoeffer probably planned to give this section the heading "The Law."[56] It should be observed that nothing so far has been said about concrete ethical teaching for the world. The discourse on the mandates was meant to define the given place for ethical teaching and acting, not the content of the teaching itself. According to our examination of the evidence, part three is where the passage on "Church and (Formation of the) World" was finally to follow. Although in the original organization of texts this was still to be part of the foundation, together with the problem of the law, of norms, and so on, these should now be seen to follow on from the discussion of the Penultimate.

During the course of Bonhoeffer's working on the *Ethics*, the structure of the whole became more differentiated. No longer did revealed reality on the one side and the construction of a renewed ethical teaching on the other confront each other. Elements of a structured reality were included to make responsible action possible. In other words, the task of teaching the concrete command is exclusively and more clearly bound to the mandate of the church. And what the church means for the world can only be carried out after the concept of the mandates has been dealt with. This is quite obvious in the introductory passage of the third part: "On the Possibility of a Word of the Church to the World." Now Bonhoeffer has to deal with the question of how God's demand is made known to the world. There is no other means by which the world can know what God wants. Bonhoeffer rejects natural law, human rights, and the law of reason altogether.[57] The Word of God is one, and it is the function of the church to proclaim it.

---

56. *Ibid.*, 282 and 455, note 103.
57. 359ff.

Bonhoeffer's work on this topic came during his greatest involve-ment with the resistance and its attempt to assassinate Hitler. So Bon-hoeffer had on his mind what the church would say when the deed was successfully done. Therefore it is helpful to refer to a manuscript which was meant to be handed out after the execution of the plot, entitled "Proclamation from the Pulpit."[58] In this the church is called to repen-tance, "renewal of life according to his holy will." We read, "In all places preach and listen to the comfort of the love of God, which forgives sins in Jesus Christ. In all places preach and listen to the healing command of God, calling to a new life." It is the twofold Word of God, Gospel and Law, that is expressed here. Bonhoeffer is using Barth's reverse of the traditional order of both sides of God's revelation. Ministers are called to a new order of life. Perceivably, behind this lies the insight of a "task without example" that the church is confronted with after the overthrow of Nazism.

The only example of concrete proclamation of the law to the world that Bonhoeffer was able to write is found in "What Does It Mean to Tell the Truth," written in prison.[59] Here the concepts of reality and of the mandates are concretely applied: "The usual definition, according to which the knowledgeable contradiction between thinking and saying is to be called a lie, is entirely insufficient." To tell the truth means that "the real is to be said in words." The person who has a relationship with the ethical person, like father with son, is entitled to hear the truth. "The qualification to say the truth always rests within the boundaries of a given mandate which I am endowed with." More cannot be said about the third part of Bonhoeffer's *Ethics,* as he was taken away to prison.

Religionless Ethics

After being taken into custody Bonhoeffer attained important new insights which could and probably would have been incorporated into the *Ethics* had he lived to return to this work. If the Word of the church is to be relevant for the whole of reality, and if the whole world is to understand it, then the church must not use a language which has

---

58. *DBW,* vol. 16, 2, 15. Cf. also "Draft of a New Ordering of the Church after the End of the Church Struggle," 2, 16. Both papers date from the end of 1942.

59. *DBW,* 2, 19, particularly note 1 in the manuscript.

become obsolete. What the world can no longer understand is religious language.

The catchword of "religionlessness"[60] is not merely theoretical for Bonhoeffer, it has to be seen in the context of future preaching of the Law to the world, which he sees as the main task of the church in times to come. And if it can be said that religion is not essential to the church,[61] but only a garment appropriate for that time when religion was a universal reality, then the church needs to revise its language. In the present, religion is merely a loophole for some rather than a universal means of communication. And so a new religionless language is needed, one which even means keeping "arcane"[62] some of its most treasured values or concepts. That means that these matters have to remain within the walls of the church, to be kept in secrecy and not used in public preaching.

But the church's credibility rests not exclusively with its language. It also concerns its way of living:

> After these years, when the church was only fighting for its self-preservation, as if this was to be an aim in itself, it has become incapable of being the carrier of the redeeming and saving word for humankind and the world. Therefore former words will become powerless and must be silenced. Our being Christian today will exist in two things: in prayer and doing the just among humans. All thinking, talking and organizing in the matters of Christendom must be reborn out of this prayer and this kind of deed.[63]

It seems to me that Bonhoeffer was aware of the fact that the passage on "Church and (Formation of the) World" needed to be rewritten. Therefore he wrote to Bethge that he would like to write a new essay in which he would point out that

> the church is only church when it exists for others. To begin with, it must give away all of its property to those who are in need. Ministers must live exclusively on the freely given donations of their congregations, perhaps taking up some profession. The church must participate in all worldly tasks of the human communities — not reigning, but

---

60. *WE,* 306ff. See *LPP,* 280ff.
61. *WE,* 307.
62. *Ibid.,* 306 and 312.
63. *Ibid.,* 328.

helping and serving. It must proclaim to people of all professions what it means to live with Christ, what it means to exist for others.[64]

There can be no doubt that this is a new discourse on the topic of "Church and Formation of the World." If the church follows this advice, then hope is at hand:

> It is not our calling to predict the day—but the day will come when humans will be entitled again to preach the word of God in such a way that the world changes itself through it and is renewed. It will be a new language, maybe entirely unreligious, but liberating and saving, like the language of Jesus himself, by which humans were frightened and nonetheless overwhelmed by its power. It is a language of new justice and truth, the language which preaches the peace of God with humankind and which announces the coming of his Kingdom.[65]

64. *Ibid.*, 431ff.
65. *Ibid.*, 328.

"Who Stands Fast?" Dietrich Bonhoeffer and Thomas Merton on Obedience

WILLIAM D. APEL

"Who stands fast?" Dietrich Bonhoeffer asked this question in his essay entitled "After Ten Years," written during Christmas 1942 for fellow conspirators in the plot against Hitler. In one of the most famous of his passages, Bonhoeffer directly, and without equivocation, answers his own question.

> Who stands fast? Only the man whose final standard is not his reason, his principles, his conscience, his freedom, or his virtue, but who is ready to sacrifice all this when he is called to obedient and responsible action in faith and in exclusive allegiance to God — the responsible man, who tries to make his whole life an answer to the question and call of God.[1]

Who stands fast? For Bonhoeffer the answer resides in obedience to God in responsible action. But this is no facile submission, and it requires of the individual an often unconventional response. Standing fast in radical obedience means to be transformed. The one who stands fast must ironically be the one who is prepared to move. Standing fast means acting in freedom, and actually moving ahead, all the while trusting God for the forgiveness and grace which such obedience necessitates.

---

1. *LPP*, 5.

Thomas Merton also discovered that to "stand fast" meant to move forward in freedom, trusting God for the rest. In 1958, a decade and a half after his decision to remove himself from "the world" to the Trappist Abbey at Gethsemani, Thomas Merton the monk learned this same lesson. While in the city of Louisville to see about printing a postulant's guide for his monastery, Merton had an epiphany which brought about a revolution in his entire outlook on life. This defining moment caused him to be transformed and brought him to a deeper understanding of obedience:

> In Louisville, at the corner of Fourth and Walnut, in the center of the shopping district, I was suddenly overwhelmed with the realization that I loved all those people, that they were mine and I theirs, that we could not be alien to one another even though we were total strangers.[2]

Merton understood he could no longer turn his back on the world — and although he maintained his vocation as a monk, his renewed commitment to people resulted in a new form of obedience which led him to embrace the world beyond his monastic walls. "To think," wrote Merton, "that for sixteen or seventeen years I have been taking seriously this pure illusion [a separate holiness] that is implicit in so much of our monastic thinking."[3] With this reorientation Merton became an active voice for peace, justice, and racial reconciliation during the Cold War era — all the while maintaining a transformed monastic life.

The nature of obedience which emerged in the lives of Bonhoeffer and Merton was truly paradoxical: it involved acts of both obedience and disobedience. According to conventional categories, these would appear to be contradictory. But ultimately they were not, and herein lies my thesis. From Bonhoeffer's work on *The Cost of Discipleship* through the remainder of his life, his conflicts and crises gave rise to a transforming type of obedience which was simultaneously a "yes" to God and a "no" to various kinds of human authority. Likewise, from Merton's work *The Seven Storey Mountain* to the close of his life, his transformations also related to a struggle to remain obedient to God, a struggle that often placed him in conflict with lines of authority both inside and outside the church.

2. Thomas Merton, *Conjectures of a Guilty Bystander* (New York: Doubleday, 1966), 156.
3. *Ibid.,* 157.

Two Preliminary Questions

First, is there legitimacy in studying Bonhoeffer and Merton together: do they really have that much in common, or are we forcing the comparison? In responding, we begin with the fact that Bonhoeffer and Merton are among the most influential religious thinkers in the twentieth century. Yet, it is true at first glance that they seem to have so little in common. They are of different nationalities and religious traditions, and appear to be at odds in their basic theological perspectives. Bonhoeffer is often celebrated as the theologian who argued for "a world come of age" in which believers are encouraged to embrace an emerging secular world and find God in its midst — or not at all; Christ becomes "the man for others." On the other hand, Merton is frequently portrayed as a sort of modern mystic and teacher, calling believers back from a meaningless modernity to the religious richness of an enduring pattern of spirituality.

Such characterizations, of course, are wholly inadequate. But these misguided generalizations may account for why so little comparative work has been done. It has also been noted that Merton, who outlived Bonhoeffer by several decades, appeared to distance himself from Bonhoeffer's theology. Writing twenty years after Bonhoeffer's death, Merton expressed deep reservations about what he called Bonhoeffer's "Christian worldliness." Upon more careful examination, however, it becomes clear that Merton's true criticism was reserved for some of Bonhoeffer's self-professed "disciples" — namely, the British and American "death of God" theologians. Merton affirmed that Bonhoeffer's engagement of the modern world did not represent a denial of guilt, but rather an "entering into the fellowship of guilt for the sake of other men." Merton noted, "This is surely quite a different optimism from the free-wheeling and breezy propensity of some Christians to accept the torn and anguished world of the twentieth century as the flowering of Christian humanism and happiness."[4]

It may be that Merton's rejection of a line of thought which had little, if anything, to do with Bonhoeffer, has caused some to think of Merton as anti-Bonhoeffer. Nothing, in fact, could be farther from the truth. In *Conjectures of a Guilty Bystander,* Merton makes over a dozen references to Bonhoeffer in a positive and constructive manner. For

4. *Ibid.,* 253.

whatever reasons, however, little comparative work has been done on these two theological giants of the twentieth century. Comparative works in the English language are scant. They cannot be found in the excellent Bonhoeffer Bibliography compiled by Wayne Whitson Floyd, Jr. and Clifford Green, nor do they appear in Michael Mott's extensive bibliography of English-language sources on Merton.

The second preliminary question concerns the inherent difficulties of doing comparative biographies for theological study. At best, writing about Dietrich Bonhoeffer and Thomas Merton is a humbling experience, and at worst it is a very presumptuous undertaking. Indeed, to write about another's life is always to accept a sobering responsibility for the interpretation of his or her thoughts and actions. In truth, we can never fully enter another's life — especially the soul of a person. Like beggars at the gate, we must wait on the outside, and can only gain entrance when it is granted to us from the inside. But enter we must, especially in the case of Bonhoeffer and Merton, for both have clearly demonstrated to the world that theology and life cannot be separated. Because of the very nature of Bonhoeffer's and Merton's contributions, we can never again develop theology and ethics apart from biography — if indeed we ever could.

There are, without question, numerous problems inherent in comparative biography. In comparative study we always run the risk of distorting lives by defining or measuring one in terms of the other. But in reality, we do this all the time. We take what we have learned from one individual and compare it quite naturally to what we have learned from another. We continue to do this until we have gathered a variety of human experiences, each informing and shaping the other.

With all these caveats in mind then, let us press ahead, for it remains my conviction that the life and thought of Dietrich Bonhoeffer and Thomas Merton cry out for comparison. More than a quarter of a century has passed since the untimely deaths of Bonhoeffer and Merton (fifty years and twenty-seven respectively). Enough time has now elapsed for the settling of the first generation of scholarship, and perhaps we are in a better position to see the whole picture more clearly. To use an analogy from Peter Brown's biography on Augustine, viewing the life of Bonhoeffer and Merton today is much like being "led along the side of a mountain-face"[5] (in this case two mountain-faces). We are distant

5. Peter Brown, *Augustine of Hippo* (Berkeley: University of California Press, 1967), 9.

enough for the general contours to become more evident. In our particular examination, one of these basic contours takes the shape of transforming obedience. It is along this rock face that Bonhoeffer and Merton have carved out a road to ultimate freedom — a pathway marked by acts of obedience which led ultimately to God while not leaving the world behind.

Our comparative study begins with Bonhoeffer and then turns to Merton. In the process, we shall chart the fascinating trajectory of their life commitments, and seek to understand them in terms of transforming obedience. In the end, we will discover just how significant this major contour of transforming obedience is on the mountain face of the experiences of Dietrich Bonhoeffer and Thomas Merton.

Bonhoeffer and Obedience

Dietrich Bonhoeffer was born into an upper-class German family in 1906. He was one of eight children (a twin) raised in a happy and secure home; he had the advantages of an excellent education, and he benefited from his well-placed position in his nation and culture. Bonhoeffer's father was a noted professor of psychiatry, and his mother was the product of a proud Prussian family whose paternal head had been the chaplain in the court of William II.

The First World War, beginning in his eighth year, interrupted Bonhoeffer's otherwise sanguine childhood. He saw two of his older brothers march off to war; one returned badly wounded, and the other did not return at all. Living in Berlin, the Bonhoeffer family heard daily reports from the front. Young Dietrich was deeply affected by the war. He later recalled, "Death stood at the door of almost every house."[6] As a result of these early experiences, he had no taste for war and in his early adulthood years embraced a pacifist position.

Bonhoeffer's religious training was typical of the bourgeois families of Germany in the first quarter of the twentieth century. Christian holidays were observed, but beyond that the family rarely attended church. Within the home itself Bonhoeffer received religious instruction from his mother. However, when at the age of seventeen young Dietrich announced that he would study theology, the entire family was surprised.

6. *No Rusty Swords* (London: Collins, 1972), 78.

Perhaps he was carving out space for himself within a professional family of attorneys and scientists.

In any case, by the age of twenty-one he had completed his doctorate, and shortly thereafter he finished the additional academic work necessary for becoming a university lecturer.

As Eberhard Bethge has so brilliantly demonstrated in his biography of Bonhoeffer, Bonhoeffer's adult years were marked by two significant turning points. The first change occurred about 1931-32 when Bonhoeffer the theologian became Bonhoeffer the Christian. It was during this period, shortly after a year's study abroad at Union Theological Seminary in New York City, that Bonhoeffer "consciously grasped the fact that he was a Christian."[7] He never said publicly precisely when, or how, that turning point came, but the conversion is mentioned in a letter written to a close friend, Elizabeth Sinn, in the winter of 1935-36.

In this letter, Bonhoeffer referred to the period of time around 1931-32 and confessed:

> I hurled myself into my work in an unchristian and an unhumble manner. . . . Then something else came along, something which has permanently changed my life and its direction. . . . I had often preached, I had seen a lot of the church, I had talked and written about it, but I had not yet become a Christian. I know that until then I had been using the cause of Jesus Christ to my own advantage. . . .[8]

Thus, in the early 1930s, Bonhoeffer discovered his calling and his voice. According to Bethge, "In 1932 he found the unmistakable language in which he wrote his characteristic contribution to theology: well-rounded books, *The Cost of Discipleship* and *Life Together*."[9]

After becoming a Christian, Bonhoeffer approached his academic work quite differently. He surprised his students at the University of Berlin by opening his lectures with prayer. He encouraged his students, for the first time, to gather with him in a fellowship of study and prayer. It was at this time that Bonhoeffer also became much more active in the

---

7. Eberhard Bethge, *Dietrich Bonhoeffer: A Biography* (London: Collins, 1970), 581.

8. Peter Vorking, ed., *Bonhoeffer in a World Come of Age* (Philadelphia: Fortress Press, 1968), 80.

9. Bethge, *Dietrich Bonhoeffer*, 581.

life of the church. Bethge has reported that "the young theologian engaged himself in a disciplined church life which was quite unfamiliar to his family and theological teachers."[10]

During this period, Bonhoeffer the Christian also turned his attention toward the menace of Nazism which was permeating Germany. In 1933 Hitler had gained control of the German nation, and the universities and churches (Bonhoeffer's two primary communities) offered faint resistance to this new form of tyranny. From the beginning, Bonhoeffer believed that the Third Reich, the proposed thousand years of Aryan domination of the world, was an enemy of Jesus Christ and the church, as well as an enemy of the German people themselves. Hitler preached hatred, while the message of Christ was love and reconciliation.

Bonhoeffer challenged the Nazification of German society and his church in what he called "the great masquerade of evil."[11] Working with the Confessing Church, a small segment of Protestant Christians within Germany who questioned Nazi domination, Bonhoeffer claimed that Hitler must be opposed from the very center of the Christian faith. The non-Aryan laws of 1933 compelled him to speak out publicly against Hitler. These racist laws led to the definition of Jews as nonpersons in Germany. Bonhoeffer understood the deadly implications of these laws, and from a theological perspective noted that whenever anyone is victimized by another individual or group, then Jesus Christ himself is victimized. He called the churches of Germany to action against the Third Reich:

> . . . when the church sees the state exercising too little or too much law and order, it is its task not simply to bind the wounds of the victims beneath the wheel, but also to put a spoke in the wheel itself.[12]

In 1939, Bonhoeffer became an active participant in a major political conspiracy against Hitler within Germany. Its ultimate aim was to remove the Führer from power, by assassination if necessary. According to Bethge, Bonhoeffer the young Christian theologian had reached a second major turning point in his life.

If in 1932 Bonhoeffer answered his calling, then in 1939 he realized

10. Vorking, *World Come of Age,* 79.
11. *LPP,* 4.
12. Eberhard Bethge, *Costly Grace* (New York: Harper and Row, 1979), 62.

his destiny. The steady movement in Bonhoeffer's life, as understood by Bethge, proceeded from theologian to Christian to contemporary. In 1939 Bonhoeffer had an opportunity to remove himself from the dangers of Nazi Germany by remaining at Union Seminary in New York City where ecumenical contacts had offered him a safe harbor, but he decided instead to return to his homeland to be with his people. With a "contemporary" conscience, he wrote of his brief New York stay and sudden decision to return to Germany:

> I have made a mistake in coming to America. I must live through the difficult period of our national history with the Christian people of Germany. I will have no right to participate in the reconstruction of Christian life in Germany after the war if I do not share the trials of this time with my people. . . .[13]

Bonhoeffer had already been banned from university lecturing at Berlin, and soon he would be prevented from publishing in Germany. As early as 1937, he had been harassed, arrested, but not held, by the Gestapo. Now Bonhoeffer determined that he must help place "a spoke in the wheel." He painfully concluded that no other responsible course of action remained, and entered the conspiracy.

During this tumultuous period, he still managed to write if not to publish. What resulted were his two most important works, *Ethics* and *Letters and Papers from Prison*. Both were published posthumously: the first being a fragment of what he had hoped to be his life's work, and the second consisting of a collection of letters written during his imprisonment — several of which contained important theological reflections written to Bethge, his closest friend and colleague. When the attempt on Hitler's life failed in July of 1944, Bonhoeffer, already imprisoned under suspicion of sedition, was linked to the assassination plot. On April 9, 1945, only weeks before the war's end, Bonhoeffer was hanged along with fellow conspirators by orders of the Führer.

As a Christian, Bonhoeffer had sought in all things to be obedient and faithful to God. He came to understand this obedience in relation to a world in which there seemed to be no solid ground upon which to stand. The first turning point had sealed his calling as a Christian and its course was relatively predictable. This, according to Bethge,

---

13. Bethge, *Dietrich Bonhoeffer*, 559.

". . . had put Bonhoeffer into a world where things were comparatively clear-cut, where it was a matter of confessing and denying, and therefore in his case of the one church for the whole world and against its betrayal to nationalist particularism."[14] It required a form of single-minded obedience — one which was transformative, but one which moved mostly along traditional lines of responsibility and accountability.

The second turning point, however, was of a different order. It required of Bonhoeffer that his Christian vocation become contemporary, meaning he could no longer experience the luxury of clear-cut choices. Life was far more complex than could be accounted for in the easy delineation of pious good from earthly evil. Bonhoeffer could no longer stand at a distance from moral ambiguities. He refused to stand with one foot tentatively placed on earth and the other safely located in heaven. He knew now that he must stand squarely in the midst of life, in the center of the world, without secure footing. His ground, and the source of his obedience, would continue to be God — but it would be the God who "let himself be pushed out of the world onto the cross" for the sake of that world. Bonhoeffer understood that he must release himself fully into the world and love it as completely as God did. This opened him to great misunderstanding among many of his churchly colleagues and friends whose theology had not been so radicalized. But writing from prison, Bonhoeffer was convinced that ". . . the Bible directs man to God's powerlessness and suffering; only the suffering God can help."[15] In Bethge's words:

> In 1939 he [Bonhoeffer] entered the difficult world of assessing what was expedient, of success and failure, of tactics and camouflage. The certainty of his calling in 1932 now changed into the acceptance of the uncertain, the incomplete and the provisional. The new call demanded quite a different sacrifice, the sacrifice even of a Christian reputation.[16]

This new calling required an even deeper form of obedience from Bonhoeffer. It, too, was transformative, but far more costly. It exacted a tremendous price — it cost him his life and called into question for some

14. *Ibid.*, 582.
15. *LPP*, 360-61.
16. Bethge, *Dietrich Bonhoeffer*, 582.

his very right to be called a Christian pastor. It is a type of obedience which Robin Lovin has referred to as "complex obedience."[17] The stance involves continuing firm obedience to God, but the footing appears far less secure. In Bethge's assessment:

> To want to be a Christian, a disciple who follows timelessly — that now became a fatal privilege. To become a contemporary standing in his right place was so much more liable to misinterpretation, so much duller and more cramped — that alone was what it now meant to be a Christian.[18]

For the sake of obedience itself, it became necessary to act in truly unconventional ways. To be an obedient contemporary Christian meant to be at one and the same time obedient and disobedient — obedient to God but disobedient to national, and even ecclesiastical, authority. In the end this caused Bonhoeffer to risk his most prized treasure — his own identity and reputation as a follower of Christ. It meant he had to act in obedience without immediate certainty of the rightness or efficacy of his actions. A very similar process is evident in the life of Thomas Merton.

Merton and Obedience

Thomas Merton was born in Prades, France, in 1915 and spent half of his fifty-three years in the secular world and the other half as a cloistered monk at the Trappist Abbey of Our Lady of Gethsemani near Louisville, Kentucky. In the first line of his autobiography, he wrote: "On the last day of January 1915, under the sign of the Water Bearer, in a year of a great war, and down in the shadow of some French mountain on the border of Spain, I came into the world."[19] His father, a New Zealand artist, and his mother, an American artist, were Bohemian in temperament and outlook. Merton observed that he inherited from his father "his way of looking at things and some of his integrity." From his mother

17. Robin W. Lovin, "A Complex Obedience," *Christian Century* 112/14 (26 April 1995), 446-47.

18. Bethge, *Dietrich Bonhoeffer,* 582.

19. Thomas Merton, *The Seven Storey Mountain* (New York: Harcourt Brace Jovanovich, 1948), 3.

he said he gained "some of her dissatisfaction with the mess the world is in, and some of her versatility."[20]

The untimely death of Merton's mother in his sixth year, and the subsequent death of his father in his fifteenth year, left Merton an orphan to the world and almost rootless. However, before his agonizing death from a brain tumor, Merton's father had provided for his son's education, first in France, and then at an English public school. His American grandfather later supported his education at Cambridge and Columbia Universities, where he proved to be a bright and precocious student.

Merton's unquenchable thirst for intellectual stimulation was matched only by his desire for all kinds of experiences — especially pleasurable ones. Although there was a serious side to Merton, as evidenced in his surprising discovery of Christ in the churches of Rome in 1933, his teenage years for the most part lacked meaning and direction.[21] Later on, Merton was to note the transiency of his experience in Rome and bemoan his frame of mind back at his grandparents' home in America:

> When I got back to New York I had lost most of my temporary interest in religion. My friends in that city had a religion of their own: a cult of New York itself, and of the peculiar manner in which Manhattan expressed the bigness and gaudiness and noisiness and frank animality and vulgarity of this American paganism.[22]

At this point, Merton's and Bonhoeffer's biographies could not have been much different. Aside from the fact that they had both experienced New York City in the 1930s, they had little in common. The earnest Bonhoeffer, living securely within his family's care and support, worked with purpose and direction, while a more youthful Merton lived essentially out-of-control. His start in higher education at Cambridge in 1933 was a disaster. When his grandfather learned of Merton's low grades, carousing, and the pregnancy of a young woman, he ordered Merton back to America. Enrolled subsequently at Columbia University, Merton found an intellectual and social climate more to his liking. In this setting, he became a promising writer and journalist. But still something was missing.

20. *Ibid.,* 3.
21. *Ibid.,* 109.
22. *Ibid.,* 117.

Following his very brief association with campus communists, Merton and a small group of friends became interested in Catholicism and Catholic writers. Then, in August of 1938, Merton began attending Mass at "the little brick church of Corpus Christi, hidden behind Teachers College on 121st street." Soon after, his life was to be changed forever. "What a revelation it was," wrote Merton, "to discover so many ordinary people in a place together, more conscious of God than of one another: not there to show off their hats or their clothes, but to pray, or at least to fulfill a religious obligation, not a human one."[23] In November of 1938 Merton was baptized at Corpus Christi; what came next shocked even his closest friends. Merton was determined to enter a religious order and eventually joined the austere, silent Trappists of Gethsemani in December of 1941.

In June of 1939 Bonhoeffer and Merton were both in New York. They were each in the process of making a decision which would determine the course of the rest of their lives; Bonhoeffer deciding to return to Germany to stand with the Christian people of his nation during a time of war, and Merton making preparations for a religious vocation which would separate him from the world and its global conflict. Once again, it appears from their actions that Bonhoeffer and Merton had little in common with each other. Merton, rejected by the Draft Board because of his "lack of teeth," was now free to enter a Trappist monastery. He had even been denied the noncombatant objector's position for which he had applied.[24]

At Gethsemani Merton discovered the only true home he ever knew. He was fully prepared to leave his old life behind, and for the next fifteen years or so he reveled in his monastic life. His best-selling autobiography, *The Seven Storey Mountain*, remains a testament to the single-minded obedience which he discovered during this period. In fact, *The Seven Storey Mountain* was written as an act of obedience by Merton to the instruction of his abbot. He himself did not want to write an autobiography, for he had left the old life behind and had no desire to revisit it. The daily life of the monastery was difficult and very austere, but things were very clear-cut. Under these conditions, Merton could pursue the holiness and contemplation which he sought, while enduring the little annoyances of what he considered to be a too busy cloistered

23. *Ibid.*, 208.
24. *Ibid.*, 311-15.

existence. Here he could strive toward what he had earlier thought quite impossible — sainthood. Later he would even enter a hermitage.

Merton, however, wondered how he could become a saint and remain a writer; indeed, he was the celebrated author of a popular religious autobiography which sold an unheard-of 600,000 copies in its first year of publication. In his Epilogue to *The Seven Storey Mountain*, Merton complained of "this writer who had followed me into the cloister":

> He is on my track. He rides my shoulders, sometimes, like the old man of the sea. I cannot lose him. He still wears the name of Thomas Merton. Is it the name of an enemy? He is supposed to be dead.[25]

Merton undoubtedly struggled during this period of renunciation with "the writer" in him who was an unwelcome intruder and reminder of an undesired past. Yet, it was the very writer in Merton that gave voice to his new life and helped him to explore its depths. In the supportive community of Gethsemani, he grew to understand the seeds of contemplation which God had spread in his life, and which blossomed into his monastic vocation. Carefully, he charted the meaning of a life consciously lived before God. In one of his most famous passages, Merton recorded the unlimited potentiality of saintliness as he knew it during these halcyon years.

> Every moment and every event of every man's life on earth plants something in his soul. For just as the wind carries thousands of invisible and visible winged seeds, so the stream of time brings with it germs of spiritual vitality that come to rest imperceptibly in the minds and wills of men. Most of these unnumbered seeds perish and are lost, because men are not prepared to receive them: for such seeds as these cannot spring up anywhere except in the good soil of liberty and desire.[26]

Paradoxically for Merton, it was only in his cloistered and constrained life that he believed himself free enough for the growth of God's seeds of love and saintliness. Such growth he now found to be possible. His desire for these seeds was clear: "If they would take root in my liberty, and if His will would grow from my freedom, I would

---

25. *Ibid.,* 410.
26. Thomas Merton, *Seeds of Contemplation* (New York: Dell, 1949), 11.

become the love that He is, and my harvest would be His glory and my own joy."[27]

A book like *Seeds of Contemplation,* from which this quotation comes, and *The Seven Storey Mountain* represented a period of tremendous spiritual growth. Such books provide an extensive testimony to the monk who aspired to saintly existence. Other works such as *The Spirit of Simplicity, What is Contemplation? The Ascent to Truth,* and *The Sign of Jonas* also attest to Merton's single-minded sense of obedience during this time. Like the earlier Bonhoeffer, Merton became a teacher of others within his religious tradition. His instruction of novices at Gethsemani was somewhat akin to Bonhoeffer's instruction of Lutheran seminarians at Finkenwalde. Both realized that the difficult vocation they asked of their students required a life of personal discipline and obedience to God. The circumstances certainly differed, but in each case the necessity for firm spiritual moorings was undeniable. Just as the first turning point in Bonhoeffer's life had sealed his calling as a Christian pastor, so too the first major turning point of Merton's life had confirmed his life as a Trappist monk. Neither man would ever depart from these commitments.[28] Neither would ever abandon his newfound faith, although both would have it greatly challenged in the years ahead.

The next turning point in Merton's life, like that in Bonhoeffer's, was of a more radical nature. Merton the traditional monk of Gethsemani was about to become Merton the contemporary Christian. Much like Bonhoeffer, Merton would have to learn how to relate to the world in a new way — a way which would require a form of obedience that was even more transformative and costly than his initial monastic calling.

At the time of his "Louisville vision," Merton's life changed dramatically. This event marked the end of the first stage of his adult years of monastic vocation and ushered in the second, and last, period of his life's journey. Merton wrote of this paradigmatic shift, "It was like waking from a dream of separateness, of spurious self-isolation in a

---

27. *Ibid.,* 12.

28. My working assumption in relation to both Bonhoeffer and Merton is that there exists more continuity than discontinuity in their lives. However, to speak of turning points makes good sense, for it recognizes change while not denying that ultimately a person's life is of one piece.

special world, the world of renunciation and supposed holiness. The whole illusion of a separate holy existence is a dream."[29] He could no longer conveniently separate himself from the contemporary world. Like Bonhoeffer before him, he realized he would have to write and relate to the world in a new and far more costly and complex manner.

Merton now realized that obedience to God was to bring him closer and closer to a genuine love for a suffering and fragmented world. Just as Bonhoeffer, writing from prison, had viewed *The Cost of Discipleship* as "the end of that path" of living a life of traditional holiness and obedience,[30] so, too, Merton noted the limitations of his earlier work in *The Seven Storey Mountain.*

> Life is not so simple as it once looked in *The Seven Storey Mountain.* Unfortunately, the book was a best-seller and has become a kind of edifying legend or something — that is a dreadful fate. It is a youthful book, too simple, too crude: I'm doing my best to live it down. I rebel against it and maintain my basic human right not to be turned into a Catholic myth for children in parochial schools.[31]

In truth, neither Bonhoeffer nor Merton could, or would, fully reject their previous writings. These works contained too much of their own callings as Christians for that to happen. But they knew instinctively that a deepening commitment to a suffering world demanded further personal transformation — an obedience to God in direct service to the world beyond church and monastery.

With his new commitment, Merton's writings exploded in a rich literary output during the later 1950s and early 1960s. He addressed the most pressing social problems of his day. According to Paul Wilkes, "Once he [Merton] was again aware of the pains and struggles of the world outside, he wrote forthrightly about the antiwar and civil rights movements, the nuclear arms buildup, and the crucial need for peace and justice in the modern world."[32] These writings, which often criticized

29. Merton, *Conjectures,* 157.

30. *LPP,* 369.

31. This quotation is taken from *Merton: A Film Biography,* produced by Paul Wilkes and Audrey L. Glynn and distributed by First Run Features, 153 Waverly Place, New York, NY 10014.

32. Paul Wilkes, ed., *Merton: By Those Who Knew Him Best* (San Francisco: Harper and Row, 1984), xvi.

the church's timidity in addressing issues of peace and justice, placed Merton directly in conflict with his own ecclesiastical authorities.

When Merton was silenced by his order's censors in the early 1960s, it was clearly because he had disturbed the conservative Catholic establishment. He insisted that peacemaking is a religious obligation and not one option among many for Christian people. Because of this, Merton was forbidden to publish his completed manuscript called *Peace in the Post-Christian Era.*[33] (It has yet to see the light of day.) He had faced censorship before within the Trappist order, and had been silenced in the 1950s, when it was felt his spiritual life needed a rest from writing. But this time it was different. Many inside and outside the church accused Merton of being a Communist, primarily because of his early and persistent opposition to the war in Vietnam. According to Merton himself, the abbot general in Rome had been informed by the F.B.I. that this misguided monk was being used by Communists.[34]

It is in response to his silencing that we gain insight into Merton's transformed understanding of what obedience to God would involve in the complexities of the larger world outside the monastery. True to his monastic vows of obedience, Merton publicly accepted the censorship and silencing. But privately he did not. In a clandestine plan, he permitted his correspondence with personal friends to be mimeographed and distributed to hundreds as the "Cold War letters." He also published in the *Catholic Worker* under other names. According to James Forest, editor at the time, Merton became "the parish priest of the Catholic Peace Movement."[35] All of this was quite remarkable for a cloistered monk living in the hills of Kentucky.

Transforming Obedience and Freedom

Merton, like Bonhoeffer, had arrived at a point where to stand fast in obedience meant to move forward in responsible action. True obedience for Merton, in his new-found public voice, demanded acts of both obedience and disobedience. He had to place his credibility as a Christian monk in question. Unusual times demanded uncommon responses, and

33. *Ibid.,* 59.
34. *Ibid.,* 59.
35. *Ibid.,* 47.

Merton was quicker than most to recognize the prophetic tenor of his day. Like Bonhoeffer, he realized that responsible persons could not permit themselves to be worn out by daily conflicts over duties and decisions. But in response to the big picture, extraordinary responses were indeed necessary — along with thoughtful strategies. Using Bonhoeffer's language, Merton sensed that he "stood at a turning-point in history" in which "something new was emerging." He wrote in the early 1960s:

> We are living in the greatest revolution in history — a huge, spontaneous upheaval of the entire human race; not the revolution planned and carried out by any particular party, race, or nation, but a deep, elemental boiling over of all the inner contradictions that have ever been in man, a revelation of the chaotic forces inside everybody. This is not something we have chosen, nor is it something we are free to avoid.[36]

In 1965 Merton gained approval for the publication of *Conjectures of a Guilty Bystander*, perhaps the most representative piece of his new writings. This work brought Merton the contemporary closer to Bonhoeffer the contemporary. Derived from his personal notebooks kept since 1956, *Conjectures* drew directly upon insights from Bonhoeffer's *Ethics* and his *Letters and Papers from Prison*. It reveals to us a transformed Merton. His years as a "petulant ascetic" had passed, and now his transformed obedience linked him in solidarity with movements for peace and justice throughout God's wider world.

In Merton's words, the writings in *Conjectures* "are not of the intimate and introspective kind that go to make up a spiritual journey." This would have been the earlier Merton. Rather, represented here are notes which he said "add up to a personal vision of the world in the 1960s."[37] Like Bonhoeffer in his prison letters, Merton had come to reject all simple answers in response to the complexity of the present situation. He now reasoned, "I think a man is known better by his questions than by his answers." Indeed, for Merton, the sort of questions asked in a time of "spontaneous upheaval" become living indicators of how involved the questioner was willing to be in the present sufferings. Merton argued,

36. Merton, *Conjectures,* 66-67.
37. *Ibid.,* 1.

"To make known one's questions is, no doubt, to come out in the open oneself."[38] Without doubt, the questions asked do disclose whether the questioner is prepared to deal concretely with contemporary reality.

In his most important chapter in *Conjectures,* Merton quoted freely from Bonhoeffer. He bemoaned what Bonhoeffer referred to as "the failure of reasonable people to perceive either the depths of evil or the depth of the holy."[39] Sounding a great deal like Bonhoeffer, Merton continued, "We are living under a tyranny of untruth which confirms itself in power and establishes a more and more total control over men in proportion as they convince themselves they are resisting evil."[40] Noting the insanity of the nuclear arms race, the rampant violence in American society, and America's racism and brutal escalation of the war in Vietnam, Merton found few in his Catholic tradition willing to stand firm against the particular "masquerade of evil" he confronted in American militarism abroad and racism at home. In short, Merton had discovered Bonhoeffer's observation that most "reasonable people" would rather acquiesce to the "tyranny of untruth" than ask the hard questions which would uncover the Lie.

Ultimately, the issue of obedience was related to the question of freedom. Genuine freedom for Bonhoeffer and for Merton could only be found on the other side of transforming obedience. Freedom for self and for others was located in responsible, albeit oftentimes ambiguous, actions. In the final analysis, a transforming obedience led to a liberating freedom on both the personal and societal level. Merton, influenced by Bonhoeffer, expressed it this way:

> Freedom from domination, freedon to live one's own spiritual life, freedom to seek the highest truth, unabashed by any human presence or any collective demand, the ability to say one's own "yes" and one's own "no" and not merely to echo the "yes" and the "no" of state, party, corporation, army, or system. This is inseparable from authentic religion.[41]

Three years after the publication of these words on obedience and freedom, Thomas Merton was dead. In 1968 he died an accidental death

38. *Ibid.,* 1.
39. *Ibid.,* 62.
40. *Ibid.,* 68.
41. *Ibid.,* 90.

of electrocution in Bangkok while attending a conference of Catholic and Buddhist monks. By this time, Merton the contemporary had expanded his horizons to encounter men and women of goodwill in numerous religious traditions. Just as Bonhoeffer's peace efforts had led him to reach out to the European and American ecumenical communities, Merton, at the close of his life, reached out in peace to a broader global community.

In his address to the Bangkok conference on the day of his death, Merton spoke of how the contemplative life must "come of age" in an ever deepening form of obedient engagement with the world. He told the story of a Tibetan monk and abbot who was forced to flee his country because of a communist takeover. This monastic leader asked a nearby abbot friend what to do. Merton reported that the reply came back, "From now on, Brother, everybody stands on his own feet." Merton then told the conferees, "If you forget everything else that has been said, I would suggest you remember this for the future. 'From now on, everybody stands on his own feet.'"[42] This, according to Merton, "is what Buddhism is about, what Christianity is about — if you understand it in terms of grace."[43]

Here is the answer to who stands fast: it is the same for Bonhoeffer and Merton. The one who stands fast is the responsible person who stands in the freedom of authentic faith — a faith that prompts obedience to God which is transformative and costly, and in the end, a faith which is joyous beyond imagination. I am convinced that Merton, if he could, would have shared in the words attributed to Bonhoeffer by a fellow prisoner shortly before his death, "This is the end — for me the beginning of life."[44] These two men who, early in their religious vocations, had set out to become saints or something like that, discovered near the end of their lives through acts of transforming obedience a truth far more redemptive than saintliness, namely, the liberating experience of becoming fully human and, thereby, completely free. Obedience, and its attendant freedom, knows in this life no final resolution, only transformations.

42. Thomas Merton, *The Asian Journal of Thomas Merton* (New York: New Directions Books, 1973), 338.

43. *Ibid.*, 338.

44. Bethge, *Dietrich Bonhoeffer*, 830.

Addendum

In the personal sphere, Bonhoeffer's engagement to Maria von Wedemeyer shortly before his imprisonment signaled a "coming of age" within his own life. Entering into this relationship helped Bonhoeffer gain a greater sense of his own humanity and the moral and spiritual complexities which an intimate, loving relationship brings. As Bethge has observed in his postscript to the recently published *Love Letters from Cell 92*, ". . . Dietrich's and Maria's coming together was a prelude to those words which, in the summer of 1944, brought forth a liberated, life-affirming theology whose influence has been more profound and far-reaching than anyone would have suspected."[45]

In a real sense, it could be argued that Maria's influence upon Dietrich was part and parcel of his turning to the world as a contemporary Christian. In a liberating and life-affirming way, she helped him to see the world differently.

It is tempting to argue a similar case for Thomas Merton, who close to the end of his life fell in love with a student nurse. She cared for him at the time of his convalescence from back surgery. This unusual turn of events for the monk from Gethsemani complicated Merton's life in a manner that made him much more sensitive to life's ambiguities. In this relationship, with his own humanity painfully apparent, Merton drew closer to the contemporary world.

In both cases, these mostly self-confident men were greatly humanized by the women they loved and who loved them. They found the completion of their own humanity in what they were able to receive and give in these relationships. Certainly, this whole matter requires further careful reflection.

---

45. Ruth-Alice Bismarck and Ulrich Kabitz, ed., *Love Letters from Cell 92* (Nashville: Abingdon Press, 1994), 366.

The Enemy and Righteous Action: A Hermeneutical Reassessment

HANS DIRK VAN HOOGSTRATEN

Fundamentally, the experience of historical tradition reaches far beyond those aspects of it that can be objectively investigated. It is true or untrue not only in the sense concerning which historical criticism decides, but always mediates truth in which one must try to share.[1]

During certain episodes of history, at certain places, the social atmosphere is saturated with ideology: nationalism, racism, national security, or (even acknowledged) self-interest. State or church, sometimes both, can exercise an all-embracing ideological power. Dietrich Bonhoeffer happened to live in such an era, in the era of the German National-Socialist State. In such a dictatorial society, the dictator and others in power who surround him are omnipresent in daily life as well as in people's consciousness. For those who feel comfortable under the dictator's guidance and control he is a godsend, friend, or father. For those who feel uncomfortable, however, he is the very opposite. In this context, liberation means becoming free from this all-embracing power, from life's total control, from Big Brother's watching eye.

When Bonhoeffer decided to join the resistance group which planned to assassinate the *Führer*, he had a clear image of Hitler as *the*

---

1. Hans-Georg Gadamer, *Truth and Method* (New York: Continuum, 1994), xxiii.

175

enemy of the German people, of humanity, and of God. It was, of course, very dangerous to communicate his opinion that the "generally honoured and worshipped German Leader," this "representative of the German people and race, the *Volksgemeinschaft*," had to be radically reinterpreted as the incarnation of evil.[2] Despite the fact that this view appeared to be anti-patriotic, it was precisely the opposite; though it looked like a revolution against the true Lutheran belief, it was actually a reintroduction of Martin Luther's doctrine concerning the killing of the "insane" tyrant.

For Bonhoeffer this was the political form of "righteous action" which had to be continuously accompanied by prayer. As he observed in *Letters and Papers from Prison*. ". . . our being Christians today will be limited to two things: prayer and righteous action." This represents, from Bonhoeffer's point of view, a radical new beginning: "All Christian thinking, speaking, and organizing must be born anew out of this prayer and action."[3] "Righteous action" in a situation of ultimate danger and destruction of traditional values and common norms, namely, in an apocalyptic world, presupposes a deep reflection of one's relation to the enemy in the light (and space) of God's covenantal relation with human beings. This is, as Bonhoeffer repeatedly calls it, "prayer."

The Captive God

Questions concerning the enemy, nationalism, religion, and "righteous action" are parts of a tricky field — especially when these concepts are ideologically interconnected. This is perfectly clear, for example, in the traditional link between throne and altar. Once Christian faith became a firm state ideology under the Roman emperor Constantine the Great, the enemy of Rome was identified as Christ's enemy, and thus could be named Total Evil, which had to be erased *in God's name* and *for God's sake.* The beginning of the so-called Constantinian Era marks the start of a long and continuing tradition, in which western supremacy, arrogance, and colonialism were identified with the occidental inheritance of the gospel of Jesus Christ. The crusades were the most notorious historical examples until the more recent identification of America as "God's own country" and Soviet Russia as the "empire of evil." As is well known, Columbus understood his

2. Cf. *Ethics,* 71-74: "The Despiser of Men."
3. *LPP,* 300.

expedition to the west as a new crusade, and he hoped such expeditions would furnish money for new crusades to the Holy Land.[4] Columbus's deepest motivation was the defence and expansion of the Holy Catholic Spanish Empire; he saw himself, thus, as giving his life for Christ's sake.

These political-incarnational claims have often functioned as a kind of framework for "Christian life." In premodern as well as in modern times, nature and culture have been interpreted as God's creational expressions. In medieval thought, it was quite common to identify natural law as *the* divine law.[5] As long as the premodern church controlled society and *homo religiosus* was the dominant type of humanity, God's omnipresence and his visible representation on earth were self-evident. This situation continued during the western Enlightenment, but in a more hidden, less religious way. Among others, the philosopher Friedrich Hegel presented a model of world history which was derived from trinitarian doctrine, shamelessly declaring enlightened western culture *(die Bürgerliche Gesellschaft)* to be the Spirit's emanation. Most interesting in this context is the perennial identification of western culture as a kind of Third Empire — a notion which found its perverse realization in the Nazis' Third Reich.[6] We all know what this meant for people who were considered enemies of the so-called "Holy Empire."

Dialectical Theology's Radical Claim

The twentieth century's dialectical theology, as initiated by Karl Barth, may be considered a liberating force from the God-enclosing claims of western "Christian" culture. In order to ensure the freedom of God to be God, such an effort was necessary. The weakness in this theology was a lack of interest in the human condition in the broad sense of the word. "The world is in some degree made to depend on itself and left to its own devices," as Bonhoeffer suggests in his letter from 5 May 1944, discussing what he takes to be Barth's "positivism of revelation" *(Offenbarungspositivismus).*[7]

---

4. Thwedan Todorov, *Die Eroberung Amerikas: Das Problem des Anderen* (Suhrkamp, 1982), 19.
5. R. Tuck, *Natural Rights Theories: Their Origin and Development* (Cambridge: Cambridge University Press, 1979).
6. K. Löwith, *The Meaning of History* (Chicago: University of Chicago Press, 1949).
7. *LPP,* 286.

Bonhoeffer's critical questioning of Barth can be regarded as the conclusion of his long journey with Barth in which both of them tried to save God's "aseity," along with his "pro-meity."[8] Bonhoeffer agreed with Barth's claim that God's Word is totally free from and for humans. The history of the covenant *(Bundesgeschichte)* speaks of "God in search of humanity," and not the other way around. The initiative is on God's side, and there is no mediation *(Vermittlung)* but that of Jesus Christ, the incarnate Word of God. No human institution, nature, or political and ecclesiastical power is entitled to replace or to substitute for this divine Word. The only appropriate response is discipleship in action, *Nachfolge.* In other words, whoever advocates human initiative places himself outside the covenant. The first hermeneutical task for a dialectical theologian is to restore the genuine dialectic: God's pure Word and the human "response." Barth wanted to separate the divine-human communication from the realm of human institutions and philosophy, to eschew what he took to be "natural theology."

Rather naively, Barth was convinced that the Word of God would rediscover its critical way in the world once it was freed and purified from the human inclination to keep it under control, for instance by institutionalizing it in church and in social institutions. Two main problems appeared: in the first place, Christian culture and natural theology were not taken seriously as social and ideological forces; and secondly, the new connection between the once privileged Word of God and traditional human words, actions, and institutions was highly problematic. As a kind of faithful solution, dialectical theology put forward with all its theological strength the Christian congregation as community (the *Gemeinde* as *Gemeinschaft*), but it failed sufficiently to clarify its sociological and social-psychological position.

Bonhoeffer's Intervention: Sociality and Morality

Emphasizing the "sociology of the Church" at the beginning of his theological writing,[9] Bonhoeffer showed an awareness of this weak spot

8. Charles Marsh, *Reclaiming Dietrich Bonhoeffer: The Promise of His Theology* (Oxford: Oxford University Press, 1994).

9. Cf. *Sanctorum Communio's* subtitle: *Dogmatische Untersuchung zur Soziologie der Kirche.*

in dialectical theology concerning the relation between God's revelation and human reality. Bonhoeffer fully agreed with Barth that liberal theology was a form of betrayal of the divine Word's original critical power, because it risked an increasing identification of civil society's cultural values and political ideology with God's creation and revelation. The only way to avoid such an error seemed to be the unconditional and total revelation of God in Jesus Christ, including the classical history of salvation *(Heilsgeschichte)*. This strong accent included a reservation concerning incarnation: the only place and time in which God invaded human history was in the person of Jesus Christ, which is realized in the *Gemeinde:* "Christ existing as *Gemeinde.*"

In many of his subsequent writings, Bonhoeffer continued to stress the connection of this indicative with the imperative, which meant that no identification exists without moral agency. In *The Cost of Discipleship* Bonhoeffer unequivocally condemned what he called "cheap grace": redemption means freedom from sin and from God's judgment, but this does not preempt *action*. Such penultimate action is, as a consequence of God's ultimate reality of justification, directed to the kingdom of God, the ultimate reality.

Here we meet an interesting tension in Bonhoeffer's theological-social thought, one which is rooted in Barth's "triumph of grace."[10] After having freed God from human possessiveness, from personal as well as political claims, the *chosen* human community seems to have lost its real connection with society as well as with nature. It is as if the community of Christ-believers were lifted into heaven, losing its ties with everyday earthly life. Here we are confronted with the age-old dilemma of election: does the chosen people's position include a setting apart (the *holy* people of God's covenant) from normal history? (And does election demand that the "world" perish under God's judgment?) In other words: Which is the relation—if there is any—between world history *(Weltgeschichte)* and the history of salvation *(Heilsgeschichte)?*

---

10. See G. C. Berkouwer, *De triomf der genade in Karl Barths theologie* (Kampen: J. H. Kok, 1954).

A Question of Hermeneutics

For Barth, as for Bonhoeffer, everything depended on the interpretation of the Bible as God's Word; if anywhere, an answer to this kind of question could be found there. The biblical narrative, for both theologians, was not merely a source from which we derive our moral and religious principles, but confronts our very reality; we, as Christian believers, are part of the story — just as Christ is present among the Old Testament people of God. Here we could suspect a blind spot in dialectical theology because the person's sociological, psychological, "worldly" existence is hardly part of the hermeneutical operation. It is only the person as justified sinner who has, *as such*, access to the Scriptures; redemption functions as *the* hermeneutical key. This kind of circular reasoning is typical of the doctrine of *Heilsgeschichte*.

I want to excavate the hermeneutical question, discussing on the one hand the almost blind conviction of Christ's saving/redeeming work as the critical Word in a godless world, and, on the other hand, the huge task of rethinking and reinterpreting biblical and theological concepts from a different hermeneutical viewpoint.

In order to recover the "lost half" of hermeneutics, Bonhoeffer had to take real, worldly relations seriously. "The world in sin" could no longer be summoned to *metanoia* while its major structural as well as personal problems were excluded from consideration. Up until his *Ethics* Bonhoeffer claimed a superior theological reality: Christ as *the* reality, to which the world was simply adjusted (indicative), and consequently had to adjust (imperative). Here is a representative quotation from the *Ethics*:

> It is from the real human being, whose name is Jesus Christ, that all factual reality derives its ultimate annulment *(Aufhebung)*, its justification and its ultimate contradiction *(Widerspruch)*, its ultimate affirmation and its ultimate negation. . . . In Jesus Christ, the real man, the whole of reality is taken up and comprised together; in him it has its origin, its essence and its goal.[11]

In his prison reflections, Bonhoeffer engaged in hermeneutical reassessment concerning this foundation of reality. As he wrestled with

---

11. *Ethics,* 229f.

trying to take the world-come-of-age seriously, he became convinced of the necessity of getting one's hands dirty. He had come to understand that it was impossible to be a saint, but also that it was impossible to be a redeemed sinner without action in a grim, dangerous world. The preciousness of grace thus demands suffering through righteous action.

The hermeneutical dilemma becomes perfectly clear in the example of the enemy, including the enemy's image and location. Joining several classic writers, Bonhoeffer opts in his pre-prison writings for a christological or Christocentric approach to the Old Testament. The traditional scheme of interpretation, which Bonhoeffer applies, for example, in his lectures on Genesis 1–3 (published as *Creation and Fall*) is quite simple. Adam's fall provoked humanity's separation from its original oneness with God. Sin caused an unbridgeable rupture which could only be restored by Christ's sacrifice on Golgotha. This event of salvation rules human life, and as such it has a universal meaning. Here, we are confronted with a metaphysical, inner-trinitarian state of affairs, which determines and interprets history. In God's history with Israel the coming of the Messiah Jesus Christ is foreshadowed. All that matters is Christ's reconciling work — God carrying away humanity's sins, judging God's own beloved Son. As Christ was the absolute temporal and local center of world history, his disciples and believers became the chosen people. Reading the Hebrew Bible, the Christian community was looking backward: the *whole* Bible had to be considered the revelational book of God *in Christ.*

If we want to understand Bonhoeffer's interpretation of the Old Testament, we need this background, which now may strike us as somewhat imperialistic. Why "imperialistic?" Because the Christian community is proclaimed to be the one and only *Gestaltung* of Christ in the world and overrules as such Israel as God's "firstborn son." Bonhoeffer later changes this approach, but here, in his biblical work of the 1930s, he is part of a long Christian tradition of "colonization." His studies in the Psalms exemplify this attitude. For that reason it may be useful to have a look at Bonhoeffer's dealing with the Psalms, as he did on several occasions between 1935 and 1940.

In the study *Christus in den Psalmen*[12] Bonhoeffer presents several

---

12. *Das gemeinsame Leben* and *Das Gebutbuch der Bibel,* ed. Gerhard L. Müller and Albrecht Schönherr, *DBW,* vol. 5 (Munich: Chr. Kaiser, 1987). English translation: *Life Together* and *Prayerbook of the Bible, DBWE,* vol. 5.

methodological points, which I summarize here in order to give an impression of the christological colonization of this Hebrew hymnbook:

> The Psalms, as the prayer of Jesus Christ's community *(Gemeinde)*, show us the life and suffering of Jesus Christ himself. Our prayer is not a standard for the Psalms, but vice versa. So, guided by the Psalms, our prayer is part of Christ's accomplishing the history of salvation.
>
> The individual is always part of the community, so his or her prayer is *Gemeinde* prayer. This aspect is important in *Life Together:* the individual prayer is part of a common confession — and thus of Christ himself.
>
> The Psalter is simultaneously Word of God and human word. God connected himself with this human word in Christ. God is the one who speaks and who listens. The "I" in the Psalms is Christ's voice in the Old Testament *Gemeinde.* In the Psalms Christ is at the same time the announced, the promised, the believed, and the denied one.
>
> In the godless people, Christ himself says: "Let him be crucified." We, the believers, are the ones who want to crucify Christ, but we are simultaneously the blessed ones. Bonhoeffer speaks expressively of the *"community of the cross."*

Who Is the Enemy and Where Is He Hiding?

In this context, Bonhoeffer explains the Psalms of vengeance and hatred against the enemy as interpretations of Christ's suffering for sin. The enemy is identified as sin. Bonhoeffer joins here a major line of *Christian* interpretation of the Old Testament which is already present in St. Augustine and continues until recent times.

Among the variety of expositors Luther is noteworthy; he considered the enemies as those forces which cause illness or temptations. Later Lutheranism distinguished *tentationes corporales,* such as illness and poverty, and *tentationes spirituales,* such as the tension between the holy God and fallen humanity.[13] In his struggle with these "enemies," the

---

13. Cf. Guido Fuchs, *Die christliche Deutung der Feinde in den Psalmen, dargestellt in den Psalmliedern Nikolaus Selneckers* (Würzburg, 1986).

Christian claims Christ's help, because the human struggle with the enemy is the struggle of Christ with humanity's sin, which is finally decided at the Cross. Bonhoeffer participates in this tradition of God's revelation in Christ's *pro-meity* when he discusses "the enemy" in the Psalms.

Localizing the Christian community and its enemies in the context of the history of salvation, Bonhoeffer avoids having to countenance a realistic confrontation with the enemy. In the period of resistance, however, he could not go on spiritualizing social relations. He then began to advocate a different relation between the Bible's two parts: the New Testament should give way to the Old; the nonreligious interpretation of theological concepts like creation, redemption, and resurrection should be brought into line with the Old Testament. "Unlike the other oriental religions," Bonhoeffer says, "the faith of the Old Testament isn't a religion of redemption. It's true that Christianity has always been regarded as a religion of redemption. But isn't this a cardinal error, which separates Christ from the Old Testament and interprets him on the lines of the myths about redemption?"[14] Bonhoeffer admits that redemption *is* important in the Old Testament. But redemption from enemies such as Egypt or Babylon are *historical* redemptions: "Israel is delivered out of Egypt so that it may live before God as God's people on earth."[15]

We are dealing here with a subtle but important difference in emphasis. In the letters from prison, Bonhoeffer in a certain way continues to localize the enemy within the reach of God's covenant, just as he did in the study of the Psalms.[16] This is a dominant theological position, which prevents and criticizes all kinds of hostility and war, emanating from human capriciousness, power, and selfish interests. The difference between the traditional Christian *spiritual* and the Old Testament *social* interpretation of the enemy is the historical *gestalt* of the enemy, *hic et nunc*. The acknowledgment of this difference provokes profound consequences, as may be evident in Bonhoeffer's theologically reflected engagement when he writes that "Our earlier words are . . . bound to lose their force and cease, and our being Christians today will be limited to two things: prayer and righteous action among men," and

---

14. *LPP*, 336.
15. *Ibid.*, 336.
16. *Das Gebutbuch der Bibel*, 128-30.

that "all Christian thinking, speaking, and organising must be born anew out of this prayer and action."[17]

. Once faced with the Third Reich's Mephistophelian reality of power and anguish, Bonhoeffer had no other choice than localizing the enemy in the political relations of his time. *Righteous action* meant fighting this enemy, who claimed to be the people's chosen leader. The pretension of being One People with One Leader, built on the ideological identification of the *Reich* with God's Kingdom (the "Third Reich of God's Spirit"), turned out to be endangering humanity. Focusing on the enemy in such a direct, inescapable manner brought about an unavoidable change of direction.

In Bonhoeffer's own historical context, the enemy was not widely recognized; the *Führer*-question (and all that it represents) was, on the contrary, a cause of deep controversy in the German consciousness, which continued to provoke profound differences up until long after the war. This is what happens when a generally accepted spiritual reality is converted into a controversial social *gestalt*. Claiming a strong position in the divine-human covenantal relationship while revolting against the *Reich* (prayer and action), Bonhoeffer intensifies the tension.

All this entitles us to identify Bonhoeffer as a representative of political theology in the new sense of the word, as claimed, for example, by J. B. Metz.[18] Bonhoeffer's position is opposed to that of his contemporary, Karl Schmitt, who loosens the enemy from God's covenant, thus providing the enemy with the quality of totality. Schmitt calls it "just and sensible" when a "pre-existent, unchangeable, real and total enmity provokes the divine judgement of a total war."[19] As a jurist and an author of books on political theology, Schmitt advances the National-Socialist view of the enemy — this being exactly the perspective Bonhoeffer fights against as *the* threatening enemy of humanity.

There is a sharp contrast between Schmitt's and Bonhoeffer's interpretation of "political theology." Continually speaking in terms of power, war, and killing, Schmitt presents the dictator as God's representative, fighting the collective enemy in cases of supreme seriousness. Bonhoeffer

17. *LPP,* 300.

18. Johannes Baptist Metz, *Faith in History and Society: Towards a Practical Fundamental Theology* (New York: Seabury, 1980).

19. Karl Schmitt, "Totaler Feind, totaler Krieg, totaler Staat" (1937), in *Positionen und Begriffe im Kampf mit Weimar-Genf-Versailles* (Hamburg, 1940), 239.

prefers to highlight God's superior and victorious action accomplished through vulnerability and weakness. God's representation and *Gestaltung* should be freed from all claims of "natural theology," which is so often identified with the Christian Occident as God's incarnation. This brings us to our final observation concerning Bonhoeffer's biblical hermeneutics.

God's Vulnerable and Redeeming Presence

This hermeneutical reassessment concerns the deep, intense, tension that belief in God is non-belief in generally accepted worldly power and power-structures, which implies action pro and con. The being-there *for* others involves resistance and action against the enemies of humanity. Concerning the fundamental question: "What is the relation — if there is any — between world history *(Weltgeschichte)* and the history of salvation *(Heilsgeschichte)*," we can adopt an ontological approach: we have to overcome the theological tendency to avoid seeing God as being present in the facts, socially as well as existentially. At the same time we need to question the inextricably knitting together of God and ideological power in "the twentieth-century myth."

In his prison letters, Bonhoeffer extends the meaning of his Christocentric approach to reality in two ways. On the one hand, he sees God as present in the facts; on the other hand, he sees God as revealing himself in the man Jesus Christ. This twofold aspect of divine omnipresence asks for a hermeneutical reassessment. God's challenging covenantal relation is no longer confined to the existential "promeity" which finds its context in the I-Thou relation *(Sanctorum Communio)*, and which is focused on the justification of the person. The question of a much broader engagement is at stake when Bonhoeffer writes on the enormous problem of "resistance" and "submission" *(Widerstand und Ergebung)*, 21 February 1944:

> We must *confront* fate . . . as resolutely as we *submit* to it at the right time. One can speak of "guidance" only on the other side of that twofold process, with God meeting us no longer as "thou," but also "disguised" in the "I"; so in the last resort my question is how we are to find the "Thou" in the "It" (i.e. fate), or, in other words, how does "fate" really become "guidance."[20]

20. *LPP*, 217.

Here we see that Bonhoeffer is unwilling to abandon the covenant; under no circumstance would he submit to the pull of the neo-pagan approach of historical events as nature's (blind) fate. World history, for him, cannot and should not be disconnected from the history of God with "his" humanity, of which Israel was the first-born witness![21]

Joining these thoughts with reflection on God's presence in Christ, Bonhoeffer describes in his 18 July 1944 letter, a few days before the assassination-effort, this all-empowering divine act:

> That is *metanoia:* not in the first place thinking about one's own needs, problems, sins, and fears, but allowing oneself to be caught up into the way of Jesus Christ, into the messianic event, thus fulfilling Isa. 53. Therefore, "believe in the gospel," or, in the words of John the Baptist, "Behold, the Lamb of God, who takes away the sin of the world" (John 1:29). (By the way, Jeremias has recently asserted that the Aramaic word for "lamb" may also be translated "servant"; very appropriate in view of Isa. 53!)[22]

Jesus Christ as the suffering servant is here not primarily the one who defeats human sin at the cross (the "enemy" spoken of in the Psalms) in a metaphysical, mythological wrestling between the archetypal Father and his Son in a judicial setting. God's presence is made as overwhelming and omnipresent as "the twentieth-century myth." In his famous description of the confrontation of weakness with power, Bonhoeffer opposes, in a competitive way, the biblical God in Christ with the *Führer* as a pagan god's representative. Bonhoeffer explicitly states, "He [Christ] is weak and powerless in the world, and this is precisely the way, the only way, in which he is with us and helps us."

Bonhoeffer himself enters the "battlefield of salvation," which is located in a historical time and a geographical space: National-Socialist Germany with its absolute state and dictatorial claims. God's affair with humanity definitely moves from heaven to earth, from metaphysics to history, from religion to faith. And so, Bonhoeffer draws near to the realistic meaning of "costly grace": no "letters from prison" without "cost of discipleship" (and, for a faithful understanding of the whole Bonhoeffer, the contrary may also be said).

This shift in Bonhoeffer's thought calls for a hermeneutical re-

---

21. Cf. references to Don Quixote and Sancha Panza, *ibid.*
22. *LPP*, 361f.

assessment. The "polemical oneness" of the imagined true and false gods is decisive here. What do people experience on a shallow and on a deep level? How can we, as members of the same tradition, share the good and the bad, their experience of grandeur and decay, despair and consolation? In order to understand Bonhoeffer's text and the text behind the text, we should be aware of the historical circumstances, the strong feelings of nationalism, victory, *Deutschland über Alles,* and the feelings behind these feelings, the deeper human reality in the wings.

The situation in the Third Reich from its very beginning, but especially during the last years of the war, could be described as follows. Covering the entire social as well as individual life, Hitler's dictatorial power denied an underlying weakness. Ideology was deaf to the omnipresent cry of anxiety and despair. In short: a false objective truth of the eternal *Reich* darkened the real human subjective truth of instability, disorder, faltering perspective, and aimlessness.

In this situation, the only way to experience God is in God's antipower, God's being-there for and with the suffering other. This hermeneutical experience, however, presupposes the human capacity to abandon the omnipotent Father, God as the Great Dictator, along with divine representatives like the *Führer* and his servants. Under these conditions the enemy of power, the Suffering Servant, speaks powerfully against the generally accepted power. In his suffering the servant accuses. This is the context in which we should read Bonhoeffer's famous words in his 16 July 1944 letter:

> So our coming of age leads us to a true recognition of our situation before God. God would have us know that we must live as men who manage our lives without him. The God who is with us is the God who forsakes us (Mark 15,34). The God who lets us live in the world without the working hypothesis of God is the God before whom we stand continually. Before God and with God we live without God. God lets himself be pushed out of the world on to the cross. He is weak and powerless in the world, and this is precisely the way, the only way, in which he is with us and helps us. Mark 8,17 makes it quite clear that Christ helps us, not by virtue of his omnipotence, but by virtue of his weakness and suffering.

Bonhoeffer continues:

> Man's religiosity makes him look in his distress to the power of God in the world: God is the *deus ex machina.* The Bible directs man to

God's powerlessness and suffering; only the suffering God can help. To that extent we may say that the development to the world's coming of age, outlined above, which has done away with a false conception of God, opens up a way of seeing the God of the Bible, who wins power and space in the world by his weakness. This will probably be the starting point for our "secular interpretation."[23]

This very vulnerable judging presence of the powerless God dismantles the image of the victorious, crusade-like Christ who simply exterminates his enemies, encouraging his disciples to anticipate the apocalypse by penultimate religious and ethnic cleansing. This crusade-like view of the execution of divine power is very different from the perspective Bonhoeffer encourages: "seeing the God of the Bible, who wins power and space in the world by his weakness."

All citizens of Nazi Germany were objects of the life-threatening control of the totalitarian state. Most of them joined the oppressing forces, serving the system ideologically, whether in the military or the bureaucracy. The *Führer*'s claims were metaphysical in nature. Based on fear and terror, these claims provoked a religious-obedient attitude. A few refused to be part of the system. They were not free from fear, but, for some reason, their hope and their indignation overruled the slavish, fearful attitude. Bonhoeffer belonged to the second group, but he was continuously aware of the framework within which hostility and enmity are evident: the covenant-enclosed humanity. This structure underlines the temporal character of these two groups' enmity.

Ongoing Hermeneutical Reassessment

According to Bonhoeffer, prayer and righteous action are the only possible Christian responses in this time of disastrous idolatry. In our context, localization and fighting the enemy mean first of all: recognizing humanity's enemy as God's enemy. For this reason the fixation of God's *gestalt* in the historical situation is extremely important. One should not identify the enemy of Christianity or the church or the believer as God's enemy. The fundamental truth of God's revelation is his incarnation in the weak, the suffering, those who lack power. What we need is a

23. *Ibid.*, 360f.

hermeneutical fusion of horizons: we are charged with the task of identifying the social and individual victims of the power system *as if* Israel still has to be redeemed from Egypt, *as if* Christ is crucified again. The Bible's approach to history aims at a liberation from the old relations, resulting in a new situation, in which former enemies can cooperate.

The *kairos* moment often implies an apocalyptic, destructive fight. But notice the notion of *moment* here, indicating a transition to a new situation, which is called resurrection from death, or the promised land. People are invited to share in the new situation.

We live in a different situation from that in which Bonhoeffer found himself, but the same option is valid. The post-communist or post-apartheid situation requires the establishment of democracy, which often means discourse and cooperation between former enemies, who, to say the least, still do not like each other. The establishment of a different state and social system often prompts the emergence of new enemies of humanity, a situation which should be taken as seriously *as if* God was involved. The capitalist world is far from imposing a definite ban on the enemy. The capitalist system continues to practice a kind of apartheid wherever it rules, *because* capitalism implies the setting apart of the system's enemies, people and other species, who do not (and cannot) contribute to the system's advantage. Those who frustrate a smooth, profitable organization are considered the system's enemies. South African as well as Latin American liberation theologians are very clear about this state of affairs. Pamphlets like *The Kairos Document* and *The Road to Damascus*[24] typically reverse the argument: For whom is capitalism, as a system of idolatry, the enemy? The answer is clear: the excluded people, who happen to be God's beloved children. The ultimate election, which transcends human possibilities, is revealed by Jesus' being there for others — his righteous action.

---

24. *The Kairos Document: A Challenge to the Churches* (Braamfontein, South Africa: Institute for Contextual Theology, 1986); *The Road to Damascus: Kairos and Conversion* (Johannesburg: Skotaville, 1989).

The Priority of the Other: Ethics in Africa —
Perspectives from Bonhoeffer and Levinas

ELIAS BONGMBA

Emmanuel Levinas and Dietrich Bonhoeffer have responded to the human situation in at least two comparable ways. First, their respective work in philosophy and theology can be read as a response to the tragic legacy of unbridled twentieth-century nationalism. Second, their work is a full-scale critique of the transcendental and ontological tradition which, as both argue, has privileged the thinking subject. I see them as pertinent to the issue of ethics in Africa because of Africa's continuing need to address the issues resulting from the excesses of political power and numerous ethnic conflicts. My thesis is that contextual ethics in Africa should posit a radical Other who cannot and should not be violated. Both Levinas and Bonhoeffer offer such a model in their work.

John de Gruchy has pointed out that although ecclesiology was the major concern of Bonhoeffer in *Sanctorum Communio,* his more fundamental concern in that text was to locate theology "in the context of human social and ethical relations in history, rather than in the epistemological framework of post-Kantian philosophy or the individualism of existentialism."[1] Regarding Levinas, Wayne Floyd Jr. has argued that he prioritizes ethics to theory in order that the other's questions might be

<hr/>

1. John de Gruchy, ed., *Dietrich Bonhoeffer: Witness to Jesus Christ* (Minneapolis: Fortress Press, 1991), 4.

addressed and heard by the Same.[2] We are confronted, thus, in both cases, with a new personalism which calls for recognition of otherness as a precondition for ethics while, at the same time, positing within this separateness a radical transcendence of the Other who stands over and above the subject.

Bonhoeffer and Levinas are not, of course, engaged in the same project. It is clear that Levinas articulates his positions on the issue of otherness within the western philosophical tradition and presents ethics as first philosophy.[3] Bonhoeffer,for his part, has analyzed relevant philosophical thinking on the issues in *Act and Being* and in this work he spells out his resolutions from a theological perspective. However, both call us to a new way of dealing with the human situation by seeing first what is Other than self. This Other than self for Levinas is a genuine human Other, while for Bonhoeffer it is a Thou, both human and divine, who, in the case of the God revealed in Jesus Christ, provides the path to a genuine Other. Both perspectives provide a compelling case for rethinking contextual ethics.

There are some obvious differences in the two approaches. First, Levinas's ethics is articulated within the western philosophical tradition as a development and critique of that tradition, while Bonhoeffer's philosophical analysis is a prolegomena to a revitalized theological agenda. Second, the two employ language in a slightly different manner. For example, Levinas employs key terms such as "infinity" and "transcendence" to underscore radical human difference, thus humanizing the Cartesian sublime. Transcendence for Bonhoeffer, or even the notion of the infinite, is closer to Cartesian transcendence — the divine being — even though Bonhoeffer rejects the subjectivity and consciousness that, for the Cartesian thinker, seems to call that transcendence into being.

The discussion that follows has three parts. First, I will review the critique of ontology presented by Levinas and Bonhoeffer — a presentation animated by my reading of *Totality and Infinity* and *Act and Being*. Secondly, I will argue that both Levinas and Bonhoeffer propose the notion of transcendence as a way out of the phenomenological cul-de-sac that has resulted from the path of ontology. Thirdly, in light of this

2. Wayne Floyd Jr., "To Welcome the Other: Totality and Theory in Levinas and Adorno," in *Philosophy and Theology* 4/2 (1989): 145-70.

3. Emmanuel Levinas, *Totality and Infinity: An Essay on Exteriority* (Pittsburgh: Duquesne University Press, 1969).

reading, I will offer some general proposals for the priority of an Other in contextual ethics in an African setting. It will be clear that this is a very focused reading of both thinkers. Dirkie Smit has presented a good review of the Other in Bonhoeffer's writings.[4] My interest in this essay is mainly in the philosophical arguments presented by Levinas and Bonhoeffer.

A Critique of the Excesses of Ontology

As indicated, Levinas and Bonhoeffer both respond to extreme nationalism, challenging directly thought that has glorified *being*, and thus a self-centered subject. They critique Cartesian and post-Kantian subjectivity and the philosophical tradition: Levinas declares that self-centered reflection has forced him to say farewell to Parmenides.[5] He decries the absence of morality and the state of war brought about by totality which dominates the philosophical tradition. Rather than totality, Levinas proposes "Infinity" as a path toward peace, a peace achieved in relationships based not on totality and anonymous historical utterances, but on dialogue with the Other.[6] Levinas defends a subjectivity grounded in the infinity of the Other against a Heideggerian metaphysics of being and the Husserlian horizon of consciousness.[7] According to Levinas, the ontological tradition's "I" needs to be reversed with an Other that is beyond the initiatives of being.[8]

Bonhoeffer launches a critique of "act" (by which he means outward reference), "infinite extensity," which is limited to the consciousness of the subject and discontinuity, and "being," by which he means "self-confinement, infinite intensity, transcendence of the conscious and continuity" of the subject.[9] Bonhoeffer highlights the problem of conflating act and being in the subject to the extent that the "I" or the self becomes the very basis, test, and end of knowledge.[10] He describes

4. Dirkie Smit, "Dietrich Bonhoeffer and 'The Other,'" *Journal of Theology of Southern Africa* 93 (December 1995): 3ff.
5. *Totality and Infinity*.
6. *Ibid.*, 23.
7. Adriaan Peperzak, *To the Other: An Introduction to the Philosophy of Emmanuel Levinas* (West Lafayette: Indiana University Press, 1993), 131.
8. *Totality and Infinity*, 38-39.
9. *AB*, 14.
10. *Ibid.*

Dasein's project, in which understanding is self-understanding, by calling attention to the focus on self in the transcendentalist and idealist traditions. Here, human existence is interpreted as "pure act," Bonhoeffer argues; human understanding is confined within the limits of the self.[11] These traditions put being and knowing on the same level so that, he observes, to know means to know oneself.

What is the problem with this idealist preference for thought which forms what Bonhoeffer calls the "frontier of the general existence in which man [sic] lives . . . ?" For Bonhoeffer two results flow from this idealist concentration on subjective thinking. First, such thinking imposes a self-limitation. Second, it presents what Bonhoeffer characterizes as the great temptation of philosophy, the tendency to promote itself as lord, master, and originary or the "point of departure."[12] In such a process, as Charles Marsh points out for Heidegger, *Dasein*, who has mastered the world, operates through a network of relations that is the world itself where being-in-the-world is constitutive of the being that is there.[13] Thus the world is not merely a simple objectification or something like Kant's *Ding an sich*. According to Marsh, "the world is therefore built within *Dasein*'s understanding as a *referential totality*."[14] As Bonhoeffer observes, "Heidegger has succeeded in forcing act and being into partnership in the concept of *Dasein* — that is to say, the actual decidings of *Dasein* coincide with its given decidedness."[15] The result is that Heidegger interprets being on the basis of temporality and "temporal *Dasein* is always directed upon itself in self-decision."[16]

Although Bonhoeffer demonstrates respect for Heidegger's thought, he sees it as being in accord with idealism or post-Kantian transcendentalism, a connection that has two consequences. First, the thinker, though aware of the world, loses reality. "From the original transcendental thesis has evolved a system characterized by thought's sheer self-transcendentalization or (which comes to the same thing) a monism unadulterated with reality; whether it is styled a system of pure

---

11. *Ibid.*, 22.
12. *Ibid.*, 24, 25.
13. Marsh, *Reclaiming Dietrich Bonhoeffer*, 113.
14. *Ibid.*, 116. Emphasis in the original.
15. *AB*, 64.
16. *Ibid.*

transcendence or pure immanence, the end product is materially the same."[17] Existence under this rubric is "homecoming." Even when *Dasein* comes to terms with its own death, the acknowledgment of that potentiality is always a way of appropriating itself into its own wholeness.[18] It is able to seize its most authentic possibility, which is offered by the existence it enjoys. It can arrive at itself, for it can understand itself. But this means that *Dasein* is included in the world, or rather that the world is included in *Dasein*. This sense of having understood all already does not mean that *Dasein* is not aware of others. *Dasein* is aware of others, but deliberately walks away or thinks itself away from an other in order to actualize its own authenticity. According to *Dasein*, freeing itself from others, it frees them also toward their own authenticity.[19] This is false freedom, however: *Dasein's* project is radically individual and severs inter-personal relations. It eventually loses sight of reality because the world, as we have seen, is constitutive of *Dasein*.

Second, transcendence is lost. According to Bonhoeffer, divine transcendence is lost and the subject falls into the atheism of finitude, leaving no room for revelation or, for that matter, a recognition of the creatureliness of the thinking subject.[20] The transcendence that is lost here is the transcendence of God and of Jesus Christ, who is the ultimate revelation of God to the world.

Levinas, for his part, argues that the priority of ontological thinking leads to totality, and exalts power. Its thematization and organization reduce both the earth and the Other. Although Heidegger decries the dominance of technology, Levinas insists that through thought the subject remains at home in the pre-technological powers of possession.[21] In this light it can be argued that whether one considers Hegel's *Geist* or Heidegger's *Dasein*, what is primary is the thinking subject before whose consciousness all things come for analysis. Accordingly, Levinas claims that the result of ontological thinking is loss of Otherness. War is rediscovered, and ethical life and thought become matters of mere opinion. Furthermore, ontological thinking results in an appropriation of the

---

17. *AB*, 25.

18. *Ibid.*, 61.

19. Charles Marsh, *Reclaiming Dietrich Bonhoeffer: The Promise of His Theology* (Oxford: Oxford University Press), 131.

20. *Ibid.*, 65.

21. *Totality and Infinity*, 45.

Other. Levinas deals with this issue in a critique of Heidegger's notion of being-in-the-world. *Dasein's* care leads to appropriation of otherness and the elements of the world. Levinas argues that ultimately, through contemplation, the subject limits its object. In social relations an existent ought to remain himself or herself.[22]

Thus, Heidegger's *Vorhandenheit* and *Zuhandenheit* do not go far enough because relationships construed as *Zuhandenheit* provide nourishment for *Dasein*. This results in "the transmutation of the Other into the same, which is the essence of enjoyment; an energy that is Other, recognized as Other, we will see as sustaining the very act that is directed upon it, become in enjoyment, my own energy, my strength, me."[23] Such a critique of *Zuhandenheit* targets instrumental and self-gratifying approaches to things. Self-gratification destroys difference and merely reinforces identity. *Dasein* enjoys itself from a base which Levinas calls dwelling, a place where *Dasein* conquers separateness.[24] According to both Levinas and Bonhoeffer, totality eliminates Otherness; ontological transcendental approaches to the world appropriate difference, resulting in a calculative monism which destroys ethics. This approach "comes to grief" and requires a departure from the path of Parmenides.

Recognition of a Transcendent Other

Bonhoeffer and Levinas argue vigorously for the recognition of an Other as a precondition for the possibility of ethics. This other is not projected by the thought of the same but independent of the subject's control. The ontological tradition's tendency toward idealism destroyed "paths towards a clearing" that could have opened "shapes of freedom" signaled in Kant's *Ding an sich* which recognized separateness because, in Kant's formulations, separateness presented a border for reason. Post-Kantian idealist thinkers privileged the subject's consciousness, thus assimilating being in reflection. In Hegel's *Geist* self-consciousness is asserted by consuming what stands in the way. Although slightly different from Husserl's turn to *die Sachen selbts*, objects are brought to the horizon — the consciousness of the thinker — for analysis.

22. *Ibid.*, 109.
23. *Ibid.*, 111.
24. Adriaan Peperzak, *To the Other*, 157.

Bonhoeffer argues that a genuine recognition of Otherness cannot be grounded on neo-Kantian transcendentalism because an *a priori* synthesis will lose transcendence to consciousness and become Hegel's project.[25] But Hegel's synthesis is rejected because Otherness is that which is apprehensible in the mind and overcome *en route* to self-actualization.[26] Divine transcendence suffers because this path makes God the content of consciousness and the object of the self who "locate[s] God in its non-objective I-hood, in its coming to terms with itself."[27] This Brunstad-Hegelian thesis is grounded in Hegel's angelic exposition of the *Geistes* movement in which "reason learns from itself."[28] For Bonhoeffer, even Seeberg's admission of a supramundane being falls short. Since God in Scheller's thought is still a construct of the "I" what is needed is recognition of Otherness which is not constructed through Husserlian phenomenological and eidetic reduction.[29]

According to Bonhoeffer, the focus on the subject and its projects makes Heidegger's philosophy atheistic; he argues the need for replacement with a genuine transcendentalism made possible by revelation. It is through revelation that the truth about human beings is known — they are in Adam and in Christ.[30] Genuine theological transcendentalism recognizes God as the subject, whose self disclosure is an act of freedom.[31] Marsh observes that freedom in *Act and Being* is a magnificent theme: God's freedom creates a bond of personal communion with humanity.[32] Furthermore, Bonhoeffer calls for the recognition of a human other. Theory has failed to recognize reality; hence, reality can only be experienced from the outside.[33] "Only what comes from the 'outside' can show man [sic] the way to his reality, his existence. In sustaining the 'claim of my neighbor,' I exist in reality, I act ethically; that is the sense of an ethics, not timeless truths about the 'present.'"[34] Bonhoeffer goes on to posit the Christian church as a locus for the knowledge of the revealed God.

---

25. *AB*, 35.
26. *Ibid.*, 35.
27. *Ibid.*, 37, 38.
28. *Ibid.*, 41.
29. *Ibid.*, 55.
30. *Ibid.*, 71.
31. *Ibid.*, 83, 85.
32. Marsh, *Reclaiming Dietrich Bonhoeffer*, 133.
33. *Ibid.*, 86.
34. *Ibid.*, 86.

To understand the priority Bonhoeffer gives to a human Other, one has to turn to his presentation of Otherness in *Sanctorum Communio*. Floyd argues that Bonhoeffer's personalism in *Sanctorum Communio* is a necessary condition for a new sociality of the church.[35] Although Bonhoeffer uses the I-Thou distinction used by Buber and others, Bonhoeffer is clear that the presence of the Other sets barriers to the "I."[36] What Bonhoeffer presents is an Other whose humanity prevents the subject from committing acts of violence against the Other. Instead, the Other's presence compels the subject to recognize the Other's claims in dialogue. Recognizing the barrier set by the presence of the Other remains a precondition for relations and ethics. [It is] "when the concrete ethical barrier is acknowledged, or when the person is compelled to acknowledge it, [that we are] within reach of grasping the basic social relations, both ontic and ethical, between persons."[37] The presence of the Other is an absolute demand for ethical life which overthrows the subject's preoccupation with comprehension and assimilation of the Other.

A fair reading of Bonhoeffer on Otherness requires appreciation of the continuity of his thought in both *Act and Being* and *Sanctorum Communio*. It is necessary to grasp the depth of the personalism and humanism in which he grounds sociality and sets divine transcendence and God's revelatory act in Christ — which then becomes the locus of life for Others. Divine transcendence in *Act and Being* does not eclipse this human project. According to Bonhoeffer, we speak about ourselves clearly when we first speak about God, something not done in the privacy of *Dasein*'s consciousness.[38] A genuine recognition of Otherness takes place in community — the church.[39] The church, seen as a community of persons, is the place for transsubjective relations that overthrows the thinking subject. Those who are part of this transsubjective communion experience authentic existence in relation with one another rather than facing death, which for *Dasein* is *jemeinig* (shared characteristic). What does Bonhoeffer's vision of this type of existence imply? "My neighbor confront[s] me as making some absolute claim on me from a position outside my own existence."[40]

35. Wayne Floyd Jr., *Theology and the Dialectics of Otherness* (Lanham, MD: University Press of America, 1988), 119ff.
36. *SC*, 45ff.
37. *Ibid.*, 32.
38. *Ibid.*, 96.
39. *Ibid.*, 118.
40. *Ibid.*, 139.

Levinas, for his part, has proposed replacing ontological totality with a human Other that is at once transcendent and destitute. We recognize our own humanity in the face of another human being. What Bonhoeffer characterizes as revelation, Levinas calls epiphany. This face that appears is human — not divine. The face which we encounter is transcendent, coming from outside, and thus it escapes all attempts to analyze and totalize it. Whereas Descartes recognized a transcendent divine being from the depths of his thoughts, Levinas simply presents a concrete human being in a face-to-face relationship as the transcendent one who overthrows sensibility used to grasp what is already in perception.[41] "The relation with the other alone introduces a dimension of transcendence, and leads us to a relation totally different from experience in the sensible sense of the term, relative and egoist."[42] This is a radical and absolute call in a world where individuals stress their preeminence:

> The Other remains infinitely transcendent, infinitely foreign; his [her] face in which his epiphany is produced and which appeals to me breaks with the world that can be common to us, whose virtualities are inscribed in our nature and developed by our existence.[43]

The transcendence should not be construed here to mean a severing of relations between the same and the Other. Levinas has already argued that "transcendence designates a relation with a reality infinitely distant from my own reality, yet without this distance destroying this relation and without this relation destroying this distance, as would happen with relations within the same. . . ."[44]

The Other for Levinas is also the destitute one. The move from transcendence to destitution must be seen in light of the portrait of a human Other that Levinas is unveiling. In this sense, to see the Other, according to Levinas, is to "recognize the gaze of the stranger, the widow, the orphan. . . ."[45] It is important to note that such an emphasis on transcendence and destitution allows people to realize that Otherness embraces all human beings. Both Levinas and Bonhoeffer articulate an

41. *Totality and Infinity,* 187.
42. *Ibid.,* 193.
43. *Ibid.,* 194.
44. *Ibid.,* 41.
45. *Ibid.,* 77.

ethic that includes everybody. The question is, What is human responsibility in the face of transcendence and destitution?

First, the face of the Other invites us to the truth. Truth, for Levinas, cannot be construed as equivalent to facts. Truth is being in relationship with the Other, in a life of participation that breaks the "enrootedness . . . of the sovereign categories of being."[46] Such a participation is not grounded on lack and hence is not a satisfaction of hunger.

Second, to recognize the Other is to desire the Other. Desire, for Levinas, is not the desire of Plato's *Symposium,* intent on going after what one does not have.[47] It is, rather, desire made possible by the presence of what is desirable — a presence that destroys the absoluteness of being and its schemes. Such a desire is justice which, unlike political justice, is not grounded on equality but on what Levinas calls religion, because in religion one finds an asymmetry that incorporates humility, responsibility, and sacrifice.[48]

Third, a recognition of a separate Other invites the subject to a life of dialogue. We stand face to face with another human being who speaks on his or her own terms. Levinas does not see discourse as a "modification of intuition."[49] It as an original way of relating to the Other which allows the presence of the Other to teach the subject. Given this view of discourse, Levinas argues that in discourse the Other places an interdiction on murder; announces a society which does not dissolve difference, but makes it possible to have an Other and a separate "I." Engaging in dialogue is offering the gift of communication. This act of recognizing and communicating with the Other makes justice possible.

I have indicated that Bonhoeffer presents a divine Other in *Act and Being* and a human Other in *Sanctorum Communio*. Both are transcendent to the subject. Levinas has called for a radical human transcendence. What is significant is that both interrupt the journey of transcendental idealism as a totality because it eliminates difference. Bonhoeffer's emphasis on revelation in *Act and Being* offers a theological path to ethics. He claims that God is revealed in Jesus Christ, who has established a community where responsible membership demands taking care of the needs of the Other. While grounding his argument philosophically, Levi-

46. *Ibid.,* 60.
47. *Ibid.,* 63.
48. *Ibid.,* 64.
49. *Ibid.,* 66.

nas draws freely from the rich Jewish religious tradition and argues that atheism involves disregard of the Other, while religion is constituted by a recognition of Otherness. One does not truly know God if one does not recognize the Other. While this is not the place for exegesis, there are clear parallels in the teachings of Jesus concerning love for neighbor and one's relationship to God. In *Difficult Freedom: Essays on Judaism,* Levinas argues that one can only know God in a genuine relationship with another individual where ethics is not perceived as something outside the religious dimension:

> Ethics is not the corollary of the vision of God, it is that very vision. Ethics is not an optic, such that everything I know of God and every-thing I can hear of his word and reasonably say to him must find an ethical expression. . . . To know God is to know what must be done. Here education — obedience to the Other will — is supreme instruc-tion: the knowledge of this will which is itself the basis of all reality. In the ethical relation, the other is presented at the same time as being absolutely other, but this radical alterity in relation to me does not destroy or deny my freedom.[50]

Otherness in African Contextual Ethics

I have undertaken this cursory review of Bonhoeffer and Levinas in order to argue that contextual ethics in Africa ought to take seriously the personalist and genuinely transcendental approaches of Bonhoeffer and Levinas. A number of works have been published recently that deal with contextual ethics.[51] If one takes the critiques of Bonhoeffer and Levinas seriously, a human Other ought to set the priorities in ethics in the African context. There are Other perspectives which run the gamut from Aristotelian virtue ethics to Kant's deontological rigorism. The emphasis on a human Other recaptures the possibility of ethics because such an approach recognizes and reinstates difference — not the difference of a *Ding an sich,* as promising as that thought may have been for any future

---

50. Emmanuel Levinas, *Difficult Freedom: Essays on Judaism,* trans. Sean Hand (Baltimore: Johns Hopkins University Press, 1990), 16.
51. C. Villa-Vicencio and John de Gruchy, eds., *Doing Ethics in Context: South African Perspectives* (Maryknoll: Orbis Books, 1994).

Kantian metaphysics and anthropology — but a concrete human Other who is affected by our actions.

In light of the contemporary debate on ethics, Jeffrey Stout is right that there is "Ethics after Babel."[52] In responding to what Edith Wyschogrod has called Alasdair MacIntyre's phenomenology of failed theory of morals, Stout applauds some of MacIntyre's insights without endorsing his historicism or the anxiety concerning the fragmentation of society which has led MacIntyre to dismiss the liberal society.[53] Stout proposes "social criticism" with both eyes open, and a revision of MacIntyre's three-stage analysis of virtue. In MacIntyre's formulation, an analysis of virtue should: first, recognize that goods are internal to social practice; second, recognize that goods concern "the good of a whole human life"; third, consider goods within the "concept of an on-going tradition."[54] Stout is sympathetic to this scheme but argues that MacIntyre tends to oversimplify the relationship between internal and external goods and the conflicts that arise from this distinction. Such conflicts make ethical practice difficult.[55] Stout proposes a radical critique of the failures of liberal society, but a critique which seeks to be both generous and programmatic. A generous critique should recognize the accomplishments of liberalism and yet be programmatic to the extent that it can propose a non-utopian vision for sustaining hope.

Stout rejects consequentialist approaches because internal goods suffer in consequentialism. Kantian ethics has a rather comprehensive landscape and should be rejected. Stout argues that we should see the different vocabularies decried by MacIntyre as a *bricolage*. We are engaged in a human conversation, and disagreements do not necessarily threaten moral discourse. Stout claims that within the prevailing liberal climate, we can hope for some kind of political control in the ongoing proliferation and distribution of goods. Our task is to strive to accomplish what we can realistically achieve.

If Stout's dream world were to be sketched, it would be a *bricolage* of insights from Aquinas, Jefferson, and Martin Luther King Jr.[56] For

---

52. Jeffrey Stout, *Ethics after Babel: The Languages of Morals and Their Discontents* (Boston: Beacon Press, 1988).

53. *Ibid.*, chs. 10, 11.

54. *Ibid.*, 266.

55. *Ibid.*, 275.

56. *Ibid.*, 292.

those of us in Africa it could be a *bricolage* of the vision of President Nelson Mandela, Oliver Tambo, Albert Luthuli, Steve Biko, Patrice Lumumba, the early Nkrumah and Kaunda, Nyerere, Felix Momier, Amilca Cabral, or Archbishop Desmond Tutu. Although I find Stout's position a helpful corrective to MacIntyre's dismissal of the contemporary liberal society, the paralysis of morality MacIntyre articulates still needs to be addressed. In this regard, I find Edith Wyschogrod's postmodernist revision of ethics, in the tradition of Levinas, hopeful.[57]

Wyschogrod approaches ethics from a narratological and hagiocentric rather than a theoretical perspective. She argues that, from Heidegger, we have seen that emphasis on theory can be, and has been, used as a manipulative tool.[58] According to Wyschogrod, postmodernist notions such as differentiality, which calls into question the assumption of a canon, "double coding," which allows postmodernism to criticize the past while drawing from that past to sustain continuity, and eclecticism, which brings together "conceptual positions . . . [to] bear upon the sphere of life and action," offer a new vision of ethics.[59] Wyschogrod notes that postmodernist eclecticism employs different genres, and proceeds intraphilosophically by drawing from phenomenology, postphenomenology, analytic philosophy, and the "traditional philosophy" of "Plato, Aristotle and Descartes."[60] Postmodernist ethics stresses alterity, critiques power, and upholds concrete materiality.

Given these assumptions, Wyschogrod locates a *point d'appui* of postmodernist ethics in the question of the "Other," stating categorically that, in the Other, we are not dealing with a mere "conceptual anchorage" but a human being who is very much alive as "a living force." Furthermore, "The Other is different from oneself; her/his existence will be shown to carry compelling moral weight. In the context of a post-modern ethics, the Other functions as a critical solvent in much the same way as the notion of difference functions in postmodern metaphysics."[61]

---

57. Edith Wyschogrod, *Saints and Postmodernism: Revisioning Moral Philosophy* (Chicago: University of Chicago Press, 1990).
58. *Ibid.*, xxvi.
59. *Ibid.*, xviii.
60. *Ibid.*, xix. Author's emphasis.
61. *Ibid.*, xxi.

According to Wyschogrod, the *aporias* of theory lie in the fact that theory *qua* theory does not lead to moral action. Besides, there are varied and conflicting theories. Wyschogrod's hagiography surveys saints "across a broad spectrum of belief systems and institutional practices."[62] She engages in hermeneutics to understand their practice, their bodies, temporality, gender, desire, and especially the "excessive desire . . . on behalf of the Other that seeks the cessation of another's suffering and birth of another's joy."[63] Viewing ethics from this perspective, Wyschogrod criticizes theory first because it does "not result in moral actions," and secondly because "there is no common frame of reference, no cultural consensus in terms of which these disputes can be settled."[64] On ontological grounds, Wyschogrod rejects theory because through the use of modern technology, and the all-persuasiveness of Being, theory becomes manipulation: "A relation with being other than established by ontology of technique is precluded. Within such a world, the ligatures that connect one being to another are bonds of calculation and control."[65]

Finally, Wyschogrod rejects theory because it is tied to reflection which, in the tradition, proceeds from the perspective of the thinker and has not been attentive to the difficulties of the Other.[66] When theory does not lead to ethical actions aimed at a genuine Other, it is time to raise the question of ethics in a radically new way. Accordingly, Wyschogrod argues, "saintly presence expresses itself in the intersubjective realm as a response to the *imago dei* that makes each person."[67] Legitimation is found not in theological concepts nor social concepts but the "rules of thumb immanent to the lived life itself."[68] This lived life is lived in the flesh — a real bodily existence. In proceeding this way, Wyschogrod finds through Merlou-Ponty's carnal essences and Levinas's genuine human "the power to bring about new configurations . . . authorized by the prior renunciation of power."[69]

Wyschogrod persuasively argues that, in labor, what is saintly is

62. *Ibid.,* xxiii.
63. *Ibid.,* xxiv.
64. *Ibid.,* xxv.
65. *Ibid.,* xxvi.
66. *Ibid.,* xxvii.
67. *Ibid.,* 13.
68. *Ibid.,* 29.
69. *Ibid.,* 58.

the deployment of a person's efforts to remedy the sufferings and pain of another person. Since it is done through saintly labor rather than the calculations of work, it "gives altruism its moral character."[70] Revisioning moral life calls for the recognition of a genuine Other. It is my conviction that Levinas and Bonhoeffer offer a hopeful path for the articulation of such a human Other as the basis of grounding an ethical conversation. In what follows, I shall offer a broad outline of such an ethics in the African context.

First, a contextual ethics of Otherness should be pluralistic. By pluralism I mean interdisciplinary as well as interreligious approaches to ethics. For a long time the disciplines of philosophy and theology have articulated the principles of ethics and morality, thus providing foundational tools for the subject matter. However, ethics in Africa is being considered in light of multiple disciplines, including anthropology, political science, economics, etc. This interdisciplinary approach is needed if one expects to revitalize the energy, and vitality, and hope for better times ahead than was present in Africa during the days of the so-called "winds of change." The recent demise of apartheid has rekindled such a hope. Attempting to capture such hope goes beyond mere nostalgia because, in concrete terms, the fight against apartheid was a fight for a human Other who was marginalized and balkanized to create, in Levinasian terms, a dwelling for the "same" to be at home and practice the ontological craft of enjoyment which is constitutive of totality. These exciting times in South Africa are being analyzed from a variety of perspectives, as one can see from recent works devoted to reconstruction.[71] For different regions of the continent, various disciplines will have to raise the question of a human Other in a new and dynamic way; letting that human Other rather than projects be the focus of concern. One could rightly argue that up to this point the so-called development projects have been undertaken

70. *Ibid.,* 85.

71. See Heribert Adam and Kogila Moodley, *The Opening of the Apartheid Mind: Options for the New South Africa* (Berkeley: University of California Press, 1993); Norman Etherington, ed., *Peace, Politics and Violence in the New South Africa* (London: Hans Zell Publishers, 1992); Marina Otaway, *South Africa: The Struggle for a New Order* (Washington D.C.: The Brookings Institution, 1993); David Chidester, *Shots in the Streets: Violence and Religion in South Africa* (Boston: Beacon, 1991); Charles Villa-Vicencio, *A Theology of Reconstruction: Nation Building and Human Rights* (Cape Town: David Philip, 1992).

as works of charity, or part of a comprehensive economic program for Africa, but they have not been undertaken from an ethical perspective as Levinas would define it. A human Other, understood across all the disciplines, is a *sine qua non* for any restorative project on Africa.

Interdisciplinary pluralism should be supplemented with religious pluralism. African religion has now reached a stage where many people are taking pluralism for granted. Recent works by David Chidester and John de Gruchy in the South African context are a testimony to this diversity.[72] This pluralism is not only a check on Islamic and Christian triumphalism, but provides us with new conceptual tools for looking at the ethics of *homo religiosus*. When we learn to see the person as different religious traditions see him or her, or listen to what these traditions say about a person, we will be better able to articulate within this pluralism an ethic that opens new possibilities. Employing Derridean language, one could argue that this pluralism does violence to the Christocentrism of Bonhoeffer. I would argue that Bonhoeffer's pluralism, especially his careful reading of the varied intellectual tradition available to him at the time of crisis, validates a new pluralism in our day that should certainly be expanded to include religious diversity.

Second, contextual ethics of the Other must wrestle with the twin demons of ethnicity and autocracy. In a very real sense, Africa's multiplicity of ethnic groups make it a paradigm for pluralism *par excellence*. I do not want to demolish ethnicity as such because it can and should be a powerful testimony to diversity in what has now emerged from the ruins of colonialism called the nation state. However, I do not believe we have tapped the positive values of ethnicity for the good of the political process in Africa. This is not a new claim because the literature and political rhetoric on the continent are loaded with attacks on the demon of "tribalism." We can turn this "demon" into an ally by accepting the concreteness of Otherness and separateness in a way that does justice to a human Other as a precondition for nation building.

This is a tough challenge. Jean Francois Bayart has pointed out that "the shadow theater of ethnicity" has played a far more dominant role in African politics than elsewhere, and I must add that it has done

---

72. David Chidester, *Religions of South Africa* (London and New York: Routledge, 1992); Martin Prozesky and John de Gruchy, eds., *Living Faiths in South Africa* (Cape Town: David Philip, 1995).

so with a frequency that most of us do not like.[73] The regionalism that is associated with the politics of ethnicity has in many instances given birth to the so-called new elite, or *evolues*. Bayart argues that it has also created what in Cameroon is called "the politics of the belly." The imagery here is suggestive of the critique Levinas provides of *Dasein*'s sense of dwelling at home, and enjoyment. This is a process that marginalizes and consumes the Other.

For the record, I do need to emphasize that "the politics of the belly" is not unique to Africa. In western politics something akin to that is implied in terminology related to "pork" and "bringing home the bacon," or, in its more conceptual form, in Tip O'Neal's dictum: "all politics is local." Elsewhere, we have seen extremes of selfishness and ethnicity: in the Nazi final solution and in ethnic cleansing in the Balkans. What is needed in Africa now is a recognition of difference that does not degenerate into the politics of my belly or my sister's belly. Such a narrow ethnicity has proven to be too costly, especially where people look at others and see not a human Other, but a "Hutu" or "Tutsi." In Cameroon, where the phrase "politics of the belly" comes from, people look at others and see "Beti," "Hausa," or "anglophone" and "francophone." Where this tendency has not degenerated into physical violence it has often degenerated into economic violence that will continue into the twenty-first century, leaving us to wonder if the so-called nation state or what I call the ruins of colonialism will survive. This economic violence has been aggravated by the fact that the survival strategy of the politics of the belly includes exporting "dwellings." Thus the politician of the belly is more at home with the Swiss bank manager and has physical dwelling places in Paris or Florida. The very people whose funds and resources have been highjacked must then carry the additional burden of scandalous tax expenditures on these properties. Bonhoeffer and Levinas teach us to recover difference without enmity or violence by seeing a human Other who is transcendent to us and to the concept of ethnicity. I am sure that if one were to ask Levinas, he would say that, as he imagines the gas chambers, he sees not only Jewish faces but human faces. Bonhoeffer in a similar way would say that the underground network was intended not only to save

---

73. Jean Francois Bayart, *The State in Africa: The Politics of the Belly*, trans. from the French by Mary Harper, Christopher Harrison, and Elizabeth Harrison (London and New York: Longman, 1993), 41ff.

Jews, but human beings whom God created and endowed with human dignity.

The other twin demon is autocracy. In the search for an ideal that would deal with the problematics of ethnicity, African countries established one-party states. Many leaders paid lip service to democracy while ruling through a single party that tolerated no deviation from the established party line. There is no doubt that Marxist influence had something to do with this in some countries, but in countries like Cameroon or the Ivory Coast where regimes sympathetic to the western agenda emerged, the establishment of one-party states to advance the cause of national unity and check tribalism was unwarranted. Where one-party states were not established, military dictatorships took control. A good look at most of these experiments with one-party states demonstrates that the experiment was in many ways a misuse of the "traditional" power structure where a chief ruled through a council of elders. These parties do not allow any dissent at all; consequently, dissenters are treated very brutally. To restore Otherness multiple political voices must be recognized and guaranteed. The totality of the one-party state has produced nothing more than a marginalized populace robbed of the political process and assimilated into a neatly orchestrated machinery where brutality is the order of the day. One hardly needs to read Milovan Djilas to see that the one-party bosses all over Africa have been a "new" and an Other-destroying class.

Third, contextual ethics of the Other ought to demolish outmoded theories and praxis. The grand themes of the African political experience such as *Negritude*, African Socialism, planned liberalism, Marxism, and capitalism, are all being reevaluated. All of these grandiloquent doctrines have promised a lot and delivered very little. There are attempts to recapture Pan Africanism — particularly the spirit of Padmore, Nkrumah, Garvey, etc. Intellectually, the question of othering in political and anthropological, as well as theological and philosophical dimensions is receiving heightened attention. Furthermore, a cursory look at panels organized at recent meetings of the African Studies Association suggests that development studies have made a big comeback, riding into the arena of discourse on such issues as gender roles, class, political power, and the economy of communities whose future has been highjacked by the AIDS epidemic. The path ahead lies in prioritizing a human Other who should not be marginalized and suspended in favor of one's favorite theory.

Fourth, contextual ethics of the Other should call into question systemic violence — which I consider to be one of the pivotal problems of modernity and postmodernity. The twentieth century has provided humankind with a rich diversity in thought and technology. It could be argued that while enriching our lives immensely, thought and technology have taken us down a path lit with violence. Bonhoeffer and Levinas demonstrate that the effect of ontological and transcendental thinking is the capitulation of ethics to violence. This loss of ethics has brought in ultimate violence — war. One used to think that war was much more vicious because of the threat of a nuclear night. But recent events demonstrate some startling things: for example, that smart bombs are very accurate and lethal; basic weapons such as the machete, as we have seen in the recent ethnic violence in Rwanda, are just as lethal when unleashed on a human Other. Still, the turning of technology into a tool of violence has been devastating for the twentieth century in particular. Thought and technology should serve the person. In talking of violence in the twentieth century, one has to deal with it in the broadest sense. Levinas and Bonhoeffer demonstrate that humankind can overcome that history of violence if each person recognizes the person who stands in front of him or her. Africa knows violence — the violence of colonialism, the violence of harsh climatic conditions, the violence of political corruption, violent denigration of their culture (the looting of art and cultural artifacts from the "jungle" to the museum of "man" and other places of "high culture"). By recognizing and welcoming a human Other, we open the door to a new day.

The modern state in Africa remains a totalitarian society. Its totalitarianism originated in the colonial project and has been perpetuated by the brutality of one-party demagoguery, which is animated, ironically, by the politics of ethnicity and its false sense of difference. Out of the indelible ink of Nazi totalitarianism, Bonhoeffer and Levinas provide us with a new way of coming face to face to with genuine difference — a difference not defined conceptually, but a difference encountered in another human whom we meet in a face-to-face relationship. The voice of that face cries out: do not murder me. Contextual ethics needs to broadcast that voice.

The Ethics of Responsibility: Human Rights in South Africa

N. BARNEY PITYANA

The changes that have taken place in South Africa are nothing short of phenomenal. Some even dare to say that they are revolutionary. The scale of transformation that is in process, from F. W. de Klerk's address to Parliament to the elections of April 1994 followed by the inauguration of Nelson Mandela as the first black and democratically elected President of South Africa on 10 May 1994, has captured the imagination of South Africans of all colors and persuasions.

Since then the task of government with all its ups and downs has had to be tackled: a new constitution with maximum popular participation is being drafted; the economy has to be managed and the process of social reconstruction begun. If one may fault South Africans at all, they have been inclined to underestimate the dimensions of the task as well as the achievements of the last eighteen months.

During this time the structures of government had to be set in place, in some cases from scratch: new provincial government structures and representative local government structures were formed; the civil service had to be integrated and restructured, bringing in those who had previously been excluded, and abolishing the apartheid structures while ensuring stability in the public service; and new policy initiatives like the RDP (Reconstruction and Development Program) had to be introduced in education, health, housing, and the administration of justice. A credible and consistent foreign policy, along with expanding diplomatic relations, had to be tested.

During this short period, we have seen a phenomenal rise in crime, both sophisticated white-collar crime and violent crime like car hijackings, murder, and rape. There has been senseless violence, especially in KwaZulu/Natal (and to a lesser degree in Gauteng), which is thought to have its genesis in local political contests and the changing role of the Zulu monarch. None of this, of course, justifies the brutality that has marked the massacres of recent days. South Africans today are very angry about the levels of crime. Other points of tension have been reported. There have been strikes by workers (remember the unofficial strike by nurses and other health workers, demonstration around the Labour Relations Act, and, more recently, threatened mass action with regard to proposals for the sale of state assets). There have been contests over land. Illegal occupation of land by homeless people has grown to such an extent that local authorities have now taken the extraordinary steps of evicting people who occupy land unlawfully. This has brought attention to the problems of land distribution and homelessness and the urgent need for rural development.

Given all of this, one must remember the guiding principles of the government of national unity: to extend democratic, accountable, transparent, and participatory governance to all the people of South Africa as much as possible. The final phase of the democratic vision will be accomplished once local or community elections take place in the province of KwaZulu/Natal and in the Cape Metropolitan area later this year. Accountability functions through the parliamentary processes, the role of the judiciary (especially the Constitutional Court), a vigorous opposition, a critical press, and a challenging civil society. Transparency has become one of the watchwords of our democracy. Open government is the ideal, but much still needs to be done to make that a functional reality. One hopes that the Open Democracy Bill due to be brought before Parliament at its next session will go a long way toward satisfying this principle. Participation, I believe, is one of the strongest elements of our democracy. Participation takes place not only through democratically elected representatives but also through institutions which support democracy, such as the Human Rights Commission, the Office of the Public Protector, the Land Restitution Commission, the Finance and Fiscal Commission, and the Truth and Reconciliation Commission. By this process, a wider cross-section of citizens are brought into the governing process as independent and impartial practitioners accountable, in most cases, only to Parliament. The hearings system used so extensively by parliamentary portfolio committees and by the Constitutional Assembly brings ordinary people into the process of governance.

The picture that emerges, then, in the new and democratic South Africa is that of wonderfully noble ideals in a context where reality threatens to negate those values and principles. The danger is that the idealism of the struggle, the moral character of the nation, and human values are going to be very hard to sustain in a climate where there is constant pressure for scarce resources. The purpose of this paper is to explore whether Dietrich Bonhoeffer's ethical concept of free responsibility would not provide a focus that will help sustain our values and ideals. I shall examine, first, the elements of responsibility in South African society today. This examination will be followed by a short discussion of Bonhoeffer's concept of responsibility, especially in his *Ethics.* I will then provide a detailed analysis of the work of human rights institutions in our constitution, which, in my view, are expressions of national responsibility.

The Problem of Responsibility in South African Society

One has to understand that under apartheid and earlier forms of white supremacist rule, a constant refrain in the conduct of government was the paternalistic notion that government knows it all. Parliament was ostensibly supreme but was manipulated by the executive. The result was that government was dominated by very few people. Authoritarianism, in fact, prevailed. Even though there was a semblance of democracy, critical elements of democracy, such as freedom of speech, were circumscribed. It is only now becoming clear that even though much was made of the freedom of the press and of the independence of the judiciary under the apartheid regime, freedom was possible only within the bounds of a common ideological mind-set, which many accepted uncritically. Even in the white community, therefore, behavior patterns were unquestioned. Civil society was dead.

The black community, not unlike the white community, was, by and large, gripped by fear. It was considered risky to take a position of prominence against those in authority, and yet there was grudging respect for those who did. One got the impression that people feared for

211

you. In later years, with the growth of organized political activity in the civic and labor movements as well as in the church, confrontational politics were played out in the townships which were under occupation and in the face of extreme brutality by the security forces.

By the end of the 1980s South African society was at the point of breakdown. There was lawlessness within the very security forces which were supposed to maintain law and order. They saw themselves as above the law, and they subverted the law at will. A culture of impunity had set in. In the black townships all forms of violence were raging. Black communities were under siege. The security forces and their agents were engaged in murder, torture, and arbitrary arrests. The political commissars, who were usually not democratically accountable, took it upon themselves to order the people about: illegal trials took place, informers were identified, and the law of the jungle was enforced. People were expected to conform without questioning on pain of retribution.

In such an environment the ordinary people exercised little responsibility, and expected none. The ethic was one of survival. Institutional structures in the community — the family, school, and church — were rendered ineffective. Other forms of authority outside the home nullified the task of parenting; schools were no longer places of learning but of agitation; and the voice of the church against violence, and against immoral and undemocratic behavior, was ignored.

South Africans, even today, are inclined to blame apartheid for many of our failings. Those who administered apartheid blame the insurrection and the subversive activities of the liberation movement. The common feature of our society is that no one takes the blame but we all pass on responsibility to others. The second legacy of our past is that we look up to powerful, charismatic father figures who lay down the law for us to obey. We look to government to provide. We are hesitant to do or say anything lest it be disapproved of. We take no initiatives except within a safe confine. I fear that we may be treating Nelson Mandela no differently from the way the Afrikaners deferred to Verwoerd and Vorster and P. W. Botha, with unseemly obsequiousness. This attitude may well explain the destructive trend in KwaZulu/Natal, where political figures and traditional leaders seem to have the power to use others as instruments of death almost in a robotic and unthinking manner. There are some terrible (not just bad but literally "terrifying," fear-inducing) lessons to be learned from that.

Lessons from Bonhoeffer's Ethics of Responsibility

Essential to an understanding of the ethics of responsibility in Bonhoeffer is the idea that one acts or behaves within a reality, concretely. In other words, one has to take account of the circumstances which affect and are reflected in one's actions. Those motivated by simple reasonableness often find the world less than perfectly reasonable; the fanatical purist will expend himself or herself in search of perfect truth and justice. The person of conscience may, on examining his or her conscience, fail to recognize that "a bad conscience may be healthier and stronger than a conscience which is deceived."[1] He or she continues to examine other ethical principles like freedom and virtue. Some of these lofty principles have limited effectiveness when they confront reality. For such a person, "reality cannot be helped by even the purest principles or by even the best of wills but only by the living God."[2] Virtuousness might even be a barrier to self-surrender and dependence upon God.

Responsibility, therefore, means to act in awareness of one's obligations toward others, what Bonhoeffer calls *deputyship*, and to act in *correspondence with reality*. He introduces a theological twist to the meaning of reality when he says that the truly real man was Jesus Christ and to act in correspondence with reality is to recognize that "in Jesus Christ, the real man, the whole of reality is taken up and comprised together. . . ."[3] Indeed, Bonhoeffer is heading for an affirmation of reality, the fact of the world. It is something concrete that must be taken seriously by any moral being, for it cannot be wished away.

His discussion of guilt and conscience leads to the assertion that one must always act out of a free and yet obedient exercise of conscience, for that is what marks us as human beings. When we do that, we recognize the burden of guilt and the capacity to acknowledge guilt, which is actually liberating: "When a man takes guilt upon himself in responsibility, and no responsible man can avoid this, he imputes this guilt upon himself and to no one else; he answers for it; he accepts responsibility for it. . . ."[4] The liberating character of this is spelled out in Bonhoeffer's very memorable words: "Before other men the man of free responsibility

1. *Ethics*, 48.
2. *Ibid.*, 51.
3. *Ibid.*, 199.
4. *Ibid.*, 216.

is justified by necessity; before himself he is acquitted by his conscience; but before God he hopes only for mercy."[5]

I will not attempt an exhaustive analysis of Bonhoeffer's *Ethics* within this short presentation. What I wish to underline, for my purposes, are a few points of emphasis.

First, the idea that ethical behavior begins only when we accept our own imperfection and the finitude of the world is striking. It is also critical that we take the real world seriously. Principles do not in themselves produce ethical conduct, but only when they are tested against objective reality.

Second, Bonhoeffer's apparent relativism, which might seem troubling, is in fact a warning against absolutism. The reason for this is clear. It appears that in Bonhoeffer's world there were some who believed that Christian ethics exempted them from soiling their hands or rolling up their sleeves. As a result they became co-conspirators with evil. They were guilty of complicity because they failed to examine the social conditions which had a bearing upon their ethical conduct.

Third, I believe that Bonhoeffer's ethics frees a person to be fully human. They insist on one's accepting ultimate responsibility for good in the world — not looking to others in order to evade responsibility or to shift blame. A world come of age, notes Jean Bethke Elshtain, "does not think of itself bound to leave the determining of its fate to anyone outside itself. . . ."[6] There can be no reliance on some *deus ex machina*, but, in the full exercise of what gifts God has granted, we are co-creators with God in fashioning the future. When we do that, we have to accept that we may sometimes be wrong. We may risk the future. The nature of responsible action is readiness to accept guilt and freedom.

The fourth lesson for me is in Bonhoeffer's address to the obvious — that responsible action means acting with and for others. Whether we like it or not, we are part of a community of free beings and we have mutual responsibility for one another. My conduct affects the capacity of another to be fully human. We cannot, solely, by our own power, make the world and shape our future. All our conduct affects other people's lives.

---

5. *Ibid.*

6. Jean Bethke Elshtain, "Freedom and Responsibility in a World Come of Age," in Wayne Whitson Floyd Jr. and Charles Marsh, eds., *Theology and the Practice of Responsibility: Essays in Dietrich Bonhoeffer* (Valley Forge: Trinity Press, 1994), 276.

Human Rights as Ethics of Responsibility

The Interim Constitution of the Republic of South Africa as well as the draft constitution now under discussion affirms that "South Africa is a sovereign democratic state founded on a commitment to achieve equality, to promote and protect human dignity, and to advance fundamental human rights and freedoms" (section one). The constitution then states that "the constitution is the supreme law of the Republic" (section two). Both these clauses mark a radical departure from previous constitutions. They affirm the centrality of human rights, and they vest sovereignty in the constitution rather than in Parliament. These changes will have consequences for the ordering of national life.

The advancement of human rights and freedoms is undertaken by a chapter on the Bill of Rights. The Bill is a judicious marrying of the absolute and fundamental freedoms universally acknowledged with application to the precise conditions of South Africa. The constitution places an obligation on the state to "respect and protect" the rights enshrined in the Bill of Rights. In other words, citizens may advance their rights even against the stated interests of the state. This does not mean, however, that the fundamental rights enshrined in the constitution are absolute and illimitable. In fact, the rights are often balanced and specifically limited under a general limitation clause (section 35), the application clause (section 38), and the interpretation clause (section 39). The constant refrain is that the Bill of Rights must be interpreted and applied so as to "promote the values that underlie an open and democratic society based on freedom and equality." Finally, the constitution balances the rights citizens are entitled to enjoy, stating that citizens are also "subject to the duties, obligations, and responsibilities of citizenship." These duties, obligations, and responsibilities are not specifically stated here but are implied throughout the text of the constitution. Some of us believe that it would help if they were clearly stated, as they are, for example, in the African Charter of Human and People's Rights.

What this constitution does is to establish a constitutional dispensation founded on the principles not just of democracy vaguely understood and practiced in a contradictory manner but defined in terms of human rights. Human rights are those fundamental rights due, intrinsically, to all humanity by reason of their being human and on the basis of which they may freely exercise their humanity. They are not given as a privilege but are essential to the fact of being human. All that the

215

constitution does is to acknowledge these rights. But it also commits the state to govern in accordance with them.

I believe that the constitution does something else. It makes all citizens responsible for honoring, respecting, and implementing the constitution. The constitution achieves its purpose not just when it is passed by Parliament, or even by referendum, but when it is owned and internalized by the largest possible number of citizens of South Africa. It is not a party-political document but reflects the aspirations of a wide cross-section of the citizens. In the nature of things, therefore, the constitution represents our idealism and our lofty principles.

Precisely because of that, and because of the frailty of our human nature, the constitution needs to be supported, monitored, and defended. The Constitutional Court has been established to be the sole interpreter of the constitution, especially in cases of dispute. Additionally, the Human Rights Commission has the mandate to help bring about a culture of human rights, to assist the people to understand their rights under the constitution, to monitor the implementation of the chapter on the Bill of Rights throughout all organs of state, and to receive, investigate, and, if necessary, bring about litigation in cases involving the violation of rights.

Other national institutions established in order to defend the rights of citizens include the Office of the Public Protector, the Commission on Land Restitution, and the recently established Truth and Reconciliation Commission. The constitution also provides for the establishment of a Gender Commission, which is presently under discussion. It seems to me that all these have to be seen together as representing a common resolve of our nation to uphold the rights of citizens in all respects.

Towards a Practice of Free Responsibility

Finally, I wish to make a brief summary and then conclude. Let me observe, first, that by its nature the national environment under apartheid was disabling and oppressive to all South Africans. South Africans lived for too long under this patronizing and authoritarian system. It inculcated patterns of dependency which, I suggest, formed the national psychosis which afflicted our nation.

Second, I suggest that there were no bystanders in the South African reality (or hardly any). The reality is that the Nazification of society was nearly total: compulsory conscription, a network of informers, privileges which many white people took without questioning, and the Bantustan system which co-opted many African people into its grand design. One can justify such participation in many ways, but, of the total population, just about everybody shares in the guilt and shame of apartheid. Yes, there were many desk perpetrators, but nobody can say, "We did not know."

Third, I would say that there developed a culture of impunity which continues to haunt us even today. Especially during the late 1980s, it was clear that those who perpetrated heinous violations of human rights knew, or must have known, that they were committing criminal acts, but they also knew that the system which they were defending would give them cover. There was a blanket of conspiracy throughout the system which meant that the terms "law" and "order" were meaningless. It is also clear that among those of us who were engaged in resistance, the same culture of impunity prevailed. The activities of the comrades in the course of the struggle were never revealed — certainly not to the apartheid forces of law and order. There was also often silent approval and encouragement by black communities of acts of resistance which soon became oppressive.

In the light of these factors, therefore, the task of establishing a culture of human rights lies along the path toward free responsibility. The crime wave now sweeping our country has its genesis in the culture of impunity and a discredited law and order system. The amazing thing is that many of us continue to express a desire for the values of peace and justice. There is hardly anybody who would express resistance to human rights, but whenever human rights are mentioned, many read "my rights." The necessary balance of rights advocated in the constitution is not understood. It has become fashionable in our country these days to call on the African values of *ubuntu*, the interdependence of the community for no other reason than that we share a common humanity. One could also invoke the religious values to which many in our country claim allegiance. Very laudable, indeed. But set against the values which we espouse, the reality is one of continuing violence and criminality.

There are others who suggest that the human rights agenda of our government implies our being "soft" on crime. They cite the abolition of the death penalty, the implementation of the international conventions on the rights of children (to the extent that children are not to be kept in prisons), the instatement of the right to bail, and the protection of the rights of prisoners. It is suggested that drug traffickers and the international criminal syndicates operating from South Africa do not operate within the constraints of any concern for human rights. I would readily concede that human rights are not the panacea for all sorts of antisocial conduct and societal ills. Human rights provide a context for the appreciation of human nature and the redemptive possibilities given by God. Human rights also provide a restraint to those in authority against the inclination to demonize and dehumanize especially those who fall foul of the law. Finally, and positively, human rights force us to recognize that we are under obligation to extend the humanity we value for ourselves to others. The establishment of a culture of human rights is only one aspect in a composite program of societal reconstruction and regeneration.

Another important aspect of that program is to take our past seriously. The Truth and Reconciliation Commission is genuinely essential for reconciliation. There has to be reconciliation, but on the foundations of acknowledgment. It strikes me that although the church in Germany, with the participation of Bonhoeffer in the earlier stages, underwent a process of confession from Barmen to Stuttgart, in fact the process was never completed. It was, says Eberhard Bethge, a matter of confession more than resistance (or even *instead of* resistance). This is how he puts the dilemma:

> The Barmen Declaration did not prevent the situation which made the Stuttgart Declaration necessary. Between Barmen and Stuttgart the nameless millions lie buried. By leaving out the steps from confession to resistance, one ends up tolerating crimes, turning confession into an alibi and, in view of the injustice committed, an indictment of the confessors.[7]

It may be suggested that these were the confessions of the righteous. I think Bonhoeffer might call them the confessions of the virtuous. For those who had not understood or experienced responsible conduct, living within the tension and dialectic of moral absolutes on the one hand and the fact that penultimate steps were required involved tempering that sense of purity with acts of the guilty on the other. Ethics takes place

---

7. Eberhard Bethge, *Friendship and Resistance: Essays on Dietrich Bonhoeffer* (Geneva: WCC Publications; Grand Rapids: Eerdmans, 1995), 28.

in the interplay between such realities. The victims, not only Jews but also Gypsies, were not acknowledged. The Confessing Synods, writes Bethge, "had excellent language to speak against nazification, they had no language to speak for its victims."[8] Bonhoeffer declined to sign the Bethel Declaration which he had helped to draft because the church refused to recognize a basic flaw in its theology which led to anti-Semitism. Confessions must be accompanied by penance and reparation. There is no cheap grace; no redemption without price.

Finally, I believe that we need to recover our lost innocence. The values of the struggle for justice for all and the sense that we have the responsibility of liberating not just ourselves but others need to be re-captured. Many who were engaged in the liberation struggle knew that they might be killed or tortured. They might never themselves taste the freedom they were struggling for. But they soldiered on. They did so because of the idealism and selfless purpose that constituted the hallmark of the struggle. Today we have lost the essentials of that idealism. We need to recover the high moral ground so that it may guide us in the process of establishing democracy for our land.

8. *Ibid.*

POLITICAL WITNESS
AND THE OIKOUMENE

Caesar, Sovereignty, and Bonhoeffer

JEAN BETHKE ELSHTAIN

How to bring Dietrich Bonhoeffer "thinking theologically" into an engagement with political thought and the world of what is usually called high politics, the world of states: that is the backdrop to this paper and should help to situate the paper for the reader. In part one of the essay, I lay the groundwork by unpacking, briefly, Bonhoeffer's complex relationship to modernity. In part two, I turn to classical formulations of political sovereignty, arguing that the genealogy of the idea owes a great deal — which usually goes unacknowledged — to a particular understanding of the *imago Dei* as the point of Sovereign Will and Power. Finally, in part three, I return to Bonhoeffer on government: what we owe it and what we do not.

Bonhoeffer and Modernity

Dietrich Bonhoeffer never penned a full-fledged justification of his refusal to obey the Nazi State and his determination to resist even unto death. This has perplexed later observers who not only seek, but yearn for, a legitimating principle or all-purpose rationale for resisting tyrannical or arbitrary power, up to and including a resort to violence. For Bonhoeffer and many of his co-conspirators, the determination to assassinate Hitler — to "cut off the head of the snake" — was a tormenting one, particularly for Dietrich, who had long expressed an affinity for pacifism and who had planned a sojourn in India with Gandhi before being overtaken by the terrible events unfolding in Central Europe.

Perhaps we can grapple with Bonhoeffer's reticence in this way. He understood that theorizing *in extremis* does not serve us well in everyday life. Indeed, "The commandment of God permits man to be before God. It allows the flood of life to flow freely. It lets man eat, drink, sleep, work, rest and play. It does not interrupt him."[1] If hard cases make bad law, extreme and deadly political situations cannot set the rules and mores for the quotidian. Surely he did not pen a treatise justifying violent resistance in part because he feared that such a justification might too easily become *normative,* might, therefore, be held up as the grounds for resistance to state authority and power in a situation far less dire than the one he and his compatriots faced. This is often missed in discussions of Bonhoeffer; hence, the full power and poignancy of his resistance is lost as well. Bonhoeffer was a good Lutheran in the best sense of that characterization. He saw himself acting out of faithfulness to Luther and to Luther's thought in his challenge to what Germans were being asked to render by a terrible Caesar. Bonhoeffer refused obedience in the name of responsibility. To whom or to what was he responsible?

The answer is complex, in part because of the dire uniqueness of his circumstance. In extreme circumstances, general rules and norms often fail us. There is no generic code for disobedience; no tick list that, concatenated, adds up to an immediate goad to civil disobedience. Bonhoeffer begins by rejecting a vulgarization of Luther's doctrine of the two kingdoms, a *reductio* that holds that there are two spheres, "the one divine, holy, supernatural and Christian, and the other worldly, profane, natural and un-Christian."[2] This modern reading of the two-kingdoms theory, shaped (Bonhoeffer would say deformed) by the Enlightenment, finalized the severing of that which was "Christian" from that which was secular or "profane."

Because Bonhoeffer is no simplistic basher of modernity, he understands that we cannot go behind the Enlightenment and recover distinctions or situations that pertained previously. But we can tame and chasten those profanations which the move to emancipate man and reason trailed in its wake, including the notion that human beings were masters and were, or might well become, unencumbered in their

1. *Ethics,* 283.
2. *Ibid.,* 69.

sovereign sway. This went too far as man proclaimed himself the rational master and sovereign of his own fate. Oddly enough, then, confronted with Nazi appeals to "the irrational, of blood and instinct, of the beast of prey in man," a decent rejoinder was precisely an appeal to reason, to human rights, and to culture and humanity — appeals that "until very recently had served as battle slogans against the Church. . . ."[3]

There is a deep irony here. Although the origin of totalitarianism as inhibited human striving and willing lay, at least in part, in the emancipation of reason, it is human reason that gets battered and bloodied when this mastery goes too far — when it refuses to acknowledge a limit. Bonhoeffer extends his remarks to cover the desperate ironies of the French Revolution; the twinning of freedom and terror; the upsurge of a terrible godlessness in human presumptions of god-likeness. Man begins to adore himself. He denies the Cross. He denies the Mediator and Reconciler. He is avid, eager in his regicide, idolatrous in his deicide. The radical, Bonhoeffer declares, has fallen out with the created world and cannot forgive God his creation.

Thus it is that those who would deify man actually despise him. God, who does not deify man, loves the human person and loves the world, "man as he is; not an ideal world, but the real world. . . . He [God] does not permit us to classify men and the world according to our own standards and to set ourselves up as judges over them."[4] But this is precisely what the deifiers of man's sovereignty do: they set up their own standard and the result is that human beings devour themselves. Western godlessness triumphs in the form of Nazism, Bolshevism, all modern totalizing ideologies, and ideologizers who recognize no limits.

A misinterpretation of Luther is involved, or implicated, in these developments in this sense, according to Bonhoeffer. Here are his words: "On the Protestant side Luther's doctrine of the two kingdoms was misinterpreted as implying the emancipation and sanctification of the world and of the natural. Government, reason, economics and culture arrogate to themselves a right of autonomy, but do not in any way understand this autonomy as bringing them into opposition to Christianity."[5] This misinterpretation helped to prepare the way for the triumph of a cult of reason and, with it, an idolatrous faith in progress.

3. *Ibid.,* 55.
4. *Ibid.,* 71.
5. *Ibid.,* 96.

There is much evidence of humans' wondrous deed-doing in the grand narrative of progress. But the arrogance of human beings was to presume that they could stand alone as Sovereign Selves within a Sovereign State.

For what was also born with the French Revolution and the emancipation of reason was modern nationalism. Modern nationalism — this "western godlessness" — becomes a religion and gives birth to an "unrestrained vitalism." The French Revolution was "the laying bare of the emancipated man in his tremendous power and his most terrible perversity," Bonhoeffer writes in his *Ethics.* Human beings devour, use, destroy — all in the name of creating. This is an "apostasy of the western world from Jesus Christ. . . ." What does Bonhoeffer mean? I think he means a defection from our shared recognition of finitude, an abandonment of the knowledge that we are creatures as well as creators. This apostasy helped to generate those forces out of which a Hitler and a Stalin might arise. Twentieth-century totalitarianism is a virulent manifestation of the story of nationalism, sovereignty, and unchained human hubris. In turn, these confluent forces deepened the overall quotient of "folly" in the human race, or so it seems; thus, it became all too easy for demagogues to play to human weaknesses. Weak human beings are ripe for mobilization — which is very different from acceptance of civic responsibility — and hence ever susceptible of becoming tools in the hands of tyrants. Alas, "any violent display of power, whether political or religious, produces an outburst of folly in a large part of mankind."[6] Exploiters and charlatans arise. Often they do only limited damage. But evil has many guises, and when it triumphs, as it had in Bonhoeffer's time and place, norms collapse in on themselves and traditional ethical responses seem inadequate to the task.

Sovereignty and Nationalism

At this juncture a brief review of the history of modern sovereignty and the nationalism to which it gives rise helps to situate the virulent versions of political idolatry Bonhoeffer confronted. As all students of political history know, 1648 marks the Treaty of Westphalia and the codification of the nation-state model. What makes a nation-state a state and not some other sort of entity? The answer is sovereignty, self-proclaimed and duly

6. *LPP,* 8.

recognized. The proclamation alone won't do; recognition must follow. We need not follow Hegel's bloody-mindedness in this matter, his claims that war is the definitive test of a state's existence — the time when it enters the list and, through a struggle unto death, seizes that sovereignty it has proclaimed for itself. But it is a rather bloody-minded business, when you come right down to it. For with sovereignty, rulers and states take unto themselves powers previously reserved to the sovereign God. Too often, they no longer see the nations as being under God's judgment but, instead, proclaim the state the final judge of its own affairs. Indeed, claims to state power as dominion, a notion essential to early modern theories of state sovereignty, are parasitic upon prior proclamations of God's sovereign power: I have in mind here the *imago Dei* as represented by many theologians post-Occam, or the image of God as Sovereign-Willer.

That God is sovereign, the Alpha and the Omega, the progenitor, the bringer into being is central to Hebrew and Christian metaphysics. We all know this story and recognize its power. God's sovereignty is perpetual, absolute, indivisible. From God's sovereignty comes the "right of dominion over his creatures, to dispose and determine them as seemeth him good," writes Elisha Coles in an 1835 work on *Practical Discourse of God's Sovereignty*. Coles notes: "There can be but one infinite; but one omnipotent; but one supreme; but one first cause; and He is the author of all."[7] The Reverend Professor John Murray, speaking at the First American Calvinistic Conference in 1939, notes that:

> The moment we posit the existence of anything independent of God in its derivation of factual being, in that moment we have denied the divine sovereignty. For even if we should grant that now, or at some future point, God has assumed or gained absolute control over it, the moment we allow the existence of anything outside of His fiat as its principle of origination and outside of His government as the principle of its continued existence, then we have eviscerated the *absoluteness* of the divine authority and rule.[8]

7. Elisha Coles, *Practical Discourse of God's Sovereignty* (Mobile: J. S. Kellogg and Co., 1835), 24. Early forays into the sovereignty question can be found in my piece, "Sovereign God, Sovereign State, Sovereign Self," *Notre Dame Law Review* 66/5 (1991): 1355-85.

8. John Murray, "A Biblical Theological Study," in *The Sovereignty of God, or the Proceedings of the First American Calvinistic Conference*, ed. J. Hoogstra (Grand Rapids: Zondervan, 1939), 25-44.

God's right is coterminous with his sovereign power: it is a right of dominion, rule, possession, "all-pervasive and efficient... omnipotent and undefeatable."[9] Human beings are subject to God's sovereign dominion. God's all-pervasive sovereignty misses nothing, attends to everything. This is the vision that dominated "sovereignty talk" for centuries. Ironically, or so I shall claim, it helped lay down the basis for the early modern conception of a triumphalist state as sovereignty migrated, so to speak, from God's domain — or a particular version of it — to that devised by man and arrogated by man unto himself. When human beings begin to forget that they are not God, as Vaclav Havel put it recently, sovereign mastery was the name they gave this forgetfulness. Consider Jean Bodin's discussion of sovereignty as the *summum imperium*, that which can neither be delegated nor divided: "Sovereignty is that absolute and perpetual power vested in a commonwealth which in Latin is termed *majestas.*"[10] Following Bodin, Thomas Hobbes is one of the most canny, the most inventive of all sovereign discoursers. For Hobbes:

> The only way to erect such a Common Power . . . is to conferre all their power and strength upon one Man, or upon one Assembly of men, that they may reduce all their Wills . . . unto one Will. . . . This is more than Consent, or Concord; it is a real Unitie of them all, in one and the same Person, made by Covenant of every man with every man, in such manner, as if every man should say to every man, 'I Authorize and give up my Right of Governing my selfe, to this Man, or to this Assembly of men, on this condition, that thou give the Right to him, and Authorise all his Actions in like manner. . . .' This is the Generation of that great Leviathan, or rather (to speak more reverently) of that Mortall God, to which we owe under the Immortal God, our peace and defence. . . . And he that carryeth this Person, is called Soveraigne, and said to have Soveraigne Power; and every one besides, his Subject.[11]

Hobbes goes on to enumerate the Sovereign's rights, which are his powers: to judge all opinions, to name all names, to defend all as "a thing necessary to Peace, thereby to prevent Discord and Civill

---

9. *Ibid.*, 28.

10. Jean Bodin, *Six Books on the Commonwealth*, trans. M. Tooley (New York: Macmillan, 1955), 25.

11. Thomas Hobbes, *The Leviathan* (New York: Penguin Books), 227-28.

Warre."[12] Hobbes, Bodin, and a small army of legists working for the rising monarchies helped to give "centralizing monarchies the basis they required in legal and political theory."[13] They were also working from, and appropriating to their own purposes, a whole body of pre-statist sovereign theory, some of it indebted to elaborate defences of the papacy as the site of *plenitudo potestatis*, a plenitude, an untrammeled amplitude (under the sovereign God, need I add) of power. Writes Antony Black:

> It now seems clear . . . that much of this was already created for them by papal theory. Certainly, long before this period, Roman imperial doctrine had been used by national kings and territorial princes to justify the overriding of positive laws, and a centralized system of legislation and appointment. Papal doctrine both endorsed this . . . and also supplied something of the more abstract and more generally applicable notion of sovereignty which was to be fully developed in the works of Bodin.[14]

The difference between the earthly enumerated powers and God's is that the earthly Sovereign, although untrammeled in his power in the temporal space that is history, is subject to God's grace or punishment. But having taken unto himself all the features of the deity, including, in some sense, creation of an earthly domain that never ends (for the king-dom is perpetual, hence immortality is in some sense assured as a function of sovereignty rather than of faith or grace), there is precious little constraint on enactments of sovereignty. The sovereign becomes a *dominus* over a bounded earthly territory, a space he keeps "domesticated." His is the power and the glory.

Writes Raymond Aron: "Absolute sovereignty corresponded to the ambition of kings eager to free themselves from the restriction Church and Empire imposed upon them, medieval residues. At the same time, it permitted condemning the privileges of intermediate bodies: feudal lords, regions, cities, guilds — privileges which no longer had any basis if the sovereign's will was the unique source of rights and duties."[15] In

---

12. *Ibid.*, 233.

13. Antony Black, *Monarchy and Community: Political Ideas in the Later Controversy* (Cambridge: Cambridge University Press, 1970), 30.

14. *Ibid.*, 37.

15. Raymond Aron, *Peace and War: A Theory of International Relations* (London: Weidenfeld and Nicolson, 1966), 738.

sum, then, the story goes like this: the sovereign God gets displaced in the early modern theory of sovereignty, taking up residence at a much greater remove than he had for medieval Europeans, where God's sovereignty was incessantly enjoined as a brake on the King's designs. (That and the authority of the church, too, which is another story. To say that the church was unhappy with the presuppositions codified at Westphalia is to understate.)

The modern, legalistic theory of sovereignty proclaims its own indivisibility and inalienability. It defines the supreme, the *above all else,* within a given unit of rule. Of course, this is far more than a legal theory or task: it involves civic order, identity, and images of well-being, security, or danger. Sovereignty shifts from king to state, and this state "can no more alienate its sovereignty than a man can alienate his will and remain a man," this from a rather sober proponent of the classical theory.[16] Jean-Jacques Rousseau protected sovereignty in this way through his postulation of the inalienability of the general will. The state and sovereignty are united. Popular sovereignty is, if anything, even more absolute and terrifying than that of the king, if the French Revolution and its aftermath is any indication. But that story is too well known to detail here.

Post-Westphalia, then, sovereignty signifies the freedom of a political entity to regulate its own affairs without interference. Rulers and governments come and go, but sovereignty remains. In the words of Supreme Court Justice Sutherland, in the 1936 case U.S. v. Curtiss-Wright Export Corp., 299 U.S. 304: "Rulers come and go; governments end and forms of government change; but sovereignty survives. A political society cannot endure without a supreme will somewhere. Sovereignty is never held in suspense."

Sovereign-discoursers, whatever their century or their theistic or a-theistic commitments, share a deep preoccupation with the notion of a unified will. There must be one final voice, we hear them say, one final will, brought to bear against cacophony and chaos. As God's will is singular, so must be the sovereign's, whether Hobbes's Leviathan or Rousseau's General Will. This preoccupation with the will and willing and "final say" is but one point of entry into the discourse of sovereignty, of course, but it helps us to take our bearings as we return to Bonhoeffer

---

16. Charles Merriam, *History of Sovereignty Since Rousseau: Studies in History, Economics and Public Law* (New York: Columbia University Press, 1990), 33-35.

and his principled, theologically grounded refusal to render unto Caesar in the form of an idolatrous *Führerprinzip* with its utter abandonment to the singular will of the leader.

Bonhoeffer on Government

Bonhoeffer joined a revolt in order to defeat idolaters who made travesty of Christian values and authentic German patriotism. The Nazi Caesar asked Bonhoeffer and others to render too much. Because hundreds of thousands of words have been spilled on Bonhoeffer's views on guilt, responsibility, freedom, and reality, I will not focus on those themes here. Rather, I will underscore what, for Bonhoeffer, constitutes *legitimate* state authority or, rather, the order of government. The concept of *deputyship* — presupposing the mandates of church, culture, marriage and family, and government — is central to his concerns. Parents act on behalf of the children. What they can and should do is enacted within appropriate boundaries — the order of the family. Responsible action flowing from legitimate authority is always thus limited. How do we determine what can rightfully be exercised by a deputy in the political realm? Bonhoeffer begins by reminding us that the concept of the state "is foreign to the New Testament. It has its origin in pagan antiquity":

> Its place is taken in the New Testament by the concept of government ('power'). The term 'state' means an ordered community; government is the power which creates and maintains order. . . . For the New Testament the *polis* is an eschatological concept; it is the future city of God, the new Jerusalem, the heavenly city under the rule of God. . . . The term government does not, therefore, imply any particular form of society or any particular form of state. Government is divinely ordained authority to exercise worldly dominion by divine right. Government is deputyship for God on earth.[17]

Legitimate government (divinely ordained) originates in, or is required by, the nature of man, but here Bonhoeffer introduces several complexities he does not develop. He sketches the Aristotelian-Thomist view and then goes on to fret that modern Lutheranism acquired a notion

---

17. *Ethics*, 332.

of the "natural state through Hegel and romanticism" which makes of the state not so much the fulfillment of "the universally human and rational character of man, but of the creative will of God in the people. The state is essentially a nation-state."[18] If you push this view, the state becomes its own ground of being, "the actual subject or originator of . . . the people, the culture, the economy or the religion. It is 'the real god' (Hegel)."[19] But this makes it very difficult for us to see and to understand the state's coercive power directed against citizens.

The Reformation broke from many of these concepts of the state, claims Bonhoeffer, by returning to Augustine and the origin of government in the Fall. Government is *not* coterminous with social life. Indeed, it was sin in the first instance that made government necessary. In addition, government is not that which helps the human person to flourish. There is no teleological motor that drives the engine of human political possibilities so much as an insistence on restraint and limits. This recognition undermines any notion of a Christian state, for the state possesses its character independently. It is of the authority of God, and God's authority is not limited to the world of Christians and Christianity.

Things get tricky at this point. Government is "independent of the manner of its coming into being." It is "of God," and an "ethical failure" on the part of government does not automatically deprive it of "its divine dignity." Thus, to say "my country, right or wrong," need not be an expression of political chauvinism so much as a tragic recognition that it is "my" country, right or wrong, that I am in some way responsible for even as I am in some way beholden. Government's tasks are legitimate, limited, some might say "austere" in Bonhoeffer's characterization. We owe obedience, under normal circumstances. But we do not owe government our very selves. It does not create us. It may curb, compel, and chastise us. Indeed, the individual's

> duty of obedience is binding . . . until government directly compels him to offend against the divine commandment, that is to say, until government openly denies its divine commission and thereby forfeits its claims. In cases of doubt obedience is required; for the Christian does not bear the responsibility of government. But if government violates or exceeds its commission at any point, for example by making

18. *Ibid.*, 334.
19. *Ibid.*

itself master over the belief of the congregation, then at this point, indeed, obedience is to be refused, for conscience' sake, for the Lord's sake.

But we must not generalize from this dire circumstance in order to make a strong claim or duty to *disobey*. Disobedience is always concrete and particular — in *this* singular case. "Generalizations lead to an apocalyptic diabolization of government. Even an anti-Christian government is still in a certain sense government. . . . An apocalyptic view of a particular concrete government would necessarily have total disobedience as its consequence; for in that case every single act of obedience obviously involves a denial of Christ."[20]

And so it came to pass for Bonhoeffer. This, as I noted, is a very austere argument. Many will argue that Bonhoeffer here, and elsewhere, unacceptably downplays the possibilities for good of states or governments and that he sets up a too strenuous requirement once the threshold of disobedience is crossed. But it is very much in tune with Bonhoeffer's determination to work the "in-between," in this instance in-between state idolatry and state diabolization. Action against an evil government, or a specific evil promulgated by government, is part of the realm of concrete responsibility, always undertaken in the "midst of the needs, the conflicts, the decisions of the immediate world around us from which there is no escape into general ideals and principles." In a world threatened by arrogant anthropocentrism, Bonhoeffer's minimalist anthropology may, in fact, open the way to a limited freedom and a form of appropriate but limited obedience or compliance. And that may not be bad. He is neither overachiever nor underlaborer in this.

Let me conclude by offering up a few concrete claims based upon Bonhoeffer's complex reflections on rendering unto Caesar. Bonhoeffer could never have made his peace with *any* regime (1) that promoted rabid nationalism with all its bitter fruits; (2) that eclipsed the space for the free exercise of human responsibility, for in a "world come of age" human beings are called to account; it follows that a system that leads us to surrender our identity to what Havel calls the "social-autotality" is an order whose claims on us are seriously compromised; (3) that served the ends of cynicism, collusion in evil deeds, human isolation, human desolation, and terror by contrast to trust, solidarity, and responsible

20. *Ibid.,* 343.

freedom; (4) that worshipped history and power and accepted no brake by definition on its sovereign designs. Such a regime repudiates the sovereign God who holds the nations under judgment.

To whom or what am I responsible? For Bonhoeffer, one does not answer that question in a way that guarantees that I "wear myself out in impotent zeal against all wrong, all the misery that is in the world." But neither an I "entitled in self-satisfied security to let the wicked world run its course so long as I cannot myself do anything to change it and so long as I have done my own work. What is the place and what are the limits of my responsibility?" Bonhoeffer leaves us with these questions. There are no easy answers about what we must render and to whom and under what circumstances. But we can at least banish the false pride that demands that we be "sovereign" in all things, even as we accept our real but limited responsibility.

Here, he writes from prison, the church in our tormented time is an arena of freedom; a repository of culture and quality and human decency. Such a church can and should recover its links with the Middle Ages, he tells us, leaving tantalizingly underelaborated what all that might entail. Time was not given him. He insists that "liberal theology" cannot help us here, for it is too atheological.

> The weakness of liberal theology was that it conceded to the world the right to determine Christ's place in the world; in the conflict between the church and the world it accepted the comparatively easy terms of peace that the world dictated. Its strength was that it did not try to put the clock back, and that it genuinely accepted the battle (Troeltsch), even though this ended with its defeat. . . . My view is that the full content, including the 'mythological' concepts, must be kept — the New Testament is not a mythological clothing of a universal truth; this mythology (resurrection etc.) is the thing itself. . . .[21]

Is there ground left for the church? Yes, but only in the light of Christ, a Christ who called human beings away from their sins, into strength, not weakness. To restore a rightful balance in the order of things, Bonhoeffer would insist that we must participate in the powerlessness of God in the world as a form of life even as we acknowledge God's sovereignty over all of life. I suppose this is what might be called

21. *LPP*, 327, 329.

Lutheran irony and it goes all the way down. Sadly, our adoration of sovereignty makes us weak, not strong, inviting slackness of thought, incapacitation in action, acquiescence in evil. We have rendered altogether too much, and we have gotten the Caesars we deserve. That is the solemn lesson Dietrich Bonhoeffer leaves us with in the matter of Caesar, sovereignty, and Christ.

Church versus State: Human Rights, the Church, and the Jewish Question (1933)

ALEJANDRO ZORZIN

It is surprising that a fundamental article by Dietrich Bonhoeffer,[1] a key one for theological reflection on Protestant church options in the face of state terrorism, has not yet received due attention within Latin American Protestantism. The painful course of events in the Latin American South Cone, especially during the difficult 1970s, faced Protestants here too with the reality of a "final solution," applied by the dictatorships to the question of the *"subversives."* The systematic *"disappearance* of persons" within the framework of a totalitarian ideology (National Security Doctrine) raised a challenge to our churches which has not yet been fully worked through theologically. Perhaps only now that some of us are attempting to reread the Protestant tradition in the light of our experiences in the various manifestations of Latin American state terrorism are we able to discover Bonhoeffer's value as a critical theologian up against the political reality of his day. For many of us — as for Bonhoeffer — it is a matter of speaking of God not only in a world which has come of age, but also in a world which has become tolerant of the violence directed by the powers of the day against various minorities.

In 1921, the novelist Jakob Wassermann gave free rein to his disillusionment and frustration as a German Jew:

---

1. "Die Kirche vor der Judenfrage," *GS,* vol. 2, 44-53. English translation in *No Rusty Swords* (London: Collins, 1972), 221-29.

236

It is futile to beseech the people of poets and thinkers in the name
of its poets and thinkers. Every prejudice that one thought had
been abandoned long ago brings forth a thousand worms each
day, like carrion.

It is futile to offer your right cheek when your left cheek has been
slapped. It does not in the least give them food for thought, it
does not move them, it does not disarm them: they strike your
right cheek likewise.

It is futile to throw out reasonable words amidst their frenzied
screams. They say: What? He dares make a fuss? Shut him up!

It is futile to act in an exemplary fashion. They say: We know
nothing, we have seen nothing, we have heard nothing.

It is futile to search for security. They say: The coward! He is
hiding, his bad conscience pushes him to it.

It is futile to go out to them and to offer them your hand. They
say: Who does he think he is with his Jewish importunity?

It is futile to be faithful to them, either as fellow fighters or as
fellow citizens. They say: He is a Proteus, he can do it all.

It is futile to help them, to remove the chains of slavery from their
limbs. They say: He will certainly have profited from this
somehow.

It is futile to neutralize the poison. They will brew it anew.

It is futile to live for them and to die for them. They say: He is a
Jew.[2]

Wassermann's words reflect the Jewish question from the point of view
of the Other, of the person who experiences it every day as a wound
which he cannot cure.

In his pivotal analysis of *The Churches and the Third Reich*,[3] German
historian Klaus Scholder emphasizes that racist anti-Semitism was an
essential and basic component of the national-socialist worldview. As
early as 1919/20 Hitler already believed that the secret dynamics of
universal history were based on the battle between two races: the "good"
Aryan race and the "malignant" Jewish race. For that reason, the final

2. J. Wassermann, *Mein Weg als Deutscher und Jude* (Berlin 1921, quoted by
Achim von Borries, ed., *Selbstzeugnisse des deutschen Judentums: 1870-1945* (Frank-
furt/M, 1962), 36.

3. K. Scholder, *Die Kirchen und das Dritte Reich*, vol. 1: *Vorgeschichte und Zeit der
Illusionen 1918-1934* (Frankfurt/M and Berlin, 1977, 1986), p. 333. English translation:
The Churches and the Third Reich, vol. 1 (London: SCM, 1987).

outcome of that struggle would determine the future course of history. According to Hitler's modern Manichaean-racist worldview it was necessary for the "Aryan race" to prevail once and for all over the "Jewish race." That is why — once Nazi-fascism was able to come to political power in Germany — a tragic new phase began for the "Jewish question."

The Boycott and the Anti-Semitic Legislation (March/April 1933)

The deeds which occurred in Breslau on March 11, 1933, initiated a program directed against Jewish professionals and functionaries which would soon be imitated in other German cities. An S. A. group burst into the courthouse, forcing Jewish judges, district attorneys, and lawyers to leave the building, in the midst of a tremendous ruckus. The police only intervened half an hour later, ostensibly compelling the S. A. paramilitary forces to leave. The police chief, a Nazi, offered to guarantee the court's security if the participation of Jewish lawyers and judges in the legal sphere were severely limited in Breslau.[4]

With this event, a precedent had been set for the pro-Nazi press to start carrying out its part in the task. On March 19, the *People's Observer* (*Völkischer Beobachter*) published libelous commentaries about what had happened in Breslau with the purpose of inciting others to imitate the procedure in other German cities. The technique worked: first there were paramilitary actions, later legitimized by the (Nazified) "security forces," all of this accompanied by libel and incitement to further abuses in the pro-Nazi press. However, as these sorts of operations continued, the spectrum of the professionals under attack grew: Jewish professors, artists, journalists, and medical doctors became the brunt of insults, threats, and open persecution. These discriminatory actions — added to the persecution which was being carried out against the leftist opposition — caused a much greater stir in the foreign press than in Germany.

Faced with the demands being made on him from abroad, Hitler decided to respond with an open provocation. On March 28, 1933, his government gave instructions to the Party to carry out a general boycott on April 1 against all Jewish professionals and businesses in Germany. Skillfully using the repercussions in other countries provoked by previ-

4. *Ibid.*, 323f.

ous incidents, Hitler justified the boycott as a vigorous and necessary response to the supposed anti-German campaign promoted abroad by Jewish sectors. Thus, taking advantage of a situation generated by his own party, he commenced a long series of measures that involved increasing discrimination and violence and were directed toward achieving the final goal that had been clearly expressed in the early 1920s: the total "removal" *(Entfernung)* of the Jewish population from German society.

In that context, it is no accident that only a few days after the boycott the executive branch, equipped with absolute powers by the fateful Enabling Act *(Ermachtigungsgesetz* of March 23, 1933), should decree, on April 7, 1933, a "Law for the restoration of the civil service" *(Gesetz zur Wiederherstellung des Berufsbeamtentums).* This law, which supposedly served to reorder the public service by ensuring that the state could count on suitable and loyal public officials, was actually designed to get rid of the state employees hired during the Social Democratic governments of the Weimar Republic and especially to "remove" all citizens of Jewish ancestry from public service. In its third article, the law established the following regulations: "Functionaries whose ancestors are not Aryan must be removed from active duty; insofar as they are honorary functionaries they must be dismissed from their posts."[5] This article, which established a citizen's "Aryan descent" as a criterion of suitability for public service *(Arieparagraph),* constituted an absolute innovation in terms of jurisprudence. It provided a legal framework, obviously a highly questionable one, for a discriminatory procedure by the state against a minority of the inhabitants of the *Reich.*

It can be supposed that initiatives of this sort served as an alarm to individuals such as Dietrich Bonhoeffer and those in his circle, persons belonging to Berlin's well-to-do professional and academic middle class. Given that they were linked by ties of family and friendship to persons of Jewish descent, such as Gerhard Leibholz and Franz Hildebrandt, they were able to recognize the character of the state's abuses fairly soon for what it was.[6] Above all — and this is proven by Bonhoeffer's paper

---

5. The text is in G. Kretschmar and C. Nicolaisen, eds., *Dokumente zur Kirchenpolitik des Dritten Reiches,* vol. 1: *Das Jahr 1933* (Munich: C. Nicolaisen, 1971), 35.

6. Eberhard Bethge tells about Dietrich Bonhoeffer's grandmother acting against the boycott dispositions by walking through an S.A. watch in front of the *Kaufhaus des Westens* in Berlin; cf. Eberhard Bethge, *Dietrich Bonhoeffer: A Biography* (London: Collins, 1970), 201.

— they perceived it in the progressive violation of basic civil rights inflicted on the regime's political opponents, and especially on Germans of Jewish ancestry.

"The Church in the Face of the Jewish Question"[7]

In a letter to his friend, the theologian Erwin Sutz (in Switzerland), dated April 14, 1933, Bonhoeffer writes from Berlin: "The church is much concerned with the Jewish question, which has caused even the most sensible to lose their heads and forget their Bibles."[8] To whom was Bonhoeffer referring with this comment? Bethge only points out that in early April 1933, the circle formed by a group of pastors in Berlin under the leadership of the regional bishop Gerhard Jacobi had decided to discuss the problems provoked by the "Jewish question." For this purpose they had asked Dietrich Bonhoeffer, who was an honorary lecturer of systematic theology at the University of Berlin, to provide an introduction to the topic.

Likewise Hermann Kapler, president of the Supreme Church Council of the Church of the Old Prussian Union, influenced by opinions abroad, the boycott, and the impending law regarding public servants, saw to getting theological advice on these issues. He therefore asked for a report from the church's Center for Apologetics in Berlin Spandau, whose young director, Walter Künneth, was also an honorary lecturer of systematic theology at the University of Berlin. In a conference for the Center for Apologetics general superintendents and consistory presidents, held April 11 in Berlin, Kapler distributed some notes "for purely personal information," which had been written by Künneth and were entitled "The Church and the Jewish question."[9] I consider it probable that Bonhoeffer, possibly through Jacobi himself, had access to these reflections by his colleague Künneth, and that in the letter to Sutz referred to above he was thinking of the suggestions made by Künneth

---

7. For a discussion of the latest articles dealing with this document, cf. Marikje Smid, *Deutscher Protestantismus und Judentum 1932/1933* (Munich, 1990), 416-19. She also offers a comprehensive and profound analysis of "Die Kirche vor der Judenfrage," 419-57.

8. Cf. *GS*, vol. 1, 37, and Bethge, *Dietrich Bonhoeffer*, 205.

9. Cf. Scholder, *Die Kirchen und das Dritte Reich*, 348.

as well as other commentaries on them which had been advanced in the church leadership meeting. If this supposition is correct, it would be possible to surmise that the essay written by Bonhoeffer was an attempt to offer a theological counterproposal to the other church position then circulating.[10]

The pronouncements by the first national convention of German Christians *(Deutsche Christen)*, which took place in Berlin from April 3-5, 1933, was also a matter for worry. Openly supporting the National-Socialist party politically, the German Christians demanded the establishment of a united *Reichskirche*, and within such a church the application of the single leadership principle *(Führerprinzip)*, as well as the full social and political cooperation of the Protestant church with the new *Reich* and the dismissal of pastors with "alien blood." Thus, even before the enactment of the "Law for the restoration of the civil service," which included the "Aryan Clause," one sector of the (Prussian) Protestant Church was already openly promoting its application within the church sphere.

Against this immediate background, Bonhoeffer developed a series of six brief theses as the basis for a discussion of the topic in the pastors' group in Berlin. In these theses he denied the possibility of incorporating or applying a discriminatory racial conception within the church and its congregations: "The church cannot allow the state to prescribe how to act with regard to its members." The participation and membership of Christians of Jewish ancestry in the church could neither be questioned nor limited. Whoever acted in this manner would himself or herself be acting as a *Jewish-Christian*, demanding a baptized person to fulfill a *law* as a prerequisite for becoming part of the church. The apostolic, *Christian-pagan* tradition does not recognize a distinction between Jew and Greek; for the latter tradition the only condition for becoming part of the church is to have received "the calling of God through God's Word in Christ." Bonhoeffer's conclusion in this respect is clear and categorical: "The exclusion of racial Jews from our ethnically German church would

---

10. Bethge indicates that at the end of the manuscript Bonhoeffer wrote: "finished on the 15.4.1933"; cf. *GS,* vol. 2, notes 1, 44. There is further information on the different original versions of the manuscript made by Gerhard Ringhausen, "Die lutherische 'Zweireichelehre' und der Widerstand im Dritten Reich. Zu D. Bonhoeffers Aufsatz 'Die Kirche vor der Judenfrage,' 15. April 1933," *Kirchliche Zeitgeschichte* (Berlin) 1/2 (1988): 215-44; cf. notes 13, 218.

approach the *Jewish-Christian* model. For this reason, such an exclusion becomes ecclesiologically impossible."

The paper also sets forth another argument, which holds special interest for those who have endured repressive governments in regions peripheral to North Atlantic political and economic power. Under the impact of the anti-Semitic boycott and the enactment of the "Aryan Clause" in the "Law for the restoration of the civil service," Bonhoeffer also analyzed the strictly political and state aspect of the problem. He then added this section at the outset of the six theses he had previously written, giving the whole the form of a short essay. It was first published in the June 1933 issue of the magazine *Der Vormarsch*, a small publication with a limited circulation.

In order to reconfigure the context for these reflections on the church's attitude with respect to the state, it is also important to consider the teaching activity which Bonhoeffer carried out in his seminars at the University of Berlin. In the winter semester (Oct. 1932-Feb. 1933), he had discussed with the students the ideas of the most recent theology, with comments on new publications in systematic theology.[11] In his analysis of the position of the church in relation to the state, therefore, Bonhoeffer had in mind both positions which he considered indulgent with regard to the state (Friedrich Gogarten) and positions that proposed the need for a more critical distance between the two (Karl Barth and Hans Asmussen).[12]

Speaking from a traditional Lutheran perspective, Bonhoeffer states that the church "confirms the state as an order of divine preservation in a world lacking God." Therefore, when the state generates order, the church is not called first of all to interfere in that process by offering its opinion, but rather to view it as an action based on the preserving will of God for a chaotic reality from which God is absent. For Bonhoeffer, history emerges from this ordering work of the state; the church does not make history happen. Nevertheless, "only the church, which wit-

11. The text is in G. Kretschmar and C. Nicolaisen, *Dokumente zur Kirchenpolitik des Dritten Reiches*, 35.

12. Dietrich Bonhoeffer finished his seminar on the 22th of February 1933, discussing with sympathy the pronouncement made by a group of pastors in Altona (Hamburg) on the topic of church and state the 11th of January 1933; cf. "Das Wort und Bekenntnis Altonaer Pastoren in der Not und Verwirrung des öffentlichen Lebens," in K. D. Schmidt, *Die Bekenntnisse undgrundsätzlichen Ausserungen zur Kirchenfrage des Jahres 1933* (Göttingen, 1934), 18-25.

nesses to the advent of God in history (Christ), knows what history is and therefore also what the state is." That is to say, on the basis of the unique and central Christ event, the church is able to relativize both history and the state that generates history, for it is aware of their provisional nature.

Within this framework it perceives that the state can decide to deal with the Jewish question as a historical problem and that "without doubt . . . it has the right to advance along new paths" in its attempt to resolve the problem.[13] In any case it will be the task of humanitarian groups or Christian leaders to call the state's attention to the moral dimension of its actions and, if need be, to denounce it "for threatening morality." For, in general terms, the church does not have the assignment of "acting directly in a political way," questioning or praising the measures applied by the state in its own sphere. One consequence of this theological stance is that with regard to the Jewish question the church "even today . . . cannot interfere directly in the word of the state and demand a given action that would be different. This, however, does not mean that it impassively allows political activity to pass before its eyes. . . ."

We see how Bonhoeffer, though fully conscious of the importance of the problem, still tries to preserve the relative autonomy of the state and church spheres. However, and here a substantial contribution to the theological view of the relation between church and state emerges, this function of the state whereby it generates history is not left exclusively to its own discretion. For Bonhoeffer it is a function of the church to ask "whether or not the state is generating order and a rule of law." Therefore, the church will observe the activity of the state as an ordering activity, but one that is enclosed between two extremes: a possible lack or a possible excess of law and order. For that reason, the church "can and must . . . ask the state . . . whether it is able to take on the responsibility for its actions as legitimate state actions." When the state, in the exercise of the function entrusted to it by God, surpasses those limits, the church is obliged to speak out.

Concretely, according to Bonhoeffer, a *lack* of law and order always appears "wherever a group of persons loses its (basic civic) rights." On the other hand, an *excess* of law and order is produced whenever the state "expands its power in such a way that it empties the Christian procla-

13. The English translation in *No Rusty Swords* differs slightly, saying: ". . . and without doubt the state is justified in adopting new methods here."

243

mation and the Christian faith of its own rights." This would happen, for example, if the state decided to force the church to exclude baptized Jews from the Christian communities, forbidding it also from having a mission among the Jews. Such an intervention by the state in spheres in which the church acts according its own independent norms would constitute an abuse of power. Forcing the church to crush its first loyalty to the confession of faith which upholds it, the state would place the church in a situation in which it is obligated to confess *(status confessionis)*.[14]

With this line of logic, Bonhoeffer approaches the most important point in his essay, where he sets forth three possible ways for the church to act in the face of a state which has exceeded its margins of legitimate authority:

a. The church must point out to the state the consequences of its behavior, asking it to take full responsibility for what it is doing. It is obligated to ask the state whether the latter's behavior fits within the framework of legitimacy (i.e., whether it conforms to the rule of law). For Bonhoeffer, in practice, "in relation to the Jewish question, the church must now put that question with the utmost clarity."

b. Furthermore, the church has an unconditional obligation to help "the *victims* of any social order, even if they do not belong to the Christian community." That is to say, in no way is the institution responsible only for the *victims* in its own ranks. The fact that Bonhoeffer used the term *victims (Opfer)* is noteworthy, since other theologians (the case of Künneth is illustrative here) still did not perceive the role of the state as that of a *victimizing* entity. This, however, is precisely what Bonhoeffer is implying with reference to the state's behavior in the "Jewish question."

Bonhoeffer indicates that in times of "legal transformations" the church cannot by any means escape the responsibility of acting in this fashion. By inference he is clearly arguing that the Protestant Church in Germany has no business countenancing the political behavior of the

14. Cf. Martin Schloemann, "The Special Case for Confessing: Reflections on the *Casus Confessionis* (Dar es Salam 1977) in the Light of History and Systematic Theology," ed. Eckehart Lorenz, *The Debate on Status Confessionis: Studies in Christian Political Theology* (Geneva: LWF Studies, 1983), 47-94.

state toward its citizens of Jewish ancestry.[15] The church has to do something: it has to speak out and assist the victims. Foreseeing the possibility of an even more critical unfolding of the situation, Bonhoeffer sketches out a third course of action:

c. The church should not only provide assistance to the *"victims"* which have fallen "beneath the wheel," but also herself "put a spoke in the wheel" constituted by the state apparatus.[16] This third possibility would imply a form of *direct* political action, a variation of the concrete resistance of the *communio sanctorum* up against the state's actions.

For Bonhoeffer it is clear that the first two ways "have now [as of April 1933] become demands of the present hour" with regard to the Jewish question. "On the other hand, the need for *direct* political intervention by the church should be decided in each case by an Evangelical Church Council and, indeed, can never be construed casuistically beforehand."

It is important to stress that although Bonhoeffer holds that there is room for direct political intervention by the church in the state, the place where it should be decided upon is not the individual or group sphere, but rather a church council. However, considering the New Testament reflection about the conflict between Jewish Christians and Gentile Christians which follows in the second part of his paper, the term he selects doubtless refers us to the "church council" of Acts 15. Thus, the primitive church becomes an *evangelical* paradigm for debating options for radical resistance in the face of state behavior which lacks legitimacy. I submit that Bonhoeffer's suggestion takes into account the possibility that this may happen outside of the institutional deliberating structures that in the case of his own Protestant Prussian church were called *synods*.

15. In 1933 the Jewish population was an estimated 0.9% of the whole population living in Germany.

16. Ulrich Duchrow indicates that bishop Berggrav (Norway) in his essay "'When the coachman is drunken': Luther on the duty of disobedience" (1946) refers to this expression as a statement made by Luther, but without pointing out where he used it. Cf. U. Duchrow, "Dem Rad in die Speichen fallen — aber wo und wie? Luthers und Bonhoeffers Ethik der Institutionen im Kontext des heutigen Weltwirtschaftssystems," in Christian Gremmels, ed., *Bonhoeffer und Luther* (Munich: Chr. Kaiser, 1983), 17-58, cf. notes 9, 56.

Walter Künneth's Document

It is worth briefly exploring here the suggestions made in this same context by Walter Künneth. The notes on the Jewish question, which he had composed during the first days of April 1933 at the request of Kapler, were published in a reworked form under the title "The Jewish Problem and the Church" in a collection of essays entitled, rather pompously, *The Nation before God: the Message of the Church in the Third Reich.* This book, with contributions by several authors, appeared in the summer of 1933 and within a year had achieved its third edition.[17]

For Künneth, the "Jewish question" poses a "complex problem" since the concepts "Jewish" and "non-Aryan" do not have a uniform definition in Germany. In this sense he points out that "the ethnological-racial differences" between the Jews that came from Eastern Europe (Poland) and, for example, Western Jews (from Spain), who settled in Germany centuries before, "are undeniable." Echoing the hypothesis according to which there was a relative disproportion of Jews in public and professional service with regard to their percentage in the total population, he points out that the state not only has the right to turn the "Jewish question" into a "problem regarding political-state reordering," but that it also does well in asking the question about "the essence akin to the particular type" of the German people. This is because "for decades there has been such a proliferation of the Jewish influence, that the risk has arisen of an overgrowth *(Überwucherung)* of German intellectual life and a domination by foreign influences *(Überfremdung)* of the public sphere."[18]

Concerning the church, Künneth argues that "the foundation which upholds or lets fall the meaning of the Christian message is that the determining factor for belonging to the Christian community should be faith in Christ as Lord, and not a given racial background."[19] Primitive Christianity already resolved the equality of rights for Gen-

---

17. Cf. W. Künneth, "Das Judenproblem und die Kirche," in W. Künneth and H. Schreiner, eds., *Die Nation vor Gott. Zur Botschaft der Kirche im Dritten Reich* (Berlin, 1933), 90-105. The preface to the book is dated "Pentecost, 4th June, 1933." So both articles, the one by Dietrich Bonhoeffer and the one by his colleague W. Künneth, went through a similar process from the time they were written down until their publication.

18. Künneth, *ibid.,* 94.

19. *Ibid.,* 95.

tile Christians and Jewish Christians. "To move away from this fundamental position would be nothing other than to deny the absolute character of Christian faith and would constitute a betrayal of the gospel."[20] That is why the church will not accept a political-racial criterion to evaluate whether or not its members are suited to hold a given post.[21] However, since the church in Germany is called to serve the people, in the present situation in which the "German people are profoundly disturbed," it is convenient to apply a cautious tactic momentarily limiting the access of baptized Jews to important posts. Especially missionary motivations demand that one be "a Greek to the Greeks." For that reason in the "present proclamation of the church it behoves us to be German to the Germans and thus win over the people to Christ."[22]

Concretely, the emergency legislation enacted in Germany should move the church to set forth the following demands to the state: (a) to introduce a greater gradation *(Abstufung)* in the legislation, establishing a clear difference between Jews belonging to the synagogue and baptized Jews. Why? Because if the state does not recognize this distinction, it would imply that it "devalues the meaning of the sacraments for the life of the people." A state which was openly to ignore a sacramental benefit for baptized Jews without distinguishing them from the remaining Jews, "could end up undermining the dignity of the church and its position in the German nation."[23] (b) The church should defend its right to continue the mission to the Jews. Why? Because precisely those Jews "who until now have not decided to become Christians . . . are the ones who maintain their distance from the German people, rejecting any adjustment to the people whose guests they are, attempting to preserve their racial-cultural individuality, thus openly becoming a foreign body inside of Germany."[24]

Lastly, Künneth rejects two extreme solutions to the problem: full equality of rights for minorities cannot be accepted in the life of the nation. But neither can the minority problem be eradicated by means of "oppression and persecution." The latter alternative, for example, should

20. *Ibid.,* 96.
21. *Ibid.,* 97.
22. *Ibid.,* 98.
23. *Ibid.,* 97.
24. *Ibid.,* 100.

not be encouraged because a persecution of foreign minorities in Germany could incite others "to oppress German minorities abroad."[25] In the present situation he proposes two ways for the church to take on its responsibility with regard to the problem posed by the state: (a) to offer consolation and assistance to "its Jewish Christian members," and (b) in its character of "conscience of the nation . . . the church must ensure . . . that the elimination *(Ausschaltung)* of the Jewish influence on the life of the people occurs in such a way . . . that it does not contradict the Christian ethos." For that reason it must have the courage to express its "most cutting opposition" to any kind of "violent damage or oppression of the Jews in Germany."[26]

In analyzing Walter Künneth's text, one can see that, despite a few reservations, in general terms he adopts the "ethnic-racial" perspective according to which the state has decided to present the problem. This is something that Dietrich Bonhoeffer rejects, and indeed does so explicitly when he says that from the church's perspective Judaism "is never a racial concept, but rather a religious concept. There is no reference to the questionable biological dimension of a Jewish race. . . ." Künneth's language does not distance itself in the same way as Bonhoeffer's from the ethnic-nationalist overtones common in the theological discourse of the time. But there are at least two further ways in which these two young theologians hold opposite positions: Firstly, whereas Künneth states that the church is responsible for tending to *its* Jewish Christian members, Bonhoeffer demands that the church help the *victims* of the state's actions "even if they do not belong to the Christian community." Secondly, whereas Künneth accepts that for reasons of missionary strategy the Aryan legislation should be partially accepted in the church, Bonhoeffer sets forth the situation as *status confessionis*, totally rejecting such an acceptance.

The Rejection of Bonhoeffer's Radical Proposals

From the beginning Bonhoeffer, with a greater lucidity than others, perceived these two issues as central. He held that there was no room for concessions on these points in the coming debates and struggles which

25. *Ibid.,* 102.
26. *Ibid.,* 104.

248

were imminent within the Protestant church.[27] His attitude was manifested in a suggestion made on June 22, 1933, to students at the University of Berlin in a public debate held on the burning question of the church. According to the information about the meeting offered by the *Junge Kirche* magazine,

> The most profound impression on the assembly was made by honorary lecturer Dietrich Bonhoeffer's words, when he described the possibilities and limits of a struggle within the church. This "struggle" should be waged only in a common knowledge of the forgiveness of sins and in the spirit of "Judge not." Those weak in faith, who wish to set up a law such as the Aryan Clause to block entrance to the church, should be carried along fraternally by those strong in faith, in accordance with Rom. 14. If, however, the law of the weak actually becomes the law of the church, then only an Evangelical Council could make a decision. It . . . would be the decisive authority for deciding all matters referred to the essence of the church. The Evangelical Council would then have to decide on the unity or schism of the church.[28]

This position — which Bonhoeffer and his friend Franz Hildebrandt defended vigorously in the political struggle unleashed between the factions within the (Prussian) Protestant Church — did not, however, gain the upper hand. Even the hopes expressed by Bonhoeffer in his *Bethel Confession* (August 1933) began to dissolve in the face of the evidence that consecutive "authorized" opinions successively altered the document and watered down its initial incisiveness. A letter written to his grandmother from Bethel on August 20, 1933, reflects his pessimism about the church's role and portends something of his inevitable destiny:

> It is becoming increasingly evident to me that we will have a big national and ethnic *(völkische)* church which will no longer tolerate the essence of Christianity, and that we must be prepared to traverse totally new paths. The question is actually Germanism or Christianity,

27. It was the opinion of Heinz Eduard Tödt that it was not the peace question *(Friedensfrage)* but the "Jewish question" that brought Dietrich Bonhoeffer to his first conflict with the politics of the Third Reich; cf. H. E. Tödt, "Judendiskriminierung 1933, der Ernstfall für Bonhoeffers Ethik," in W. Huber and I. Tödt, eds., *Ethik im Ernstfall. Dietrich Bonhoeffers Stellung zu den Juden und ihre Aktualität* (Munich: Chr. Kaiser, 1982), 139-83, 155.

28. *Junge Kirche* 2 (June 30): 22f.; cf. *GS*, vol. 2, 55.

and the sooner the conflict becomes an open one, the better. For this to remain veiled is the most dangerous option of all.[29]

Early on Bonhoeffer sensed the true dimensions of the conflict. He perceived that the sectors of his church willing to resist direct state intervention, even with a confessing zeal, were nevertheless trying to evade open confrontation. The attitude of the church leadership can be understood if one takes into account that rejection of the Aryan Clause would have signaled defiance of the Nazi-fascist regime. For Hitler, legislation about the "Jewish question" was not incidental but represented the beginning of an essential strategy that had as its goal the "removal" of the Jews from Germany. A church that insisted on challenging him on this particular point would be challenging him not on a secondary issue but on one of the cruxes of the National-Socialist ideology: the battle between good and evil, ciphered racially. In his April 1933 essay Bonhoeffer had raised core issues which could not be conceded, but which, for the church, could result in a bloodbath.[30] If the (Regional Prussian) Church, threatened by innumerable problems, held inflexibly to this position in opposition to the regime, it would mean its end sooner rather than later. This is why I do not agree with Scholder when he states that "the Confessing Church in formation, despite its struggle against the application of the Aryan Clause in the church, did not grasp the exemplary meaning and the scope of the National-Socialist anti-Semitism. This fault is inescapable."[31] In my opinion, Bonhoeffer and Hildebrandt represent a group that clearly did grasp the scope of National Socialist anti-Semitism. From the beginning, they attempted to move the budding Emergency Pastors League *(Pfarrernotbund)* to maintain an irreducible position with regard to this very point.[32] A good part

29. *Ibid.,* 79.

30. See his letter from London (April 28th, 1934) to Erwin Sutz, saying that this kind of opposition against the state has only a provisional character and that the time is coming for a very different kind of opposition, where only a few of the persons struggling in this first clash will be able to face that second battle, where the need will be to resist to the death. *GS,* vol. I, 40.

31. Cf. K. Scholder's article, "Kirchenkampf," in *Evangelisches Staatslexikon,* 2nd ed. (Stuttgart-Berlin, 1975), col. 1177-1200, here quoted from K. O. von Aretin and G. Besier, eds., *Die Kirchen zwischen Republik und Gewaltherrschaf. Klaus Scholder. Gesammelte Aufsätze* (Berlin, 1988), 131-70, 140.

32. See Christine-Ruth Müller, *Dietrich Bonhoeffers Kampf gegen die nationalsozialistische Verfolgung und Vernichtung der Juden. Bonhoeffers Haltung zur Judenfrage im*

of the church struggle during the summer months of 1933 had to do with the centrality of the Aryan Clause.[33]

This being said, the dynamics within the Confessing Church in its process of formation can be seen in a rather different manner. The leaders in that process, among whom there were certainly some with anti-Jewish tendencies,[34] may have sensed the essential character of the anti-Semitism of the authoritarian regime that had started to pressure them from within and without.[35] However, in the face of increasing political pressure and guided by a church survival instinct, they decided to opt for consigning discrimination against Jews to a secondary role in their suggestions and demands toward the state.[36] In that critical situation, this option probably seemed reasonable to many, since given a total of approximately 18,000 pastors, only about 30 were of Jewish descent.[37]

After this change in direction, the precise situation which Bonhoeffer had tried to avoid through his initial presentation of the problem in March/April 1933 came to pass — that is, only isolated voices speaking from a humanitarian or Christian perspective questioned the morality of the "ordering action" of the state. Given the church's progressive institutional shirking of responsibility, individuals were left to speak out from outside the safeguard of the church community. Isolated demands

---

Vergleich mit Stellungnahmen aus der evangelischen Kirche und Kreisen des deutschen Widerstandes (München, 1990).

33. See, e.g., the pamphlet "Der Arierparagraph in der Kirche," from July/August 1933, *GS,* vol. 2, 62-71, and the English version, "Appeal to the Ministers of the Old Prussian Union: The Jewish-Christian Question as *Status Confessionis,*" *GS,* vol. 6, 272-74; cf. also Christine-Ruth Müller, *Dietrich Bonhoeffers Kampf,* 19-36.

34. Cf. Hans Prolingheuer, *Kleine politische Kirchengeschichte. 50 Jahre evangelischer Kirchenkampf von 1919 bis 1969* (Köln, 1984), notes 100, 182.

35. It is noteworthy that the regional synod of Brandenburg, the most important district of the Evangelical Church of the Old Prussian Union, held on the 23rd July 1933, accepted the application of the Aryan Clause in the church by a vote of 133 to 48. This reflected the relation between the delegates belonging to the *Deutsche Christen* (75%) and to the Confessing Church (25%). But it also shows that at the beginning of the Church Struggle most of the persons belonging to the "Confessing church in its process of formation" adhered to a more radical position on this matter. See Scholder, *Die Kirchen und das Dritte Reich,* vol. 1, 593-96.

36. There was strong political pressure against those who dared to oppose the "official" line in the church favored by the Nazi-party. The pressure exerted against church historian Dr. Hans Lietzman, who voted against the Aryan Clause, is just one known example. *Ibid.,* 595.

37. Cf. Prolingheuer, *Kleine politische Kirchengeschichte,* 72.

on a terrorist state inevitably lead to concentration camps and ultimately to martyrdom. In this sense, the appeal that Bonhoeffer sent Martin Niemöller from London on December 15, 1933, reflects very well the situation toward which the process had led by the end of that year:

> The clarity with which you indicated during the summer what course we should follow has repeatedly given us [Bonhoeffer and Hilde-brandt] hopes that now, in the last minute, we might avoid "not knowing how to win" or letting ourselves be pushed away from a purely theological line. Precisely now is when we must be radical in all points, that is to say also with regard to the Aryan Clause, and not be deterred from any consequences that might bring us difficulties. If we now, at this juncture, act disloyally in any way, we will discredit our entire struggle last summer. Please, please make sure that every-thing remains clear, courageous and clean.[38]

Conclusions and Consequences

The Tacit Complicity of the Church

The enactment of the Aryan Clause by the state led to the undermining of law and order, restricting the fundamental civil rights of a group of citizens. Indeed, it deprived a minority of legal protection and produced social victims. By means of the anti-Semitic legislation, the churches were drawn into tacit complicity with the state, even when they decided not to accept the application of the Aryan Clause within their own sphere. Why? Because in 1933, despite its demands, the Nazi state did not have access to the totality of data regarding the ancestry of its citizens. The *Reich* had data in its registry offices as of 1876, that is, covering only two generations. Thus, any citizen who needed to prove his or her "Aryan ancestry" (up to the third and fourth generation) had no other alternative than to ask the parish pastor (or priest) to provide a "Proof of Aryan ancestry" *(Ariernachweis)* on the basis of the church registry. Hence, the entire debate on the application or nonapplication of the Aryan Clause among the functionaries of the Protestant Church in no way exhausted the magnitude of the problem at hand. Even when

38. *GS,* vol. 2, 152.

certain sectors of the church decided not to suspend their Jewish pastors and functionaries nor exclude baptized Jews from their communities, the church cooperated with the state in implementing this discriminatory law in the civil sphere. From the very moment in which the church supplied the state with the facts that allowed it to apply the law, it was giving it direct political support.

This history surely demonstrates how naive it is to propose a clear and precise separation between the civil or state and church spheres. When churches try to avoid any kind of direct political action upon being faced with a state of whose illegitimacy they have little doubt, they should ask themselves with considerable scrupulousness if in fact they are not cooperating directly with the state by means of which they have not yet fully become conscious. Pastor Joachim Kanitz, who was a student of Dietrich Bonhoeffer in Berlin (1932/33) and later in the Finkenwalde Seminary, comments:

> . . . at that time the theological insight was already quite clear that if the Jews were to be excluded a part of the body of Christ would be extirpated; but not only that; also at stake was: Open thy mouth for the mute (Prov. 31:8). I still remember how at that time he (Dietrich Bonhoeffer) introduced ideas about a ministers' strike into the debate and said for example that the pastors should go on strike if they were asked to (write out) those Aryan certificates. . . . What a signal it would have been if the German pastors had said, "We will not provide the certificates." It would not have been possible to throw thousands of pastors into jail. Daily the requests came: "Give me my grandmother's certificate of baptism." And if she had been baptized, then presumably she had been Aryan.[39]

Precisely here, as Kanitz points out, the Protestant Church had an opportunity for direct political action with which to "put a spoke in the wheel" of a state apparatus prepared to crush the Jewish minority. A "ministers' strike," as Bonhoeffer and Hildebrandt pointed out, could and should have been an initially feasible decision in tune with the third option that Bonhoeffer had suggested in his essay. If the pastors, sup-

---

39. Testimony of J. Kanitz in the German documentary film by Hans Joachim Dörger, *Dietrich Bonhoeffer. Nachfolge und Kreuz, Widerstand und Galgen* (Matthias-Film/GmbH, Stuttgart, 1983). The whole text appears in an additional booklet by Dieter Petri and Jörg Thierfelder (Stuttgart: Calwer, 1985), 16.

ported by their superiors (deans, superintendents, bishops), had refused to issue the "Proofs of Aryan ancestry," it would have constituted direct political action decided upon by an Evangelical Council.

The Risks of the "Casus Confessionis"

In his essay, Bonhoeffer established that the state is responsible for an *excess* in law and order when it interferes in matters that concern the church particularly and exclusively. The abuse of state power confronts the church with the need to resist on the basis of the confessional grounds to which it adheres as a Christian community of faith.[40] Now, the beginning of the church struggle shows that the state has subtle and at first glance unobtrusive resources with which to interfere in the church. Nazi-fascism meddled in church matters by means of a "faith movement," a *Deutsche Christen* party that served as its "church arm." By transferring the conflict to the bosom of the church, it also obtained a very important secondary benefit: it encouraged the church to close in upon itself.

In his March/April 1933 essay, Bonhoeffer clearly distinguished two issues to which the church must pay attention: one *ad extra*, that is, responding to state actions, and the other *ad intra*, that is, clarifying for itself why it could not accept the demand for Aryanization proposed by the German Christians. However, when the conflict erupted, the church closed in more and more upon itself, concentrating on the social problem at most from the limited perspective of *status confessionis*. These very terms that Bonhoeffer had used in sketching the problem offered the church the possibility of closing in upon itself. Why? Because the church, threatened and pressured by political power within and without, rapidly became, in its struggle for survival, an *ecclesia incurvata in se*. It became

---

40. With absolute clarity he again formulates this insight at the end of July 1933, in his "Appeal to the Ministers of the Old Prussian Union": "The Aryan paragraph in the form contained in the first programme of the 'German Christians' is a *Status confessionis* for the church. Nothing is more dangerous than for us to allow ourselves to be hoodwinked by statements as to its relative harmlessness. The constantly repeated effort to befog the questions relative to it, is intended to keep us from seeing clearly the fact, by the very substance of which the church is endangered, and thus wrest out of our hands the decision for which we are responsible to the church alone" (*GS*, vol. 6, 272).

an institution that, in order to defend itself from the abuses related to an *excess* of law and order in the state, ended up prevaricating about the *lack* of law and order that the same political regime was applying to a minority group, which in part was located outside the church (non-baptized Jews, leftist political adversaries, gypsies).

Accordingly, an especially problematic aspect was that the debate on the applicability or nonapplicability of the Aryan Clause within the church finally displaced and put an end to the theological debate about the defense of the non-Aryan minority's fundamental human rights in the civil sphere. In my opinion, this situation is repeated any time state terrorism threatens the institutional integrity of the churches. Consequently, the horizons of the *confessio* should be broadened, so that the *casus confessionis* does not receive priority or exclusive consideration as a church problem during times of persecution. Otherwise, the church risks acting in a lukewarm way with regard to the victims, whatever their social and confessional identity, of an oppressive political regime.

For us today in the peripheral reality of "low-intensity democracies" in the Latin American South Cone, this means taking up once more this discussion about the fundamental rights of all the inhabitants of a given nation, and looking at the question from a perspective that can help us avoid our apparently typical Christian shortsightedness. This shortsightedness becomes particularly acute in times in which there is open violation of basic civic rights. I believe that, precisely because for Bonhoeffer the Aryan Clause was an *articulus stantis et cadentis* for the society and the church of his day, we should continue searching out the clues that he gives us in his early essay on the "Jewish question." The latter should be reread in the light of a letter that Bonhoeffer wrote his friend Erwin Sutz on September 11, 1934, back in London:

> Once and for all, we need to put an end to our theologically based restraint with regard to the state's activity: it boils down simply to fear. "Open thy mouth for the mute" (Prov. 31:8) — who in the church today still knows that this is the Bible's minimum requirement in times such as these? And then there is the question of military service, of the war, etc., etc.[41]

41. Cf. *GS,* vol. 1, 42.

In this instance, the mute were those persecuted within the Third Reich, which Bonhoeffer had clearly come to regard as a form of state terrorism. He is referring particularly to the Jewish minority, which can be deduced from the two subsequent references that point toward the problems of another minority: the conscientious objectors confronting the issue of obligatory military service.

Implications for Contemporary Human Rights

First, inasmuch as "the church is not called first of all to interfere" in the state's ordering process by "giving its opinion," she is not called to legitimate any activity of the state either. I make this point because it is all too common when churches have gone through chaotic historical situations that they openly endorse a "strong government" which purports to restore law and order, especially order. According to its very definition, the church should rather hold to its role as a guardian, as a watchperson, as a vigilante, but refrain from adopting a legitimating, justifying, or apologetic role with regard to the state's defects or culpability.

Secondly, of key importance is the use of the term *victims* when referring to the effects of state actions. The language of victimization defines an option for the church and even a certain kind of critical self-definition in the face of the state. "Victims" means the ones who don't have a voice, who lack any power of their own to fall back upon, who are subjected to violation of their civil rights in a situation of total defenselessness. In some sense a victim is by definition innocent from an "ontological" point of view.[42] "Victims" also implies a *victimizer,* an aggressor, whereas more innocuous terminology — such as "harmed" or "damaged" persons — suggests a condition without an agent, and thus silently legitimizes the victimizer in his role as such.

The violence of state actions takes many forms. It may involve ethnic, religious, or political discrimination, but it may also include the marginalization of sectors of the population that suffer the consequences of structural adjustment policies. This means that under the more inclusive term *victims* one can establish a necessary connection between

42. Cf. Franz J. Hinkelammert, *Sacrificios humanos y sociedad occidental. Lucifer y la bestia* (San Jose/Costa Rica, 1991), especially 125-73.

the concept of the *weak* and the concept of the *poor*,[43] so crucial in Latin-American liberation theology.[44] Economic violence is in fact a kind of disguised physical violence, and therefore constitutes a violation of human rights. To put it in a more provocative manner, one could say that a parallel exists between, on the one hand, political measures and laws intended to guarantee the payment of the interest on the foreign debt, and, on the other hand, state activity that generates a "lack of law and order" in Bonhoeffer's sense. Like legislation directed against the Jewish people in the Third Reich, fiscal policies defined by the issue of foreign debt payment leave a group of people without protection, marginalizing them and excluding them from society. The poor are thus *victims* in the same way that politically persecuted persons are.

So, whenever the church is faced with a state failing to perform the function of "God's order of preservation in a godless world," that is, as long as the state keeps generating *victims,* these three possible forms of action that Dietrich Bonhoeffer pointed out pertain. In this sense his appeal in 1933 "to put a spoke in the wheel" of state apparatus continues to be current. The reflections on the "Jewish question" should serve as a paradigm to make our churches conscious of the problem, especially in situations of "low intensity democracies" being subjected to structural adjustment policies.

43. Cf. Bonhoeffer's "View from below": ". . . the outcast, the suspects, the maltreated, the powerless, the oppressed, the reviled . . . ," which he wrote either at the end of 1942 or in the autumn of the following year. The English text is to be found in *LPP,* 17. These words clearly belong to the period when he had decided to act against the Nazi regime from outside of the institutional protection of the church.

44. Cf. Franz J. Hinkelammert, "La critica de la religion en nombre del cristianismo: Dietrich Bonhoeffer," in F. Hinkelammert et al., *Teologia alemana y teologia latinoamericana de la liberacon. Un esfuerzo de dialogo* (San Jose/Costa Rica, 1990), 45-65. See especially 60f.

Sharing the Destiny of His People

ANDREAS PANGRITZ

The purpose of this paper is to inquire into the significance of theology in the context of Bonhoeffer's involvement in political resistance and especially in military conspiracy against Nazi Germany. The title contains an allusion to a letter from prison to Eberhard Bethge, where Bonhoeffer reflects on this involvement.

In a playful comment, Bethge has proposed to divide Bonhoeffer's participation in the anti-Nazi opposition movement into three periods, each characterized by the letter "p": first, the "prophet" engaged in the Confessing Church, protesting publicly against the interventions of the Nazi State into church affairs; second, the "pietist" of the Finkenwalde Seminary, concentrating on meditation on the Bible; and third, the "plotter," engaged in the military conspiracy against Hitler.

It is easy to recognize both the theological and the political dimensions of the role of the "prophet," whereas — at least at first glance — the "pietist" seems to tend exclusively to theology and the "plotter" exclusively to politics. In concentrating on the third aspect of Bonhoeffer's anti-Nazi activity, that of the "plotter," I hope to show that — in contrast to what might first appear — Bonhoeffer would never have become a plotter on political grounds alone. Rather, theology played a decisive role in his particular understanding of and involvement in political resistance.

Contextualization of the Problem

"The Church and the Jewish Question" (1933)

Bonhoeffer's April 1933 address on "The Church and the Jewish Question" can be seen as his manifesto of resistance against the racist policy of the Nazi government. In view of the conservative context of church and society in which Bonhoeffer operated, the topic of this essay — the so-called "Jewish question" — seems to be rather eccentric. In the Barmen Declaration of May 1934, the foundational document of the Confessing Church, this topic would not be mentioned at all. On the other hand, there is no doubt that the manner in which Bonhoeffer treats the so-called "Jewish question" theologically is highly problematic.

It is not my purpose to report at length about the controversies which Bonhoeffer's essay has aroused among Bonhoeffer scholars during the last years. I simply want to mention one recent discussion.

At the Philadelphia Meeting of the American Academy of Religion in November 1995, Stephen R. Haynes tried to demonstrate that Bonhoeffer can serve as a model for Holocaust education.[1] In this context, Haynes criticized Bonhoeffer's 1933 address on "The Church and the Jewish Question" because it contained elements of obvious theological anti-Semitism. In spite of such retrospective criticism I would agree with Heinz Eberhard Tödt's view, according to which Bonhoeffer "was the only one who considered solidarity with the Jews, especially with non-Christian Jews, to be a matter of such importance as to obligate the Christian churches to risk a massive conflict with that state — a risk which could threaten their very existence."[2]

I mention this controversy because Haynes criticizes particularly what he calls the Christian "witness people myth" with respect to the Jews and pleads for a "normalization" of the Jewish-Christian relationship. He claims that what he calls the "witness people myth" is only the other side of the traditional teaching of contempt. This position seems

---

1. S. R. Haynes, "A Man for Others and for Us: Bonhoeffer and Holocaust Education." Paper given at American Academy of Religion meeting, Philadelphia, 1995.
2. Cited in Eberhard Bethge, "Dietrich Bonhoeffer and the Jews," in John D. Godsey and Geffrey B. Kelly, eds., *Ethical Responsibility: Bonhoeffer's Legacy to the Churches* (Toronto/Leviston: Edwin Mellen, 1981), 63.

to ignore the specific language of theology, and typifies a rather progressive or liberal political philosophy.

Unlike Haynes, I would contend that there is no possibility of "normal" Jewish-Christian relations after the Holocaust. What he calls the "witness people myth" will remain indispensable as long as the Bible has any relevance to theology, because it is closely related to the theological concept of Israel as God's Chosen People. For Bonhoeffer, it forms the very nucleus of his theological foundation of political resistance against Nazi Germany. Haynes is right in criticizing Bonhoeffer for repeating the theological tradition of the Chosen People "bearing the curse of its deeds."[3] His alternative suggestion of "normalization" of the Jewish-Christian relationship, however, will turn out to be an illusion of liberalism.

On the grounds of the Lutheran doctrine of the two kingdoms or two realms, Bonhoeffer rejects a simplistic liberal foundation for Christian solidarity with the Jews. This is the reason he can admit to the state the right of exploring "new ways" to deal with the so-called Jewish question.[4] And, perhaps even more disquieting: this is why Bonhoeffer maintains that — for the church — the so-called Jewish question is not a matter of "morality." According to Bonhoeffer in 1933, the church would never criticize the state on the grounds of a "humanitarian ideal."[5] These disturbing formulations do not imply that, according to Bonhoeffer, there is no reason for the church to criticize the legal discrimination of the Jews. On the contrary, he is in search of a more profound basis for this criticism than "humanitarian ideals" and "moral" reasons would be in his view. And he finds this basis in theology; for the church the "Jewish question" is primarily a theological question.

Likewise, the question of how to act toward the state is a theological question for the church. And here we see Bonhoeffer exploring "new ways" of understanding the Lutheran doctrine of the two kingdoms. In spite of the fact that the state is admitted a certain autonomy, Bonhoeffer sees three possible ways in which the church can act toward the state. "In the first place, it can ask the state whether its actions are legitimate. Second, it can aid the victims of state actions. The third possibility is not just to bandage the victims under the wheel, but to jam the spoke in

---

3. *GS,* vol. 1, 49.
4. *Ibid.,* 45.
5. *Ibid.,* 46.

the wheel itself." In "the Jewish problem" Bonhoeffer argues that "the first two possibilities" are "the compelling demands of the hour. The necessity of direct political action by the church," which would involve a revolutionary reinterpretation of the Lutheran doctrine of the two kingdoms, is — according to Bonhoeffer in 1933 — "to be decided . . . by an 'Evangelical Council.'"[6]

Karl Barth on "Tyrannicide" (1938)

In his essay "Rechtfertigung und Recht" (1938) Karl Barth proposed a theological justification of political resistance on the grounds of an affinity between spiritual justification and secular justice.[7] "The phrase of the alleged equal affinity or non-affinity of any possible form of government to the gospel," Barth emphasizes, "is not only shabby but simply wrong. It is true that you can go to hell in a democracy and be redeemed under a mob rule or dictatorship. But it is not true that a Christian can affirm, wish and strive for mob rule or dictatorship as seriously as for democracy."[8]

Barth interprets the "subjection" to the will of the authorities, which Paul in Romans 13:1 allegedly demands from Christians, as simply "paying somebody the respect due to his position." This would be the self-evident other side of the "priestly service" of the Christian congregation with respect to the state, which is primarily exercised in intercessory prayers. By no means would "due respect" to the authorities have the meaning of "affirming and voluntarily supporting the intentions and enterprises of the authorities, even when these are oriented to suppress rather than protect the proclamation of the gospel of justification."[9] In this case the Christian "respect" to the authorities would assume a "critical form."[10]

6. D. Bonhoeffer, "The Church and the Jewish Question," in G. B. Kelly and F. B. Nelson, eds., *A Testament to Freedom* (San Francisco: HarperCollins, 1990), 139f.
7. K. Barth, "Rechtfertigung und Recht," *Theologischen Studien* 104, 2nd ed. (Zurich, 1979), 20. In his *Ethics*, Bonhoeffer characterizes the topic as "preparing the way" for the "ultimate" within the "penultimate." *Ethics*, 133f.; cf. *Ethik, DBW*, vol. 6, 155.
8. Cf. Barth, "Rechtfertigung," 44f., note 30b.
9. *Ibid.*, 38f.
10. *Ibid.*, 40.

Barth does not, therefore, make a plea for tyrannicide, referring to the Zurich reformer Zwingli and to the *Confessio Scotica.* In Zwingli's *Schlußreden* (1523) we read that "a faithless government, which has abandoned the rule of Christ, must be *dismissed with the help of God."* And the Calvinistic *Confessio Scotica* (1560) makes it the task of the Christian "to support the life of the good people, *to oppress the tyrant,* and to defend the weak against the violence of the malicious" (44f.).[11]

Bonhoeffer probably knew Barth's essay, and it is likely that he was encouraged by it to participate in political resistance even without support by the church.[12] Yet, Barth's way of reasoning is not his. In the context of the church, which interpreted the Lutheran doctrine of the two kingdoms in a highly conservative and authoritarian way, Bonhoeffer could not see very much sense in stressing the "affinity" between the spiritual and the secular. Even his own understanding of Romans 13 in *The Cost of Discipleship* comes across in such a traditional Lutheran and authoritarian way[13] that in 1943 he would have no difficulty in referring to it during his trial at the *Reichskriegsgericht.* "If anyone wants to learn something of my conception of the duty of Christian obedience towards the authorities, he should read my exposition of Romans 13 in my book *The Cost of Discipleship.* The appeal to subjection to the will and the demands of authority for the sake of Christian conscience has probably seldom been expressed more strongly than there. That is my personal attitude to these questions."[14]

Another reason Bonhoeffer could not fully agree with Barth's conception may be seen in the political attitudes of the anti-Nazi conspirators. The majority of them were not "democratic" in a western sense or at least "democratic" only with some qualifications. Their concepts of how to reconstruct Germany after a successful *coup d'état* tended toward Romanticism and authoritarianism.

Obviously, Barth's "democratic" reasoning in favor of political resistance is — in Bonhoeffer's view — still affected by the utopian expectations of historical progress in the years immediately after World War I, when the intention was to establish a democratic administration in

---

11. *Ibid.,* 44f.
12. Cf. Bonhoeffer's letter to G. Leibholz (March 3, 1940) smuggled via Switzerland to Oxford, *GS,* vol. 3, 35.
13. Cf. *Nachfolge, DBW,* vol. 4, 256-59.
14. *LPP,* 60.

Germany for the first time. In contrast to this perspective Bonhoeffer seeks "conservative" grounds for political resistance, a foundation which would be able to save a society running self-destructively to the abyss. So we read at the end of the chapter called "Inheritance and Decay" (1940) in his *Ethics:*

> Two things alone have still the power to avert the final plunge into the void. One is the miracle of a new awakening of faith, and the other is that force which the Bible calls the "restrainer," *katechon* (2 Thess. 2:7), that is to say the force of order, equipped with great physical strength, which effectively blocks the way of those who are about to plunge into the abyss. . . . The "restrainer" is the force which takes effect within history through God's governance of the world, and which sets due limits to evil. The "restrainer" itself is not God; it is not without guilt; but God makes use of it in order to preserve the world from destruction.[15]

It was not the imminent defeat of Germany which troubled Bonhoeffer most. Rather, he experienced Hitler's military successes as a catastrophe which had to be restrained. Therefore he claimed the allied armies as "restrainers" in the biblical sense, as well as the circle of military conspirators within the German *Abwehr*. When Bonhoeffer emphasizes the difference between the "miracle of a new awakening of faith" on the one hand and the "restrainer," who is "not without guilt" on the other, we again recognize the structure of the Lutheran two-kingdoms doctrine in his argument.

No wonder Bonhoeffer's "conservatism" in search of a theological foundation of political resistance provoked Barth's "democratic" suspiciousness. As Barth informed Bonhoeffer via Charlotte von Kirschbaum, he was distrustful of "any attempt to rescue Germany by the means of further 'national' enterprises from its immeasurable misery." Among these he explicitly counted "also the attempts which possibly would be made by the military generals."[16]

---

15. *Ethics,* 108; cf. *Ethik, DBW,* vol. 6, 122f.
16. Cf. Ch. v. Kirschbaum, letter to D. Bonhoeffer (May 17, 1942), in D. Bonhoeffer, *Schweizer Korrespondenz 1941-42. Im Gespräch mit Karl Barth* (Munich, 1982), *Theologische Existenz heute,* no. 214, 18.

Political Motives in Bonhoeffer's Decision

"Patriotism" in the Moment of Decision (June 1939)

We turn to Bonhoeffer's letter from prison to Eberhard Bethge (December 22, 1943), where he reflects on his decision to return to Germany in 1939. Bonhoeffer writes:

> Now I want to assure you that I haven't for a moment regretted coming back in 1939 — nor any of the consequences, either. I knew quite well what I was doing, and I acted with clear conscience. I've no wish to cross out of my life anything that has happened since, either to me personally . . . , or as regards events in general. And I regard my being kept here . . . as being involved in Germany's fate, as I was resolved to be.[17]

This is the phrase I have alluded to in the title of this paper, though I have translated it by "to share the destiny of his people" (instead of "being involved in Germany's fate"). The phrase may remind us of Bonhoeffer's letter to Reinhold Niebuhr on the occasion of his return to Germany in July 1939 on the eve of World War II: "I have made a mistake in coming to America. I must live through this difficult period of our national history with the Christian people of Germany. I will have no right to participate in the reconstruction of Christian life in Germany after the war if I do not share the trials of this time with my people."[18]

The nostalgia for Germany is obvious in this passage. But what would be the precise meaning of "sharing the destiny of Germany" even in the "trials of this time" of war? Do we see Bonhoeffer here submitting to a fate predetermined by *Vorsehung* (Providence)? Does he give way to the tide of *Volksverbundenheit* (Romantic nationalism), as Kl.-M. Kodalle has put it?[19] Such an interpretation could be supported by an even more problematic phrase in Bonhoeffer's diary (June 22, 1939):

> It is unbearable over here for a German; one is simply torn in two. To stay here during a catastrophe is quite inconceivable, unless it is or-

---

17. *LPP*, 174.
18. *A Testament to Freedom*, 504; *GS*, vol. 1, 320.
19. Kl.-M. Kodalle, *Dietrich Bonhoeffer. Zur Kritik seiner Theologie* (Gütersloh, 1991), 73f.

dained. But to be responsible oneself, to have to reproach oneself, for having come out unnecessarily, is certainly crushing. We cannot separate ourselves from our destiny. . . .[20]

For Bonhoeffer, the patriot who does not leave his people alone in a "difficult period" of its "national history" — it would be easy to settle for this simplistic political portrait. But Bonhoeffer's seemingly obvious patriotism is contradicted by some other statements.

Elements Contradicting Patriotism

It seems obvious from Bonhoeffer's diary that the reasons for his decision to return to Germany were not as clear to him in the moment of decision as he would later pretend. In the moment of decision the motives for his return were hidden even before his own conscience. In his diary of summer 1939 we can find the traces of a painful process of decision-making. We would search in vain for traces of what he later called his "clear conscience" in that moment. On the contrary, on July 20, 1939, the day of decision, Bonhoeffer notes:

"It is remarkable how I am never quite clear about the motives for any of my decisions. Is that a sign of confusion, of inner dishonesty, or is it a sign that we are guided without our knowing, or is it both?" And then he continues:

> Today the reading speaks dreadfully harshly of God's incorruptible judgment. He certainly sees how much personal feeling, how much anxiety there is in today's decision, however brave it may seem. The reasons one gives for an action to others and to one's self are certainly inadequate. One can give a reason for everything. In the last resort one acts from a level which remains hidden from us. So one can only ask God to judge us and to forgive us.[21]

Only a few months later it turned out that Bonhoeffer's decision to "share the destiny" of his people implied his participation in political resistance. Already the letter to Reinhold Niebuhr from July 1939 quoted

---

20. *A Testament to Freedom*, 497 (translation altered); cf. *GS*, vol. 1, 305f.
21. *Ibid.*, 496.

above reveals that Bonhoeffer was "willing the defeat" of Germany in the war. The quotation continues:

> Christians in Germany will face the terrible alternative of either willing the defeat of their nation in order that Christian civilization may survive, or willing the victory of their nation and thereby destroying our civilization. I know which of these alternatives I must choose; but I cannot make that choice in security. . . .[22]

Even more explicit is the recollection of Willem A. Visser 't Hooft, who, during Bonhoeffer's journeys to Switzerland on the instruction of the conspiracy group within the German *Abwehr* in 1941 and 1942, repeatedly met him in Geneva. When Visser 't Hooft asked him in September 1941, "What are you praying for in the present situation?" Bonhoeffer answered: "If you want to know it, I am praying for the defeat of Germany, because I believe this is the only possibility to pay for the suffering which my country has brought upon the world."[23]

It seems to be obvious from this recollection that Bonhoeffer's political attitude (if it can be characterized as patriotic at all) implied a very special kind of patriotism — and this in obvious contrast to the attitude of other members of the resistance movement who had joined the conspiracy in order to prevent the defeat of Germany. I want to illustrate this difference by an episode from Bonhoeffer's journey to Sweden on behalf of the *Abwehr* in Spring 1942. On May 31, 1942, he met his friend, Bishop George Bell, in Sigtuna.

---

22. *Ibid.*, 504; *GS*, vol. 1, 320.

23. W. A. Visser 't Hooft, "Begegnung mit Dietrich Bonhoeffer," in *Das Zeugnis eines Boten. Zum Gedächtnis von Dietrich Bonhoeffer* (Geneva, 1945), 7. Cf. Visser 't Hooft's note after his encounter with Bonhoeffer in Spring 1941: "Inside the Confessing Church there is a certain difference of conviction with regard to the stand which the Church should take. . . . With regard to the attitude to the war, it is generally recognized among believing Christians that a victory of their government will have the most fateful consequences for the Church. . . . On the other hand, they consider that a defeat of their country would probably mean its end as a nation. Thus many have come to believe that, whatever the outcome of it all will be, it will be an evil thing for them. One hears, however, also voices which say that after all the suffering which their country has brought upon others they almost hope for an opportunity to pay the price by suffering themselves." Bethge, *Dietrich Bonhoeffer. Eine Biographie* (Munich: Chr. Kaiser, 1967), 819.

Hans Schönfeld, a member of an ecumenical research center in Geneva and cooperating with the resistance group *Kreisauer Kreis,* had come to Sweden as well in order to present a memorandum of the German opposition to George Bell. In this "Statement by a German Pastor," Schönfeld maintains that "the internal circumstances are becoming now peculiarly favourable to a coup d'état. . . ." He suggests that

> it would help and quicken this process toward the change of power . . . if the Allies would make it clear whether they are prepared for a European peace settlement. If otherwise the Allies insist on a fight to the finish the German opposition within the German Army is ready to go on with the war to the bitter end in spite of its wish to end the Nazi régime.

Among other ambiguous demands which, in view of the military situation, indicated the vision of a unified Europe under German hegemony, the Schönfeld "Statement" announces the readiness/willingness of the German opposition to "co-operate with all other nations for a comprehensive solution of the Jewish problem."[24] At a time when the so-called "final solution" of the Jewish question was already underway there was — in this perspective — a "Jewish problem" waiting for solution. Obviously this wing of the German opposition had no idea of the fact that the so-called Jewish question was primarily a German question.

In his account of the meeting, however, Bishop Bell recollects:

> Here Bonhoeffer broke in. His Christian conscience, he said, was not quite at ease with Schönfeld's ideas. There must be punishment by God. We should not be worthy of such a solution. Our action must be such as the world will understand as an act of repentance. "Christians do not wish to escape repentance, or chaos, if it is God's will to bring it upon us. We must take this judgment as Christians."[25]

It is obvious from this account that Bonhoeffer — in contrast to the major part of the opposition — does not reject the Allied demand of

24. Cf. H. Schönfeld, "Statement by a German Pastor at Stockholm (31st May 1942)," *GS,* vol. 1, 380.
25. Cf. George Bell, "The Church and the Resistance Movement" (1957), in *GS,* vol. 1, 405. Cf. also G. Bell, "The Background of the Hitler Plot" (1945), *ibid.,* 395.

"unconditional surrender."[26] In view of the German guilt piling up day by day there is no time left for negotiations. Immediate action is demanded. And obviously, Bonhoeffer has no difficulty with regarding the Allied armies as well as the conspiracy group as instruments in the hand of God, helping to execute his judgment.

In Bonhoeffer's drama fragment written during the first months of his imprisonment we find "Germany" among the besmirched terms which should be honored by silence for a time. Here we read from the dramatic persona Christoph, who can be largely identified with Bonhoeffer: "Which right-thinking man would bring himself today to utter the besmirched words Liberty, Brotherhood, even the word Germany? . . . Let us honor the great values for a time by silence, let us learn to do the right thing for a time without words."[27]

In this quotation we have — as the Bethges put it — "a kind of secular, political dimension of 'arcane discipline.'" This points us to the theological dialectic of "arcane discipline" — the discipline of the secret of faith — and "doing justice among the people" in Bonhoeffer's prison writings. In "Thoughts on the Day of Baptism" of Bonhoeffer's grand-nephew (May 1944), Bonhoeffer writes:

> Our church, which has been fighting in these years only for its self-preservation, as though that were an end in itself, is incapable of taking the word of reconciliation and redemption to humanity and the world. Our earlier words are therefore bound to lose their force and cease, and our being Christians today will be limited to two things: prayer and doing justice among the people. All Christian thinking, speaking, and organizing must be born anew out of this prayer and action.[28]

Who would dare to tell when the time has come that the church will be able "to utter the Word of God" in a way "that the world will be changed and renewed by it" as Bonhoeffer expects? Or, by analogy: who would prophesy the day when it should be permitted to talk of "Germany" with pride again?

---

26. Cf. Bethge, *Dietrich Bonhoeffer*, 85.

27. Cf. *Fragments aus Tegel*, ed. Renate Bethge and Ilse Tödt, *DBW*, vol. 7 (Gütersloh: Chr. Kaiser/Gütersloh, 1994), 49.

28. *LPP*, 300.

Theological Motives

The "Brethren" of the Confessing Church

Who is this "Germany"; who are the people for whom Bonhoeffer feels responsible? Along with his reference to "Germany" in his American diary from 1939 Bonhoeffer repeatedly mentions the "brethren." So we might interpret that his sentiment of responsibility for the "brethren" of the Confessing Church is the main reason for his decision to return to Germany. This would correspond to Bethge's second "p": Bonhoeffer the "pietist," who became involved in political resistance on the grounds of solidarity with his church.

Yet the notion of "brethren" could arouse our suspicion as well. Solidarity with an oppressed church may be reason enough to honor a person as a saint, a holy man, and finally a martyr. However, this motive would be a narrowing of the original starting point of Bonhoeffer's involvement in resistance activities. This starting point was — as I have already mentioned — solidarity with the Jews. And besides that, at least according to today's linguistic conventions, the "sisters" seem to be dismissed from Bonhoeffer's ecclesiastical solidarity.[29]

In his *Ethics* Bonhoeffer attempts to reflect the experience of political resistance theologically. In contrast to the popular characterization of Bonhoeffer and his fellow resisters as "heroes of conscience," the notion of "conscience" does not play an important role in Bonhoeffer's ethical reflections. Rather, the conscience appears as an expression of the self-centered attitude of the sinner. The central concept in Bonhoeffer's reflection on his participation in anti-Nazi resistance is "responsibility." And in search of "the structures of responsible life" he develops the concept of "mandates."[30] It is noteworthy that Bonhoeffer counts among these "mandates" the church, the family, culture, and government;[31] the notion of "people" or "nation" is lacking in his list. Asking how it was possible that Bonhoeffer's solidarity with the "destiny of his people" assumed such a paradoxical shape involves taking into

---

29. Cf. L. Siegele-Wenschkewitz, "Die Ehre der Frau, dem Manne zu dienen: Zum Frauenbild Dietrich Bonhoeffers," ed. R. Jost und V. Kubera, *Wie Theologen Frauen sehen — Von der Macht des Bildes* (Freiburg, 1993), 98ff.

30. *Ethics*, 207ff., 286ff.

31. *Ibid.*, 286.

account the "confession of guilt" which was formulated as part of his *Ethics* in 1941.

The *"Confession of Guilt"*

If we recall Bonhoeffer's address "The Church and the Jewish Question," we may realize that the most explosive point, the hope that an Evangelical Council would decide on the necessity of "direct political action" in solidarity with the Jews, had turned out to be an illusion. The Confessing Church had never felt in a position to assume responsibility for such a decision. This is the point where Bonhoeffer sees the church becoming guilty: the church has failed to accept the role of "restrainer" and "to jam a spoke in the wheel" of a disastrous history. Instead, even the Confessing Church had proclaimed that participating in Hitler's criminal war was a "patriotic duty."

Thus, Bonhoeffer in the course of 1941 feels compelled to formulate a "Confession of Guilt," where we read:

> The Church confesses that she has witnessed the lawless application of brutal force, the physical and spiritual suffering of countless innocent people, oppression, hatred and murder, and that she has not raised her voice on behalf of the victims and has not found ways to hasten to their aid. She is guilty of the deaths of the weakest and most defenceless brothers of Jesus Christ.[32]

According to Eberhard Bethge, "there is no doubt that Bonhoeffer's primary motivation for entering active political conspiracy was the treatment of the Jews by the Third Reich."[33] "With this terminology, 'the brothers of Jesus Christ' Bonhoeffer by the very act of confessing his own and his church's guilt enters into deep solidarity with the victims of the Holocaust; and he shows at the same time a respect, or a self-imposed restraint, towards the victims, the Jews."[34]

Probably at the same moment he formulated this confession of guilt Bonhoeffer inserted into his chapter "Inheritance and Decay" the fol-

---

32. *Ethics,* 114; cf. *Ethik, DBW,* vol. 6, 129f.
33. Eberhard Bethge, "Dietrich Bonhoeffer and the Jews," in *Ethical Responsibility,* 76.
34. *Ibid.,* 80.

lowing phrase: "An expulsion of the Jews from the West must necessarily bring with it the expulsion of Christ. For Jesus was a Jew."[35] With the beginning of the war the problem was no longer "expulsion." It now became more and more clear that the so-called "final solution" was the extermination of the European Jews. Now each moment of hesitation to "restrain" the catastrophe would mean another moment of guilt.

We are able now to understand more precisely which "destiny of Germany" Bonhoeffer had decided to share. It is not primarily the destiny of "his people," not even solidarity with the "brethren" of the Confessing Church, which turns out to be central for Bonhoeffer's decision to return to Germany, but the destiny of the Jewish "brothers of Jesus Christ." Without a theological conception of the close relationship between the church and Israel, without the so-called "witness people myth," Bonhoeffer probably would not have been able to develop such a paradoxical form of "patriotism." "Western history is, by God's will, indissolubly linked with the people of Israel, not only genetically but in a genuine uninterrupted encounter. The Jew keeps open the question of Christ."[36]

And in the essay "After Ten Years" he notes for his fellow conspirators in December 1942:

> We are not Christ, but if we want to be Christians, we must have some share in Christ's large-heartedness by acting with responsibility and in freedom when the hour of danger comes, and by showing real compassion that springs, not from fear, but from the liberating and redeeming love of Christ for all who suffer. . . . The Christian is called to compassion and action not in the first place by his own sufferings, but by the sufferings of the brothers, for whose sake Christ suffered.[37]

"Compassion": Participating in the Suffering of God

After his imprisonment, Bonhoeffer's "sharing the destiny of his people" assumes primarily the form of compassion. One aspect of this compassion is political, as he writes in the "Thoughts on the Day of Baptism" of his grandnephew (May 1944):

35. *Ethics*, 90; cf. *Ethik*, *DBW*, vol. 6, 95.
36. *Ethics*, 89; cf. *Ethik*, *DBW*, vol. 6, 95.
37. *LPP*, 14. Translation slightly altered.

It will not be difficult for us to renounce our privileges, recognizing the justice of history. We may have to face events and changes that take no account of our wishes and our rights. But if so, we shall not give way to embittered and barren pride, but consciously submit to divine judgment, and so prove ourselves worthy to survive by identifying ourselves generously and unselfishly with the life of the community and the sufferings of our fellow-men. . . . "Seek the welfare of the city . . . and pray to the Lord on its behalf" (Jer. 29:7).[38]

This identification with the life of the community is pulled from the political into the theological light in the last letter to Eberhard Bethge before the failure of the *coup d'état* (July 16-18, 1944). Now he writes on "participation in the sufferings and powerlessness of God" himself in the "secular life." Bonhoeffer interprets a line of the poem "Christians and Pagans":[39] "The poem . . . contains an idea that you will recognize: 'Christians stand by God in his hour of grieving'; that is what distinguishes Christians from pagans."[40]

And Bonhoeffer explains this "standing by" in what follows as "participation":

It is not the religious act that makes the Christian, but participation in the sufferings of God in the secular life. That is *metanoia:* not in the first place thinking about one's own needs, problems, sins, and fears, but allowing oneself to be caught up into the way of Jesus Christ, into the messianic event, thus fulfilling now Isa. 53. . . . This being caught up into the messianic sufferings of God in Jesus Christ takes a variety of forms in the New Testament. . . . The only thing that is common to all these is their sharing in the suffering of God in Christ. That is their "faith." There is nothing of religious method here. The "religious act" is always something partial; "faith" is something whole, involving the whole of one's life. Jesus calls men, not to a new religion, but to life.[41]

The announced explanation of "this life" in "participation in the powerlessness of God in the world" can be found in the following letter to E. Bethge, the letter from July 21, 1944, the day after the failure of the plot:

38. *Ibid.*, 299.
39. Cf. the poem "Stations on the Road to Freedom," *LPP*, 370f.
40. *Ibid.*, 361. Translation slightly altered.
41. *Ibid.*, 361f.

One must completely abandon any attempt to make something of oneself, whether it be a saint, or a converted sinner, or a churchman (a so-called priestly type!), a righteous man or an unrighteous one, a sick man or a healthy one. By this-worldliness I mean living unreservedly in life's duties, problems, successes and failures, experiences and perplexities. In so doing we throw ourselves completely into the arms of God, taking seriously, not our own sufferings, but those of God in the world — watching with Christ in Gethsemane. That, I think, is faith; that is *metanoia;* and that is how one becomes a human being, a Christian.[42]

In his "Outline for a Book" (August 1944) Bonhoeffer finds the most provocative formulation of the thought, nearly identifying Christian life with Christ himself: "Our relation to God is not a 'religious' relationship to the highest, most powerful, and best Being imaginable — that is not authentic transcendence — but our relation to God is a new life in 'existence for others,' through participation in the being of Jesus."[43]

In my view, such "existence for others" in "participation in the being of Jesus" reflects the tradition of mysticism to a problematic extent. The question might be asked whether the identification of a Christian life with the life and death of Jesus Christ would not result in excessive demands. The reason for this identification, however, seems to be the discovery that in the first place it was Christ himself who, in his suffering, identified himself with the life and sufferings of his people. This is the meaning of Bonhoeffer's remark on the "messianic event" that Isaiah 53 — the song of the suffering Servant of God — is *now* being fulfilled. Eberhard Bethge writes in his essay "Dietrich Bonhoeffer and the Jews": "Isaiah 53 is 'now' ... fulfilled in the representative suffering of Israel for the nations. Not just in ancient times, 'then,' but 'now' in the present there is a 'life of participation in the powerlessness of God in the world.' In this way the Jews really 'keep open the question of Christ.'"[44]

---

42. *Ibid.,* 369. Translation altered.
43. *Ibid.,* 381.
44. Bethge, "Dietrich Bonhoeffer and the Jews," 84f.

"Operation 7"

In this context it seems appropriate to recall one of the activities of the conspiracy group, which in larger historical perspective might appear as irrelevant. I think of the so-called "Operation 7," which simply consisted of the attempt to rescue a small number of human lives. By this conspiratorial activity in September 1942 — at a time when the mass deportations of Jews already were underway — the Bonhoeffer-Dohnanyi group within the *Abwehr* succeeded in sending a group of fourteen people of Jewish faith or Jewish descent across the Swiss border, into security camouflaged as spies of the *Abwehr*.[45]

The question has been asked whether by this successful rescue activity the conspiracy group had not threatened the more important project of the plot against Hitler. A postwar correspondence between Hans Bernd Gisevius and Fritz W. Arnold, the speaker of the rescued, clarifies the theological dimension of "Operation 7": In the beginning of 1946, Gisevius maintained that the *Ausland/Abwehr* office had been "extraordinarily unsuitable for such things." It was "primarily in a position to prepare for the assassination attempt." He therefore described it as "highly questionable to let oneself be diverted from this great goal by any independent action, even if the intention was well-meant."[46] Fritz W. Arnold replied that he was convinced that "rescuing one human life — one grain of sand in an ocean of murdered — was much more important than any plot, independently of how great the goal was. . . ." In reaction to this letter Gisevius could not see any sense in continuing the correspondence, because, as he put it, Arnold was arguing in a "talmudic" way.[47]

Unfortunately, Gisevius did not explain what he intended by "talmudic." But it is clear that in his opinion this must be something even more stupid than "normal" theological thinking. However, it was such "talmudic" thinking that obviously motivated Bonhoeffer — in contrast to other members of the resistance movement, Gisevius himself included.

45. Cf. W. Meyer, *Unternehmen Sieben. Eine Rettungsaktion für vom Holocaust Bedrohte aus dem Amt Ausland/Abwehr im Oberkommando der Wehrmacht* (Frankfurt, 1993).

46. H. B. Gisevius, letter to Fr. W. Arnold (January 5, 1946); cited in W. Meyer, *Unternehmen Sieben*, 457f.

47. Fr. W. Arnold, letter to H. B. Gisevius (January 9, 1946); cited in *ibid.*, 590 (note 670).

It is not by chance then that "Operation 7" was one of the reasons Bonhoeffer was prosecuted and finally sentenced to death. Bonhoeffer became a martyr not simply as a political resister, but especially as a rescuer. I agree with William J. Peck, who said: "Deeds must precede words." Bonhoeffer therefore — according to Peck — "took back his sentence about the curse laid on the name of the Jews, in the only way in which he could take it back, by entering into solidarity with the victims of the Holocaust through his death."[48]

The Politics of Memory

On the occasion of the fiftieth anniversary of the day of Bonhoeffer's assassination, Bishop Wolfgang Huber has recently added another political "p" to Bethge's series: Bonhoeffer, the "patriot." This characterization is remarkable, particularly in view of the fact that Bonhoeffer's participation in military conspiracy has been vehemently disputed in postwar Germany. In the 1950s and early 60s Bonhoeffer was regarded as a traitor of his nation. Even his own church, the church of Berlin-Brandenburg, in a message of July 20, 1945, felt it was necessary to condemn the plot. The church allegedly could never approve of a political plot, no matter what the purpose was. Among the people who had suffered from persecution by the Nazis were many who would never have wished for such a conspiracy. Consequently the name of Bonhoeffer was not mentioned, because for the church he was no martyr in the full sense of the word.[49]

It now seems, however, that not just the German Protestant Churches but German society as a whole is ready to make peace with a person who has been honored internationally already for a long time as a representative of the "other Germany," a defender of "freedom and democracy" against totalitarianism.

It is difficult for some of us not to feel a little bit uneasy about this rapprochement. "What can . . . a past thing be rescued from?" asked the

---

48. William J. Peck, "Response," in *Ethical Responsibility*, 100.

49. Significantly, the judges who had sentenced Bonhoeffer to death were acquitted of guilt by the supreme court in the fifties, whereas Bonhoeffer has never been rehabilitated. This proves a certain continuity of legal institutions between Nazi Germany and the West German democracy after 1945. No Nazi judge was ever sentenced for the part he had played.

Jewish philosopher Walter Benjamin. His answer is: The past has "not just to be rescued from the disrepute and disrespect it may fall into, but from a certain way of being handed down. The way it is honoured as 'inheritance' may be even more disastrous than oblivion ever could be."[50] It is my suspicion that the unification of Germany has functioned as a kind of legitimization for patriotic language with respect to Bonhoeffer. I would contend, however, that his treatment as a traitor in the 1950s in Germany comes closer to the historical facts; it was in fact *as* a traitor in Nazi Germany that he proved himself a "good German," a political resister in the full sense of the word.

A German newspaper headline, written on the occasion of the fiftieth anniversary of Bonhoeffer's death, reads: "A death for Germany."[51] This headline turns out to be a quotation from George Bell's sermon in the commemorative service at Holy Trinity Church in London on July 17, 1945. But let us hear the quotation in context:

> His death is a death for Germany—indeed for Europe too . . . his death, like his life, marks a fact of the deepest value in the witness of the Confessional Church. As one of a noble company of martyrs of differing traditions, he represents both the resistance of the believing soul, in the name of God, to the assault of evil, and also the moral and political revolt of the human conscience against injustice and cruelty . . . it was this passion for justice that brought him, and so many others . . . , into such close partnership with other resisters, who, though outside the Church, shared the same humanitarian and liberal ideals. . . . For him and Klaus . . . there is the resurrection from the dead; for Germany redemption and resurrection, if God pleases to lead the nation through men animated by his spirit, holy and humble and brave like him; for the Church, not only that in Germany which he loved, but the Church Universal which was greater to him than nations, the hope of a new life.[52]

The use of Bell's sermon to prove the alleged "patriotism" of Bonhoeffer seems to me highly questionable. More precisely, in my opinion, simply quoting the "patriotic" beginning of this sermon and

---

50. Walter Benjamin, *GS*, vol. 1, 1242. Cf. W. Benjamin, "Das Passagen-Werk," *GS*, vol. 5, 591: "Es gibt eine Überlieferung, die Katastrophe ist."

51. Klaus von Dohnanyi, in *Die Zeit*, April 9, 1995.

52. Cited in Bethge, *Dietrich Bonhoeffer*, 1041f.

ignoring its ecumenical perspective constitutes an improper political use of this sermon. If we may find elements of patriotism in Bonhoeffer's decision, these have nothing to do with what is usually understood by this term. In order to avoid political instrumentalization and other misrepresentations we should rather abstain from using the unclear expression at all to characterize Bonhoeffer's attitude. His unusual theological "patriotism" includes elements such as solidarity with the Jews and high treason against the political administration, which, at least in Germany, have never before been associated with patriotism.

Bonhoeffer's Reception in East Germany[1]

JOHN A. MOSES

Any history of the collapse of the German Democratic Republic (GDR) in the autumn and winter of 1989/90 that fails to pay due attention to the role of the church, in particular the Protestant church, is bound to be out of focus. By the same token, any assessment of the church's self-perception and role in its relations with the State of so-called Real Existing Socialism (RES) that neglects the theological and political influence of theologians such as Karl Barth, but particularly Dietrich Bonhoeffer, is also going to be inadequate. Moreover, the Socialist Unity Party's (SED) own response to Bonhoeffer's political-theological legacy played a central part in shaping official church policy. Consequently, given the impact of Bonhoeffer's thought for both church and state in the GDR, he can be ignored neither by the theologian nor by the historian.

In explaining the behavior of the Protestant church in Eastern Germany from 1945 to 1989 the historian is obliged to evaluate theological ideas as much as s/he would attend to social, political, and economic factors. Historical explanation demands that the investigator be receptive to all these aspects with sufficient understanding to be able to attribute to them their relative importance to the overall course of

1. The preparation of this paper was greatly facilitated by the friendly assistance of Professor Michael Lattke and the Reverend Dr. Maurice Schild.

events. And precisely because in the history of the GDR the church occupied a peculiar status in society as the one agency outside the direct control of the regime, theology took on yet again in contemporary German history an efficacious significance. This presents a problem for the less theologically literate historian. Not all have felt entirely at home in having to take theological perspectives into account. Nevertheless, the attempt has to be made. It is perhaps not surprising that in the former GDR some of the most prominent historians and analysts of the subject are also in fact pastors.[2]

These have contributed greatly to the ongoing debate concerning the so-called Protestant Revolution in the former GDR. Among them, Edelbert Richter (Weimar) has proffered one of the most convincing explanations.[3] He identifies the Protestant church as having constituted an irreducible, independent ideological element in GDR society which developed in the course of time under the changing internal and external conditions into a genuine "public sphere." In it more and more dissident groups were able to coalesce into a vocal opposition which could not, in the end, be silenced, as much as the regime would have wished to do so. Since the regime had abandoned its initially moderately accommodating policy toward Christians, with a view to collaboration in building a new society, and replaced it with one of rigorous marginalization of the church, Christians found in time that they were being increasingly forced into opposition.

Since the formation of the Task Force for Church Questions in the Central Committee of the SED *(Arbeitsgruppe Kirchenfragen)* in March 1954, which operated on the principle of "claim to total truth" by the Party *(totaler Warheitsanspruch)*,[4] the Church was confronted with the decision whether to submit to the policy of ultimate "ghettoisation" or

---

2. An exhaustive list of publications by pastors here would be impracticable. Some of the most outstanding writers include Erhart Neubert, Edelbert Richter, Friedrich Schorlemmer, Rudi Pahnke, Richard Schroeder, Detlef Pollack, and Kurt Nowak. However, see John A. Moses and Greg Munro, "Assessing the Role of the East German Churches in the Collapse of the GDR," in *Rewriting the German Past*, ed. Reinhard Alter and Peter Monteath (London: Humanities Press, 1996).

3. Edelbert Richter, *Christentum und Demokratie in Deutschland — Beiträge zur geistigen Vorbereitung der Wende in der DDR* (Leipzig/Weimar: Verlag Gustav Kiepenhauer, 1991), 274-77.

4. Joachim Heise, in the introduction to *SED und Kirche* (Band 1:1946-67), ed. Frédéric Hartweg (Neukirchen/Vluyn: Neukirchener Verlag, 1995), 8, 11.

to try to become pro-active in the proclamation of the gospel. Indeed, Bishop Otto Dibelius already identified the problem in 1949 when he observed that, "At the present time we are oppressed more than anything else by the concern that the form of State which is emerging around us evinces so many of the characteristics which in the period of National Socialism, for the sake of God, merited our resistance."[5] This unleashed an internal church debate on the question whether the State of RES should be regarded as the genuine "powers-that-be" *(Obrigkeit)* in the sense intended by St. Paul's epistle to the Romans, chapter 13.

This debate was never concluded, and with the enforced break with the all-German Church, *Evangelische Kirche Deutschlands* (EKD), and the subsequent establishment in 1969 of the *Bund der Evangelischen Kirchen* (BEK) with jurisdiction limited to the borders of the GDR, it took on an even more intensified form. This was because one could never gain complete agreement as to what the concept adopted by the Church in its relation to the regime, *Kirche im Sozialismus,* really signified. There were those who regarded it in practically the same terms as the organization of the German Christians in relation to the Third Reich (i.e., total submission to the State) and quoted Reich Bishop Ludwig Müller from February 1934: "We exist not beside or against the state but rather we stand in its midst as its most loyal servants and firmest pillar."[6] The point of this, of course, was to depict the State of RES in its attitude to the church as essentially indistinguishable from the Nazi state, the obvious differences notwithstanding. And such a state was no *Obrigkeit* for those who thought like Dietrich Bonhoeffer or Otto Dibelius. However, for others such as Bishop Moritz Mitzenheim of Thuringia, who represented an extreme understanding of the doctrine of the two kingdoms *(Zwei-Reiche-Lehre),* the SED-State[7] was unconditionally to be obeyed. Between these two poles opinion oscillated. Was it legitimate to oppose the state which clearly wanted to marginalize the church, or was it one's Christian

---

5. Quoted in *Bericht der Enquete-Kommission "Aufarbeitung von Geschichte und Folgen der SED-Diktatur in Deutschland,"* Deutscher Bundestag 12. Wahlperiode, Drucksache 12/7820 (31 May 1994), 166. (Hereinafter cited as *Enquete-Kommission.*) See also the narrative thereto by Gerhard Besier, *Der SED-Staat und die Kirche: Der Weg in die Anpassung* (Munich: C. Bertelsmann Verlag, 1993), 66.

6. *Enquete-Kommission,* 168.

7. The expression SED-State *(SED-Staat)* is frequently used to describe the regime in power in the former GDR. *SED = Sozialistische Einheitspartei,* the Socialist Unity Party, the communist party in power.

duty to submit to it? In the end the idea that one had to oppose the state of "liars and robbers" came to dominate. The legacy of Dietrich Bonhoeffer's opposition to the Third Reich was in this regard a central factor.

However, this legacy was a dual one. Remarkably, the regime actually tried to apply a selection of Bonhoeffer's later texts to legitimize the ideology of Marxism-Leninism. This attempt by regime-friendly theologians to harness the authority of the great opponent of fascism in the service of a different kind of totalitarianism was, in the end, not crowned with the success its few champions had hoped for, but it is instructive as an example of the opportunism to which the regime of RES would resort in order to have its power sanctioned.

The second dimension of Bonhoeffer's legacy was, of course, for those who perceived the church to have been under existential threat or at least under severe pressure. This paper will draw attention to these two ways in which Bonhoeffer's legacy was applied during the history of the GDR.

"Apologist" for the State of Real Existing Socialism (RES)

The official communist attitude to Dietrich Bonhoeffer was initially determined by the fact that he was remembered as a heroic fighter against fascism who had courageously given up his life for the cause of freedom as he understood it. As an individual of such prominence he was difficult to ignore; the other conspirators of 20 July 1944 had been consigned to historical oblivion because they were of aristocratic or bourgeois origin and hence had clearly not been inspired to act on behalf of the working class. Precisely why it was legitimate to remember Bonhoeffer, whose bourgeois origins could not have been more apparent, is only explainable within the framework of Marxist-Leninist casuistry.

A prime example is supplied by the communist writer Gerhard Winter, who took the occasion of Bonhoeffer's seventy-fifth birthday (4 February 1981) to spell out why such a bourgeois and a Christian was worthy of remembrance in a society destined to become entirely atheistic.[8] The preoccupation with Bonhoeffer, one suspects, is rooted in a fear that he could become a focus of opposition to the regime. This would

---

8. Gerhard Winter, "Dietrich Bonhoeffer — Kämpfer gegen Krieg und Faschismus," *Beiträge zur Geschichte der Humboldt-Universität zu Berlin* 5 (1981): 9-26.

explain why a communist apologist like Gerhard Winter would seek, on the one hand, to dignify Bonhoeffer's memory while, on the other, emphasizing the inadequacy of his motivation for resistance because it was, after all, Christian rather than "scientific" and, as such, had only limited efficacy. Nevertheless, since Bonhoeffer's views could be said to point in the direction which led to Marxism-Leninism, communists and Christians in the GDR could find common cause. As Winter argues:

> This awareness of responsibility, this preparedness to sacrificial action, this determination to struggle against a society in which human rights are being trampled under foot binds the communists with the faithful Christian. However, in contrast to Bonhoeffer *we* identify the spiritual/intellectual means for the establishment of a society commensurate with human dignity in Marxism-Leninism, the scientific *Weltanschauung* of the working class. So, while we do not ignore this contrast we remain aware of that which binds us.[9]

Clearly, Winter and other party strategists investigated Bonhoeffer's writings such as *The Cost of Discipleship, Ethics,* and *Letters from Prison* and gleaned ideas and values which they felt coincided sufficiently to be of use in communist propaganda. Obviously, the faithful Christian and the communist both strove for world peace. This and other elements, such as the demand for social justice, enabled a Christian/communist dialogue, and Bonhoeffer's witness and martyrdom, despite his obvious limitations from a communist point of view, were valuable sources for such collaboration. One thing in particular commended Bonhoeffer as a role model for the present. While he was never able to locate the root causes of imperialism he did wage a consistent struggle against bourgeois nationalism; this was important because of the way nationalism had always been used to manipulate the population for war — turning people into willing cannon fodder so that capitalists could reap the profits of war.[10] So, by emphasizing Bonhoeffer's commitment to world peace and in particular his efforts to mobilize the ecumenical movement to that purpose, the communists invoked Bonhoeffer's memory to persuade the contemporary international ecumenical movement to make common cause with them against the warmongering West.

9. *Ibid.,* 15.
10. *Ibid.,* 18.

A second field of Bonhoeffer's activity from 1933 which the communists tried to exploit was his critical role within the Confessing Church and his uncompromising repudiation of German Christians. The racial ideology which much of the German church justified as a component of the Christian faith, its identification of the Nazi Reich with the Kingdom of God, its adulation of the Führer as virtual savior, and finally its transformation of the Evangelical Church into a fascist state Church were consistently and energetically opposed by Bonhoeffer. Indeed, his critique of the Third Reich from his radical Christian standpoint made Bonhoeffer a most attractive kind of bourgeois for the communists, and his doctrine of passive resistance developed in *The Cost of Discipleship* stamped him as a foremost opponent of fascism.

And if that were not sufficient justification for communist recognition of a bourgeois anti-fascist, there were elements in Bonhoeffer's political theology which led him to endorse certain goals of the labor movement. This emphatically pro-labor direction in Bonhoeffer's thinking is adumbrated in sections of *Ethics* which indicate that the experience of fascism led Bonhoeffer through the barriers which under ordinary circumstances would have hindered him from collaboration with communists. So, Winter argued, the lesson to be drawn from an investigation of Bonhoeffer's thought was that Christians should work in good conscience together with communists in building up a new and genuinely humane society.

Gerhard Winter's interpretation of Bonhoeffer seems to have been designed to convince the thoughtful Christian layperson in the GDR of the legitimacy of collaboration with the SED-State. Hanfried Müller, as a regime-friendly professional theologian with a particular Bonhoeffer expertise, on the other hand, directed his analysis of Bonhoeffer's career to convincing the pastorate in general to accept the rule of RES as perfectly consistent with the essence of the gospel. He did this by seeing Bonhoeffer's church struggle as a repudiation of the nationalist tendencies in German Protestantism which had led in a linear progression from Luther to Hitler.[11] So, for Hanfried Müller, the path of German Protestantism, allied as it was in the past to the military monarchies and

---

11. Hanfried Müller, "Dietrich Bonhoeffer — Christuszeuge in der Bekennenden Kirche für die mündige Welt," *Beiträge zur Geschichte der Humboldt Universität zu Berlin* 5 (1981), 33.

capitalism, and currently to NATO in the Federal Republic, had been historically disastrous.

By the time of Hitler's seizure of power two rival parties competed for the domination of the church; one Müller termed the "clerical fascists"; the other, the "German Christians." The clerical fascists wished to monopolize the social influence of the church, namely to use its position to keep the *petit bourgeois* and peasant masses loyal to the ruling classes so that they would continue to vote for conservative forces in peacetime, and in wartime volunteer to serve in the armed forces as cannon fodder. By this means the clerical fascists hoped to avoid ceding their religious authority to the Nazis. They wanted to be partners with the state and to participate in the exercise of power. They supported the anti-Versailles foreign policy and the anti-communist domestic policy of the Nazis but wished to preserve the social prestige of the church and to erect a dam against the process of secularization. They admired the successes of Mussolini and Franco.

In contrast to the clerical fascists the German Christians accepted the Nazi party's church policy and wanted less to use fascism in the service of the church than to place the church totally in the service of fascism. In this rivalry, argues Müller, the German Evangelical Church disintegrated. Out of this situation arose the "Confessing Church," which owed much to Bonhoeffer's rigorous biblical commitment but which was unable to extricate itself entirely from the legacy of the past clericalism. As Müller comments:

> The church struggle was carried out *in* the Church *for* the Church and *against* the Church: against the Church, which as a secularised Church wanted to sacralise the world, and out of fear of the emancipation of society from ecclesiastical tutelage, repeatedly aligned itself with re-actionary forces until it even resorted to collaboration with the Nazis for fear of the communists.[12]

Only gradually could the Confessing Church free itself from the clericalism which defined it, and one of its most radical and self-critical champions was, of course, Dietrich Bonhoeffer. In his *Letters and Papers from Prison,* according to Hanfried Müller, Bonhoeffer enabled pastors to free themselves inwardly from the clerical tradition in Lutheranism and

---

12. *Ibid.,* 37.

the religious illusions of its *Weltanschauung.* Indeed, those letters pointed the way to a new orientation toward Marxism-Leninism as the revolutionary world movement.[13]

Just how many people were taken in by this highly propagandistic interpretation cannot, of course, be quantified, but it was probably a negligible number. However, as Wolf Krötke has pointed out, the communists believed it was necessary to lay exclusive claim to Bonhoeffer and to project him as a champion of proletarian liberation so that residual counterrevolutionary elements in the GDR could not enlist him in the service of anti-communist propaganda.[14]

Of central relevance to this discussion is Wolf Krötke's recent essay "Der zensierte Bonhoeffer,"[15] in which he reports how official state censorship in the GDR, which monitored all publications, affected the reception of Bonhoeffer's work. Krötke has spent some time at the Federal Archives in Potsdam going through the files of "expert opinions" on the publication of Bonhoeffer's work and on literature about Bonhoeffer. Some of the more important of these were prepared by theologians Christoph Haufe and Kurt Meier, who allegedly belonged to the "most progressive" younger faction to come out of the seminar of the regime-friendly Professor Emil Fuchs (1874-1971) at the university of Leipzig.

It is worth noting that their negative opinions were sometimes overturned by the literature board of the ministry of culture (*Amt für Literatur des Kulturministeriums,* later called *Haupt-Verwaltung Verlage*). As a consequence, *Letters from Prison* was finally published in 1957 as the third Bonhoeffer publication in the GDR, the others being *Life Together* (1954) and *The Cost of Discipleship* (2nd edition, 1956).[16] The generally negative opinions by the expert readers clearly resulted from their anxiety that Bonhoeffer's readers might draw parallels between the sit-

---

13. *Ibid.*
14. Wolf Krötke, "Bonhoeffer als Theologe der DDR. Ein kritischer Rückblick," in *Protestantische Revolution?* ed. Trutz Rendtorff (Göttingen, 1993), 295-99 passim. This was among the objects of the communist-oriented *Bund evangelischer Pfarrer in der DDR,* founded in Leipzig, July 1958. It had sent invitations to 6,000 pastors to attend the foundation meeting. Only 60 (i.e., 1%) appeared. It never achieved popularity and was dissolved in 1971. See Gerhard Besier, *Der SED-Staat und die Kirche — Der Weg in die Anpassung* (Munich, 1993), 294, 301.
15. *Die Zeitschrift für Theologie und Kirche* 92 (1995): 3, 329-56.
16. *Ibid.,* 333.

uation under National Socialism and that under RES. The literature board, on the other hand, clearly decided that in these cases, the public would understand that Bonhoeffer's critique was against the Nazi system, which, as every well-schooled communist would know, was the antithesis of socialism.[17]

It was, from the point of view of ideological class struggle in the GDR, a not unimportant ploy on the part of the regime to promote Bonhoeffer's thought as eminently compatible with Marxism-Leninism. The common humanism of the two belief systems was a feature worth exploiting in order to bring the remaining Christian element in the GDR population into alignment with the goals of the regime. This gave rise to a curious theological enterprise based chiefly on the Humboldt University, directed by Professor Hanfried Müller, who engaged in an intensive "Bonhoeffer industry." Futhermore, Müller, supported by his wife, Rosemarie Müller-Streisandt, and like-minded colleagues, formed the so-called Weissensee Circle, which was designed to persuade the wider Protestant pastorate to accept a pro-communist version of a "refunctioned" Bonhoeffer theology of church and state. According to their argument the cause of the gospel would be best served by advancing the realization of communism and abandoning the traditional role of the church in society. Here is where Bonhoeffer's concept of "religionless Christianity" was advanced, unsuccessfully as it turned out.[18] Pastors were generally unimpressed by such efforts to reinterpret Bonhoeffer, and so the enterprise of the Weissensee Circle achieved only marginal success.

---

17. *Ibid.*

18. When in March 1963 church leaders in the GDR began seriously to appreciate that the communist system was no mere passing phase, they drew consciously on the Barmen Declaration of 1934 to state their position vis-à-vis the new form of totalitarian and atheistic state. They did so in "Ten Articles on the Freedom and Service of the Church." The regime saw in this a hostile act, and the regime-friendly theologian Hanfried Müller drafted a rebuttal formulated as the "Seven Articles" of the Weissensee Circle. This made much of the "religionless" interpretation of Bonhoeffer's theology. They had next to no effect on the wider pastorate. See the account of this episode in Gerhard Besier, *Der SED-Staat und die Kirche — Der Weg in die Anpassung* (Munich, 1993), 540-53. The respective texts are reproduced in *Kirchliches Jahrbuch der EKD* (1963), 181-98. For the theological discussion of Bonhoeffer's concept of "Religionless Christianity," see Peter H. A. Neumann, ed., *"Religionloses Christentum" und "Nicht-Religiöse Interpretation" bei Dietrich Bonhoeffer* (Darmstadt: Wissenschaftliche Buchgesellschaft, 1990).

Meanwhile, alongside this ideological undermining of traditional Christianity by means of the less than subtle promotion of what surely amounts to heresy, the state set about intimidating the church and individual Christians by means of the elaborate and extensive activities of the Secret State Police *(Stasi)*, which perceived itself as the "sword and shield" of the ruling party. This policy of targeted oppression, as Professor Richard Schroeder[19] has pointed out, indicates that the state perceived the church as a source of ideological opposition which needed to be rendered as ineffectual as possible. Indeed, the entire policy of the regime toward the church was attributable to the anxiety of the party leadership that Christianity could delay the socialization of the population, particularly the children and youth, into "new species beings" in accordance with Marxist-Leninist ideology. Certainly, the aim was to create conditions in which the continuance of traditional Christian consciousness would be very difficult. But since the churches had a constitutional right to exist, every available method of frustrating the growth of Christianity was called into service. For this reason the state maintained six theological faculties at the universities in the GDR which fostered a form of religion based on the premise that "socialism" and Christianity were mutually reinforcing. But regardless of whether the staff were responsible for or committed to teaching "Bonhoeffer," they had to subscribe to the sole validity of Marxism-Leninism, which meant that officially at least they all had to bring the gospel into alignment with that ideology.[20] For the conscientious Christian this situation was fraught with difficulties. The system was clearly oppressive and hence posed an existential challenge to the church.

Wolf Krötke attests that overall the investigation of Karl Barth and Dietrich Bonhoeffer among the pastors of the GDR has been only slight. Neither was the teaching of their theology at any of the six "theological sections" at the universities or the three church theological colleges particularly significant because traditional Lutherans had reservations about both men.[21] But having noted that, Krötke goes on to observe that

19. *Deutschland schwierig Vaterland* (Freiburg: Herder Verlag, 1993), 135-43.

20. For information concerning the SED attitude toward the teaching of theology in the GDR at universities, see Dietmar Linke, *Theologiestudenten der Humboldt-Universität — Zwischen Hörsaal und Anklagebank. Darstellung der parteipolitischen Einflussnahme auf eine Theologische Fakultät in der DDR anhand von Dokumenten* (Neukirchn-Vluyn: Neukirchener Verlag, 1994), 10-75.

21. Wolf Krötke, "K. Barths und D. Bonhoeffers Bedeutung für die Theologie in der DDR," *Kirchliche Zeitgeschichte* 7/2 (1994): 282.

it is nothing to be proud of that the first complete analysis of Bonhoeffer's theology was that produced by Hanfried Müller in 1961.[22]

Müller justified his manuscript, *Von der Kirche zur Welt*, as follows:

> I have sought to show in my work how the bourgeois opponent of Hitler, Bonhoeffer, who was loosely associated with the circle of conspirators of 20th July 1944 and who was initally ideologically closely aligned with them, progressed to an advanced bourgeois anti-fascism under the immediate influence of the great social changes of this time which were chiefly influenced by the final defeat of fascism at Stalingrad. This anti-fascism can at the present time mediate to the Church new perspectives for openness with regard to the forward-driving movements of our time. . . . What is qualitatively new in Bonhoeffer's view of the world and places him apart from all previous theologians is his acknowledgement of the existence of recognizable laws in nature and history.

As Wolf Krötke observes, for Bonhoeffer to be of any use to the communists it was necessary to locate in his thought an arguable openness to the idea of the regularity of laws in history which conformed to those discovered by Marx. According to Hanfried Müller, perceiving this connection would liberate Christians to adopt an atheistic, nonreligious *Weltanschauung*.[23]

Müller's justification for his study must have been persuasive because, after the censors' demands for some rewriting had been met, the work was published. This in turn enabled him to become established in the theological faculty of Humboldt University, from which position he came to exert great influence on the censorship process, usurping the former preeminence of the Leipzig faculty. From the early 1960s, all Bonhoeffer literature, to the extent it was theologically censored, had to satisfy the so-called "Berlin interpretation."[24] This, of course, did not mean that there would be a sudden increase in the publication of Bonhoeffer's works in the GDR. *Schöpfung und Fall* had appeared in 1960; *Das Gebetbuch der Bibel* had to wait until 1967, while a new edition of *Letters*

22. *Ibid.*, 293. See Hanfried Müller, *Von der Kirche zur Welt. Ein Beitrag zu der Beziehung des Wortes Gottes auf die societas in Dietrich Bonhoeffers theologischer Entwicklung* (Leipzig: Koehler & Amelang, 1961).
23. Krötke, "Der zensierte Bonhoeffer," 335-36.
24. *Ibid.*, 339.

from Prison came out in 1977. All titles were quickly sold out. A selection of Bonhoeffer's writings in one volume, *Christus für uns heute. Eine Bonhoeffer-Auswahl,* after much wrangling with the censors, appeared in 1970 and was reissued a year later, edited by Walter Schultz.

As indicated, Bonhoeffer's thought had to be presented in such a way as to conform to the party line. For example, it was deemed necessary, in the view of the Müller/Müller-Streisandt group, to insist that there had been a break in Bonhoeffer's thought to allow for a change in a Marxist direction. When authorities such as Albrecht Schönherr maintained there was no such hiatus, but demonstrable continuity in Bonhoeffer's thinking, there were strenuous objections to publication. However, precisely such contrary views as those of Schönherr were, in the event, permitted to be published in the aforementioned selection.[25]

Why the party authorities overruled the censors is a question of the SED church policy which was characterized by a certain capriciousness, sometimes ruthless, sometimes conciliatory and tolerant. There were times when it was considered prudent to make concessions toward the church if these would serve the interest of the state.[26] Nevertheless, officially, theology had to be written in such a way as to conform to the situation in the GDR as judged ultimately by the Central Committee of the SED (ZK). This had the effect of causing scholars to write in vague or impenetrable language when it was necessary to make reference to the political situation.[27]

---

25. *Ibid.,* 340.

26. See John A. Moses, "The Church Policy of the SED-Regime in East Germany 1949 to 1989: The Fateful Dilemma," *Journal of Religious History* (University of Sydney) (forthcoming). For example, in the 1980s the regime was particularly concerned to build bridges to the church and to portray Martin Luther as a national hero, indeed a forerunner of proletarian revolution, so it comes as no surprise that in the first half of the 80s permission was granted for the complete works of Bonhoeffer to be published. Between 1986 and 1988 volumes 1, 2, 5, and 9 had appeared. See Krötke, "Der zensierte Bonhoeffer," 339 and note 38, as well as 351 and note 91, where it is suggested that the positive personal response of the then Secretary of State for Church Affairs, Klaus Gysi, to Albrecht Schönherr, who was a Bonhoeffer pupil, helped to dampen the "fanaticism" of the Berlin censors and thus allow the publication of these volumes — including Eberhard Bethge's famous biography which finally appeared in the GDR in 1986. See Klaus Gysi, "Meine Begegnung mit Albrecht Schönherr," in *Glauben lernen in einer Kirche für andere* (Gütersloh: Chr. Kaiser/Gutersloher Verlagshaus, 1993), 76-85.

27. Krötke, "Der zensierte Bonhoeffer," 344.

In this, of course, the theologians of the GDR were in the same situation as all creative writers who had first to submit their work to political censorship. But if it was not possible to seal off the entire GDR from outside influences completely, it was even less possible to isolate the church and to obstruct forever the publication of Bonhoeffer's work and work about him. This was particularly the case in view of the fact that increasingly by the late1970s and early 80s, the church was becoming de facto the public sphere, that is, effectively the only place where critical public discourse could take place.[28]

A benchmark in the church's "public sphere" activity was to be the fourth International Bonhoeffer Congress held in the church's retreat center outside Berlin at Hirschluch, 12-17 June 1984. Bonhoeffer scholars from both the eastern bloc and the capitalist west attended. That this occurred with the official sanction of the ZK indicates that the church policy of the regime was still driven by the notion that Bonhoeffer could be instrumentalized to promote the acceptance of socialism by Christians. Even publication of the congress proceedings was sanctioned.[29]

It was in this context that a further publication, *Bonhoeffer Studien*,[30] appeared in 1986. The volume encompassed seventeen contributions in an ideologically pluralistic manner. Clearly, it had to satisfy the authorities, and so it contained essays by regime-friendly theologians such as Hanfried Müller. But scholars who maintained a considerable distance from him and his usual associates were also included.[31] This theological

28. Wolf Krötke, "Dietrich Bonhoeffer als Theologe der DDR — ein kritischer Rückblick," 308, where he speaks of the role of the church in the disintegrating GDR as positive for a better kind of state. For a more critical view of the role of the church in the GDR, see Detlef Pollack, *Kirche in der Organisationsgesellschaft* (Stuttgart: Verlag W. Kohlhammer, 1994). See also note 2, above.

29. See *Newsletter of the International Bonhoeffer Society* (English Language Section) 28 (November, 1984). The SED's Secretary for Church Affairs, Klaus Gysi, even dignified the event by inviting some of the delegates to a special reception. The conference papers were edited by Pastor Martin Kuske, *Weltliches Christentum. Dietrich Bonhoeffers Vision nimmt Gestalt an* (Berlin: Evangelische Verlagsanstalt, 1984).

30. Albrecht Schönherr and Wolf Krötke, eds., *Bonhoeffer Studien — Beiträge zur Theologie und Wirkungsgeschichte Dietrich Bonhoeffers* (Berlin: Evangelische Verlagsanstalt, 1986).

31. For Krötke's account of the difficulties in producing this volume, created, of course, by the need to include disparate assessments of Bonhoeffer and at the same time to satisfy the censors, see his contribution, "Dietrich Bonhoeffer als Theologe der DDR. In kritischer Rückblick," 299.

pluralism in the midst of RES bears witness to the fact that the church had successfully resisted the *totaler Wahrheitsanspruch* of the SED and thereby de facto enforced the separation of state and party, the former unity of which characterized all states of RES. In this process, the investigation of Bonhoeffer's theological-political legacy proved of central significance. Once intellectual-ideological pluralism was a reality accepted by the SED, its claims to be the sole authority to legislate what occurred in the world of ideas were overthrown. This is why the vagaries of the church policy of the SED merit close attention in any explanation of the ultimate failure of the regime to win the hearts and minds of the population.

Theologian of the "Church in Socialism"

Wolf Krötke's statement that the influence of Karl Barth and Dietrich Bonhoeffer on theologians in the GDR was only slight because their thought was alien to the traditional Lutheran mind, has to be balanced by the observations of those who identify Bonhoeffer as the theologian of the "Church in Socialism."[32] Krötke would count himself among their number. Indeed, he observes that wherever the church in the GDR struggled with its independent identity and wherever individual pastors and Christians encountered Barth and Bonhoeffer, they discovered the essential possibilities for the freedom of the church and its fundamental ability to meet the challenges imposed by the system of RES. In other words, some bishops and other high profile churchmen drew inspiration from these theologians in their struggle to maintain loyal witness to the gospel against the strenuous efforts of the state to marginalize the church. In addition, a significant number of parishes engaged in serious reflection on the question of what it meant to be the church in an atheistic state, and were similarly affected.[33]

All this had a cumulative effect when leading personalities began to

---

32. Wolf Krötke, "Karl Barths und Dietrich Bonhoeffers Bedeutung für die Theologie in der DDR," *Kirchliche Zeitgeschichte* 7/2 (1994), 282. Here the author addresses the question whether there was a widespread investigation of Barth and/or Bonhoeffer in the GDR and concludes that it was "fairly thin." Even in the theological sections in the universities, broadly speaking, the concern with Barth and Bonhoeffer was not particularly strong.

33. *Ibid.*, 296.

make synodal charges and addresses which unequivocally appealed to Bonhoeffer. It was then a case of the church actively implementing a specific tradition, namely that of the Confessing Church during the Third Reich.[34] And, when church leaders founded committees dedicated to Bonhoeffer studies, such as that founded in 1977 by the BEK, there was evidence of a groundswell of interest. This fifty-member-strong committee (which included members from Hungary and Czechoslovakia) coordinated the work of previously existing scattered groups, thus indicating that there were significant Bonhoeffer "cells" around the country.[35] Church historians in the former Federal Republic make the point that a full comprehension of the behavior of the church in the GDR with regard to the state is only possible if Bonhoeffer's legacy is taken into account.[36]

Quantification is here a less than helpful tool of inquiry. Ideas, faith, and conviction are categories which do not lend themselves readily to statistical analysis. What the historian can observe, however, is the effect of these mental/spiritual factors. The political circumstances of the GDR were particularly oppressive for the church. It was as though there was an irreconcilable rivalry between two claimants for the custody of absolute truth. Indeed, Edelbert Richter has observed that in a real sense there were two denominations in the GDR, Marxism-Leninism on the one hand and Christianity on the other.[37] Certainly, the representatives of the state perceived themselves and wanted to be perceived as bringers of salvation *(Heilsbringer)*.[38] The pastorate and the various dissident groups which they fostered, directly or indirectly, however, obstructed the state in its mission, and this obstruction became increasingly more determined the more the legacy of Dietrich Bonhoeffer was appropriated.

34. Albrecht Schönherr, "Die Bedeutung Dietrich Bonhoeffers für das Christsein in der DDR," in *Glauben lernen in einer Kirche für andere,* ed. Ernst Feil (Gütersloh, 1993), 42.

35. Schönherr and Krötke, *Bonhoeffer Studien — Beiträge zur Theologie und Wirkungsgeschichte Dietrich Bonhoeffers* (Berlin: Evangelische Verlagsanstalt, 1986), 10. This committee was responsible for the production of the collection in 1986. In the Foreword the editors draw attention to the fact that "numerous parishes and churches" in the GDR bear the name of Bonhoeffer, and that books about him and by him were usually quickly sold out.

36. Personal communication to the author by Professors Leonore Siegele-Wenschkewitz (Arnoldshain, Schmitten) and Christoph Klessmann (Potsdam).

37. Edelbert Richter, *Christentum und Demokratie* (Leipzig: Weimar, 1991), 275.

38. Wolf Krötke, "Die Kirche und die friedliche Revolution in der DDR," *Zeitschrift für Theologie und Kirche* 87 (1990): 4, 539.

The peculiar situation of the church in the GDR is summed up in the ambiguous title which it acquired, namely *Kirche im Sozialismus.* This designation derived from an admonition to the Church from the Secretary of State for Church Affairs, Hans Seigewasser, after the revised GDR constitution of 1968 was allegedly approved by 94.49% of the population.[39] At that time he said that the conclusion to be drawn by the men of the church was that they could only do justice to the spiritual commission of the *Church in Socialism* if they abstained from denigrating socialism and its humanistic policies, especially foreign policy.[40]

For good or ill, the church continued to employ this designation. The former Bonhoeffer student and later bishop of the eastern section of the Berlin Brandenburg Church, Albrecht Schönherr, made the point at the BEK synod at Erfurt, 1971, that the church defined its position in the GDR society as neither beside nor against it. This was to express at once loyalty to the state and the intention of the church to preserve its autonomy. The state, however, expected that the church would now abandon any attempt to assert itself in public life, to become literally a niche church, marginalized and without social or political relevance. However, the repeated instances of state abuse of human rights, including discrimination against Christian children and students, compelled church leaders to take a stand. In this the "freedom speech" address of the Erfurt prior *(Domprobst)* Heino Falcke at the BEK synod, June 1972, in Dresden under the title "Christ Liberates, therefore Church for Others" was a milestone. It proclaimed defiantly that the church was not going to assume the supine role which the SED regime had assigned to it. It was virtually a demand for freedom and social emancipation, and drew heavily on Bonhoeffer's *Ethics.*[41] Falcke characterized the future role of the church as one of "critical loyalty" toward the state, implying that real existing socialism required the critical input of Christians — in other words, it stood in need of improvement. His address did not go unnoticed by the authorities. It was seen as serving notice on the SED that the church now determined to assume the role of

39. Cf. Hermann Weber, *Die DDR 1945-1986* (Munich: Oldenbourg Verlag, 1988), 235.

40. *Zum Gebrauch des Begriffes "Kirche im Sozialismus,"* Information und Texte der Theologische Studienabteilung beim BEK 15 (März, 1988), 2.

41. Erhart Neubert, "'Obwohl der scheinbar tiefe Frieden . . .' Zur Genese der systemimmanenten protestantisch geprägten Opposition in der DDR — 1972 bis 1978," in *Rückblicke auf die DDR,* ed. Gisela Hellwig, *Edition Deutschland Archiv* (Köln: Verlag Wissenschaft; Politik Claus-Peter von Nottbeck, 1995), 48.

a political-ideological opposition against the "leading *Weltanschauung* of the working class."[42]

Not all evangelical churchmen were in agreement with this stance derived from the Bonhoeffer heritage, but it was a statement of position from which there was no turning back. A pro-active element was aroused in the church which belatedly, so it seemed, had arrived back at the views expressed by Otto Dibelius in the decade 1949 to 1959.[43] This was made possible by an increasing awareness of Bonhoeffer's thought. That it made a difference is evidenced by the spirited statements of bishops and ordinary pastors such as Albrecht Schönherr, Wolf Krötke, Heino Falcke, Erhart Neubert, Edelbert Richter, and others.[44] There can be no doubt that Bonhoeffer's ideas contributed massively to a radical learning process within the leadership of the German Evangelical Church in both parts of the nation, but it was particularly crucial in the East because, paradoxically, this regime, as we have seen, wanted to adapt aspects of Bonhoeffer's thought to legitimize the state, the social structure, and the *Weltanschauung* of the GDR. But men such as those just mentioned refused to identify "real existing socialism" with the "world come of age"; they challenged the prevailing notions that militant atheism equaled "hopeful Godlessness" or that the building up of socialism could be understood as "immanent righteousness."

Wolf Krötke sums up in four key points where the challenge of RES to the church had to be confronted, employing Bonhoeffer's categories:

1. The State of RES with its claim to absolute power in all spheres of life and society came to be assessed as an opportunity for the

---

42. See *SED und Kirche: Eine Dokumentation ihrer Beziehungen*, vol. 2, 1968-89, ed. Frédéric Hartweg/Horst Dohle (Neukirchen-Vluyn: Neukirchener Verlag, 1995), 211-12.

43. Krötke, "Karl Barths und Dietrich Bonhoeffers Bedeutung für die Theologie in der DDR," 294. Krötke implies strongly that the church was guilty of a grave error in judgment in refusing to accept the challenge of Dibelius's agenda back in the 1950s. Partially responsible at least for this was Karl Barth's encouragement to the pastorate to adopt an attitude of "loyal" opposition to the regime. See the detailed discussion in Gerhard Besier, *Der SED-Staat und die Kirche — Der Weg in die Anpassung,* 301-26.

44. For a selection of key synod statements and resolutions of the BEK, see Roswitha Bodenstein et al., *Gemeinsam Unterwegs-Dokumente aus der Arbeit des Bundes der Evangelischen Kirchen in der DDR 1980-1987* (Berlin, 1989); and Christoph Demke et al., *Zwischen Anpassung und Verweigerung-Dokumente aus der Arbeit des BEK in der DDR* (Leipzig: Evangelische Verlagsanstalt, 1994).

Church to abandon its own claims to power and social privileges and finally to rely completely on God through Jesus Christ to rule.

2. Historical and dialectical materialism, as the official ideology, was accepted as a militant declaration of "coming of age of the world" and could thereby be interpreted as "hopeful Godlessness." It was "hopeful" because fundamentally it rested on the concept of building up a more just society. And precisely because of that Christians were called to collaborate as autonomous individuals. Indeed, this was not a privilege but a duty imposed by Christ by virtue of His propitiatory sacrifice on the cross.

3. The Church was not a haven of retreat from society but "Church for others." It lived in solidarity with "the others," who, as the religionless, were pledged to build up socialism (though obviously not "socialism" in the manner defined by the SED). In this sense, as Albrecht Schönherr formulated it, the Church was not a Church *beside*, not *against*, but *in* socialism.

4. The Church should witness in this society without fear for its own existence by concentrating on its crucified Lord who is and continues to be the ruler of the world.[45]

This appeal to Bonhoeffer enabled the church to see in its oppressed situation the opportunity and promise to be the church, purified and unencumbered. What indeed appeared to be designed to enslave the church was in reality liberating and empowering it. This was not an encouragement to those who adhered to an extreme form of the doctrine of the two kingdoms[46] to withdraw into hibernation; on the contrary, the obligation to collaborate with the religionless in the construction of a more just society required a pro-active response from Christians. And this response made itself most publicly apparent on 30 April 1989 at the Dresden synod where a twelve-point manifesto was proclaimed that addressed itself to all the problem areas in both the domestic and foreign policies of the GDR.[47]

Erhart Neubert has designated the manifesto as the *Magna Carta*

---

45. Wolf Krötke, "Dietrich Bonhoeffer als Theologe der DDR," 302-3.

46. Edelbert Richter, "Die Zweideutigkeit der lutherischen Tradition," *Deutschland Archiv* 4/26 (1993): 407-17.

47. For the text of the so-called manifesto, see *Ökumenische Versammlung für Gerechtigkeit, Frieden und Bewahrung der Schöpfung* (Dresden 1989), published by the Kirchenamt der Evangelischen Kirche in Deutschland (Hanover, 1991), 23-108.

of all the dissident groups because it provided both the justification and the practical goals for what became the totally unexpected "Protestant Revolution."[48] Its publication and reception were arguably the key event in spurring on the burgeoning conciliar process then taking place all over the GDR.[49] So, there was an undeniable line of continuity between the witness of the persecuted Bonhoeffer in the Third Reich and the opposition movement which contributed so much to the overthrow of communism in the GDR. Indeed, Neubert, as the preeminent champion of the idea of the "Protestant Revolution" among the pastors then active against the SED regime, identifies the elements of opposition in the GDR as having been both directly and indirectly influenced by Protestant thought. In other words, the dissidents, including the Marxist ones, drew on the ideas and example of Protestant critics whose voices were being heard from 1972 onward.[50] These were the intellectual/spiritual precursors *(Vordenker)* of the revolution in whose formation as Christian leaders Bonhoeffer's legacy had played a key role. And because of their existence they were able, by 1988, to bring the disparate voices of opposition in the GDR increasingly into focus. They were in fact the internal opposition latent within the "system," that is, an element which, in the face of the all-powerful instruments of repression at the disposal of the state, could still reproduce and assert itself.

The pastorate of the eight provincial Churches in the GDR was heir to a number of theological traditions, all of which affected their

---

48. See also David Steele, "At the Front Lines of Revolution: East Germany's Churches Give Sanctuary and Succor to the Purveyors of Change," in *Religion, the Missing Dimension in Statecraft*, ed. Douglas Johnston and Cynthia Sampson (Oxford: Oxford University Press, 1994), 128, where he confirms that the so-called *Magna Carta* was forged as the consequence of deliberations at three ecumenical assemblies (Dresden, February 1988; Magdeburg, October 1988; and Dresden, April 1989). Here the German churches, including the Roman Catholic Church for the first time, were responding to the World Council of Churches' advocacy of addressing the issues of Justice, Peace and the Integrity of Creation. Steele reports that the original designation of the twelve-point manifesto as the *Magna Carta* for the revolution of 1989 stems from the Chairman of the Presidium of the Ecumenical Assembly and Church Superintendent of Saxony-Dresden, Christof Ziemer.

49. Erhart Neubert, "Sozialethische und charismatische-evangelikale Gruppen in der Kirche aus soziologischer Sicht," in *Das Recht der Kirche* 3, ed. Gerhard Rau et al. (Gütersloh: Gütersloher Verlagshaus, 1992), 311-12.

50. See note 36, above; and Erhart Neubert, *Eine Protestantische Revolution* (Osnabrück: Kontext Verlag, 1990), 14-17.

attitude to the state. Among them were residual conservative elements which, as Edelbert Richter has pointed out, cultivated a radical form of the doctrine of the two kingdoms.[51] Their preferred mode of behavior was virtual hibernation in order to preserve the purity of the gospel as they understood it. Another group of conservatives were prepared to see in the SED-State a legitimate *Obrigkeit*, to which the only opposition in the 1950s came from Bishop Otto Dibelius. Others, obviously conscious of the legacy of the Confessing Church, were ready to take the advice given to them by Karl Barth in 1958, and, for a time at least, really believed that it was possible to support the regime as a kind of "loyal opposition."[52] Hanfried Müller and the Weissensee circle, as we have seen, tried to instrumentalize Bonhoeffer's theology to implement what would have been the most extreme form of the doctrine of the two kingdoms: the church would have eventually merged into the state. Finally, there were the other heirs of the Confessing Church for whom Bonhoeffer became the preeminent prophet of emancipation. These came to prevail in the *Kirche im Sozialismus*, which proved to be, in the words of Wolf Krötke, the representative for a better form of state. "Es war—wenn wir das Ende des Sozialismus betrachten—auch aus heutiger Sicht kein Zufall, dass die Kirche am Ende in einer Art Stellvertreterfunktion für ein besseres Staatswesen dastand."[53]

Certainly, the stance adopted by the church, always insisting, against the express wishes of the state, that Christians had a right and duty to collaborate in the realization of freedom, withstood and discredited the regime's ideological terrorism. It was the church which was prepared, following Bonhoeffer's notion of collaboration with the religionless, to accept the state, but the ideologically ossified custodians of the state refused to accept such a gracious offer.

51. See note 40, above.
52. See Karl Barth and Johannes Hamel, *How to Serve God in a Marxist Land*, with an introductory essay by Robert McAfee Brown (New York: Association Press, 1959), for an explanation of Barth's position at that time and the response it provoked.
53. Krötke, "Dietrich Bonhoeffer als Theologe der DDR . . . ," 308.

The Idolatrous Enchainment of Church and State: Bonhoeffer's Critique of Freedom in the United States

GEFFREY B. KELLY

Throughout its history the United States has endlessly claimed that it is not only a country where "freedom" reigns but also the champion of "freedom" throughout the world. Americans tend also to view themselves as the God-blessed force that has liberated captive peoples from their repression at the hands of totalitarian ideologies and evil dictatorships. At the same time, the United States has a sorry record of supporting ruthless dictatorships as long as they constitute a friendly outpost against Marxist ideology.

In the name of a bogus national security, murderous death squads, trained in the United States and supported by the CIA's "black budget," have roamed Latin American countrysides terrorizing poor peasants, native Indians, labor organizers, catechists, and just about anybody that might stand in the way of the business interests of the ruling oligarchies and multinational corporations. In short, the United States has yet to face up to the ambivalence in the way it declares itself the "torch bearer" of freedom around the world.

During Dietrich Bonhoeffer's abbreviated stay in the United States in 1939, he observed and attempted to articulate this ambivalence. He wrote in his diary that Americans and their churches were not really as free as they claimed. He had witnessed firsthand instances of America's racism during his year at Union Theological Seminary in 1930-31, and his criticism of the churches' boast about their unique possession of freedom went hand in hand with his indignation at America's brand of bigoted violence directed against African Americans a mere seventy years after the "Emancipation Proclamation."

The background for Bonhoeffer's remarks was a Sunday worship service that he had attended at a prominent Riverside church in New York. In his diary he bemoaned the fact that Americans used their sermons to preach excessively about freedom. "Freedom," he wrote, "is a doubtful thing for a church. . . . Freedom for the church comes from the necessity of the Word of God. Otherwise it becomes arbitrariness and ends in a great many new ties. Whether the church in America is really 'free,' I doubt it."[1]

Given the current political and religious climate in the United States, Bonhoeffer's words seem to have acquired a renewed relevance for Christians and their churches. There is evidence today that a less-than-holy communion has been forged between politicized religious denominations and clever but mean-spirited politicians eager to exploit the voting prowess of these groups for their own self-serving ideology. Despite the veneer the Religious Right spreads on this ideology, their blustery solutions to social ills often appear to run counter to Jesus' own example and his teaching of compassion for the poor and the oppressed, the sick and the outcast, during his public ministry. Indeed, the proponents of the so-called "Republican Revolution" threaten the well-being and, therefore, the freedom of the most helpless citizens of the country.

Drawing on Dietrich Bonhoeffer's theological critique of the injustices of the Nazi era, I will attempt to expose three idolatries that seem to have sparked this much vaunted "Republican revolution" with its so-called "Contract with America": the worship of material prosperity; the homage paid to consumerism and government's increasing harshness toward the nonproductive people of society; and the idolatry of national security with its consequent militarism and cult of violence as a means of solving national and international problems. My tentative conclusion is that reconciliation of the disparate segments of American society and a deeper sense of Christian community are needed if the freedom promised by Jesus Christ will ever be a reality in the United States.

1. G. B. Kelly and F. B. Nelson, eds., *A Testament to Freedom* (San Francisco: HarperCollins, 1990), 76.

The Religious Right and the "Contract with America"

Several church leaders, along with liberal news commentators and many members of the Democratic opposition, have called the "Contract with America" a declaration of war on America's most helpless citizens by well-fed, well-paid, and well-cared-for political and corporate elites who form the bastion of the Republican Party's strength at the polls. Political analyst Herbert Gans has likewise depicted the stringent budgeting priorities of Congress in battlefield terms, claiming that, in their veritable "war on the poor," the affluent stereotype the poor as indolent and undeserving of programs designed to provide a safety valve for the destitute.[2] Author Richard J. Barnet writes of *The Global War Against the Poor*[3] in acerbic phrases that contrast the good economic news for the few with the bad news for the many who do not benefit from the largesse that the new legislation promises to generate.

There is a dark hole in this political agenda that is often missed by those who rally around the flags of what is well advertised as a moral crusade. Conservative politicians fulminate about their intention to have less government interference with money-making, less regulation of polluting industries, toleration of, and even more tax breaks for, cannabalistic corporations and their executives, and a tough line against those whom the Religious Right considers a blight on the nation's potential affluence and greatness (the two are interrelated!). There is likewise a vapid nostalgia in both the Christian Coalition (including its subsidiary, the Catholic Alliance) and the G.O.P., that "Grand Old Party" for a mythical, ideal time in America in which, as the dream goes, effort was always rewarded with prosperity and lack of prosperity could always be traced to a lack of effort. Those dependent for their subsistence on welfare are often considered either shiftless or parasitical. America, the argument goes, must be freed from the weight of the welfare system and the intolerable burdens of supporting these laziest of all citizens.

But can a nation be truly free when nearly all of its wealth is flowing to those at the top fifth of the income scale? Or if churches have difficulty mustering prophetic anger when the poor are ill-clothed and ill-fed?

2. Herbert J. Gans, *The Underclass and Antipoverty Policy* (New York: Basic Books), 1995.
3. Richard J. Barnet, *The Global War Against the Poor* (Washington, D.C.: Servant Leadership Press, 1994).

Here I believe Bonhoeffer's theology can still be of value as a counterfoil against those who think along the lines of the right wing in American politics and religion.

During his brief but informative stay in America in 1939, Bonhoeffer expressed serious misgivings about the so-called freedom that seemed to be America's proudest boast. "The freedom of the church," he wrote,

> is not where it has possibilities, but only where the Gospel really and under its own power makes room for itself on earth, even and precisely when no such possibilities are offered to it. The essential freedom of the church is not a gift of the world to the church, but the freedom of the Word of God itself to gain a hearing. . . . The American praise of freedom is more a praise which is directed to the world, the state and society, than a statement about the church.[4]

Leaving aside the question of how often American churches have succumbed to the lure of blind patriotism in this century, one might legitimately ask whether this "Contract" really bestows on the churches the freedom to promote religious and family values, as its proponents claim. Other critical questions are likewise in order. For example, does an excessively armed military guarantee freedom through the potential for overkilling any putative enemy? Does the death penalty inject fear into the hearts of criminals and make Americans secure in their homes and safe in their streets? If Isaiah's warnings about putting one's trust in "horses and chariots" and Jesus' teachings about loving one's enemies have any credence, the answer would have to be negative. That is, unless one identifies freedom, "family values," and peace with unlimited acquisitions, tougher penalties for criminals, and doling unlimited funds to an already overstuffed military.

While politicians hawk these deceptions to a credulous public, the truth is that the promised freedom is a mere chimera of the freedom of Christ and the freedom that comes from discipline, action to achieve justice for all, self-sacrifice and suffering for the sake of others, and the giving of one's life out of love for God and God's people, to paraphrase Bonhoeffer's often quoted poem from Tegel prison.[5]

---

4. *A Testament to Freedom,* 524.
5. See "Stations on the Way to Freedom," *A Testament to Freedom,* 516-17.

In his commentary on the Sermon on the Mount, moreover, Bonhoeffer observes that reliance on earthly possessions for our security is a grandiose delusion. "Earthly possessions dazzle our eyes and delude us into thinking that they can provide security and freedom from anxiety. Yet in all truth they are the direct source of anxiety. If our heart is dependent on possessions for its satisfaction, we will receive as a result an overwhelming burden of worry."[6] Seeking security in possessions, he says, becomes an iron chain that binds us to a life of anxiety. Might we add that so many of the campaign promises of politicians come down to an appeal to voters coveting an increase in material possessions and willing to snap at the bait of reduced taxes? These promises are a distant cry from Bonhoeffer's more sober judgment that above all the material cares "we must seek the righteousness of Christ."[7]

In detailing the "cost of following Jesus" Bonhoeffer argues that obedience to Jesus' mandates in the Sermon on the Mount must always include the compassion that provides for the needy and the practical effort to lift people from their incarceration within the material cares that often overwhelm them. Bonhoeffer contradicts the hollow promises of political manipulators that would offer tangible physical benefits in exchange for party loyalty. Instead, he calls for an ethic of suspicion against the enthroned mighty and a broader vision drawn from the victims "below." Hence Bonhoeffer's reminder to his family and fellow conspirators, that they had at last been able to see things "from below, from the perspective of the outcast, . . . the powerless, the oppressed, the reviled,"[8] is apropos in judging the pledges of politicians and their sycophantic supporters.

Bonhoeffer's reminder has been echoed today in the feelings of betrayal of those who have seen their well-being eroded by the corrosive inequities they must face daily. They are the marginalized people who have lost faith in the American system of government. They cannot get a job and, therefore, cannot boast of prosperity with the flag-wavers, nor can they pledge with hand over heart that this nation has either liberty or justice for all, much less that it is one nation under God. These poor and powerless people have come to know with increasing indignation and bitterness that their needs and rights have been restricted by the

6. *CD*, 197; translation slightly altered.
7. *Ibid.*, 201.
8. *LPP*, 17.

affluent power brokers and by politicians who have neither class nor religious links to them and little appreciation of what it means to live in the grinding poverty of the crime-infested ghettos of North America.

The problem is compounded by ignorance of what poverty really does to people. The affluent and most of the middle class know of welfare only from what their political leaders, the Religious Right, and conservative editorials have told them. If Congress were truly serious about lifting people out of their dependency on welfare, it would go far beyond time limits on benefits to the unemployed and seemingly unemployable. It would admit in all honesty publicly that to end welfare dependency will cost far more in the short term. It would involve providing a job to any welfare recipient who continues to be unable to find work. That would cost billions of dollars, money that the United States Congress prefers to spend on superfluous weapons and members' own pensions. Instead of seriously examining the plight of the millions of Americans trapped in seemingly inescapable poverty, including some 14 million who subsist on "Aid to Families with Dependent Children" (AFDC), right-wing Republicans in the House of Representatives have built their plan on the dogma that government lavishes too much on poor people, especially those on welfare.

Congressional speeches of the right-wing representatives and senators laud the diminution of aid to America's poorest citizens in tones that exude sincerity. Yet one of the most glaring bits of evidence of their duplicity lies in their announced intention to cut the earned income tax credit that helps poor people work their way out of poverty, while attempting to bestow tax breaks worth 245 billion dollars on the most affluent Americans under the rubric of the already discredited trickle-down economic theories and the now sacred grail of a "balanced budget," all within the idealized and absolutized time span of seven years. *Time* Magazine called this "a sop to G.O.P. moralists who bemoan the dissolution of the family."[9]

There is, of course, a dividend for the rich in the legislation that would come as the growing concentration of poverty in inner-city neighborhoods has exacerbated problems of already existing discrimination, unemployment and underemployment, inadequate education, teenage promiscuity and resultant pregnancies, and increased dependency of

9. *Time* Magazine, December 25, 1995/January 1, 1996, 93.

families on government support, drug-related criminality, and the perpetuation of the vicious cycle of destitution, inequality, violence, and despair.

Even arch-conservative William Bennett, former Secretary of Education in the Bush administration, has admitted his uneasiness over the manner and speed of the Republican downsizing of governmental care for the poor. "What's come across quite clearly is that we Republicans are smart and serious and that we are going to shrink the government. What hasn't come across is a lot of compassion. It's not enough to bring down the welfare state; you have to say what replaces it. We lose if we come across as a bunch of mean-hearted creeps. We have to say yes to something. We have to cut welfare for the rich."[10] It is refreshing finally to hear a conservative Republican spokesman mention "welfare for the rich." Indeed, welfare for corporations and their executives, for the rich patrons of the G.O.P., and for the plutocratic military-industrial complex appears not to bother the architects of this proposed legislation.

What does Bonhoeffer's theology have to say to churches in the face of this kind of legislation and the evident toughening of attitudes toward the most hurting of America's citizens? If we are speaking of the *victims* of governmental legislation, Bonhoeffer's words in that often quoted essay, "The Church and the Jewish Question," are especially pertinent. In a comment that could easily pertain to the latest legislative proposals. Bonhoeffer argued that "the church has an unconditional obligation to the *victims* of any ordering of society." That obligation, he goes on to state, includes an official protest or, alternately, a demand that the state justify its action, the provision of aid to the victims, and, failing an adequate response from the government, a direct confrontation that could include steps to bring down that government.[11] It is highly significant that Bonhoeffer emphasizes the word "victims" when speaking of state legislation. The Jews were the *victims* of the repressive anti-Jewish legislation passed in Germany. It is not beyond logic to suggest that the poor will be the prime "victims" of the proposed budgetary cuts.

This view is supported by a new "Kairos" document that is intended, like the *Kairos Document* that denounced South African apartheid, to address a prophetic message to our elected officials. The text directs

---

10. *Ibid.*
11. *A Testament to Freedom,* 132.

forceful criticism to the policies of the Republican-dominated Congress and asks members of the movement to "find more ways to speak and act in defense of our brothers and sisters." The document declares:

> The policies currently being enacted by Congress — massive cuts in welfare and social services — are an assault on poor Americans. We are convinced that these policies will directly result in greater suffering for our most vulnerable citizens. We also are convinced that the God of the Bible speaks and acts passionately in defense of the poor. Policies which abandon the poor are an assault on the heart of God.[12]

To see how the message of this "Kairos" document intersects with Bonhoeffer's own defense of the downtrodden, it is helpful to go back to his first experience of raw poverty during his Barcelona ministry. In a memorable conference he told his parishioners that the way of Christ to God was the divine light shining "down on those who are ever neglected, insignificant, weak, ignoble, unknown, inferior, oppressed, despised. . . . Here the light of eternity has been cast on the toiling, struggling, and sinning masses." Bonhoeffer concluded that conference with the observation that Christianity must invert the value systems of society by preaching the "unending worth of the apparently worthless and the unending worthlessness of what is apparently so valuable. The weak shall be made strong through God and the dying shall live."[13]

In his Christology lectures Bonhoeffer returned to the same point when he asked his students to look for Jesus as the "humiliated one" who enters the world "in such a way as to hide himself in it in weakness and not to be recognized as God-man . . . He goes incognito as a beggar among beggars, as an outcast among outcasts, as despairing among the despairing, as dying among the dying."[14] Not incidentally, that metaphor of the beggar has been used by both Pope Paul VI and Pope John Paul II to contrast the scandalous affluence of the many who sit at well-spread tables of plenty to the poor Lazaruses of this world who have only the crumbs that fall from those tables and only the master's dogs to lick their wounds. If in 1933 Bonhoeffer's statements could be applied to the hated Jew or the despised African American, it is fitting that in 1995 Bonhoeffer's Christology can direct us to the poor of America now being

12. *Kairos/USA* (Advent, 1995), 2.
13. *A Testament to Freedom*, 52.
14. *Ibid.*, 122.

305

faulted for their own misery. There is apparently little effort on the part of the United States Congress to help the Jesus who hangs out in the back streets, slums, and Galilean hills of modern America.

It might bolster the courage of church leaders opposed to the legislation were they to read significant passages of Bonhoeffer's *The Cost of Discipleship*, particularly that uncompromising passage in which he directed his attention to the brutalizing of Nazi Germany's own hated *Untermenschen*: "Those who are now attacking the least of the people are attacking Christ."[15] Here too one can refer to that passage from the Book of Proverbs that Bonhoeffer cited to explain his own having made common cause with the Jewish people: "Who will speak up for those who have no voice?"[16] There is more. In a frequently overlooked passage in Bonhoeffer's *Ethics*, he makes the connection between poverty and injustice:

> To allow the hungry to remain hungry would be blasphemy against God and one's neighbor, for what is nearest to God is precisely the need of one's neighbor. It is for the love of Christ, which belongs as much to the hungry as to myself, that I share my bread with them and that I share my dwelling with the homeless. If the hungry do not attain faith, then the guilt falls on those who refused them bread.[17]

These are strong words but perhaps the kind of rebuke needed by the apathetic, cost-cutting congressional legislators who balk at providing food stamps for the indigent.

Bonhoeffer's unabashed solidarity with the victims of unjust laws offers a clear and inspiring direction to several church efforts now underway to defend the poor from seemingly heartless ideologues who wish to build up a strong, free America through harsh restrictions on programs for the destitute and lavish benefits on the richest of Americans! Less than a year before his death, Bonhoeffer spoke in poetry about the suffering of God, oppressed because God's children were being oppressed. In that poem he described this God as one in "need and dread, a God poor, despised, without roof or bread."[18] The attitude that God

---

15. *CD*, 341.

16. Eberhard Bethge, "Bonhoeffer and the Jews," in John D. Godsey and Geffrey B. Kelly, *Ethical Responsibility: Bonhoeffer's Legacy to the Churches* (Toronto/Leviston: Edwin Mellen, 1981), 71-73.

17. *Ethics*, 137.

18. "Christians and Pagans," *A Testament to Freedom*, 515.

is in those who are "poor, despised, without roof or bread," might give an altogether different spin to the listing of congressional virtues and defects by leaders of the Religious Right.

Christian Discipleship and American Consumerism

If juggling America's priorities for the benefit of the more affluent, productive members of society is a plank in the Republican promise to bring a new tomorrow of greatness for Americans, the totems of that greatness are unlimited acquisitions, increased capital gains, more bank dividends, and the end of frugality for those already enjoying a comfortable life. Their euphoric promises entice big business interests and plutocratic supporters everywhere who are filled with dreams of unparalleled wealth. For many church leaders, however, these dreams of the prosperous are nightmares for the have-nots of American society. For the affluent, the amassing of goods constitutes the most conspicuous badge of economic honor as they also purport to be the pathway to the only "freedom" that really counts, *freedom from want.*

But, one can ask, is that freedom? "Getting and spending, we lay waste our powers," Wordsworth wrote in 1807, long before the era of telemarketing, mall rats, and what Michael Jacobson, founder of the Center for the Study of Commercialism, and his coauthor Laurie Ann Mazur have aptly called "marketing madness." It is Jacobson's contention that the 30-second commercials and thousands of billboards, sneaking their messages into our lives, waste both our money (because the $150 billion that advertisers spend each year is ultimately paid for by consumers) and our time. Jacobson asks: "What if $150 billion a year was spent on persuading us to go to the library, to save money, to be nice to our parents, to volunteer at a nursing home" — wouldn't it change the way we think? He insists that "living in a culture where companies spend $150 billion a year on these powerful messages has to affect values: The underlying message is 'BUY!'" This, he concludes, fosters materialism, wreaks havoc with frugality, and persuades us that whatever ails us can be fixed by *buying* something.[19]

Noam Chomsky takes this argument to another level in his allusion

---

19. Cited from Michael Jacobson and Laurie Ann Mazur, *Marketing Madness: A Survival Guide for a Consumer Society,* in Patricia McLaughlin, "Buy! Buy! Buy! Buy!" *The Philadelphia Inquirer Magazine,* July 6, 1995, 23. Emphasis mine.

to what he has labeled Thomas Jefferson's worst nightmare. Jefferson had warned of the dangers posed by a "single and splendid government of an aristocracy, founded on banking institutions and moneyed incorporations," through which the few would be "riding and ruling over the plundered ploughman and beggared yeomanry."[20] Chomsky maintains that this nightmare is being realized beyond anything conjured up by Jefferson. Boundaries are clearly being drawn between the communities of the privileged few and the barrios of the many. The escalation of economic inequality is, indeed, at its most disturbing level today, summarized in the phrase that has become a truism in societies around the world: the rich are getting richer and the poor, poorer.

Two additional phenomena must be laid on the scales weighing the damage done to ordinary people in the United States in recent years: the shrinking of the middle class in terms of growth in income and the shrinking of a working class able to reach middle-class standards of living. The era of high-paying jobs for low-skilled workers seems nearly over before it has had a real chance to take hold. Further, though the production of material wealth across the world is booming, billions of human beings are sinking into the economic quicksands of a relentless poverty. Nearly a billion people, mostly children, live at the edge of starvation; and 30,000 children die each day because they lack sufficient food and clean water. In the midst of all this, the steps taken by politicians to address budgetary allotments continue to cause pain, spawn despair, and diminish the quality of all our lives. And all this is happening as the supporters of the Christian Coalition's ideals and the Republican "Contract" hasten to parade their own success stories as exemplary of the moral values promulgated from their pulpits all over America.

The impact of this consumerism on the present frenetic concern over the deficit-obliteration bills Congress wants to enact into law has been dramatically exposed by Richard Barnet in his *The Global War Against the Poor*. During the 1980s, he notes,

> American consumers went on a binge, encouraged by easy access to credit, cheered on by the affable big spender in the White House who greatly expanded government expenditures even as he kept denouncing government and cutting taxes. Except for the growing number of home-

20. Noam Chomsky, "Democracy's Slow Death," *In These Times,* November 28, 1994, 25.

less, welfare recipients, and those in the working poor without access to credit the country was living well beyond its means. Government and corporations encouraged our collective mania for accumulating things of every description, and offered a dizzying array of painless ways to do it. But all the schemes had the same bottom line: go into debt. Families did. And so did the Treasury. Soon everyone was talking about The Deficit, a word that would be used again and again both to deny money, education, or health care to the poor and to block community efforts to attack the causes of poverty. The very notion of economic entitlements — the right to nourishing food, the right to a decent place under a roof, the right to public education and essential public services — was once again declared to be unaffordable and un-American.[21]

Barnet's remarks, despite their exaggerations, may help explain why legislators in the U.S. Congress have become so concerned over the deficit.

Senator Paul Simon has complained of this misdirection of priorities to satisfy the few at the expense of the many. Speaking about health care, he noted that this is a $1.4 trillion industry. "*Newsweek* has reported that $400 million was spent to defeat President Clinton's health care bill. . . . Meanwhile, the voices of 41 million Americans who are not covered by health insurance, who are not going to be contributors to campaigns, are muted." Simon also observed that the Religious Right's equating their political beliefs with God's commands constitutes an abuse of religion harmful to the political process.[22]

This is precisely where Bonhoeffer's theology can serve as a prophetic critique not only of consumerism but also of that false freedom which is associated with it. Certainly, one of the reasons so many Germans paid homage to Hitler during the 1930s was that he had delivered them from the economic deprivation hanging over from the "Great War" and the ravages of the depression. Hitler had promised the German people a "new world order"; the Republican Congress has made a similar promise through its "Contract with America."

Bonhoeffer countered that these "world orders" were already superseded by the "new order" of Jesus Christ. This is the gist of his sermon for the first Sunday after Trinity Sunday, 1932. Against Hitler's highly

---

21. Richard J. Barnet, *The Global War Against the Poor*, 34.
22. "Throw Out the Pollsters: An Interview with Paul Simon," *The Christian Century*, October 18, 1995, 958.

popular slogans for the "new world order," Bonhoeffer preached that those blessed by Jesus include

> you outcasts and despised, you casualties of society, you men and women without work, you broken and ruined ones, you lonely and forsaken, you who endure violence and unjustly suffer, you who suffer in body and soul. . . . That is the gospel of the dawn of the new world, the new order, that is the world of God and the order of God. The deaf hear, the blind see, the lame walk, and the gospel is preached to the poor. . . . So seriously does God take suffering that God must immediately destroy it.[23]

The sermon then goes on to show how God destroys that suffering through the compassion of Christians toward the poor of this world who are like the biblical Lazarus, victims of the indifference of the rich. That is the Christian order — works of mercy, not national selfishness; love of enemies, not blind patriotism and vilification of enemies such as was preached by Hitler.

It is equally instructive to note Bonhoeffer's insistence on integrating suffering for the sake of justice into his theology, community life, and pastoral care. In 1934, for example, he told his parishioners that suffering is holy, "because God suffers in the world through human beings and whenever God comes God has to suffer from human beings again. God suffered on the cross. Therefore, all human suffering and weakness is a sharing in God's own suffering and weakness in the world. We are suffering! God is suffering much more. Our God is a suffering God."[24] Those inspiring words from the pulpit of St. Paul's Church in London presage the more often cited letter from Tegel prison in which he declared that: "Only the suffering God can help us." To which he adds in the very next letter: "We are called to share in God's sufferings at the hands of a godless world."[25] It is not unreasonable to suppose that God suffers in the person of those who have been made to languish through the pitiless legislation of an insensitive government. Or that Christians are called to share in that suffering by making common cause with those whom society victimizes in the name of maximizing corporate profits and garnering more wealth for the

---

23. *A Testament to Freedom*, 204. For the complete sermon, see *GS*, vol. 4, 50-59.
24. *Ibid.*, 182.
25. *LPP*, 361.

already well-to-do. In Bonhoeffer's opinion Christians can never be truly free unless they are willing to engage in brave deeds for the sake of those who cannot defend themselves against rapacious manipulators.

The community that is Christian, according to Bonhoeffer, does not flinch from being associated with those whom respectable society looks upon as less than worthy citizens or even *Untermenschen*. In one of the most powerful sections of his *The Cost of Discipleship*, therefore, Bonhoeffer put it to his seminarians that Christians need to "have an irresistible love for the downtrodden, the sick, the wretched, the wronged, the outcast and all who are tortured with anxiety.... In order that they may be compassionate they cast away the most priceless treasure of human life, their personal dignity and reputation."[26] The Religious Right, on the other hand, claims great personal dignity by staking out the sacred ground through their claims to represent the will and the ways of God. But if Bonhoeffer is correct, then Christians are urged by Christ not to be overly concerned with their "dignity and reputation" as they make themselves a nuisance to those who threaten with political and economic mayhem the downtrodden, the wronged, and outcasts of all sorts.

Finally, it is clear from Bonhoeffer's legacy that the church is truly church only when it is willing to suffer for those who are bereft of strength before the exploitive machinations of the powerful. The Jesus he heralded in his prison letters as "the man for others" has challenged Christians to "a new life in 'existence for others' through participation in the being of Jesus."[27] In a remarkable passage in his *Ethics* Bonhoeffer insists that "it is with the Christ who is persecuted and who suffers in his church that justice, truth, humanity and freedom now seek refuge."[28] While it is not fully accurate to speak of the plight of America's poorest people as a form of "persecution," it is not too far off the mark to claim that when legislators, backed up by the Religious Right, single out the poorest, weakest citizens to bear the brunt of the suffering inevitable in any budget-slashing legislation, there is an injustice that must be redressed.

26. *CD*, 124-25; translation slightly altered.
27. *LPP*, 381.
28. *Ethics*, 59.

Militarism and the Evil of Blind Patriotism

All of our discussion thus far, centered as it has been on domestic issues, is inevitably related to the sphere of international relations and, in particular, the United States' military role. Hence our focus of attention must, of necessity, shift to the problem of militarism and the blind patriotism which accompanies it. What, we must ask, has happened to the "peace dividend" promised by the politicians following the demise of the communist empire? The money then being squandered on excessive weaponry, so we were told, would now be free to provide aid where it was most needed in our society. Instead, the Pentagon and CIA have pumped exorbitant amounts into armaments to defend the national interest against "terrorist nations." As in the case of materialism and consumerism, so this third form of idolatry is a robbing of the poor under the guise of national security.

During the period of the Persian Gulf War I gave talks in several churches on the prophetic theology and spirituality of Bonhoeffer. Because so many Americans have turned Bonhoeffer into a folk hero and modern martyr in a just cause, they seemed to expect me to associate Bonhoeffer's opposition to Hitler with the newfound cause, getting rid of the "Hitler-like" tyrant, Saddam Hussein. My audiences were for the most part surprised to find that the writings of Bonhoeffer and his actions leading up to his eventual arrest and execution at the hands of the Gestapo could just as well be directed against the American overkill of Iraqis and the massive destruction, unrelated to the liberation of Kuwait, that took the lives of countless civilians, including an estimated 49,000 children. Indeed, Bonhoeffer's legacy to the churches stands as a bracing reminder to pretentious "patriots" that war, however well orchestrated by self-serving politicians and military propaganda teams, is still a denial of the gospel teachings of Jesus Christ.

For Bonhoeffer, a church that prizes fidelity to the aims of the nation above the commands of the gospel is a church enchained to an idol, "even if it believes itself to be free."[29] Yet too many churches in tandem with the Religious Right have permitted the blessing of peacemakers in Jesus' Sermon on the Mount to be shunted into a dustbin of irrelevancy in favor of the unquestioning, biblicized patriotism that flourishes during a popular war. In Nazi Germany such an

29. *A Testament to Freedom*, 524.

acquiescence by the churches helped open the way for unwavering obedience to clearly immoral orders. Thus, SS commandos could, with few qualms and no rebuke from their churches, kill Jews with icy disdain for any Christian compassion for their innocent victims in the mass graves and death camps of World War II. They were only following orders from above.

More immediately, the dulling of moral sensitivity in the churches of the United States for the people of Iraq made palatable to many Christians the destructive bombing of defenseless villages and the consequent killing of innocents either through the bombing itself, or through the lingering effects of having obliterated the industrial infrastructure needed to provide for the babies, children, and weakest citizens of Iraqi society. That massive terrorizing of the civilian population was, of course, dismissed by the Orwellian double-speak of the Pentagon as mere "collateral damage." Such double-speak was typical of how Jesus' preaching of agapeic love for and sensitivity toward one's supposed enemies could be suppressed by Christians who should know better and by churches who neglected their duty to proclaim the prophetic word of Jesus. The enemy had been demonized and brutality justified.

In like manner in the troubled nations of Latin America, right-wing death squads have scoured the countrysides in order to terrorize into submission the poor peasants and indigenous peoples who are the backbone of the working force. Those who banded together for better wages and self-defense were considered a threat to the national security of those countries and of their powerful patrons, the CIA and United States business interests. Such atrocities were declared "justified" because the killing was done in the name of "national security."

It is not surprising that national security is still invoked by the United States Congress and the Religious Right to justify outlandish funding of expensive weaponry. Bonhoeffer once spoke with prescience of the sufferings about to befall Europe through the idol of national security. His words from an ecumenical address in Gland, Switzerland, in 1932, are remarkable for their contemporary relevance.

> It is as though all the powers of the world had conspired together against peace: money, business, the lust for power, indeed, even love for the fatherland have been pressed into the service of hate . . . and behind it all a world which bristles with weapons as never before, a

world which feverishly arms to guarantee peace through arming, a world whose idol has become the word security....[30]

When one ponders the number of times politicians have trotted out national security needs to justify everything from the CIA's secret budget of billions of dollars, the military's expenditures at over 258.2 billion dollars per annum and climbing, the additional 70% of all research directed toward military weaponry, the money poured into arms sales as the core of foreign aid to despotic leaders, and the denial of funds for the more pressing "war zones" at home, Bonhoeffer's words have a perennial accuracy about them. United States militarism is of a piece with materialism and consumerism in the harm it does to the poor.

Bonhoeffer takes his criticism of the idolatry of national security a step further not only by opposing the malevolence of a criminal government but also by blaming the churches for their complicity in the horrors perpetrated by Hitler and his like-minded ideologues. Bonhoeffer was himself frustrated by his inability to convince the churches of Germany and the ecumenical churches abroad that they had the power to mobilize as a counterforce to Nazism and to save innocent victims from the murderous violence Hitler was preparing to unleash on Europe. These same churches in Germany pandered to the popular mood of the vast crowds of ordinary citizens who were enamored of Hitler's achievements and lost in admiration for his promotion of what seemed to be solid family values, law, and order in the streets and national pride.

It is no wonder, then, that Bonhoeffer directs most of his anger against these same churches. Bishops and clergy alike should have been a more vibrant force in Germany, making it impossible for such evil to be perpetrated by their churchgoing people. Bonhoeffer's indictment of the churches for their failure either to prevent or to bring an end to the repression of human rights and the killings that enshrouded a world at war offers a lesson on how the churches can lose their vocation to be the prophetic Christ to the world.

It was the "Jewish Question," Bonhoeffer insisted, that became the test of the authenticity of Christian faith for the churches. The church's failure to defend the Jews, apart from nonoffensive resolutions, was, in Bonhoeffer's opinion, construed as acquiescence in the unspeakable brutalities against that people. "The church confesses that ... it is guilty of

30. *A Testament to Freedom,* 104.

the blood of the weakest and most defenseless brothers and sisters of Jesus Christ," he would write in his *Ethics*.[31] The guilt, he said, stemmed from its silence "while violence and wrong were being committed." The church, he complained, "was silent when it should have cried out because the blood of the innocent was crying aloud to heaven."[32]

That "confession of guilt" was crafted as reprisals against the Jews and the denial of their civil rights had become official state policy. Bonhoeffer was privately bemoaning the denial of Christ by the churches because of their silence while Jews and dissenters were being persecuted and the conquering troops, the SS elite brigades, and the Gestapo were celebrating their bloody victories. The principal noise from the churches came from the gonging of their bells over the jubilant, flag-waving crowds.

Bonhoeffer's earlier demands that the church rush to the aid of the victims and even jam a spoke in the wheel of state had gone unheeded. During the years of the church struggle, Bonhoeffer would make defense of the Jews the test case for whether church synods had succeeded or failed. "Where is Abel, your brother," became his question.[33] To the churches, he argued, belonged the mission of defending the dignity denied those targeted for extinction in Hitler's Third Reich.

If Christians in America are to thrill at Bonhoeffer's forthright criticism of Hitlerism and claim him as exemplifying "American ideals," we might also ask, as he would, who among the American bishops went public with such a lament or such a "confession of guilt" during the wild celebrating of the American victory in the Persian Gulf? Only a handful of editorial writers complained about the huge costs of the self-congratulatory parades. Americans whose opposition to the Persian Gulf War was lonely and frustrating had the right to ask where the critical voices and prophetic actions of their bishops had gone once the war was underway.

To be sure, one can cite the American Catholic Bishops and the Pope himself to document at least one church's stand on this crucial moral problem. They stated clearly that, in their opinion, the war about to begin could not be justified "as a last resort," or, given the consequences of initiating the military violence with the modern weaponry of today, in terms of proportionality, one of the other "conditions" for

31. *Ethics*, 114.
32. *Ethics*, 113.
33. See note 16, above.

the war to be declared "just." But once the war was underway and its popularity among the people became clear, even some prominent Bishops joined the President in rummaging around for reasons to declare its justification. Only the most stout-hearted would ask whatever happened to Jesus' blessing the peacemakers, turning the other cheek in resisting violence, forgiving enemies (even his executioners), and refraining from calling on the twelve legions of angels to reduce the Sanhedrin and the Roman soldiery to body parts. Except for a handful, the Catholic bishops sounded more like phlegmatic lawyers than outraged prophets.

What is needed to counteract America's uncritical homage to war and military heroism is some of the fire of Bonhoeffer's own efforts to goad church leaders to more prophetic, self-sacrificing action on behalf of peace. From early on in his teaching career Bonhoeffer had made the achievement of peace a central focus of his energies. Speaking before the German Student Christian Movement in Berlin in 1932, for instance, he linked following Christ with "becoming witnesses for peace." The thought that in war one can step around the command of God, "You shall not kill," and the word of Jesus, "Love your enemies," makes "grace cheap."[34] The violence from which countless peoples suffered was, in Bonhoeffer's opinion, the inevitable outcome of the churches' pursuit of the "cheap grace" that he excoriated so vehemently in *The Cost of Discipleship*.

Bonhoeffer put the cost of living that gospel squarely to the delegates of the ecumenical conference in Fanö, Denmark, in 1934. The setting was a morning sermon in which he asked these church leaders not to miss a serious opportunity to act as the one church of Jesus Christ in addressing an issue so clear as the promotion of peace and the condemnation of war. He pushed those present to abandon their usual staidness and stop couching their resolutions in inoffensive, polite, and easily ignored platitudes.

Bonhoeffer's sermon on peace supports the observations of historians of the ecumenical movement that Bonhoeffer's "Ecumenical Youth Commission" was the most radical of all the groups at Fanö.[35] In that sermon he attacked attempts to downplay or ignore Christ's teachings on peace by appealing to national security or legitimate defense of one's

34. *A Testament to Freedom*, 94f.
35. R. Rouse and S. C. Neill, *A History of the Ecumenical Movement, 1517-1948* (London: SPCK, 1954), 583.

country. God was not to be identified with the idol of national security. Bonhoeffer went on to point out that "this church of Christ exists at one and the same time in all peoples, yet beyond all boundaries, whether national, political, social, or racial." When nations take up arms against one another, they are in reality taking up arms against Jesus Christ, who lives in the German, the English, the French, and in all those who are the targets of militarized slaughter. And so he beseeched the ecumenical council to speak out, "so that the world, though it gnash its teeth, will have to hear, so that the peoples will rejoice because the church of Christ in the name of Christ has taken the weapons from the hands of their sons, forbidden war, proclaimed the peace of Christ against the raging world." A significant sentence from that sermon remained forever emblazoned in the memories of Bonhoeffer's students: "Peace must be dared; it is the great venture!"[36]

One can only wonder what might have happened to the march toward war in the Persian Gulf if the American bishops had stated in dramatic language, such as we read in Bonhoeffer's 1934 sermon, that the Iraqi people were our brothers and sisters in Jesus Christ and that the deadly force used against them was a violence done to Christ himself.

One of the problems Bonhoeffer faced throughout his life was how to arouse the church from its political quietism in order to stir up outrage at the abuses of human rights beyond the more self-serving determination to defend only its own limited interests. For Bonhoeffer, abuses of human rights anywhere had to be the church's concern, whether the victims be Christian or not, German or not. Bonhoeffer had, indeed, urged the churches early on in the Hitler era to recognize that Jesus Christ encounters us in human needs and pleads for our help in the persons of those who are not of one's nation or of one's race or of one's "class."

In an essay he wrote shortly before his arrest, he states dramatically his conviction that, to be faithful to the gospel, Christians must adopt as their own the compassion of Christ toward those who suffer. "We are not Christ," he said, "but if we want to be Christian, we must have some share in Christ's large-heartedness by acting with responsibility and in freedom when the hour of danger comes, and by showing a real compassion that springs, not from fear, but from the liberating and redeeming love of Christ for all who suffer."[37]

36. *A Testament to Freedom*, 228-29.
37. *LPP*, 14.

There is no doubt that Bonhoeffer's decision to join the political conspiracy against Hitler was an effort on his part to conform to the example of Jesus Christ. His willingness to risk his life for the victims of Nazism in that struggle became the ultimate expression of that faith. Bonhoeffer's opposition to Hitler was further motivated by a keen sense that the church should be where Christ has always been: among the outcasts, the despised, the oppressed, the victims of nationalist-military bloodletting and an immoral war. His suffering and death for these victims are a lesson to Americans that when the well-being of vulnerable citizens is threatened by harsh government policies, it is the Christian calling to resist.

It is heartening to know that Bonhoeffer's witness to Christian faith and compassion for the downtrodden have been of use and encouragement to the thinkers and the activists of South Africa who have resisted systemic evil and given hope to oppressed peoples everywhere. The people of America have much to learn from these South Africans who offer an example of courage and social, theological insight as America struggles to be itself a just society promoting human dignity, economic justice for all, and the kind of community in which Christ exists and is cared for in the person of those in need. Thanks in part to the agitation and protests of my colleagues here, the churches of South Africa did, indeed, come out of their stagnation to say the controversial word and to oppose the entrenched evil of apartheid head-on. The churches of America have yet to shake completely loose from their secularized patrons and their alliances with the affluent. It is my hope that the crisis stirred up by the "Contract with America" may arouse within these churches the fortitude to live the "costly grace" of following Jesus Christ. That cross can be for the churches, as it was for Bonhoeffer, the taking of an unpopular, risky stand against the evil now being structured into the fabric of discriminatory legislation. In asking the churches to see things from the perspective of those who suffer, Bonhoeffer was unwittingly charting a faith-filled way of life for his own time, for our time, and for Christians in every age.

Bonhoeffer and the Ecumenical Movement

KONRAD RAISER

In the mainline discussion about the significance of Dietrich Bonhoeffer, his involvement in the ecumenical movement has received relatively little attention. Apart from the early study by Jørgen Glenthøj (1956),[1] the treatment of the relevant facts in Eberhard Bethge's biography (1966), and Armin Boyens's comprehensive account of the *Church Struggle and the Oikoumene* (1969 and 1973),[2] no further in-depth analysis of this subject has been published, at least to my knowledge. The historical details have been fully reconstructed, and the materials which were published in the new edition of Dietrich Bonhoeffer's writings have added nothing substantially new. But the ways in which Bonhoeffer's thinking and the witness of his life have influenced the ecumenical movement in the second half of this century still have to be elucidated more fully. In particular, the organized ecumenical movement still has to claim Dietrich Bonhoeffer as one of its great sources of continuing inspiration. Obviously, this paper cannot satisfy that

---

1. Jørgen Glenthøj, "Bonhoeffer und die Ökumene," in *Die Mündige Welt* 2 (Munich: Chr. Kaiser, 1956): 116-203.
2. Eberhard Bethge, *Dietrich Bonhoeffer. Eine Biographie* (Munich: Chr. Kaiser, 1967); and Armin Boyens, *Kirchenkampf und Ökumene, Darstellung und Dokumentation*, vol. 1, *1933-39* (München: Chr. Kaiser, 1969); vol. 2, *1939-45* (1973).

demand. All I can hope to do is to initiate some reflections which should be pursued further.

The International Bonhoeffer Committee has promoted and made visible at the same time the reception of Dietrich Bonhoeffer beyond the German context. In its meeting in Geneva in 1976, commemorating the 70th birthday of Dietrich Bonhoeffer, it became apparent that Bonhoeffer's influence on new ways of doing theology in situations of oppression and conflict has probably been stronger in the southern hemisphere (Latin America, South Africa, and South Korea) than in Europe, and especially in Germany, where he is mainly seen as one of the martyrs of the German resistance movement. This was the focus of the events of 1995 commemorating his death fifty years ago. The one exception, at least in Germany, was the discussion about a "council of peace" inspired by Bonhoeffer's meditation in Fanø (1934). I shall come back to this point later.

The inspiration which the South African movement of Christian resistance against apartheid received from Dietrich Bonhoeffer is in itself an ecumenical fact. It is very appropriate, therefore, that we should assemble for this congress commemorating Bonhoeffer's 90th birthday in the new South Africa and reflect, among other topics, about Bonhoeffer's role in the ecumenical movement.

Historical Reconstruction

The study by Jørgen Glenthøj on *Bonhoeffer and the Oikoumene* has carefully surveyed the documentary evidence. Even though Bethge and Boyens have provided further details and clarified the wider context, they have not significantly changed this first attempt at historical reconstruction. I can limit myself, therefore, to recalling the main phases of Bonhoeffer's ecumenical involvement. His active participation in ecumenical activity was limited to the six years between 1931 and 1937. His later writings, especially the posthumously published *Ethics* and the *Letters and Papers from Prison*, do not mention explicitly his continuing links with the ecumenical movement.

Jørgen Glenthøj structured his presentation around four texts in which Bonhoeffer gives an account of his own evolving ecumenical reflection. I shall follow Glenthøj's outline and summarize the main elements of the context of the four texts of 1932, 1935, 1939, and 1941.

First Phase

Even though most of the German actors in the ecumenical movement were located in Berlin, and especially at the faculty where Bonhoeffer completed his studies in 1927 with his innovative doctoral dissertation *Sanctorum Communio,* he does not seem to have been aware of or influenced by the emerging ecumenical movement. Thus the year of postdoctoral studies at Union Theological Seminary in New York, 1930-31, was his first direct ecumenical exposure. Some of the friendships formed there became important sources of support during his later ecumenical activity.

The first point of contact with the organized ecumenical movement was his participation in the joint meeting of the World Alliance for Promoting Friendship among the Churches and the Life and Work movement in Cambridge, September 1931. Bonhoeffer had been sent to this meeting by his supervisor in the Berlin church, Superintendent Diestel, who was himself engaged in the work of the World Alliance. In Cambridge, Bonhoeffer was appointed one of three regional secretaries of the Joint Youth Commission of these two ecumenical bodies. This remained his main structural link with the ecumenical movement until 1937.

One might have thought that the young German assistant professor of Systematic Theology would have been more at home in the serious theological discussion of the Faith and Order movement. Instead, his first — and his last — ecumenical commitment concerned the question of peace. For him, this was the decisive issue for the young generation of his time. But it was also the point of entry for him to raise fundamental questions about the understanding and purpose of the ecumenical movement as a whole. His addresses in Ciernohorské Kúpele and Gland[3] and his later meditation in Fanø,[4] as well as his ecumenical activities in Germany from 1931-33, demonstrate that he was passionately engaged in clarifying and strengthening the theological and ecclesiological self-understanding of the ecumenical movement so that it could address with authority God's commandment of peace to a world which had lost its sense of a viable order.

---

3. Dietrich Bonhoeffer, "Zur theologischen Begründung der Weltbundarbeit," *GS,* vol. 1, 140ff., and "Ansprache in Gland," *ibid.,* 162ff.
4. Dietrich Bonhoeffer, "Kirche und Völkerwelt," *GS,* vol. 1, 216ff.

Second Phase

With the arrival of Hitler to power, a new challenge arose. Bonhoeffer's perceptive critical analysis of the *Führer* concept in a broadcast only two days after Hitler's appointment[5] and his immediate response to the preparation of racist legislation against the Jews in his article "The Church and the Jewish Question"[6] show that Bonhoeffer was prepared to draw the consequences from his understanding of the prophetic role of the church. While he was distressed about the inability of his own church to face this challenge, he found support among his friends in the World Alliance, who, in Sofia in September 1933, passed a strong resolution on the measures against the Jews in Germany.

His decision in this critical situation to accept the appointment as pastor of the German congregation in London was sharply criticized by his new mentor Karl Barth and led to a temporary cessation of their correspondence. However, the move intensified Bonhoeffer's ecumenical involvement, particularly through friendship with George Bell, Bishop of Chichester and since 1932 President of the Universal Council for Life and Work, which was formed during these eighteen months. It was Bonhoeffer's insistence which led, only weeks prior to the first synod meeting of the Confessing Church at Barmen at the end of May 1934, to the famous "Message regarding the German Evangelical Church to the Representatives of the Churches on the Universal Council for Life and Work from the Bishop of Chichester."[7] This was followed in August 1934 by the joint meeting of the World Alliance and Life and Work in Fanø under the presidency of Bishop Bell, with Bonhoeffer's address "The Church and the World of Nations"[8] (in which he sharpened his earlier positions regarding the theological basis of ecumenical work for peace), his famous meditation during morning prayers on 28 August 1934, "The Church and the Peoples of the World,"[9] and the resolution of the conference on the German church. In declaring "its conviction

5. Dietrich Bonhoeffer, "Der Führer und der einzelne in der jungen Generation," *GS*, vol. 2, 22ff.

6. Dietrich Bonhoeffer, "Die Kirche vor der Judenfrage," *GS*, vol. 2, 44ff.

7. "A Message regarding the German Evangelical Church . . . ," in Dietrich Bonhoeffer, *GS*, vol. 1, 192ff.

8. Dietrich Bonhoeffer, "Die Kirche und die Welt der Nationen, Theses for a Presentation in Fanø," *GS*, vol. 1, 212ff.

9. See note 4, above.

that autocratic Church rule, especially when imposed upon the conscience in solemn oath; the use of methods of force; and the subversion of free discussion are incompatible with the true nature of the Christian Church,"[10] the Council not only endorsed the clear message by Bishop Bell, but acted according to Bonhoeffer's understanding of the calling of the church in this situation.

It is against this background that Bonhoeffer's correspondence in the summer of 1935 with Canon Leonard Hodgson, the Secretary of the Continuation Committee of the Faith and Order movement, about participation in the preparatory meeting for the 1937 Edinburgh Conference has to be seen.[11] Bonhoeffer's fundamental disagreement with Hodgson led to his article "The Confessing Church and the Oikoumene," published in August 1935,[12] which has remained the most explicit theological account of his understanding of the ecumenical movement.

Third Phase

After having returned from London in March 1935, Bonhoeffer assumed responsibility for the programme of ministerial training of the Confessing Church. The demands of this new responsibility, the growing repression in Germany, also against the activities of the World Alliance, and doubts about the will of the ecumenical organizations to act according to the convictions expressed at Fanø, led Bonhoeffer to a gradual withdrawal from his active involvement in international ecumenical work. In 1936, he went once more to a meeting of Life and Work in Chamby, the last session before the Oxford Conference in 1937. His reservations about the attitude of the official ecumenical bodies regarding the situation in Germany were confirmed there, and in 1937 Bonhoeffer asked to be relieved of his responsibilities as regional youth secretary and member of the executive committee.

In his own assessment, Bonhoeffer remained firm and even sharpened his position in 1936 with his essay *"Zur Frage nach der Kirchengemein-*

10. Minutes of the Meeting at Fanø, 51
11. See correspondence with Faith and Order, *GS*, vol. 1, 230ff.
12. Dietrich Bonhoeffer, "Die Bekennende Kirche und die Ökumene," *GS*, vol. 1, 240-61.

schaft,[13] which culminates in the provocative affirmation: "Whoever consciously separates himself from the Confessing Church in Germany separates himself from salvation."[14] For Bonhoeffer himself, this was the obvious conclusion from the position he had already developed one year earlier in his article "The Confessing Church and the Oikoumene."[15] But in Germany his situation became increasingly difficult, even among his friends in the Confessing Church. His academic license was withdrawn, and in September 1937 the seminary in Finkenwald was closed. Bonhoeffer continued his work, but the situation of illegality became more and more risky.

In this situation, after the events of 1938 (annexation of Austria, occupation of Czechoslovakia, and the November pogrom against Jews) and under the threat of being called up for military service, Bonhoeffer tried to leave Germany with the help of ecumenical friends. While attempts via Canon Hodgson in London to receive an appointment as liaison person of the Confessing Church to the ecumenical organizations failed, he received an invitation to come to the U.S.A. After only one month (12 June — 6 July 1939), he returned to Germany convinced that it had been a mistake to go to America. In a letter to Reinhold Niebuhr, he wrote: "I must live through this difficult period of our national history with the Christian people of Germany. I will have no right to participate in the reconstruction of Christian life in Germany after the war if I do not share the trials of this time with my people. . . . Christians in Germany will face the terrible alternative of either willing the defeat of their nation in order that Christian civilization may survive, or willing the victory of their nation and thereby destroying our civilization. I know which of these alternatives I must choose. . . ."[16] His essay "Protestantism without Reformation,"[17] reflecting on his impressions during the four weeks in the United States, is rightly considered by Jørgen Glenthøj as Bonhoeffer's third account of his ecumenical convictions. All the issues which had caused him, since 1931, to challenge the Anglo-Saxon influence on the ecumenical

13. Dietrich Bonhoeffer, "Zur Frage nach der Kirchengemeinschaft," *GS,* vol. 2, 217-41.

14. *Ibid.,* 238.

15. Cf. *GS,* vol. 1, 244f.; see also "Letter to Karl Barth," *GS,* vol. 2, 286.

16. See *GS,* vol. 1, 320.

17. Dietrich Bonhoeffer, "Protestantismus ohne Reformation," *GS,* vol. 1, 323-54.

movement are addressed here in a very succinct way: unity of the church and denominationalism, church and state, peace, etc.

Fourth Phase

Already in February 1938, Bonhoeffer had been in touch with the emerging resistance movement among high-ranking officers and generals through his brother-in-law Hans von Dohnanyi. After the beginning of the war and once the continuation of his work for the Confessing Church had become impossible, these contacts grew closer, and from February 1941 Bonhoeffer was on leave of absence from his church responsibilities to assume special missions on behalf of the resistance movement under the cover of a member of the military secret service.

This was the last context in which Bonhoeffer's ecumenical connections became important. In 1938, the World Council of Churches in the process of formation had been established, bringing together Faith and Order and Life and Work. Willem A. Visser 't Hooft had been appointed the first General Secretary. During his visit to London in March 1939, Bonhoeffer met Visser 't Hooft for the first time, and they immediately established a close and trusting relationship.[18] Visser 't Hooft was determined to continue the support which Bishop Bell and Bishop Amundsen had given to the Confessing Church. This made him one of the important contact persons for the resistance movement in Germany in their efforts to establish links with the British and later the allied governments.

Three missions of Bonhoeffer during this last period before he was detained deserve to be mentioned. Already in February 1941, he travelled a first time to Switzerland to see Karl Barth, Friedrich Siegmund-Schultze, and in particular Visser 't Hooft. He gave Visser 't Hooft detailed information about the political and church situation in Germany and about the aims of the resistance movement. The encounter helped to reestablish the former relationship of trust with his ecumenical friends which had been clouded for Bonhoeffer since 1937. Already in September 1941, he came back for a second visit. Meanwhile, William Paton had published a book, *The Church and the New Order,* which reflected the discussion in the British peace aims group. Visser 't Hooft and Bonhoeffer

18. Cf. Willem A. Visser 't Hooft, *Zeugnis eines Boten,* 6ff.

jointly prepared a memorandum responding to this publication which gave Bonhoeffer the opportunity to introduce the perspective of the German opposition into the wider ecumenical discussion about the responsibilities of the church for a new international order after the war. Bonhoeffer's own German draft of this memorandum is his last explicit statement in the ecumenical context.[19]

In May 1942, Bonhoeffer met with Bishop Bell in Sigtuna, Sweden. He shared with him details about plans and persons involved in the German resistance movement and urged Bell to obtain some positive signal from the British government. But Bonhoeffer was not interested in an easy compromise. Bell later recalled Bonhoeffer having said: "We do not want to escape repentance. Our actions must be understood as an act of repentance."[20] This was Bonhoeffer's last personal encounter with his closest ecumenical friend. Bishop Bell was also the addressee of Bonhoeffer's last words before he was taken away for his execution, and which were reported by Payne Best: "Tell him . . . that for me this is the end but also the beginning. With him, I believe in the principle of our universal Christian brotherhood which rises above all national interests, and that our victory is certain — tell him, too, that I have never forgotten his words at our last meeting."[21]

Bonhoeffer's Legacy for the Ecumenical Movement

The historical reconstruction has already touched upon the main themes around which Bonhoeffer's ecumenical thinking crystallized. Rather than simply summarizing and reproducing Bonhoeffer's arguments, I shall concentrate in this second part of my paper on four issues which have been central in the process of reception and indicate Bonhoeffer's continuing influence on the ecumenical movement. These issues are, in a certain chronological order: peace, the church and the oikoumene, confession and resistance, and the challenge of modernity.

19. Dietrich Bonhoeffer, Gedanken zu W. Paton, "The Church and the New Order," *GS,* vol. 1, 355-60.

20. See *GS,* vol. 1, 395.

21. Quoted from Eberhard Bethge, *Dietrich Bonhoeffer. Eine Biographie,* 1037, note 54.

Peace— The Concrete Commandment

The most recent context in which Bonhoeffer's legacy has been redis-covered has been the ecumenical discussion about the responsibility of the churches for peace. Since the Oxford Conference in 1937, the ecu-menical movement has been caught in a dilemma: while all churches acknowledge — as the Amsterdam Assembly in 1948 put it — that "war is contrary to the will of God," they were divided about the concrete consequences to be drawn from this affirmation. The conflict between the three positions outlined for the first time in Oxford has continued until today. There are, on the one hand, the classical position of the just war and, on the other, the opposing tradition of radical pacifism. The third position is advocated by those who maintain that modern warfare fought with weapons of mass destruction can never be considered a just war and therefore must be resisted on ethical grounds.

Of course, the ecumenical discussion has evolved since Oxford and Amsterdam. In particular, the intensive discussion about the ethical is-sues posed by the possibility of nuclear war has led to the conclusion that the time had come for the churches to declare "that the promotion and deployment as well as the use of nuclear weapons are a crime against humanity and that such activities must be condemned on ethical and theological grounds. The nuclear weapons' issue is, in its import and threat to humanity, a question of Christian discipline and faithfulness to the gospel."[22] The statement of the Vancouver Assembly, "Peace and Justice," from which this quotation has been taken, is still the most comprehensive account of ecumenical thinking on war and peace.

The Vancouver Assembly is important, however, in our context because of the conciliar process on justice, peace, and the integrity of creation which was initiated there. This process was an indirect response to a proposal submitted by the delegation from the churches in the former German Democratic Republic that the WCC should consider whether the time had come for a "universal Christian council of peace" along the lines of the appeal by Dietrich Bonhoeffer in Fanø almost fifty years earlier.[23] This powerful witness for peace by Bonhoeffer had almost been

---

22. See David Gill, ed., *Gathered for Life*, Report of WCC Assembly, Vancouver (Geneva: WCC, 1983), 137.

23. See "Vancouver 1983," *Beiheft zur Ökumenischen Rundschau* 48 (Frankfurt, 1984): 206.

forgotten. Its reactivation half a century later shows that Bonhoeffer had developed an approach to the issue of war and peace which cuts across the conflicting positions and has lost nothing of its power.

The issue of world peace was at the center of Bonhoeffer's first contribution to ecumenical discussion in 1932 and 1934. He takes issue, on the one hand, with the approach represented by the Anglo-Saxon tradition of the World Alliance for which peace was an ideal to be realized following the teaching of Jesus, especially the Sermon on the Mount. The Alliance, therefore, sought to promote international encounter and understanding, but this, in Bonhoeffer's assessment, was not specifically Christian. It avoided articulating the "one great reconciling message." Where international peace was turned into an ideal state, an end in itself, the essential relationship between peace, justice, and truth was lost.

But Bonhoeffer also took issue with the continental European tradition which approached the issues of war and peace by reference to the orders of creation. In this tradition, the designation of an order as a manifestation of God's will would justify its defense also by going to war. Bonhoeffer argues that any order is at best an "order of preservation" for the sake of Christ, but never an unchangeable order of creation, and accepting the reality of struggle and conflict in a broken world must never lead to the justification of war, to the affirmation of war as inevitable or even as a principle. "War in our day,"Bonhoeffer says already in 1932, "no longer falls under the concept of struggle, because it is the certain self-annihilation of both combatants."[24] Because war can in no way be understood as one of God's orders of preservation, "war today and therefore the next war must be utterly *rejected* by the church."[25]

Decisive for Bonhoeffer's own approach to the issues of war and peace is his concept of the "concrete commandment." The church as the new community of Jesus Christ has the commission to proclaim with authority God's word as gospel and as commandment. While the gospel, for example the proclamation "your sins are forgiven," becomes concrete and alive as it is accepted by the hearer, the commandment must become concrete through those who proclaim it. The church has to enter as fully

24. Dietrich Bonhoeffer, *Zur theologischen Begründung der Weltbundarbeit, GS,* vol. 1, 140-58, 155 (English quotation follows *No Rusty Swords* [London: Collins, 1972], 166).

25. *Ibid.*

as possible into the conditions of contemporary life in order to move from the general statement of God's will for all everywhere to the proclamation of the concrete commandment for today. Articulating the concrete commandment means to discover what are God's "orders of preservation" for today. "Today God's commandment for us is the order of *international peace.* To say this is to express a quite definite recognition of the will of God for our time."[26] It is this understanding of the concrete commandment which enabled Bonhoeffer to cut through the deceptive identification of peace with security and to maintain that the struggle for peace must never compromise with the demands of justice and truth. But he is not afraid of being called a pacifist. "As certainly as we leave the making of the last peace to God, so certainly should we also make peace to overcome war. It is obvious that struggle as such will not be driven out of the world in this way, but here we are concerned with a quite definite means of struggle which today stands under God's prohibition."[27]

Bonhoeffer was clearly ahead of his time and also of the ecumenical discussion with his position that today the order of international peace is God's commandment for us. His insight that this commandment could be proclaimed with authority only by a "universal Christian council" was revolutionary in 1934 and has remained so even during the conciliar process fifty years later. Bonhoeffer was concerned about the faithfulness and obedience of the church to its Lord, who is the revelation of God's commandment for us. But he was equally concerned about the urgent need for peace in the political situation of his time and after the war had broken out, about the conditions for reestablishing a peaceful order. His unequivocal theological basis with its emphasis on the concrete commandment provided him with clear criteria, and in 1941-42 he was involved in exploring conditions for a new order of international peace after the war. The joint memorandum with Visser 't Hooft of September 1941 says:

> The commandments of God indicate the limits which dare not be transgressed, if Christ is to be Lord. And the Church is to remind the world of these limits. For a long time, it has not exercised this ministry, but more recently it has again begun to do so, as in different countries

---

26. *Ibid.,* 152 (English translation, 163).
27. *Ibid.,* 155 (English translation, 166).

it has taken a strong stand against the violation of God's commandments in political life. . . . The Church cannot and should not elaborate
detailed plans of post-war reconstruction, but it should remind the
nations of the abiding commandments and realities which must be
taken seriously if the new order is to be a true order, and if we are to
avoid another judgement of God, such as this present war.[28]

The legacy of these insights still has to be reclaimed by the ecumenical
movement.

The Church and the Oikoumene: Unity and Truth

For several years now, the WCC has been engaged in a process of
reflection on the "Common Understanding of the WCC" in the context
of the wider ecumenical movement. This process is an indication of the
fact that fifty years after the first Assembly at Amsterdam, the WCC is
in need of taking stock and reassessing its aim and its task as we move
into the twenty-first century. In its Basis, the WCC defines itself as a
"fellowship of churches." During the last two decades, however, the
WCC has been more commonly defined through its programs and activities, particularly in the areas of social justice, resource sharing, development, conflict resolution, etc. For many, the WCC is an international organization which pursues activities that go beyond what the
churches can do separately. Yet, it is merely an organization with no
ecclesial significance.

However, what is intended when the WCC is being called a "fellowship of churches"? What are the nature and quality of this fellowship?
Is the relationship between the churches, which has been established
through the formation of the WCC, merely instrumental or task-
oriented, or does it participate in what it means to be the church? While
this question is not being asked for the first time, the answers so far have
been inconclusive or evasive.

Against this background, it is significant to recall Bonhoeffer's reflections about the church and the oikoumene. Already the opening sentences
of his first statement in an ecumenical context are characteristic:

28. Memorandum on "The Church and the New Order in Europe," *GS*, vol.
1, 363.

There is still no theology of the ecumenical movement. As often in history as the Church of Christ has reached a new understanding of its nature, it has produced a theology appropriate to this self-understanding. A change in the Church's understanding of itself is proved authentic by the production of a theology, for theology is the Church's self-understanding of its own nature on the basis of its understanding of the revelation of God in Christ, and this self-understanding of necessity always begins where there is a new trend in the Church's understanding of itself. If the ecumenical movement stems from a new self-understanding of the Church of Christ, it must and will produce a theology. If it does not succeed in this, that will evidence that it is nothing but a new and up-to-date improvement in church organization. No one requires a theology of such an organization, but simply quite definite concrete action in a concrete task.[29]

Bonhoeffer was unequivocal that the oikoumene, even in the form of the relatively loose World Alliance, was not an instrumental organization *(Zweckorganisation)* with specific tasks, but a manifestation of the church itself. It is church to the extent that it has its raison d'être in faithfully and authoritatively proclaiming God's word, both as gospel and as concrete commandment.

This early position regarding the oikoumene as a manifestation of the church itself was radicalized in his critical correspondence with Leonard Hodgson, whose insistence on the ecclesiological neutrality of the Faith and Order movement has remained valid for the way in which the WCC is being understood in broad sections of its membership. For Bonhoeffer, on the other hand, the emergence of the Confessing Church had crystallized in a decisive way what it means to be the church.[30] In his essay "The Confessing Church and the Oikoumene," he interprets the resolution of Life and Work at Fanø as the recognition that the struggle of the Confessing Church in Germany is at its center the struggle about the proclamation of the gospel and that the Confessing Church is struggling vicariously for the whole church. The oikoumene cannot remain neutral to this situation. Rather, the Confessing Church and the oikoumene in their encounter are called to mutual accountability regarding the basis of their existence.[31] Is the oikou-

---

29. See above, note 24; quotation, 140 (English, 32).
30. Dietrich Bonhoeffer, "Die Bekennende Kirche und die Ökumene," *GS*, vol. 1, 240-61.
31. *Ibid.,* 242f.

mene in its visible manifestation church? Are the ecumenical organizations the visible and appropriate expression of the ecumenicity of the church according to the witness of the New Testament?

Obviously, this claim would be inappropriate where the ecumenical organizations are being understood only as associations of "Christian personalities" for the purpose of engaging in dialogue and conversation. In this perspective, the ability of the ecumenical organizations to foster open dialogue would be endangered if they were to take definitive positions, especially on matters of doctrine and confession. Dialogue, it was being said, is possible only as long as exclusive truth claims are being overcome, for the full truth can only be found in unity.

For Bonhoeffer, this "romantic-aesthetic-liberal" understanding of the oikoumene had been challenged through the experience of the Confessing Church. Here it had become clear that the church has no existence apart from the act of confessing its Lord and standing against his enemies. The church's confession is not an abstract theological affirmation, but a concrete, living act. The truth of the confession is manifested in struggle which leads to the separation of truth from falsehood. There can be no unity apart from the concrete affirmation of the truth. Oikoumene is church when it participates in this struggle for true confession, trusting in God's forgiveness.

Once this has been said, the reverse challenge must also be formulated: Can the Confessing Church claim to be truly church apart from the oikoumene? Is its participation in the ecumenical movement only pragmatic, or does it reflect a theological necessity? Indeed, should the Confessing Church so isolate itself in its claim to stand for the truth that its confession leaves no room for ecumenical dialogue, it would provoke the serious question whether it is truly the Church of Jesus Christ. The oikoumene, that is, the fellowship of those who are bound together through baptism, is the limitation of any absolute truth claim. This affirmation of the one baptism places the grace of God above the doctrine of the church and leads the church to the confession of sin and to repentance. In the ecumenical movement, the churches listen to one another's confession and call one another mutually to repentance. No church exists in and out of itself. The oikoumene is the manifestation that each church receives its life, the validation of its confession, from outside through the community of the whole church. Therefore, the participation of the Confessing Church in the ecumenical movement is the consequence of an inner necessity.

Never since this essay of Bonhoeffer in 1935 has the question of the ecclesial character of the ecumenical movement been addressed with such penetrating sharpness. To be sure, the context of the German church struggle was exceptional, and Bonhoeffer's argument is based essentially on an understanding of the church in the tradition of the Reformation. But his insight that the ecumenical movement cannot evade the question of the truth of the gospel by wanting to keep the dialogue open and that it participates in what it means to be the church when it joins the struggle for truth is as relevant today as it was then. Unity and truth cannot be separated from one another, just as peace cannot be separated from justice and truth. Unity is no end in itself; it is sustainable only if it is rooted in the truth. But the reverse must also be affirmed: no truth claim can be validated apart from the community; each church is dependent on the ecumenical fellowship to be challenged or confirmed in the truth of its confession. This mutual accountability which is rooted for Bonhoeffer in the bond of the one baptism is the decisive ecclesial mark of the fellowship of churches, also in the WCC. Bonhoeffer's reflections, therefore, have immediate relevance for the contemporary ecumenical discussion.

Confession and Resistance

Ten years ago, the South African *Kairos Document* was published and the South African Council of Churches issued the "call to prayer for the end of unjust rule." These two events mark the rediscovery of the inseparable link between confession and resistance. The ten affirmations of the World Convocation on Justice, Peace, and the Integrity of Creation in Seoul in 1990 have reaffirmed this insight. Clearly, the South African struggle against apartheid is the most notable example where Christians, in drawing on the experience of the struggle against the Nazi regime, have rediscovered the inseparable link between confession and resistance.

In a recent paper entitled "Between Confession and Resistance," Eberhard Bethge has retraced the experiences of his contemporaries in the German church struggle, leading them from confession to resistance. He recalls how little he and his friends who had received the Barmen Declaration as a liberating message were prepared for something like political resistance. "We had neither experience with nor conceptions of such activities, and, frankly, most of us still believed during Hitler's first years that his efforts and goals were in the best interests of Germany. When this belief began to be shaken, nobody spoke of resistance, even less so when some conscious acts of resistance were in fact committed. For by now the word had to be avoided until after 1945."[32] In fact, he recalls that some of those who were closely associated with the conspiracy against Hitler first heard the term "resistance movement" being applied to their activities after the end of the war. Indeed, most of our Christian traditions still have difficulty accepting that active political resistance can be an expression of Christian obedience. Retracing the witness of Bonhoeffer can help us to renew for our contemporary situation those vital insights which can guide Christians in their efforts to lead a life of moral responsibility under the conditions of unjust rule.

Bonhoeffer was among the first to identify the fundamental challenge which the so-called "Aryan clause" posed to the self-understanding of the church and its relationship to the state. In an article, "The Church and the Jewish Question," already in April 1933, he discussed the question of how the church can and should respond to this challenge based on its own mandate, which is distinct from that of the state. He maintains that the church has no right to interfere directly with the political actions of the state, but the church is called upon to act when the state does not serve its function to maintain law and order. This can be the case when there is either too much or too little law and order as a consequence of the policies of the state.

In the specific case in question, Bonhoeffer saw an example of too much law and order. "That means that the state develops its power to such an extent that it deprives Christian preaching and Christian faith . . . of their rights — a grotesque situation, as the state only receives its peculiar rights from this proclamation and from this faith, and enthrones itself by means of them. The Church must reject this encroachment of the order of the state precisely because of its better knowledge of the state and of the limitations of its actions. The state which endangers the Christian proclamation negates it."[33]

On the basis of this fundamental understanding of the respective roles of the church and the state, Bonhoeffer then outlines three possible

---

32. Eberhard Bethge, "Between Confession and Resistance," *Friendship and Resistance* (Geneva: WCC, 1995), 19f.

33. *No Rusty Swords*, 220f.

ways in which the church can act toward the state. This analysis has become a classical statement of the forms of Christian resistance, and it already foreshadows the way which Bonhoeffer was going to be led himself. In the first place, Bonhoeffer says, the church "can ask the state whether its actions are legitimate and in accordance with its character as a state, i.e., it can throw the state back on its responsibilities. Secondly, it can aid the victims of state action. The church has an unconditional obligation to the victims of any ordering of society, even if they do not belong to the Christian community. . . . In both these courses of action, the church serves the free state in its free way and at times when laws are changed, the church may in no way withdraw itself from these two tasks."[34] What Bonhoeffer describes here are the traditional ways for the churches to exercise a critical political responsibility. Most Christian traditions would limit the mandate of the church to these two forms of action.

It is, therefore, of decisive importance that Bonhoeffer adds a third possibility which he describes as: ". . . not just to bandage the victims under the wheel, but to put a spoke into the wheel itself. Such action would be direct political action, and it is only possible and desirable when the Church sees the state fail in its function of creating law and order, i.e., when it sees the state unrestrainedly bring about too much or too little law and order. In both these cases it must see the existence of the state, and with it its own existence, threatened. There would be too little law if any group of subjects were deprived of their rights, too much where the state intervened in the character of the Church and its proclamation, e.g., in the forced exclusion of baptized Jews from our Christian congregations or in the prohibition of our mission to the Jews. Here the Christian Church would find itself in *status confessionis,* and here the state would be in the act of negating itself."[35] It is this third possibility, which Bonhoeffer envisages in 1933, which has become the model for declaring a *status confessionis* in the struggle against apartheid in South Africa as well as in the conflict about nuclear arms and nuclear deterrence in Europe and North America. The reasons developed by Bonhoeffer to legitimate this third way of acting have been eloquently restated and unfolded in the confrontation between the South African churches and the apartheid state.

34. *Ibid.,* 221.
35. *Ibid.*

While Bonhoeffer remained a lonely voice during the first years of the church struggle in Germany with his prophetic insight of the possibility of Christian resistance, he was joined in 1938 by Karl Barth with his essay "Justification and Law," and shortly afterwards with his letter to Josef Hromádka referring to the impending occupation of Czechoslovakia by German troops. In December of the same year, Karl Barth went even further in a lecture at Wibkingen, where he developed his understanding of the relationship of church and state in a specific situation. Shortly after the night of the pogrom against Jews in Germany, he says: "Whoever is in principle an enemy of the Jews reveals himself as an enemy of Jesus Christ. Anti-Semitism is sin against the Holy Spirit."[36] Barth openly admits that he has supported in this way the prayer of the church against the oppressive powers and that he has considered this prayer as the "decisive action of the Church in view of the political challenges of the time."[37] This statement of 1938 found a late echo in the call to prayer for the end of unjust rule issued on 16 June 1985 in South Africa.

Bonhoeffer himself does not come back to the question of confession and resistance in his later writings, particularly in his *Ethics*, for the very reasons mentioned already by Eberhard Bethge. But his own life is a telling witness of the sincerity of his convictions formulated as early as 1933. The fragments of his *Ethics*, written during his active involvement in the conspiracy against Hitler, however, add the decisive dimension that responsible living includes the acceptance of becoming guilty, trusting in the forgiveness of God.[38] There is no doubt that the question of the link between confession and resistance, raised for the first time by Dietrich Bonhoeffer, remains a very pressing issue for the ecumenical movement today.

The Challenge of Modernity

Bonhoeffer exercised his most widespread ecumenical influence through his reflections on "religionless Christianity," which are contained in his letters from the prison. While his friends in the ecumenical movement

---

36. Quoted from Eberhard Busch, *Karl Barths Lebenslauf* (Munich: Chr. Kaiser, 1978), 304 (author's translation).

37. *Ibid.*

38. *Ethik, DBW*, vol. 6, "Die Struktur des verantwortlichen Lebens," 256-89, esp. 275-83.

are exercised about the corrosive influences of secularism and neo-paganism, Bonhoeffer tries to come to terms with the disappearance of the traditional religious consciousness from the life of modern society and begins to explore what an interpretation of the Christian faith could look like without making use of the categories of metaphysical religion. He is sharply critical of all theological attempts to reserve a space for God in private religious experience and wants to discover the presence of God in Christ in the midst of everyday life. How can the reality of God be articulated in a cultural situation which has lost the evident sense of transcendence? It is in this context that he develops a keen interest in the philosophical consequences of modern scientific research, in particular in nuclear and quantum physics, which represent, as it were, the hard core of modern consciousness.

It is, however, not only in his letters from the prison, but already in the fragments of his *Ethics* that he demonstrates his acute interest in taking the conditions of modern life seriously. Over against the Barthian rejection of natural theology, he develops a keen sense for the integrity of "natural life," and his famous distinction between the ultimate and the penultimate represents a revolutionary reinterpretation of the distinction of the two kingdoms in his Lutheran tradition. It is in the light of the ultimate message of the gospel of justification by grace alone that he arrives at an ethical reevaluation of the penultimate and the significance of human historical existence.

However, this constant effort to come to terms with human existence under the conditions of secular modernity from which he sees no escape makes him all the more sensitive to the inner contradictions of the modern spirit which has succeeded in pushing the reality of God to the very periphery. Where Karl Barth, reflecting the theology of the Calvinist tradition, proclaims the kingship of Christ over all human history, Bonhoeffer, drawing on his Lutheran heritage, begins to affirm the presence of God in the suffering of Christ who shares the place of those who dare to live with God in a world without God. Not the kingly rule, but the powerlessness of God in the suffering of Christ is the point at which Bonhoeffer breaks through the closed system of modernity.

It is in this context that in a fragment which is probably part of his account "After Ten Years" on the eve of 1943, he has articulated an insight which has become a decisive starting point for much of the contextual and ecumenical theological reflection of our time. It was Gustavo Gutiérrez who, in an article in *Concilium* in 1979,[39] drew attention to this passage. Bonhoeffer there speaks of a learning experience which he had made recently and which he describes in the following terms:

There remains an experience of incomparable value. We have for once learned to see the great events of world history from below, from the perspective of the outcast, the suspect, the maltreated, the powerless, the oppressed, the reviled — in short from the perspective of those who suffer. The important thing is that neither bitterness nor envy should have gnawed at the heart during this time, that we should have come to look with new eyes at matters great and small, sorrow and joy, strength and weakness, that our perception of generosity, humanity, justice and mercy should have become clearer, freer, less corruptible. We have to learn that personal suffering is a more effective key, a more rewarding principle for exploring the world in thought and action than personal good fortune. This perspective from below must not become the partisan procession of those who are eternally dissatisfied; rather, we must do justice to life in all its dimensions from a higher satisfaction, whose foundation is beyond any talk of "from below" or "from above." This is the way in which we may affirm it.[40]

Bonhoeffer was not allowed to live long enough to unfold the full implications of this learning experience, of this decisive change of perspective. However, he has reached, from his limited vantage point, the decisive insight from which any theology beyond modernity has to start. He has begun to acknowledge the victims of the emergence of the modern industrial society, and he has liberated himself from the understanding of world history from the perspective of the powerful and the beneficiaries. Gustavo Gutiérrez called his own theological critique of modernity a "theology from the underside of history," and he has acknowledged that it was Bonhoeffer who in his generation took the first step in this direction. What we can learn from Bonhoeffer even today is the insight that Christianity and Christian theology will come to terms with the ambivalent challenges of modernity not through an attitude of defensive anti-

39. Cf. Gustavo Gutiérrez, *Die historische Macht der Armen* (Munich: Chr. Kaiser,1984), "Die Grenzen der modernen Theologie: Zu einem Text von Dietrich Bonhoeffer," 190-203.
40. *WE,* 26; *LPP,* p. 17.

modernism, but only by penetrating to the center of modern human existence.

It does not minimize the decisive character of Bonhoeffer's insight that his interpretation of modern culture as being "religionless" seems to be contradicted by the reemergence of religion in contemporary society. Bonhoeffer was interested in an analytical understanding of modernity and not in an empirical description. He would have been the first to assess critically his understanding of "the world come of age." However, it is precisely his experience of the perspective "from below" which opens the way for a new look at the role of religion in coming to terms with the challenges of modernity.

These four indications do not exhaust the continuing significance of Bonhoeffer for the ecumenical movement. Other impulses which directly or indirectly have their origin in Bonhoeffer's reflections could be added. It was my intention to show that Bonhoeffer's contribution to the ecumenical movement is not only a decisive feature of ecumenical history, but has continuing validity for today. Hopefully, a fuller exposition will be made one day.

Dialogue with the Orthodox World: A Further Journey for Bonhoeffer

KEITH CLEMENTS

It has become a truism to describe Dietrich Bonhoeffer as a truly *ecumenical* Christian — one whose life and thought were intensely bound up with his particular historical and national context, yet who has become a figure of universal significance. Not only to Protestants, but to many Roman Catholics also, he represents a challenge to integrity of thought and action in the modern world. Nor is such interest confined to the "north." Few European theologians have drawn so much respect from the so-called Third World, especially from those wrestling with political and liberation theologies, in Latin America and indeed here in southern Africa. This ecumenical dimension to his influence, however, is liable to overstatement. Or, put another way, it assumes a somewhat partial understanding of what "ecumenical" means. Even if we confine ourselves to the Christian *oikumene,* vast areas of church and society outside the western, Latin-based world and its progeny in the south are frequently overlooked. Prominent in these other spheres is the other great legacy of Christendom, the Eastern or Orthodox Churches and the societies in which they have been such formative forces.

Study of Bonhoeffer has so far impinged little on the Orthodox world.[1] Indeed, the typically western discussion of Bonhoeffer has largely

1. To substantiate this view critically would require a thorough bibliography. One has the impression that most Orthodox scholars who have attended to Bon-

ignored that world. For example, the Fifth International Bonhoeffer Congress at Amsterdam in 1988 focused on Christian ethical responsibility in Europe.[2] One of the main parameters of that discussion was the situation, still prevailing then, of a Europe politically divided between the capitalist west and the socialist east. There was no mention that eastern Europe, as well as being the sphere of Soviet-style socialism, was also in large measure, in Christian historical terms, the world of Orthodoxy.

To acquiesce any longer to this state of affairs is, I believe, to evade a major challenge both to the integrity of our Bonhoeffer studies — including the claims we make for his wider significance — and to a properly ecumenical responsibility. It could also mean missing out on a creative and enriching theological encounter. Our African context at this Congress also underlines the importance of taking Bonhoeffer on this further journey. The ancient Coptic and Ethiopian Churches have played an immensely important role in Africa. Although they belong to the Oriental Orthodox (non-Chalcedonian) family rather than the Orthodox communion itself, their ethos has much in common with that of eastern Christianity as a whole. Moreover, this century has witnessed the dramatic growth of the African Orthodox Church of Kenya, Uganda, and Tanzania.

In this paper I can do little more than indicate where some of the main lines of an encounter between Bonhoeffer and Orthodoxy might take us, and where some of the main questions might arise. First, however, some brief remarks about the context of my own interest are in order, followed by a review of relevant biographical information about Bonhoeffer himself and his own experience of Eastern Christianity.

---

hoeffer are located in the west. John Zizioulas, e.g., in *Being as Communion: Studies in Personhood and the Church* (London: Darton, Longman and Todd, 1985), has clearly taken note of Bonhoeffer's ecclesiology and Christology. The most explicit recent exploitation of Bonhoeffer by an Orthodox theologian is by the Armenian Vigen Guroian (see note 20, below).

2. For the papers of that Congress, see *Bonhoeffer's Ethics: Old Europe and New Frontiers*, ed. G. Carter et al. (Kampen: Kok Pharos Publishing House, 1991).

The Contemporary Context:
A Reemergent European Divide

Why am I (and I hope others also) now so concerned about the Orthodox world? Much of it has to do with the changes in Europe that now make that Amsterdam meeting of 1988 seem, in some respects, such a long time ago. The Berlin Wall has come down. The Soviet Empire is no more — and even the figure who was so crucial in bringing it to an end, Mikhail Gorbachev, has gone from the public scene. The reverberations of those changes played no small part, it seems, even in the great shift that at last took place here in South Africa. In central and eastern Europe, new forms of cultural and ideological identity — or in some cases at least old ones now resurrected — are competing for allegiance to fill the void left by official Stalinist doctrine. Nationalism is on the rise again, and in the grasping after national identity it is to historic Orthodoxy that many are returning as the carrier of that identity. The beautiful cathedrals in the Kremlin, for decades silent museums, are once again resounding to the timeless chants of the Orthodox liturgy. To this resurgence there are both positive and negative sides. Deep spiritual wells are again being drawn upon. So too are atavistic forces intolerant of anything savoring of "foreign." And on the larger scale, after the initial euphoria at the dismantling of the so-called Iron Curtain, many in Europe are afraid again as an even older divide reemerges, between the Catholic and Protestant west on the one hand, and the Orthodox east on the other. In some ways, I believe, this divide is at least as potentially explosive as that between capitalist west and communist east — precisely because of its appeal to deep religious emotions and historical memories. What we have seen in the tragedy of the conflicts in former Yugoslavia is in part the reassertion of the potency of that divide, represented by Catholic Croatia and Orthodox Serbia, with the Muslims of Bosnia caught between. The old dividing line drawn by Emperor Theodosius in the fifth century between the western and eastern empires, between the spheres of Rome and Byzantium, is that which today runs through Bosnia.

That is my immediate context, as a European, for wishing dialogue with the Orthodox world as a matter of urgency.

But can Dietrich Bonhoeffer help us here? Is he, in this respect too, "of any use"? At first sight the signs are not propitious. What possible common ground, it may be asked, can there be between, on the one hand, one who is regarded as the apostle of faith amidst secular modernity, advocating a gospel stripped of all "religion"; and on the other hand, a church which seems to embody traditional religion and other-worldliness at their most exotic? With Bonhoeffer, surely, we are encouraged to leave the church and enter into secular life and political responsibility under the open sky "as if God were not given"; Orthodoxy, by contrast, invites us to enter the candle-lit darkness of the sanctuary, surrounded by the icons of saints from past ages, and to take part in a liturgy unchanged for centuries and in which the crucial action takes place behind the iconostasis, hidden from view to most of the worshippers. "Who is Jesus Christ, for us, today?" asks Bonhoeffer. The Orthodox, if they ask that question at all, will be expected to give only one answer: Jesus Christ is the one he has always been, as proclaimed in the Niceno-Constanti-nopolitan Creed, symbol of the unchanging faith of the one church down the ages and to all eternity. These, however, are surface impressions. Beneath them lie other elements, both on the side of Bonhoeffer and of Orthodoxy.

Bonhoeffer and Eastern Christianity

It is true that Bonhoeffer had relatively little direct contact with Or-thodoxy, and that dialogue with Orthodox thought barely surfaces in his theological writings. He was, however, sharply aware of the significance of the Eastern Churches. During his studies in Berlin in 1924-27, his teacher Karl Holl not only infected him with an enthusiasm for Luther but also directed him toward an interest in Orthodox Christianity.[3] Holl, in fact, had learned Russian in order to read Tolstoy in the original. Bonhoeffer himself had read Tolstoy as a schoolboy, and now also plunged into Dostoyevsky. Dostoyevsky had been vital to Karl Barth's rediscovery of the strangeness of the God who is encountered most truly by the godless. Bonhoeffer, for his part, was particularly impressed by Dostoyevsky's identification of a Russian spirituality which, paradoxi-cally, was a "supranational post-humanism."[4] Bonhoeffer also quickly acquired the successive volumes of Hans Ehrenberg's *Eastern Christianity*. In addition, in 1927 Holl brought Stefan Zankow, the leading Bulgarian

---

3. E. Bethge, *Dietrich Bonhoeffer*, 47f.
4. *Ibid.*, 47.

theologian, to Berlin to give lectures on "The Orthodox Christianity of the East"—a series which was later published.

The Orthodox churches were already beginning to participate in ecumenical conferences, and Bonhoeffer was to meet Zankow and others in the Life and Work movement and in the World Alliance for Promoting International Friendship through the Churches. His furthest reach into actual Orthodox territory would have been at Sofia, Bulgaria, where the World Alliance met in September 1933. Would it have been there that he acquired a favorite icon which Wolf-Dieter Zimmerman, to his chagrin, confesses to have accidentally knocked off the wall and broken at Finkenwalde?[5]

From these biographical indications of an awareness and appreciation by Bonhoeffer of Eastern Christianity, let us turn to some features of his theology which might well be appreciated in turn by Orthodox theologians. I will identify at least four main elements.

Ecclesiology

"The Church is one and the same with the Lord—his body, of his flesh and of his bones. The Church is the living vine, nourished by him and growing in him. Never think of the Church apart from the Lord Jesus Christ, from the Father and the Holy Spirit." So wrote St. John of Kronstadt (1829-1908), one of Russia's great nineteenth-century saints, a priest of the poor and sick in St. Petersburg. His words capture the Orthodox emphasis on the church as a human community spiritually one with and indwelt by the triune God: an icon of the Trinity, of unity in diversity. This incarnational emphasis on the Body of Christ mystically united with its Head is underscored by the Greek theologian Christos Androutsos, who describes the Church as "nothing else than the continuation of [Christ's] prophetic, priestly and kingly power. . . . The Church and its founder are inextricably bound together. . . . The Church is Christ with us."[6] It is a strongly communitarian view, self-consciously opposed to what it sees as the essentially hierarchical un-

5. W.-D. Zimmermann, in *I Knew Dietrich Bonhoeffer*, ed. W.-D. Zimmermann and R. Gregor Smith (London: Collins Fontana, 1973), 110f.

6. Quoted in Timothy (Bishop Kallistos) Ware, *The Orthodox Church* (London: Penguin, 1993), 241.

derstanding of the Roman Church, and to the Protestant view of a human community gathered *under* the Word of its absent Lord. Bishops and people are joined in an organic unity, neither having any meaning without the other. Bishops are called to teach the faith, but it is the whole people of God, in and with God, who are its guardians. For the Russian Orthodox this sense of togetherness is expressed in the beautiful if almost untranslatable word *sobernost.*

"The Church is Christ existing as community," states the young Bonhoeffer of *Sanctorum Communio* and *Act and Being*. Revelation is not the momentary invasion of human consciousness by a Word *ab extra*. It is concretized, made flesh, in the humanness of a community which retains a continuity of identity, the fellowship of the forgiveness of sins. This is not Orthodox language, but neither is it dissimilar from Orthodox concerns. Behind it lies an attempt to do justice not only to the sovereign freedom of God which Barth and the dialectical theologians had rediscovered in reaction to the immanentism of liberal Protestantism, but also to the God who shows his freedom precisely as a freedom to *turn to* and *be with* his creaturely, human world. Orthodoxy would claim that it has never lost this insight into the God who dwells in and with humankind, above all in the Church, yet remains the transcendent God — "God is beyond in the midst of our life," in Bonhoeffer's own words.[7]

God as Redeemer and Sanctifier of All Creation

"The 'religious act' is always something partial; 'faith' is something whole, involving the whole of one's life. Jesus calls not to a new religion, but to life," writes Dietrich Bonhoeffer in his prison letters.[8] Earlier, in his *Ethics*, he had rejected the pseudo-Lutheran notion of "thinking in two spheres." In Christ, God and reality are united. There is only the one world, reconciled by and to God in Christ, which means "that there is no real possibility of being a Christian outside the reality of the world and that there is no real worldly existence outside the reality of Jesus Christ."[9] Nor can humanity itself be sundered into compartments, inner

7. *LPP*, 282.
8. *Ibid.*, 363.
9. *Ethics*, 172.

345

and outer, spiritual existence and bodily existence.[10] It is the whole person whom Christ claims and redeems. It is in the this-worldliness of life that we learn what faith is.[11]

It is precisely at those points where to western eyes it appears at its most "other-worldly" that Eastern Christianity in fact makes its own boldest claims to a holy worldliness. Much of the symbolism of Orthodox worship, for all its seeming strangeness to everyday secular life, is expressive of a theology which sees salvation as embracing the material and physical no less than the spiritual, and the whole of cosmic reality no less than the individual human being. Iconography is not just pious artistry. It represents a belief in the sanctity of creation as a medium of the divine, right down to wood, paint, and oil. The sanctuary may appear to be a darkened haven from the real world, lit only by a dim religious light, but in fact it is seen as the cosmos in microcosm, and the liturgy the celebration of the redemption of that whole cosmos. For example, in the liturgy on the feast of Christ's baptism, the descent of the Spirit at the Jordan River is celebrated as God's recreating activity on all the waters of creation. It should be no surprise, then, that a number of Orthodox theologians have in recent years attended to theologically based ecological ethics. Even that aspect of Orthodox spirituality which appears to liberal western Protestants as the worst obscurantism — the veneration of the relics of the saints, even to the least fragment of bone — is defended in similar terms. "This reverence for relics," says Kallistos Ware, "is not the fruit of ignorance and superstition, but springs from a highly developed theology of the body."[12]

The Secret Discipline

Well had [the biblical Fathers] learnt the lesson that the awful dignity of the mysteries is best preserved by silence. What the uninitiated are not even allowed to look at was hardly likely to be paraded about in written documents. . . . Moses was wise enough to know that contempt attaches to the trite and to the obvious, while a keen interest is naturally associated with the unusual and the unfamiliar. In the same

10. *Ibid.*, 346f.
11. *Ibid.*, 369f.
12. Ware, *The Orthodox Church*, 234.

manner the Apostles and Fathers who laid down the laws of the church from the beginning thus guarded the awful dignity of the mysteries in secrecy, for what is bruited abroad at random among the common folk is no mystery at all.[13]

So wrote Basil of Caesarea in the fourth century. Other church fathers, of both west and east, spoke in similar vein of what in later western Protestantism became known as the *disciplina arcani,* the "discipline of the secret" or (less accurately) the "secret discipline." It is the Eastern Church which has preserved most fully this sense of a mystery at the heart of faith, to be found in right *doxa* — worship — at least as much as right doctrine.

Dietrich Bonhoeffer's call, in his prison letters, for a new kind of *disciplina arcani* is well known. He argues that the great Christian doctrines have become strange to us. We are like little children having to learn to understand them all over again for the modern world. We cannot as yet proclaim them to nonreligious people. Until we can do so — and one day, in God's good time, we assuredly will do so — the Christian life will be one of prayer and righteous action. It is important to see that Bonhoeffer was *not* saying that the totality of Christian truth consists *only* of prayer and righteous action, and that the great tradition of faith must be jettisoned. Rather, much of that tradition must be preserved in a patient, waiting silence for the time being. His criticism of what he saw as Karl Barth's "positivism of revelation" was similarly based on his insight that Christian truth cannot be delivered as a ready-made package of beliefs: "There are degrees of knowledge and degrees of significance; that means that a secret discipline must be restored whereby the *mysteries* [Bonhoeffer's emphasis] of the Christian faith are protected against profanation."[14] And Bonhoeffer's anxieties about profanation through overenthusiastic popularization go right back to *The Cost of Discipleship.*[15]

13. Basil of Caesarea, *De Spiritu Sanctu,* 27, 66, in H. Wace and P. Schaff, eds., *St Basil: Letters and Select Works,* Library of Nicene and Post-Nicene Fathers (James Parker, 1985), 42.

14. *LPP,* 286.

15. *CD,* 166.

Salvation: Theiosis, the Image of God in Us and Humankind's Coming of Age

This last reference to *The Cost of Discipleship* aptly leads us to consider where Bonhoeffer puts the emphasis in his understanding of salvation. At the risk of oversimplification, it can be said that while western theology — certainly since Augustine — sees the work of Christ as restoring the perfection and innocence lost in the Fall, eastern theology typically sees Christ as bringing humankind to the fullness of life which Adam and Eve had *in potential*, a potential for growth which they forfeited in their disobedience. (Recently, at an exhibition in London of "Africa in Art," I was intrigued to see an ancient Coptic figure in wood, of Adam carrying the cross.) The west sees the Fall as a lapse into depr*a*vation, the east sees it as misdirection into depr*i*vation, a perpetual childhood deprived of growth into maturity.

It is striking that the final chapter of *The Cost of Discipleship* is titled "The Image of Christ"; in it Bonhoeffer describes the work of Christ less in terms of his bringing us to a state of heavenly bliss than of his restoring the image of God, his own image, in us:

> God saw himself in Adam. Here, right from the beginning, is the mysterious paradox of man. He is a creature, and yet he is destined to be like his Creator. Created man is destined to bear the image of uncreated God.[16]

The language throughout the chapter continues to be that of Irenaeus, the great second-century Greek father and martyr-bishop of Lyons, and himself an important link between east and west. It is his use of Irenaean Christology and soteriology which enables Bonhoeffer to depict Christ as the one who enters into solidarity with the entire human race in its sin and need, the one through whom God recreates his image in humankind. Discipleship therefore entails a like entry into solidarity with the world in God's *philanthropia*. This chapter forms a pivotal connection between the theology of discipleship and the world-orientation which follows in the *Ethics* and the prison writings.

It is too little appreciated in the west just how daring Orthodoxy is in its account of the destiny of (redeemed) humanity. Sanctification

---

16. *Ibid.,* 269.

reaches to *theiosis,* the deification of humanity in union with God's own self. "In his unbounded love, God became what we are that he might make us what he is," says Irenaeus. Human persons by the grace of God become a "created god," still human but partaking of the divine nature. Far from being a purely mystical, still less a magical, state beyond moral discipline, it is a state which is deeply ethical and indeed social, because it means expressing the divine love in action. What divinization means is expressed in the saying of one of the desert fathers: "If it were possible for me to find a leper and to give him my body and to take his, I would gladly do it. For this is perfect love."[17]

There is ample room therefore in eastern theology for a deeply affirmative vision of human possibility and destiny. Human beings are meant for adulthood and maturity in the responsibility of love. It would be wrong to draw a direct link, or even an exact parallel, between the notion of *theiosis* and Bonhoeffer's view of the "coming of age" of humankind. But in both there is a decided rejection of the premise that divine and human strengths are mutually derogatory.

These, then, are just four points of affinity between Bonhoeffer and main features of Orthodox theology. There are also, undeniably, important differences. Orthodoxy will doubtless find much of Bonhoeffer's writing overly Christocentric at the expense of a truly trinitarian perspective,[18] and ineluctably Lutheran in its *theologia crucis.* But there is surely also common ground for dialogue. Bonhoeffer, like Orthodoxy, is concerned for continuity and identity as we apprehend the tradition for today. Orthodoxy, like Bonhoeffer, affirms the totality of human, creaturely existence and the cosmos as the locus of encounter with God.

Church and Nation: The Critical Point of Dialogue

I return to the contemporary European context, of revived nationalisms frequently seeking historic religious traditions as their foundation. The crucial point here, and one which westerners find very hard to apprehend, is that in many of these cases not only is the Orthodox faith claimed

---

17. Quoted in Ware, *The Orthodox Church,* 237.
18. Cf Zizioulas, *Being as Communion,* 110n. Zizioulas is appreciative of Bonhoeffer's Christology but finds a pneumatological dimension lacking throughout his work.

as the faith of the majority of the population, nor even the Orthodox Church acknowledged as the national or even state church: Orthodoxy and nationality are actually one and the same thing. "No-one who is not Orthodox can be Bulgarian," I was told while in Sofia earlier this year. There are historic reasons for this. Especially among the Russian and other Slav peoples, the beginnings of their national stories are effectively dated from the espousal of the Byzantine faith, which brought with it an almost ready-made civilization to be enculturated in the life of their people. Within the territories ruled by the Ottoman Empire the faith was even more significant than that. The Turkish rulers delegated the civil administration of Christian populations to the churches, which thereby became virtually coterminous, politically and culturally no less than geographically, with the "Christian nation." In the Balkans the dynamic of this identity between faith and nation survived long after the demise of the Ottoman Empire. It persisted right through the communist period when it gave the churches a powerful *raison d'être*, namely, to be the carriers of national cultural identity in the face of imposed ideological uniformity. It was certainly this role which helped keep the Serbian Orthodox Church alive during the Tito period in Yugoslavia. Unfortunately, adopting that role also left the Serbian Church with little theological or political muscle to resist the nationalistic political opportunism of Serbia's post-Tito leaders — and indeed in some eyes the church has itself actually aided and abetted that nationalism by providing justification for the "Greater Serbia" project.

The Christian nation, or the nation pervaded by the spirit of which the church is the visible focus, is a noble vision. Unfortunately, history tends to produce a nationalized Christianity rather than a Christianized nationality. "[Orthodox Slavs] have sometimes tended to think of their faith as primarily Serb, Russian, or Bulgar, and to forget that it is primarily Orthodox and Catholic; and this has also been a temptation for the Greeks in modern times."[19] The mission of the nation and the mission of the church become hopelessly confused, with tragic results for both. No space is left for the church's prophetic mission of calling its rulers to account according to the standards of justice and peace. Rather, those interests of justice and peace become totally subsumed under the supposedly national interests, which can take the form of aggression, or of brooding self-pity for past wrongs suffered and requiring redress. Above

19. Ware, *The Orthodox Church*, 77.

all, there is a deep distrust of everything foreign. The nation must be ethnically and religiously pure.

One can readily see why Dietrich Bonhoeffer poses a challenge to such a view, waging as he did in his own life and thought a battle against the nationalist and racist ideology of National Socialism. But Bonhoeffer can only be of use if he can be taken seriously by Eastern Christianity as a theologian on his own merits, in tune with certain of the east's deepest concerns, and not seen simply as yet another westerner lecturing others on their shortcomings. The reason Bonhoeffer can be seen as a potential partner in *dialogue* with the east is that, as we have seen, he takes *the church as community* so seriously and, at the same time, takes the social context of the church equally seriously as the realm where God's redemptive and sanctifying work operates. Salvation, the restoration of God's image in humankind, is the re-creation of community. Bonhoeffer stresses this, right from *Sanctorum Communio* to *Ethics.* In the earlier work, far from dismissing the idea of the national church, he suggests that the real question is whether the national church can find its way to becoming a confessing, gathered church. In the later work, he sees the gathered congregation as the community which stands with the Word of God on behalf of all people: in solidarity with them yet also in *critical* encounter, alongside the Word, with the powers of this world.

In what I hope is a foretaste of much else to come, Vigen Guroian, an Armenian Orthodox theologian at Loyola College, Baltimore, has opened up the issues which Bonhoeffer's critique of religious nationalism presents to his own Armenian church and nation.[20] In fact, he draws a parallel between Bonhoeffer's critique and that of Archbishop Tiran Nersoyan (1904-89), who trenchantly criticized the mythology upon which depended much of the identification between Armenian nationhood and the Armenian Orthodox Church. More positively, Nersoyan envisaged a national life which would allow autonomous civil institutions to pursue secular goals, the church seeking neither to embrace nor control all these, but revitalizing the life of the people by its preaching of the gospel, its moral teaching, and its inspirational example.

Dietrich Bonhoeffer himself knew that the church, as holy, catholic, and apostolic, is in the nation and for the nation, but not of the nation.

---

20. Vigen Guroian, *Ethics After Christendom: Toward an Ecclesial Christian Ethic* (Grand Rapids: Eerdmans, 1995), ch. 5, "Church and Armenian Nationhood: A Bonhoefferian Reflection on the National Church."

It is first and foremost the one church of Jesus Christ, gathered across all the nations.[21] In his last recorded words — his message to Bishop George Bell — he repeated his bedrock belief in the one universal Christian fellowship which rises above all national interests and boundaries. An increasing number of Orthodox thinkers are troubled by the fact that, ironically, it is precisely in their tradition, which has made such large claims for the indivisibility of the church catholic, that such insistence should today be placed upon *national* churches, often deeply jealous of their sovereignty. For our part, we who are western Protestants know that for a very long time we shall have to live with Bonhoeffer's critique of "Protestantism without Reformation,"[22] that fragmentation of Christianity into competing denominations and, ultimately, individuals, under the guise of "freedom." Bearing that in mind, and maybe saved thereby from a liberal arrogance, we can encourage a future dialogue between Bonhoeffer and what he might have called the "Orthodoxy without Catholicity" of the east. That could serve the renewing of both western and eastern Christianity, their greater unity, and, moreover, the peace of the world.

21. See in D. Bonhoeffer, *No Rusty Swords,* "A Theological Basis for the World Alliance" (157-73); "The Church Is Dead" (182-89); "The Confessing Church and the Ecumenical Movement" (326-44).

22. "Protestantism Without Reformation," in Bonhoeffer, *ibid.,* 92-108.

Bonhoeffer, Apartheid and Beyond: The Reception of Bonhoeffer in South Africa

JOHN W. DE GRUCHY

In an essay entitled "Bonhoeffer and South Africa" (published in Eberhard Bethge's book *Bonhoeffer: Exile and Martyr*, which contains the lectures he gave in South Africa in 1973), I told a story which has been repeated subsequently by others. "As we listened to Bethge's lectures," I wrote, "it became increasingly obvious how relevant Bonhoeffer's life and thought are for our situation today. Some laymen who attended a seminar on Bonhoeffer, but who had no previous knowledge of him, innocently enquired: 'When did Bonhoeffer visit South Africa? He knows our situation from the inside.'"[1] The appropriateness of Bonhoeffer's theology and witness for South Africa was already becoming obvious to a handful who were familiar with his legacy. But his significance for our situation was to become even more apparent in the years which followed. It was not just the case that there were always aspects of Bonhoeffer's life and thought which provided insight for the struggle against apartheid, but that his example and writings challenged us to greater commitment and more faithful engagement.[2]

Having said that, two qualifications need to be made at the outset

---

1. Eberhard Bethge, *Bonhoeffer: Exile and Martyr* (London: Collins, 1975; New York: Seabury, 1976), 26.
2. See John W. de Gruchy, *Bonhoeffer and South Africa: Theology in Dialogue* (Grand Rapids: Eerdmans, 1984).

about the reception of Bonhoeffer's legacy in South Africa. The first is that it would be wrong to give the impression that the reception has been solely in the hands of professional theologians, or of those who have been particularly interested in his work. In an introductory essay to *Bonhoeffer: Exile and Martyr,* entitled "The Response to Bonhoeffer," Bethge focuses largely on the scholarly reception of Bonhoeffer in eastern and western Europe, for very good reason. But that cannot be our chief focus in South Africa, any more than it is in Latin America or, as John Moses has indicated elsewhere in this volume,[3] in the former German Democratic Republic. Certainly there has been some academic work done on Bonhoeffer's theology in South Africa, and I do not wish to underplay its importance. But more significant has been the appropriation of Bonhoeffer by those whose witness to Jesus Christ and involvement in the struggle for justice and liberation have led them along a similar path, and who, as they have journeyed along that path, have discovered fragments of his theology which have helped them to remain faithful and hopeful.

In this respect we must say that Bonhoeffer's contribution to theological existence and witness in South Africa has been made more in the arena of struggle than in academic study. But any dichotomy between theological reflection and praxis is inappropriate if we are to take Bonhoeffer's legacy seriously. The academic study of Bonhoeffer's legacy in South Africa, as in other countries of the south or what used to be called the Third World, has been inseparable from the life of the ecumenical church and involvement in the struggle for justice and peace. Perhaps that is the reason his legacy has become so important in contexts such as South Africa, but less so in countries where theology and praxis have been kept in separate compartments.

The second qualification is that we must not overestimate Bonhoeffer's direct or overt influence. After all, the vast majority of Christians in South Africa have not even heard about him. It is important that we constantly remind ourselves that those of us who may think we are informed about, or who regard ourselves at the "cutting-edge" of contemporary theological developments, are by no means the majority in the church. Moreover, the churches to which most of us belong no longer represent the majority of Christians. So when we talk about the influence of Bonhoeffer in South Africa we have to recognize that no matter how

3. See John Moses, "The Reception of Bonhoeffer in East Germany," 278-97 in this volume.

real and important it has been, it has been confined to a relatively small circle, however influential in certain respects. Bonhoeffer's main challenge has been directed, in fact, to those of us who, like himself, were usually (though not only) white, privileged, academically trained, and therefore numbered among an elite minority in South Africa — though an elite which sought, in some way, to be in solidarity with those who struggled for liberation and, insofar as it is ever possible, who expressed solidarity with those who suffered both as victims of apartheid and on account of their role in the struggle. The fact of the matter is that Bonhoeffer helped to liberate us to be of some use. But now, in a new time and context, he forces us to ask of ourselves: "Are we still of any use?" And if so, in what way? So let us reflect on those elements or, better, fragments in his legacy which have been of particular importance for us in the past, and which may still be of use in helping us to discern our responsibility in the present and future.

Confessing Christ Concretely Here and Now

In talking of the reception of Bonhoeffer in South Africa there is no doubt that we must begin with the testimony of Beyers Naudé. I know that comparisons are invidious; I also acknowledge Naudé's unease with comparisons between himself and Bonhoeffer. But we cannot be true to the story of the church struggle in South Africa if we fail to note Naudé's Bonhoeffer-like role. The reason for the comparison derives, initially, from the fact that both Dietrich Bonhoeffer and Beyers Naudé sought to be faithful in their witness to Jesus Christ within their respective contexts, and that their contexts — Nazi Germany and apartheid South Africa — bore a striking resemblance.[4] It was not by chance that Beyers Naudé was at the very first International Bonhoeffer Congress in 1971 in Düsseldorf.

Bonhoeffer's influence can be seen, early on, in the formation of the Christian Institute in the post-Cottesloe period.[5] Again and again,

---

4. See John W. de Gruchy, "Patriotism, True and False: Reflections on Bonhoeffer, Oom Bey and the Flag," in Charles Villa-Vicencio and Carl Niehaus, eds., *Many Cultures, One Nation: Festschrift for Beyers Naudé* (Cape Town: Human and Rousseau, 1995).

5. See John W. de Gruchy, "A Short History of the Christian Institute," in Charles Villa-Vicencio and John W. de Gruchy, eds., *Resistance and Hope: South African Essays in Honour of Beyers Naudé* (Cape Town: David Philip, 1985).

Naudé wrote and spoke about the need to develop a "confessing church" movement in South Africa which would oppose both the policy of apartheid and its theological legitimation and ecclesiastical support. The publication of *The Message to the People of South Africa* in 1968, inspired in large measure by Naudé, with its radical critique of apartheid as a false gospel, rightly reminded many of the Barmen Declaration. At the heart of *The Message* was a strong confession of Christ as Lord over against the idolatrous claims that apartheid could provide a way of salvation for South Africa.

The Message had two major consequences. First, it gave impetus to the development of a confessing theology and witness within the ecumenical church in South Africa. Yet it went beyond Barmen by focusing not primarily on the church but much more specifically on the political sphere. In doing so it was following Bonhoeffer's dictum that confessing Christ had to be done in the most concrete way possible. It was insufficient to speak in theological generalities. What was needed was to say precisely what Christ required here and now in relation to the issues at hand. Hence *The Message* not only set in motion a study project on social, political, and economic issues (Spro-cas), but also led to greater political activism on the part of some, and to the state's subsequent banning of the Christian Institute, Beyers Naudé, and other leaders such as Theo Kotze. Indeed, it eventually led to the attempt to put a spoke in the wheel of the apartheid regime.

Confessing Christ concretely here and now meant resisting apartheid in all its forms. It meant rejecting any attempt to provide a theological justification for racism, oppression, and injustice. So it always must whenever and wherever such idolatry rears its head. Racism, oppression, and injustice, especially in the economic sphere, have by no means disappeared from our South African society. Hence, even in the new South Africa, a genuine confession of Christ will require a critical witness which ever seeks to prevent the destruction of human life and dignity. Confessing Christ today means, at least in part, participating in the struggle for a culture of human rights and opposing any attempt by the state to become the sole arbiter of good and evil, right and wrong. Bonhoeffer still has much to teach us in this regard.

Putting a Spoke in the Wheel

The hagiographic picture of the German Confessing Church has long since been deflated. Yet those of us who were not involved in the German church struggle have no right to judge those who were. Theirs was a courageous testimony, and many of the Barmen confessors paid for it with their lives. The Confessing Church did not fail to confess Christ against Nazi ideology and the attempt by the German Christians *(Deutsche Christen)* to control the Evangelical Church. For Hitler, certainly, Barmen was a threat, in the same way as *The Message to the People of South Africa* was perceived as a threat by Prime Minister John Vorster.[6] Nonetheless, as is widely acknowledged, Barmen did fail to confess Christ concretely against the persecution of the Jews, and in the end the Confessing Church did not live up to its confession at Barmen and Dahlem. Hence Bonhoeffer's growing disenchantment with the Confessing Church.

So it was that he began to move outside the parameters of the Confessing Church and became involved in the resistance and the conspiracy against Hitler. Already in 1933, in his essay on the Jewish Question, Bonhoeffer had recognized the possibility of a time when the church would not only have to help the victims of Nazism, or warn the state that it was failing in its duty to protect a just order, but also actively resist and, if possible, "put a spoke in its wheels." And, sure, enough, the time came when confession had to become resistance. The metaphor of "putting a spoke in the wheels" of government was certainly quoted many times in South Africa by those Christians who were familiar with Bonhoeffer's essay and who were convinced that the apartheid regime was illegitimate.

The illegitimacy of the white minority government in South African had long been recognized by Africans and others who rejected the formation of the Union of South Africa in 1910. But it was not until the implementation of apartheid and resistance to it began in earnest in the 1950s that the issue attracted more widespread attention. This was especially so after the Sharpeville massacre in 1960 and the subsequent banning of the African National Congress and the Pan Africanist Congress. Yet it was only as a result of the Black Consciousness Movement,

---

6. See John W. de Gruchy and W. B. de Villiers, eds., *The Message in Perspective* (Johannesburg: SACC, 1969).

the WCC Programme to Combat Racism, and, finally, the Soweto student uprising in 1976, that the question of state legitimacy began to find a tentative place on the agenda of the ecumenical church which was still dominated by white perceptions and interests. Slowly and painfully it began to dawn on a handful that a way had to be found to put a spoke in the wheel of the state and not just bandage up the victims of apartheid.[7]

Indicative of this new perception was the conscientious objection debate in which a handful of young white males argued, much in the tradition of Dietrich Bonhoeffer, that they could not serve in the South African army, not on pacifist grounds but because they rejected the moral authority and legitimacy of the state in defending apartheid.[8] Complementary to this was the debate about the use of violence to overthrow the state, and therefore the legitimacy of the armed liberation struggle.[9] The time had come not just to minister to victims, not just to remind the state of its proper role, but to recognize the illegitimacy of the apartheid regime and take steps to remove it. The banning of the Christian Institute and the growing harassment of the South African Council of Churches were indicative of the extent to which the state now regarded their witness on such issues as a threat to its continued existence. Then, belatedly, but no less significantly, came the declaration in the 1980s that apartheid was a heresy, and the call to pray for the end of unjust rule.[10] This was a direct assault on the legitimacy of a state which claimed that its policies were Christian.

The publication of the *Kairos Document* in 1986, as repression and resistance intensified, was the final crossing of the Rubicon. Now the lines were clearly drawn: first, between the church which supported apartheid and the church which rejected it; but also, secondly and most significantly, between the church which rejected apartheid in principle yet stopped short of political solidarity with the liberation struggle, and the church which rejected the government as tyrannical and unequivo-

7. See Charles Villa-Vicencio, *Civil Disobedience and Beyond: Law, Resistance and Religion in South Africa* (Grand Rapids: Eerdmans, 1990).

8. See John W. de Gruchy, *The Church Struggle in South Africa,* 2nd ed. (Grand Rapids: Eerdmans, 1986), 138ff.

9. See Charles Villa-Vicencio, *Theology and Violence: The South African Debate* (Johannesburg: Skotaville, and Grand Rapids: Eerdmans, 1987).

10. See John W. de Gruchy and Charles Villa-Vicencio, eds., *Apartheid Is a Heresy* (Grand Rapids: Eerdmans, 1983); Allan Boesak and Charles Villa-Vicencio, eds., *When Prayer Makes News* (Philadelphia: Westminster Press, 1986).

cally took sides with the oppressed in their struggle for justice.[11] There could be no cheap reconciliation. Bonhoeffer's doctrine of costly grace was fundamental to the argument.

The *Kairos Document* was also reminiscent, however, of Bonhoeffer's blunt distinction between the true and false church, and his categorical insistence that outside the Confessing Church there was no salvation.[12] For Bonhoeffer there could be no compromise between the Confessing Church and the official church in trying to achieve reconciliation and unity without speaking out clearly against Nazism and also taking a stand on behalf of the Jews and other victims of Nazism. Bonhoeffer, of course, finally decided to engage in the struggle beyond the relatively clear boundaries of the Confessing Church, entering the shadow world of resistance and conspiracy; the *Kairos Document* reflected the fact that this was already taking place in South Africa. Christians were no longer simply engaged in a church struggle, but identifying with the liberation struggle. The question we now have to consider is: How should this "Kairos theology" inform our praxis in a new day? Are those who signed the *Kairos Document* still of any use?

Learning to See Things from Below

As previously indicated, the reception of Bonhoeffer in South Africa has been largely restricted to a small group of elites. But it is precisely to this group that Bonhoeffer's challenge has had a particularly sharp cutting-edge. For us, his challenge has been, and remains, above all else to see things from below, from the perspective of those who suffer. This, I suggest, is where the legacy of Bonhoeffer has had a particular impact, both consciously and unconsciously, on those South African Christians who, first, began to listen to the black voice; who, secondly, recognized the legitimacy of the liberation struggle; and who, thirdly, identified, however inadequately, with that struggle.

For Bonhoeffer, learning to see things from the perspective of those who suffer as victims of racism and oppression grew out of his identification with them — from the time he first encountered the struggle

11. *The Kairos Document: Challenge to the Church*, 2nd revised ed. (Johannesburg: ICT, 1986).

12. Dietrich Bonhoeffer, *The Way to Freedom*, 94.

against racism by African Americans in New York until he finally identified with the victims of the Holocaust. That was the ultimate act of solidarity or deputyship, a sharing in the sufferings of Jesus and his Jewish brothers and sisters. Not all of us, indeed very few of us, may share in solidarity to this extent. Martyrdom is not, in any case, something which one chooses, even though it is sometimes the consequence of solidarity, as we well know in our context, which has been so terrifyingly rich in martyrs. But even if not all suffer to the same extent, all are called to learn to see things from this perspective and to act accordingly. This is the call to costly discipleship, a lifelong journey of learning, a journey full of temptations, failures, and yet joys, victories, and celebrations.

The painful journey along the way of solidarity, step by agonizing step, is known to many in South Africa, even if they remain few in the totality of things. As was the case with Bonhoeffer, it has been the case also in South Africa that some of those who have been privileged have learned, have often been forced to learn, to see things differently from below. This learning process is still taking place as we are made aware of, and challenged by, new or different perspectives from our own. Certainly the transition to democracy and, even more, the struggle for democratic transformation are forcing many white people to see things quite differently, and to change even if reluctantly. I am quite sure that Bonhoeffer, more than any European theologian of his generation, would have been open and willing to respond positively, yet also critically, to the challenges raised by Professor Chung and others at this Congress — especially if he had survived to marry Maria! Despite his patriarchal views, his whole life was lived on a sharp learning curve, as he sought to see things from the perspective of others, especially those who suffer. There is no reason to assume that the rest of his life would have been different. The fundamental continuities in his theology were precisely those which enabled him to change as he experienced the challenge of reality in new ways.

Let us be clear that, for Bonhoeffer, solidarity did not mean rejecting his own identity, culture, or education. Bonhoeffer always treasured the best in his own upbringing and culture, just as he relished every opportunity to experience other cultures and to learn from them. It was not in his nature to indulge in any form of false shame or guilt. But those who are privileged, Bonhoeffer recognized, have a special responsibility within society. In some cases it is the responsibility of resistance, but in all cases it is responsibility of service in solidarity with others. This is of critical importance for South Africa at this time of reconstruction when many, especially but not only whites, who have been privileged with a good education and training are tempted to withdraw from public responsibility and pursue the goals of self-interest.

But Bonhoeffer also addresses his challenge to the new elites of our society, those who were powerless but who are now powerful; those who were in solidarity with the poor, but who are now fast becoming numbered among the rich. "Are we still of any use?" Have our swords become rusty? Has the iron in our souls turned to gravy?

Acknowledging Our Own Guilt

Learning to see things from below, identifying with victims, and acknowledging one's own identity and background have a third dimension, namely, taking the initiative in dealing with the past. The failure of the Confessing Church in Germany to live up to its early promise led Bonhoeffer, already in 1937, to consider the need for a confession of guilt. Of course, even ten years before that, in his doctoral dissertation *Sanctorum Communio*,[13] he had written about the need of the church to confess the sins of the nation vicariously. But that was before the rise of Nazism and the *Kirchenkampf.* So the question of guilt took on a new and urgent aspect when, in his *Ethics,* he wrote about the need of the church to confess both its own guilt and that of the nation for the sake of its rebirth and renewal.[14] In so doing he anticipated, though with much greater concreteness and power, the Stuttgart Confession of Guilt of the Evangelical Church in 1945.

The obligation of South Africans to deal with their past, especially through the recently appointed Commission on Truth and Reconciliation, has led in recent months to a great deal of discussion about the need for a confession of guilt on the part of the church. The necessity of such a confession was recognized already by some within the ranks of the South African Council of Churches in 1988, though there was considerable debate as to whether the time was appropriate. But those who were familiar with Bonhoeffer's witness and writings recognized that a confession of guilt could not be delayed until there was a more

13. *SC,* 83.
14. *Ethics,* 110ff.

propitious moment.[15] Such a confession was necessary not just as a way of dealing with the past, but as a way of actually bringing about change. Confessing guilt was, in other words, a way of hastening reconciliation rather than simply repenting at leisure later.

The potential impact of a confession of guilt was evident at the Rustenburg Conference in 1990 sponsored by the National Conference of Church Leaders, which spanned the ecclesiastical spectrum in the country. On that occasion, a leading white Dutch Reformed theologian, Professor Willie Jonker of the University of Stellenbosch, in his address to the Conference, offered a confession of guilt for the sins of his church, and especially for its complicity in apartheid.[16] This was a moment of intense emotion, given the history of that complicity and the fact that this was the first occasion when the Dutch Reformed church was formally involved in ecumenical discussions with the SACC since the 1960s. Archbishop Tutu, in an ad hoc response to Jonker, mentioned how deeply he was touched by the confession.

Although Jonker was supported by his colleagues at Rustenburg, he came under considerable criticism from both politicians and other Dutch Reformed church leaders after the Conference. Indeed, not many leaders of the previous regime have been willing, or found it easy, to confess their guilt for the past. Moreover, the Conference itself made it very clear that confession without reparation would amount to little more than "cheap grace." Nonetheless, Jonker's brave confession opened up a new dynamic at the Conference, pointed the way beyond the impasse of the past, and led to further reflection on the extent of the church's guilt in South Africa. It is not surprising, then, that the Declaration adopted by the Conference included a far-reaching statement of confession on the part of the church, reminiscent of the concreteness which Bonhoeffer always sought, and of his own confession in the *Ethics*.[17] Not only did the confession include reference to the sins of the colonial and apartheid church, but also the sins of the victims of apartheid who, inter alia, "acquiesced in and accepted an inferior status," and tolerated the sins of white dominance.[18]

---

15. See *Confessing Guilt in South Africa: The Responsibility of Churches and Individual Christians* (Johannesburg: SACC, 1989).

16. Louw Alberts and Frank Chikane, eds., *The Road to Rustenburg: The Church Looking Forward to a New South Africa* (Cape Town: Struik, 1991), 87ff.

17. *Ethics*, 110ff.

18. *The Road to Rustenburg*, 276ff.

However much previous attempts to confess guilt achieved, or failed to achieve, it is of vital important that the church should now take the lead on behalf of the nation in dealing with the past. In this regard Bonhoeffer's insights on confessing guilt have been central to the discussion among those theologians who have been involved in helping to clarify the role of the Truth Commission.[19]

Becoming a Church for Others Beyond Privilege

The final point of contact between Bonhoeffer and South Africa is one which comes late in his legacy and which, within our context, is only really now becoming a matter of urgent concern for the church and Christian witness. Bonhoeffer's prison insights into the nature of the church within a post-Christendom secular society are of considerable importance for us in South Africa as we begin to discover the role of the church and of Christian faith in a new democratic, multi-faith and multi-cultural South Africa.

But it is perhaps precisely here that some might begin to have difficulty in the reception of Bonhoeffer in South Africa at this time. On the one hand, of course, we are rapidly shedding our Constantinian heritage and becoming a secular society; on the other hand, we remain a very religious society, though now more fully aware than before of the multi-faith dimension of this religious character. Of course, it is widely recognized that Bonhoeffer's anticipation that we are headed for a time of no religion at all, and that we therefore have to begin to conceive of a Christianity in a "world come of age," has not proved to be as true statistically as he suggested. Or, should we say, not as true elsewhere in the world as it is in western Europe. This has raised the question as to whether Bonhoeffer's theology, not just that of the church struggle period but even of the prison letters, is still of any use to us in South Africa today. We are no longer engaged in a church struggle in the way we were, and our society is by no means a religionless one.

---

19. See my essay "Bonhoeffer and South Africa," in *Bonhoeffer: Exile and Martyr,* 32; see also John W. de Gruchy, "Confessing Guilt in South Africa Today in Dialogue with Dietrich Bonhoeffer," *Journal of Theology for Southern Africa* 67 (July 1989); Johan Botha, "Skuldbelydenis en Plaasbekleding," D.Th. dissertation, University of the Western Cape, 1989.

Yet if we properly understand what it was that Bonhoeffer had in mind in his reformulation of Christianity in a world come of age, then we soon discover that his Tegel theology remains pertinent for us as we participate in the shaping of a secular state and society. The church in South Africa has to learn, and learn quickly, how to be the "church for others" in a post-Constantinian, multi-faith context where the privileges of dominance are fading, and where there is already considerable antipathy toward Christianity because of the dominant role it played in colonialism and throughout the apartheid era. Within such a context Bonhoeffer's fragmentary thoughts on the "discipline of the secret," and the connection he made between prayer and righteous action, are particularly relevant.

Much has been written about Bonhoeffer's spirituality and, for many people, especially those attracted largely to his *Cost of Discipleship* and *Life Together*, it is this dimension to his life and theology which remains compelling. That spirituality was, of course, the spirituality of the church struggle. What is clear, however, even from a cursory reading of the *Letters and Papers from Prison*, is that Bonhoeffer's spirituality, despite his reservations about *The Cost of Discipleship*, remained fundamental to his existence, even if it began to change in significant ways along with his theology. His ongoing reading of the Bible and his prayers, despite moments of intense dryness and darkness of soul, provided the sustenance which kept him going — just as it has enabled so many others, including many in apartheid's prisons, to hope against hope.

Bonhoeffer's recovery of the ancient *disciplina arcani* or "discipline of the secret" provided a counterpoint to his thoughts on the "church for others."[20] If the church was to be truly open to the world, engaged in its struggles for justice and peace, and yet remain the church of Jesus Christ, it had to be firmly rooted in the Word, in prayer, and in the Eucharist. At the same time, if it were truly for others, it could not thrust its spirituality on the world in a triumphalistic, pietistic manner, any more than it could thrust its dogmas on the world in a "take it or leave it" way. What was required in the world was "righteous action," which, as Bonhoeffer had long before indicated,

---

20. *LPP*, 281, 286, 300. See Gisela Meuss, "Arkandisziplin und Weltlichkeit bei Dietrich Bonhoeffer," in Eberhard Bethge, ed., *Die Mündige Welt*, vol. 2 (Munich: Chr. Kaiser Verlag, 1960), 8ff.

interpreted itself;[21] what was necessary in the church was a disciplined life of reflection on the Word and prayer for the world. This model of spirituality is vital to the ongoing life and witness of the church in the modern secular world, and, indeed, perhaps even more in the postmodern world of multi-faith and multi-cultural societies such as South Africa. As such, Bonhoeffer's fragmentary prison reflections on "Who is Jesus Christ, for us, today?" — which bind together his theology and his spirituality in the service of the world — remain important for the church in the new South Africa, just as his confessing theology and spirituality were so vital in the struggle against apartheid.[22]

Bonhoeffer's question, "Are we still of any use?" was not asked, of course, about any aspect of his theology, but about the future role of those elites of which he was a part, who had given leadership in the struggle and who were now engaged in the conspiracy. So we end with that question in our hearts and minds. What is the role of those of us who were involved in the struggles, debates, and issues of the past, now that South Africa has entered into a new era? And does Bonhoeffer still have something to say to us, to the churches, to people of other faiths or no faith, and to the new generation of women and men who must take responsibility for the future? Hopefully, if the Seventh Bonhoeffer Congress has accomplished nothing else, it has enabled the dialogue with Bonhoeffer to continue in South Africa in such a way that it might continue to prove fruitful.

21. "Das Wesen der Kirche," in *Ökumene, Universität, Pfarramt 1931-1932,* Eberhard Amelung and Christoph Strohm, eds., *DBW,* vol. 11 (Munich: Chr. Kaiser Verlag, 1994), 285; see also note 320.

22. See Russel Botman's appropriation of Bonhoeffer's theology in this regard in his "Discipleship as Transformation? Towards a Theology of Transformation," D.Th. dissertation, University of the Western Cape, 1994.

AFTERWORD

Is Bonhoeffer Still of Any Use in South Africa?

H. RUSSEL BOTMAN

On 12 January, 1996, the Seventh International Bonhoeffer Congress moved from the Breakwater Campus of the University of Cape Town to assemble for its final plenary session at the University of the Western Cape. This historically black university has been in the forefront of the struggle against apartheid and the processes of transformation. It boasts a population of 14,650 students, of whom only 1.2% is white; more than 53% of the students are women. The social world of the students and staff is not so much "nonreligious" as interfaith, with the Christian and Muslim communities as the numerical majorities. This university, nevertheless, also represents — like any other South African university — all the contradictions of South Africa. It experiences many racial, class, and gender conflicts together with creative community transformation debates and action. Four members of the community of the University of the Western Cape participated in the events of the last day of the Congress, namely Denise M. Ackermann, Jaap J. F. Durand (Vice-Rector Emeritus), myself, and a student, John Klaasen. They formed part of a panel, with Jaap Durand as chair and Molefe Tsele, from the Lutheran Theological Seminary, Umphumulo, as co-panelist. The panel discussion followed John de Gruchy's presentation, "The Reception of Bonhoeffer in South Africa."

The panelists approached the Congress theme: "Are We Still of Any Use?" by creatively stating the problem in different ways, focusing attention on various issues, highlighting different areas of Bonhoeffer's theology in relation to past struggles and future hopes, and pointing to particular critiques offered by some of the papers presented at the Congress. Denise Ackermann saw the main problem as described in the question "*Who* are we?"; John Klaasen asked, "*Where* are we situating the question?"; Molefe Tsele wanted to know, "*When* is the crucial time for this question?"; and I reflected on, "*To whom* are we called to be of use?"

Agency, Gender, and Power

Denise Ackermann called our attention to the question of agency in ethics and theology. She questioned the exclusive focus on circumstances and suggested a much-needed emphasis on agency and choice. The question of agency is extremely important in the search for an ethic of resistance and responsibility. We should no longer ignore the implications of Bonhoeffer's theological anthropology, ethics, and spirituality. She referred to the issue of violence against women as a case in point. Once this form of violence is explained in terms of people's circumstances, the solution is sought through changing the circumstances. Urgent appeals are then made to the might of the state for more stringent laws and more punitive law enforcement. However, Ackermann stated, "The politics of violence requires that we understand and recognize the question of will in acts of violence as well as understand the circumstances in which they happen." When we ask, "Are we still of any use?" the answer must touch base in anthropology and agency to get a clear description of who we are.

She then criticized the fact that the seminar and the plenary sessions she attended, excluding the presentation of Chung Hyun Kyung, seemed not to take the seriousness of this question for granted. She found the presenters to be trapped in the limitations of "malesteam theology," with scant gender analysis even from theologians who are alive to the consequences of gender blindness in the theological endeavor. The general question, "Who is Jesus Christ, for us, today?" must be narrowed down through gender analysis because the answer depends on one's context and the particularities of one's experience as much as it does on universal truth claims made by Christianity. The incisiveness of this criticism was expressed in her statements: "I did not hear much about my Jesus," and "What can be useful for me as a white woman doing theology in a post-apartheid South Africa at the end of the twentieth century, whose interest lies in the areas of feminist theology, the relationship between our theological theories and praxis, and, last but not least, spirituality?"

She referred to the fact that Bonhoeffer scholars from other contexts might pose two kinds of questions in response to her position, namely, what does gender analysis have to do with Bonhoeffer studies? and, given that violence against women *is* a terrible reality, what has theology to do with it? Both these question, she insisted, are in essence about our struggle to clarify what we understand by theology and *who* we are in this endeavor. In fact, the answer lies in the difference between malestream theology and inclusive theological enterprises. Combining the positions stated by Chung Hyun Kyung and Jean Bethke Elshtain, she concluded that Bonhoeffer would have understood this difference in the light of his theological anthropology and his views on power.

The New Kairos

For Molefe Tsele, Bonhoeffer's question, "Are we still of any use?" should be understand as a Kairos question: "Are we *still* of any use?" He referred to attempts in the past to use Bonhoeffer in such a way that the sharp edges of his theology are suppressed. Our question is, "Are we, after Kairos I, still of any use?"

Molefe Tsele's commitment to this question goes beyond his presentation at this Congress. He coordinated the second Kairos gathering held in September 1995 which celebrated the tenth anniversary of the *Kairos Document.* The event of the new democracy in South Africa represents a new kairos. This formed the background of Tsele's incisive analysis and evaluation of "our usefulness." He highlighted three major areas of future hopefulness that South Africans may want to appropriate from Bonhoeffer. The first is the notion of the mature believer; second, how we relate to land; and third, the issue of power.

South African Christians have to learn the art of being Christian at a time when the government is set on establishing a secular society. Out of a history in which every major Christian celebration was a public holiday, South Africans now celebrate secular public holidays rather than primarily Christian ones. Maturity is required among Christians in relating to a secular state and a secular society. Bonhoeffer's theology, Tsele suggested, could assist South Africans in this task.

Secondly, the crucial place of the land issue in South Africa draws us to the struggles in Bonhoeffer's theology. How does one promote and continue to empower people in their respect for land without falling into the idolatry of living and dying "for God, blood, and fatherland" in an uncritical manner? Tsele regarded this as a major area of concern for South African theology. South Africa has no real future unless the land question is settled. However, this very necessity carries its own national dangers. How are restitution and respect for land to be done at this kairos moment in South Africa, and what are the task and role of the church in this?

Thirdly, Tsele referred to the issue of power. His concern was particularly with the issue of the all-pervasive global political and economic power of the west in South Africa. This all-pervasive form of power that respects no national boundaries or contexts creates a situation where economic and political quality is not determined by the caliber of a nation's leadership. Real political and economic power lies else-where. This fact means that it may make very little difference to the poor of the country that Nelson Mandela is South Africa's President as long as the global economic grip on South Africa remains in place. This new moment or kairos requires a theo-political engagement with issues related to the global economy. Yes, concluded Molefe Tsele, we are still of use, but only if we can refocus our energies in the light of the new kairos moment.

Young, Black, and Disadvantaged

As a young black student, John Klaasen admired Bonhoeffer's witness as a young person in Germany. He is a significant role model in South Africa, Klaasen emphasized, because young people form a large part of the disadvantaged community of the country. He called attention to estimates that indicated that more than fifty percent of the potential voters of South Africa are young people. Bonhoeffer's question, "Are we still of any use?" should be properly located in relation to this reality if a lasting response is sought. South Africa has not been successful in its attempts to integrate young people into the mainstream of society. Youth remain the most marginalized section of the community.

Klaasen found that the Congress did not do justice to Bonhoeffer's own commitment to oppressed people. "People are still homeless, a lot of people still go to bed with little or no food, there are still people who have no running water and no electricity and are still exposed to violence. We cannot close our eyes to these realities when we ask ourselves, "Are we still of any use?" he claimed. "This Congress has not adequately addressed this kind of context." He also focused on two areas of central importance to young people which were not adequately addressed. Although the issue of truth and reconciliation was addressed in some of the papers, the fundamental concerns regarding restitution were absent. How young people must deal with the past and guilt, and come to terms with the necessity of restitution, is crucial for the future of this country.

A second area of concern related to the ecumenical and interfaith scene. He expressed concern that the ecumenical movement in South Africa is becoming less effective because of limited resources and stagnation of its vision. Bonhoeffer's witness underlines the important role the ecumenical movement can play in the lives of young people in South Africa. Apart from the need for a stronger ecumenical movement for and of young people, there is also the need for more exposure to the interfaith reality in South Africa. Young people should be involved in a constructive religious dialogue in South Africa, he concluded. This, he insisted, requires a revisitation of the christological question in the country.

The Question of Usefulness

My presentation focused the Congress theme on the question: "Of use, yes, but to whom?" In a situation in which evil is clearly defined and established, and resistance is called for, the question has a familiar ring to it. However in a situation like ours where President Mandela, on that beautiful day of 10 May 1994, committed the nation to the ideal of the formation of a new community, we are faced with a different reality. Mandela said: "Out of the experience of an extraordinary human disaster that lasted too long must be born a society of which all humanity will be proud."[1] South Africans are facing the question, "Are we still of any use?" at the dawn of this newly found democracy.

---

1. Nelson Mandela, *Long Walk to Freedom* (Johannesburg: Macdonald Purnell, 1994), 613.

As a Christmas gift for Colonel Oster and Hans von Dohnanyi (both of whom were executed on the same day as Bonhoeffer), Bonhoeffer wrote his celebrated essay from prison entitled "After Ten Years. Are We Still of Any Use?" The background to this question is his total commitment to the building of a new Germany after Hitler. He believed that the building of a new society required a particular type of person. "What we shall need," he wrote, "is not geniuses, or cynics, or misanthropes or clever tacticians, but plain, honest, straightforward men [sic]."

However, we have to face another side of this question. The South African nation is still divided, internally torn between the interests of so many different sectors and ideologies. There are so many areas that require building, reconstruction and transformation. There are so many voices demanding to be recognized, demanding our usefulness. To whom ought we to be of use? I ask this question as a black person who has discovered that the demands placed on black people in our post-apartheid society have become increasingly strenuous and varied. Government expects our usefulness, civil society requires our usefulness, and employers demand our usefulness. Even within society the issue is not that clear. Society is a divided reality, with class, race, and gender demands. Each sector calls for a particular and, sometimes, exclusive usefulness to its own agenda. The usefulness question is a scary one in a world of so many voices. The most attractive voices are not necessarily those worth following.

Congress participants from the west may also experience this dilemma. I have heard people talk about the demands of their institutions of higher learning in the west. These institutions place demands on them to do research, to publish, to study, to become comfortable in the ivory tower. The result is that we see less of these people in the struggles of the communities crying out from below. Commitments can easily become more parochial, institutional, and individualistic. How do we discern the voices worth following at this time in the history of the world and of South Africa. We will have to face the challenge raised by Bonhoeffer in the "After Ten Years" essay, namely:

> Will our inward power of resistance be strong enough, and our honesty with ourselves remorseless enough, for us to find our way back to simplicity and straightforwardness?

The "to whom" question has also torn the prophetic church in South Africa apart. In responding to this question many have left the church and the ecumenical movement for parliament, business, consultations, foundations, and lucrative institutions. This "upward" movement of black leadership is happening at a risk to civil society, community-based activities, and the church. Are we heeding the right voices? Bonhoeffer's theological leadership can guide in responding to this difficult question. He answered this question consistently with reference to "the coming generation":

> Thinking and acting for the sake of the coming generation, but being ready to go any day without fear or anxiety — that, in practice, is the spirit in which we are forced to live.[2]

What shall we say to all these questions which remain at the end of the Congress? They point, undoubtedly, to the same type of experiential foundation that led Bonhoeffer to the "Are We Still of Any Use?" question in the first place. Like him, we must also admit that: ". . . experience has made us suspicious. . . ." What separates us from Bonhoeffer has to do with the fact that we are not yet prepared to give up the hermeneutics of suspicion. In our judgment there is no real epistemological conflict between a hermeneutic of suspicion and our sociopolitical usefulness, between suspicion and straightforwardness. Our usefulness will necessarily be grounded in the suspicion that we inherited as a legacy of the resistance and the confessing movement — the Kairos movement — in South Africa.

2. *LPP*, 15.

Abbreviations

The many editions and translations of Dietrich Bonhoeffer's writings, together with the multinational character of the essays in this volume, have made it difficult to achieve consistency in our references to Bonhoeffer's works. Authors have had the freedom to use whatever editions they have found appropriate. Moreover, the publication of the new critical edition of Dietrich Bonhoeffer's works *(DBW)* in 16 volumes and their translation into English *(DBWE)* mean that we are in a transitional phase in referencing Bonhoeffer's writings. Since only *Life Together* and the *Prayerbook of the Bible* had been translated by the time of the Seventh International Bonhoeffer Congress, they are the only books in the *DBWE* which are used in this volume. Regerences to the German volumes, both old editions and those now available in the *Dietrich Bonhoeffer Werke*, are indicated as such in the footnotes.

AB   Dietrich Bonhoeffer, *Act and Being.* Trans. Bernard Noble. New
         York: Harper & Row, 1961; London: Collins, 1962.

CD   Dietrich Bonhoeffer, *The Cost of Discipleship.* 2nd edition. Trans.
         R. H. Fuller. London: SCM, 1959; New York: Macmillan,
         1960.

DB   Eberhard Bethge, *Dietrich Bonhoeffer. Theologe — Christ — Zeit-*
         genosse. Eine Biographie. Munich, 1968. English translation:
         Dietrich Bonhoeffer: A Biography. Abridged from the 3rd German

ed. Trans. Eric Mosbacher, Peter and Betty Ross, Frank Clarke, and William Glen-Doepel, under the editorship of E. T. Robertson. New York: Harper and Row, 1970; London: Collins, 1970.

DBW   *Dietrich Bonhoeffer Werke.* 16 vols. Ed. E. Bethge et al. Munich, 1968– .

DBWE   English translation: *Dietrich Bonhoeffer Works.* 16 vols. Ed. Wayne Whitson Floyd Jr. Minneapolis: Fortress Press, 1996– .

GS   Dietrich Bonhoeffer, *Gesammelte Schriften* (Collected Works). 6 vols. Ed. E. Bethge. Munich, 1958-74. English translation of selected material: *No Rusty Swords.* London: Collins, 1965; *The Way to Freedom.* Trans. and ed. Edwin H. Robertson. London: Collins, 1966; *True Patriotism.* London: Collins, 1973.

LPP   Dietrich Bonhoeffer, *Letters and Papers from Prison.* 4th ed. Trans. Reginald H. Fuller. Revised by Frank Clarke et al. Additional material trans. by John Bowden for the enlarged edition. London: SCM Press, 1971; New York: Macmillan, 1972.

LT   Dietrich Bonhoeffer, *Life Together* (Dietrich Bonhoeffer Works, vol. 5). Ed. Geffrey B. Kelly. Trans. Daniel W. Bloesch. Minneapolis: Fortress Press, 1996.

SC   Dietrich Bonhoeffer, *Sanctorum Communio: A Dogmatic Inquiry into the Sociology of the Church.* Trans. Ronald Gregor Smith. London: Collins, 1963.

WE   Dietrich Bonhoeffer, *Widerstand und Ergebung. Briefe und Aufzeichnungen aus der Haft.* New edition. Ed. Eberhard Bethge. Munich: Chr. Kaiser Verlag, 1985.

Contributors

Denise Ackermann — University of Western Cape, South Africa

William Apel — Linfield College, Oregon, U.S.A.

Eberhard Bethge — President of the International Bonhoeffer Society

Jean Bethke Elshtain — University of Chicago, U.S.A.

Elias Bongmba — Rice University, Houston, Texas, U.S.A.

Russel Botman — University of Western Cape, South Africa

Chung Hyun Kyung — Ewha Women's College, Seoul, South Korea

Keith Clements — Council of Churches for Britain and Ireland

James Cochrane — University of Natal, Pietermaritzburg, South Africa

John de Gruchy — University of Cape Town, South Africa

Frits de Lange — Kampen, Netherlands

Barry Harvey — Baylor University, Texas, U.S.A.

Geffrey Kelly — La Salle University, Philadelphia, U.S.A.

John Klaasen — University of Western Cape, South Africa

John Moses — St Mark's National Theological Centre, Canberra, Australia

Andreas Pangritz — Free University, Berlin, Germany

Hans Pfeifer — Christusgemeinde, Freiburg, Germany

Barney Pityana — South African Commission on Human Rights

Konrad Raiser — World Council of Churches, Switzerland

Peter Selby — Durham University, England

Molefe Tsele — Lutheran Theological Seminary, Umphumulo, South Africa

Hans Dirk van Hoogstraten — University of Nijmegen, Netherlands

Ralf K. Wüstenberg — Humbolt University, Berlin, Germany

Alejandro Zorzin — Instituto Superior Evangelico de Estudios Teologicos, Buenos Aires, Argentina

List of Papers presented at the 7th International Bonhoeffer Congress Not Published in This Volume But Housed in the Archives of Union Theological Seminary, New York, U.S.A.

1. Andrew Stirling, United Church of Canada: *Who Is "Christ the Centre" for Us Today?*
2. Russel Botman, University of the Western Cape, South Africa: *Who Is "Christ as Community" for Us Today?*
3. Deotis Roberts, Eastern Baptist Theological Seminary, Pennsylvania, U.S.A.: *Bonhoeffer and King: Their Message for Today*
4. Hans Goedeking, Wuppertal, Germany: *". . . Teilnehmen an dem Schicksal Deutschlands . . ."*
5. Mary Glazener, Author, North Carolina, U.S.A.: *On Being a Christian Today*
6. Jurjen Wiersma, Faculty of Protestant Theology, University of Brussels: *Bonhoeffer's Concept of the Mandates Re-examined*
7. Ruth Zerner, City University of New York: *Called: Bethge, Bonhoeffer, and an American Triptych*
8. Sabine Bobert-Stützel, Humbolt University, Berlin, Germany: *"Pastoral Counselling" in Dietrich Bonhoeffer*
9. Charles Marsh, Loyola College, Baltimore, Maryland, U.S.A.: *The Self for Others in Lived Experience: Questions to Bonhoeffer from the American Civil Rights Movement*
10. Johan Botha, Uniting Reformed Church, Belhar, South Africa: *On Dealing with South Africa's Past — Bonhoeffer and Guilt*

11. Traugott Stahlin, Bielefeld, Germany: *Ecumenical Spirituality and Secularisation: On the Relationship between Bonhoeffer's Piety and Theology*

12. James S. Scott, York University, Ontario, Canada: *Prison in Writing and Writing in Prison: Ruth First's 117 Days, Dietrich Bonhoeffer's Letters and Papers from Prison and the Ambiguities of Resistance*

13. Martin Hüneke, Bad Iburg, Germany: *The Theological Relevance of Bonhoeffer's Pacifism*

14. Larry Rasmussen, Union Theological Seminary, New York, U.S.A.: *Earth and Its Distress: The Christian's "Song of Songs"*

15. Jeffrey C. Pugh, Elon College, North Carolina, U.S.A.: *What Is Christianity for Us Today? Dietrich Bonhoeffer and Contemporary Theology*

16. Stacey Ake, Pennsylvania State University, U.S.A.: *A Twist of Faith: The Christian at the Centre of the Ethical*

17. Carel Anthonissen, Dutch Reformed Church, Stellenbosch, South Africa: *Credibility versus Relevance*

18. Charles Sensel, United Methodist Church, U.S.A.: *Discipleship and Friendship in the Letters of Dietrich Bonhoeffer and John Wesley*

19. Martin Rumscheidt, Halifax, Canada: *The Letters of Dietrich Bonhoeffer and Maria von Wedemeyer: An Attempt to Understand Them*